STUDIES IN CHINESE LITERATURE AND SOCIETY

Editors

Irving Yucheng Lo
Leo Ou-fan Lee

Joseph S. M. Lau
Eugene Chen Eoyang

BLOOMING
AND
CONTENDING

BLOOMING AND CONTENDING

Chinese Literature in the Post-Mao Era

MICHAEL S. DUKE

INDIANA UNIVERSITY PRESS
Bloomington

For Josephine Chiu–Duke

This book was brought to publication with the aid of a grant
from the Andrew W. Mellon Foundation.

Manufactured in the United States of America

Library of Congress Cataloging in Publication Data

Duke, Michael S.
   Blooming and Contending.

   (Studies in Chinese literature and society)
   Bibliography: p.
   Includes Index.
   1. Chinese literature––20th century––History and
criticism. I. Title. II. Series.
PL2303.D84 1985   895.1'5'09   84–48641
ISBN 0–253–31202–7

1   2 3   4   5   89   88   87   86   85

Contents

Acknowledgments

I wish to thank Mason Y.H. Wang and the editors of the Green River Press for permission to incorporate portions of "The Second Blooming of the Hundred Flowers: Chinese Literature in the Post-Mao Era" from *Perspectives in Contemporary Chinese Literature* (1983) into chapters two and three, and the editors of *Chinese Literature: Essays, Articles, and Reviews* for permission to incorporate all of "A Drop of Spring Rain: The Sense of Humanity in Pai Hua's *Bitter Love* (vol. 5, no. 1) into an expanded discussion of Bai Hua and resurgent humanism in chapter five. For institutional or financial support I would like to thank the National Endowment for the Humanities for a Research Grant for 1981–82 that enabled me to begin work on this project; the Department of East Asian Languages and Literature, University of Wisconsin, Madison and William H. Nienhauser, Chairman, for making me an honorary NEH Fellow for 1981–82 and for inviting me to speak at the Midwest Seminar on Chinese Arts in April 1982; the Office of Research Services of the University of British Columbia for generous research and travel grants for the years 1982–85; St. John's University for a travel grant to attend their May 1982 Workshop on Contemporary Chinese Fiction; the organizers of the Fourth International Comparative Literature Conference at Tamkang University, Taipei, Taiwan for their hospitality during the week of August 21–27, 1983; and the Department of Asian Studies here at U.B.C. for a generous use of Distinguished Lecturer Program funds to sponsor a two day conference on Modern Chinese Literature and Society on March 22 and 23, 1983.

Many people have read portions of this manuscript and offered both encouragement and helpful criticisms. I would like to thank the following teachers and colleagues: Cyril Birch of the University of California, Berkeley; Howard Goldblatt of San Francisco State University; C.T. Hsia of Columbia University; Jeffrey Kinkley of St. John's University; Joseph S.M. Lau and Yü-sheng Lin of the University of Wisconsin, Madison; Leo Ou-fan Lee of the University

of Chicago; Perry Link of U.C.L.A.; and Wai–leung Wong and
William Tay of the Chinese University of Hong Kong. Professors
Hsia, Lau, and Lee deserve special thanks for reading the entire
manuscript. My debt to Professor Joseph S.M. Lau encompasses
much more than any short note could ever acknowledge. I would also
like to thank Ms. Rachel Rousseau and Olga Betts for typing portions
of the manuscript as well as helping me use a word processor and Mr.
Frank Flynn of UBC Arts Computing for teaching me the easy parts
and setting up the hard parts of the Textform program with which this
book has been prepared. The decorative Chinese title characters, with
the words *mingfang* (blooming and contending) in the Oracle bone
style, are by Kenichi Takashima of UBC, and I am most greatful to
him for them.

Finally, although she asked me repeatedly not to write anything in
dedication, I must acknowledge that the very existence of this book and
whatever portions of it may shine a little brighter than the rest is
primarily due to the efforts of my most exacting critic and my most
constant supporter — Josephine Chiu–Duke — to whom this book is
greatfully dedicated.

Introduction

The study of modern Chinese literature from the People's Republic was an uninspiring affair throughout the Cultural Revolution years of 1966–76 when literature was little more than crude propaganda and those scholars who read and wrote about it regarded their work more as a species of sociology or political science than literary criticism. The situation has changed sufficiently since 1977 to allow for scholarly studies that attempt to at least balance literary and social or political criticism. The nature of PRC society and its literature makes it virtually impossible to avoid all political comment — both the state and the writers themselves insist on the social relevance of their works — and so this book, which attempts to survey the most significant works of literature to appear in the PRC from 1977 through the summer of 1984, also contains rather more political comment than might be found in a similar book on literature from Taiwan or Japan, to name just two areas of the Far East where modern literature flourishes without the necessity of being politically tendentious. Regardless of our attitude toward the politics of the PRC and the entire communist experience of the past thirty–five years in China, it is nevertheless extremely important that we study the literary works of the immediate Post–Mao Era in order to understand the problematic nature of life in the PRC as it is presented by its own writers to its own citizens. Thus I have summarized a great many works that have not yet appeared in translation, if indeed they ever will. My intention throughout has been to write a book that would be of interest both to specialists in the field and to students of modern Chinese society and comparative literature who do not read Chinese.

There are more than thirty literary journals publishing hundreds of stories and poems every month in the PRC, and no one person could reasonably claim to have covered them all. In this book I have tried to deal with the most significant literary events in the PRC from 1977–84 and I believe that my conclusions concerning the works surveyed present the main literary trends likely to be followed at least throughout the 1980s if not for the rest of this century. Chapter one details the significant changes in the Chinese Communist Party line on literature and art during this period, and the events related therein, however dry and dull at times, must be kept in mind while reading the remaining chapters just as PRC writers and editors have to keep them in mind whenever they write or publish anything. Chapter two presents a group of well known PRC writers' own critique of their nation's literature since "liberation," a critique strikingly similar to that made previously by non–Chinese or non–Marxist literary critics throughout the years since 1949. Chapter three is a literary critique and a survey of the neo–realist fiction that burst upon the scene in 1979 and 1980 and significantly altered the perception of PRC society among Chinese reading scholars throughout the world. I have chosen to use the term neo–realism, first used in this context by Lee Yee and Bi Hua in Hong Kong, in order to differentiate this particular body of post–Mao fiction from the decidedly unrealistic "Socialist Realism" and "Revolutionary Romanticism" that preceded it. To the extent possible under present political conditions, post–Mao neo–realism represents a renewed attempt to write literature that tells the truth about social reality as the individual writer sees it. The material in chapter four necessitates a decidedly political treatment because it deals with the basically non–fiction works of a courageous investigative reporter for the *People's Daily*. Chapter five introduces the important theme of humanism that has become one of the dominant trends in the PRC since Bai Hua's *Bitter Love* became the object of official criticism. Chapter six continues the discussion of humanism through an exami- nation of Dai Houying's fictional presentation of "Marxist humanism," a topic taken up in 1983 by none other than Zhou Yang himself. The final chapter presents the longings of the post–Mao "thinking genera- tion" of younger writers who are trying to create works that go beyond the narrowly ideological boundaries of the past and reach toward a better future for modern Chinese literature. Their task is a difficult one, but the future greatness, if any, of modern Chinese literature from the People's Republic depends upon the extent to which they are able to continue blooming and contending.

Although I have given one full chapter to an analysis of Bai Hua's *Bitter Love*, I do not, however, wish to leave the mistaken impression that his work is superior to that of Dai Houying or the many writers discussed in chapters three and seven. *Bitter Love* is important for its expression of humanism by a dedicated communist and for the political repercussions of that expression rather than for its intrinsic literary merit. From an artistic point of view the best writers being published in the PRC today are those younger writers between the ages of twenty-five and forty whose many poems, short stories, and novellas, whether in the "realist," "romantic," or even "modernist" modes, are less and less blatantly tendentious. If allowed a modicum of artistic freedom, some of them may be expected to develop into world class writers.

The truth of the aphorism that art is long but life is short seems never more apparent than in the study of contemporary Chinese literature. Having surveyed the main trends of this recent period, I must now confess that there are still many topics that are not included in this volume. Most regretably I have been unable to deal with the newly emerging poetry and the great polemic concerning so-called "obscure poetry" that raged from 1979 well into the 80s. An entire book could and should be written about this remarkably good post-Mao verse. I have not dealt with the "literature of the special areas" — *Tequ wenxue* being a new journal title — which seems to have some particular characteristics such as the frequent depiction of foreigners and overseas Chinese that differentiate it from most other PRC fiction. Nor have I discussed the significance of the sometimes controversial emergence of science fiction and crime stories as popular subgenres. An even larger area that I've only touched on in passing is the post-Mao spoken drama that has, like neo-realist fiction, revised many of the pre-Jiang Qing conventions of Chinese drama and adapted many new (for China) western techniques to the Chinese stage. Finally, I have said almost nothing about the embryonic practice of genuine literary criticism or aesthetic criticism as distinct from politically motivated ideological critiques of particular works. The bibliography is intended to aid the reader interested in these uncovered areas: for "obscure poetry," refer to the works of Bonnie S. McDougall, William Tay, Yeh Wei-lien, and Bi Hua; for science fiction, see Rudolf Wagner's excellent paper; for crime stories, see Jeffrey Kinkley's article; and for drama, see Edward M. Gunn's paper and anthology. For *tequ wenxue,* there is only Joseph Lau's short unpublished paper; and there is next to nothing on literary criticism. I hope that the general reader will forgive me for not including more than the present volume contains and that the specialist will kindly overlook any omission of his/her chosen topic or favorite work.

I. Political Background: The Second "Hundred Flowers" Policy

"Literature and art are subordinate to politics, but in their turn exercise a great influence on politics . . . What we demand is unity of politics and art, of content and form, and of the revolutionary political content and the highest possible degree of perfection in artistic form." Within this famous formulation from Mao Zedong's 1942 literary catechism, *Talks at the Yan'an Forum on Literature and Art*,[1] there lurked a deceptive paradox and a tragic dilemma. While they seemed to accord due respect to purely artistic values, in order to win the support of those humanistic leftist and Marxist writers and intellectuals who already viewed the Chinese Communist Party (CCP) as the best hope for a war-ravaged nation, Mao and his literary bureaucracy paradoxically emphasized only the first or political half of the formula while systematically persecuting those very revolutionary CCP member writers who took the second half seriously and put artistic, humanistic, and individualistic values ahead of the exigencies of the Party's political and economic policies. The tragic dilemma of the self-proclaimed revolutionary intellectual writer was a choice between maintaining his/her personal and artistic integrity at considerable risk by writing in a realistic (i.e., personally truthful) fashion about the hard life of the workers, peasants, and soldiers under communism or becoming propaganda spokesmen for (after 1957) increasingly unpopular and ineffectual government policies. In spite of the prevailing slogans, a deep conflict of values was inherent in the Maoist conception of art and the revolutionary humanist writers' conception of politics: the writers attempted to use art to influence Party policies while the Maoists employed power politics to control art and reduce it to propaganda.

As a direct consequence of this conflict of values, the history of modern Chinese literature in the People's Republic of China (PRC) during the Maoist Era (1942–1976) involved an increasingly dogmatic and mechanical application of a narrowly determinist and anti-humanistic ideology to control the literary output and the very lives of all Chinese writers. One inspiring feature of that era, however, was the continued refusal of some of China's finest writers to ever completely abandon their artistic and humanistic values and ideals — values which they believed to be compatible with the Marxist philosophy of life — in favor of a thoroughgoing Maoist reductionism. These Chinese writers' commitment to the fundamental values of human dignity and the primacy of individual conscience was met with increasingly violent rectification and thought remolding campaigns from the 1942 Rectification Movement in wartime Yan'an, through the Anti-Rightist Campaign of 1957-58, and culminating in the Cultural Revolution period of 1966-76 when scores of writers were hounded to death and the writing of literature in any meaningful sense of the word ceased completely.

The literary policies of the Cultural Revolution period can be traced directly to statements in the *Yan'an Talks* in which Chairman Mao rejected most of the primary values of Chinese and Western humanism as bourgeois and reactionary.[2] The very idea of a common humanity — human nature — is rejected in favor of a crude class analysis:

> In a class society there is only human nature that bears the the stamp of a class, but no human nature transcending classes . . . What they [bourgeois intellectuals] call human nature is in substance nothing but bourgeois individualism, and consequently in their eyes proletarian human nature is contrary to their human nature. (90)

As a corollary to this vulgar Marxist schema, human sympathy, the Mencian spirit of commiseration or love of mankind, is cynically rejected as a ruling class hoax:

> As to the so-called 'love of mankind,' there has been no such all-embracing love since humanity was divided into classes. (91)

The honest presentation of a personal vision of truth in literature — objective truth or personal knowledge, and along with it moral autonomy — is rejected in favor of Party dictated praise or exposure:

> Only truly revolutionary artists and writers [by CCP defini-tion and with CCP imprimatur] can correctly solve the prob-lem whether to praise or to expose. All dark forces which

endanger the masses of the people must be exposed while all
revolutionary struggles of the masses must be praised . . . (91)

The possibility that the "dark forces" endangering the Chinese people
might emanate from the CCP itself, as Ding Ling, Xiao Jun, Ai Qing,
and Wang Shiwei had maintained in Yan'an, was brushed aside with
Mao's assertion that democracy prevailed in Yan'an and there was no
longer any need for Lu Xun–style satirical essays in the communist
controlled areas. Finally, recognizing that there is such a quality as
artistic excellence apart from political considerations, the Chairman
deliberately rejected literary excellence that is not in conformity with
Party policy:

> Some things which are basically reactionary from the
> political point of view may yet be artistically good, but the
> more artistic such a work may be, the greater harm will it do
> to the people, and the more reason for us to reject it. (89)

After the Great Helmsman's death and the fall of the Gang of Four
late in 1976, an extended period of relaxation of Party policies toward
writers, artists, and other intellectuals began. This period of relaxation
lasted from late 1977 to late 1981, with the period of greatest freedom
for writers coming in 1979 and 1980. This period of the Second
Hundred Flowers policy is not officially over, but a greater degree of
control over literature and art has been established since the summer of
1981 and the overall quality of the literature written since 1982 (with a
few notable exceptions) does not match that of 1979 and 1980. The
five years from 1977 to 1982 represent, I believe, yet another cycle of
relaxation and control so familiar to students of Chinese communist
literature since 1942.[3] In fairness one should add that the control is not
as rigid as during the Cultural Revolution period or perhaps even the
seventeen years prior to it; and that, although bleak by Western
European and North and South American standards (not all such
bleakness being due to direct political control), the prospects for PRC
literature may be brighter today than at any time since 1949. As a
prelude to our study of particular works, this chapter will present a
survey of the most important CCP policy changes relating to literature
and art from 1977 to 1982.

In July 1977, nine months after the "smashing" of the Gang of
Four, Hua Guofeng was confirmed as Mao Zedong's "hand picked"
successor for Chairman of the CCP Central Committee at the same
session that reinstated Deng Xiaoping as Vice–Chairman. In August,

Hua delivered a rambling 32,000 character political report to the 11th National Party Congress in which he announced the official end of the Cultural Revolution, pronounced it a "great victory" over the "revisionism" of the Gang of Four, surveyed all of China's internal and external problems, and offered a list of eight things that had to be done to attain "great order across the land."[4] Two points are important for literary and artistic freedom. In point five — "We must make a success of the revolution in cultural and educational spheres" — he quoted from two "significant conversations" with the Great Helmsman in July 1975 in which Mao, seemingly bored with reading Cultural Revolution literature, had offered the following critique of Jiang Qing's "bourgeois cultural autocracy": "No longer are a hundred flowers blossoming . . . People are afraid to write articles or produce plays. There is nothing in the way of novels and poetry." With this divine imprimatur established, Hua announced the CCP's return to the policies of "letting a hundred flowers blossom and a hundred schools of thought contend," of "making the past serve the present and things foreign serve China," and of "weeding through the old to bring forth the new."[5] He concluded by reaffirming Mao's "correct policy of uniting with, educating and remolding intellectuals and harnessing their enthusiasm for socialist construction" in order "to build up a vast army of working–class intellectuals."[6] In point seven — "We must promote democracy and strengthen democratic centralism" — he called for a balance between "freedom" and "discipline" and between "democracy" and "centralism," among the people and within the CCP, in order to guard against "ultra–democracy or licence," . . . "fight more effectively against our class enemies, correctly handle contradictions among the people, strengthen the Party's leading role, consolidate the dictatorship of the proletariat, [and] serve the socialist economic base." He made it emphatically clear that the purpose of promoting democracy was "by no means to weaken, much less to undermine, the Party's leading role and the dictatorship of the proletariat" or "the socialist economic base."[7]

Throughout all of the struggles for reform and change in China since that speech, struggles that have witnessed the gradual retreat of the Maoists and the victory of Deng Xiaoping's reform group, the basic structural relation between the CCP and those intellectuals who are writers and artists has not changed in theory or practice; and, as Deng Xiaoping himself has said, "practice is the sole reliable criterion for testing truth" in the PRC.

In March 1978, the Fifth National People's Congress approved a new *Constitution of the People's Republic of China*, the third since the founding of the PRC, in which the preamble was changed from the Cultural Revolution Constitution of 1975 in order to stress the goal of economic modernization in the "new period of development." Article 45 stated that among the fundamental rights of citizens are "freedom of speech, correspondence, the press, assembly, association, procession, demonstration and the freedom to strike," and article 52 stated that "citizens have the right to engage in scientific research, literary and artistic creation and other cultural activities."[8] Article 52 was identical to article 95 of the 1954 Constitution and seemed to reflect an intended improvement over the 1975 Cultural Revolution Constitution which stated bluntly: "The proletariat must exercise all-around dictatorship over the bourgeoisie in the superstructure including all spheres of culture."[9] Article 14 of the new Constitution, under the section on "general principles," was quite explicit, however, on the limits of the freedom of thought implied above: "The State upholds the leading position of Marxism-Leninism-Mao Zedong Thought throughout all spheres of ideology and culture. All cultural undertakings must serve the workers, peasants, and soldiers and serve socialism." Furthermore, Marshall Ye Jianying, considered one of the major obstacles to any speedier timetable for Deng's reforms, made it very clear in his "report on the Revision of the Constitution,"[10] that these freedoms are to be enjoyed only under the limiting control of Mao's "six political criteria" in order to promote socialist economic development, unity, the people's democratic dictatorship, democratic centralism, and the Party leadership.[11] As is customary in the PRC, with or without legal codification, the limits to free expression are murky, and are subject to final interpretation, not by an independent judiciary, but by the Central Committee or even the Politburo of the CCP. Professor Jerome Cohen's astute comments on this point provide a fine summary of the legal situation prevailing with regard to the arts from March 1978 to December 1982:[12]

> Indeed, the 1975 language represents quite an accurate description of the current Party line, even though as a factual matter much greater cultural, scientific and educational freedom exists at present than existed during the intellectual nightmare of the 1966–1976 decade . . . although the new constitutional language does not indicate the restrictions upon the freedoms currently exercised under its auspices, it

does symbolize that there has been an important change
from what is now viewed as the tyranny of the "gang of four."

For our purposes, it is sufficient to remember that such freedoms of
literary and artistic expression that exist at any given time exist under
the aegis of the CCP (or some particular leadership faction) or not at
all.

In the now famous Third Plenum of the 11th Central Committee,
held 12–18 December 1978, Deng Xiaoping began to further
consolidate his power, and the CCP came to the aid of literature and
the arts through a number of celebrated decisions. Held less than a
month after the Peking Municipal Party Committee had reversed the
historical verdict on the Tiananmen Incident — the spontaneous
demonstration of 5 April 1976 that honored the memory of Premier
Zhou Enlai, attacked the regime of the Gang of Four, and supported
Deng Xiaoping— the Third Plenum met at a time when wall posters on
Peking's "democracy wall" were attacking Mao Zedong's role in the
suppression of the Tian An Men Incident, demanding punishment for
the high officials still in office (meaning Hua Guofeng himself) who
had helped suppress the demonstration, and calling for various reforms
to curb the bureaucratic privileges of CCP cadres and solve the problems of the derusticated and unemployed intellectual youth, the
workers, and the impoverished peasants. Besides endorsing the
Politburo's decision to shift the emphasis of the Party's work from
political class struggle to economic modernization, the Plenum put
forward three slogans of great importance to the arts: "emancipation of
the mind" (the official Peking translation of *jiefang sixiang*, "liberation
of thoughts/thinking"), "seeking truth from facts" *(shishi qiushi)*, and
"practice is the sole criterion for testing truth" *(shijian shi jianyan
zhenli de weiyi biaozhun).*[13] Although these slogans were conditioned
by the equally strong emphasis on the duty of the Party to "lead and
educate" the people in the "scientific system of Mao Zedong Thought,"
as outlined in the next section, there actually was a great deal of
"emancipation of the mind" going on in literature and politics
throughout 1979 and 1980, despite several serious setbacks for those
people whom Westerners might regard as democratic dissenters.

Throughout 1979 a number of further governmental decisions
promised hope for literary, artistic, and intellectual freedoms. In
January, as further proof of the ascendancy of Deng's reform group,
Lin Biao and the Gang of Four were officially labeled "left
deviationists" and the dominant thrust of official criticism was shifted

to leftist policies (Maoism without mentioning Mao by name) rather than rightist policies (of Liu Shaoqi, Zhou Enlai, and Deng Xiaoping.)[14] Throughout the year, many cadres, writers, and other people who had been punished or harmed by the Cultural Revolution were rehabilitated, many of them posthumously. On 1 February at a mass meeting in Guangzhou, it was announced that the three young men known collectively as Li Yizhe, authors of the celebrated 1974 manifesto entitled "Socialist Democracy and a Legal System," had been completely exonerated and released from prison.[15] In June, Peng Zhen, director of the Commission for Legislative Affairs, delivered a report to the Second Session of the Fifth National People's Congress explaining the seven Draft Laws scheduled to take effect on 1 January 1980. The "Criminal Law" and the "Law of Criminal Procedure" provide formal legal protection for citizens' rights in most criminal cases, impose heavy penalties for various crimes like murder, robbery, arson, sabotage, and other "counter-revolutionary acts," and guarantee the right of public trial, legal defense, and verification of evidence in most criminal cases. Once again, however, the CCP and the state security organs are still above the judiciary and can be expected to intervene in cases involving the interpretation of vague areas in the law concerning "counter-revolutionary acts" whenever the Party hierarchy is especially interested in the outcome.[16]

During the same meeting, Hua Guofeng echoed a number of press reports when he once again stressed that strengthening "socialist democracy" and "socialist legality" could only proceed in accordance with the "Four Fundamental Principles": the socialist road of development, the dictatorship of the proletariat, the leadership of the CCP, and Marxism-Leninism-Mao Zedong Thought as the only correct ideology.[17] Political or literary criticism of any defects of Chinese socialism, such as autocracy, bureaucracy, special privileges, patriarchal work style, factionalism, lack of discipline, and so on — criticism made by Party Central in the first instance — must be subordinated to or fall within the scope of the "Four Fundamental Principles." Any criticisms deemed by Party Central to go beyond the "Four Fundamental Principles" will be regarded as unfriendly dissident criticism and dealt with accordingly, regardless of freedoms of speech, press, and assembly enshrined in the new Constitution.

The strongest statements of official support for the new literature of 1977 to 1979 and the fullest promises of further artistic freedom from direct Party control were made by then Vice Premier and Vice Chairman of the CCP, Deng Xiaoping, and Vice Chairman of the

All–China Federation of Literary and Art Circles, Zhou Yang, at the emotionally charged Fourth National Congress of Writers and Artists which convened in Peking from 30 October to 16 November 1979.[18] Mao Dun gave an upbeat keynote speech in which he proclaimed that the "ultra–leftist" line of the Cultural Revolution period had "ceased forever," that literature should serve the Four Modernizations, that only the "Hundred Flowers" policy could lead to the creation of "even more and better works of literature and art," and that Marxism–Leninism–Mao Zedong Thought "are sciences that guide practice, not dogmas" to be applied without regard to "new historical conditions that our revolutionary teachers did not encounter in their lives." (3–6)

After generously praising the literature and art of the first seventeen years of the PRC (1949–66) and of the post–Cultural Revolution period (works that played an active role in attacking the Gang of Four and their followers), Deng Xiaoping proclaimed that "the sole criterion for deciding the correctness of all work should be whether that work is helpful or harmful to the accomplishment of the Four Modernizations." The general overall function of literature, he went on, is to carry on "ideological struggle" by criticizing "the ideas of the exploiting classes, the influences of conservatism, and the narrow–minded, small–producer mentality, as well as anarchism, extreme individualism, and bureaucracy;" to satisfy "spiritual needs;" to educate "new socialist youth;" and to "raise the ideological, cultural, and moral levels of the entire society." (9)

After this catalog of generalities, Deng then listed at least thirteen specific things that writers and artists should do. They included describing and praising the fine qualities and great revolutionary victories of the Chinese people; "describing and promoting" [i.e., creating an image of] "new socialist youth;" whipping up "enthusiasm for socialism among the masses;" "vividly describing the inner and essential qualities" of Chinese social relations; expressing the people's desire for progress and the trend of historical development; educating the people in socialist ideology and imbuing them with "determination to strive for a brighter future;" considering the "social effects" of literature and "the needs of the masses;" "elevating the minds of the masses to a higher spiritual plateau;" guarding against both "Left" and "Right" pressure "to stir up social unrest and disrupt political stability and unity;" learning and applying "all the fine artistic skills and techniques, domestic and foreign;" "heeding and accepting constructive criticism and suggestions;" and "discovering and training young writers. (9–12)

Finally, Deng outlined the role of the CCP in relation to literature and art and promised an expansion of artistic freedom in accordance with "Comrade Mao Zedong's principle that art and literature should serve the people, particularly the worker–peasant–soldier masses, and follow his policies of 'letting a hundred flowers bloom;' 'weeding out the old to bring forth the new,' and 'making foreign and ancient things serve China.'" (10) Party leadership should support writers and artists in every way possible while helping them "to maintain a correct political orientation," but "the issuing of executive orders in the areas of literary and artistic creation and criticism must be stopped" because they are counter–productive. (13) "In mental endeavors as complicated as literature and art," Deng concluded, "it is absolutely essential for writers and artists to totally utilize their individual creative spirit. Writers and artists must have the freedom to choose their subject matter and method of presentation based upon artistic practice and exploration. No interference in this regard can be permitted." (13–64) One can imagine the applause that must have greeted these remarks.

After the political leader of the "new era" had presented the Party's overall position, the seemingly indefatigable 72–year old leader of the literary bureaucracy, Zhou Yang, delivered a 25,000 word speech in which he summed up the "experiences of the past" (as interpreted by the 1979 leadership) and spelled out in some detail the "tasks for the future." He repeated Deng Xiaoping's praise of the first 17 years and added further praise of the leftist writings of the 1930s and 40s, reaffirmed the correctness of Mao's *Yan'an Talks* and the "necessary and important struggles" involved in all of the criticism campaigns of the first 17 years from the attack on the film *Wu Xun zhuan* to the anti–Hu Feng movement. (15–21) In keeping with the current interpretation, he did admit, however, that the Anti–Rightist Campaign of 1957 represented a mistaken "leftist" over–extension of the class struggle which was "extremely harmful," involved "harsh and arbitrary" criticisms, and "severely curtailed" artistic democracy. (25–26)

Zhou strongly contrasted the Cultural Revolution literature of 1966–76 with the post–Mao literature of 1977–79. He characterized the literary line of the Cultural Revolution era, spelled out in the *Summary of the Forum on Literary and Art Work in the Armed Forces*,[19] as a "feudal–fascist cultural autocracy and cultural nihilism" that represented a complete "distortion of Comrade Mao Zedong's ideas on literature and art" and "enslaved the arts with counter–revolutionary politics." (21–22)[20] The literature of 1977–79, by contrast, represents a return to the "realist tradition of socialist literature and art" and poses "urgent problems in real life" thus reflecting "the people's wishes, ideals, moods, and demands." (23–24) Zhou Yang defended the "literature of the wounded" in very strong terms:

> We should not casually censure these works as literature of the wounded or exposé literature.[21] The people's spiritual wounds and the counter–revolutionary gang that inflicted those wounds are all facts. How can our writers cover them up or whitewash them? How can writers close their eyes to the contradictions in real life? Of course we [i.e., the CCP literary bureaucracy] do not condone describing the spiritual wounds in a naturalistic way that will lead to negative, apathetic and nihilistic thoughts and feelings. The people need healthy literature and art. We [the CCP] need the power of literature and art to help people better understand their bitter experience, heal their wounds, and learn their lessons so that the same tragedies will not happen again. (24)

Following Deng's example, Zhou then went on to discuss three important relationships that must be handled "correctly" in Chinese Marxist literary criticism: the relationship between (1) the arts and politics, (2) the arts and the life of the people, and (3) the inheritance of tradition and innovation in the arts. He discussed the second one first. Calling it "the most fundamental and decisive," he reiterated the standard Marxist premise that "literature and art are reflections of social life . . . and in turn exert a tremendous influence on life." Admitting that the 1962 attacks on "middle characters" was mistaken — because such people do exist in real life — he nevertheless reaffirmed "Comrade Mao Zedong's idea of combining revolutionary realism with revolutionary romanticism in literary and artistic creation . . . as a guide in helping writers observe and depict life with accuracy and foresight" provided they are "rooted in reality." "Revolutionary realism," he concluded, "often contains factors of revolutionary romanticism, especially when it reflects the future development of reality and the ideals of life." (27)[22] Nevertheless, writers should be "free to choose" their own "method of creation, . . . have the courage to expose and reflect the contradictions and struggles in life," and "both portray the bright side . . . and expose the dark side of society." (28)

Defining politics, most disingenuously, as the politics "of classes" and of "the masses" or "the people" and thus ignoring the role of the

CCP; Zhou maintained that "literature and art . . . should be suited to the political needs of a given historical period. At the present time they should harmonize with the needs of socialist modernization." (28–29) Whatever is good for modernization is good for "the proletariat and the broad masses and thus is good literature. "A writer should," aside from this general requirement "be free to write what he wants and in any way he wants." The leadership should not interfere, but should only "be good at giving guidance." (30)

In regard to the third relationship, Zhou referred to "Comrade Mao Zedong's 1956 talk to musicians" and reiterated Mao's call for a balance between the use of the literary heritage and contemporary needs.[23] He left little doubt that current needs were paramount with his assertion that modernized versions of traditional operas should continue to "impart historical knowledge and teach people how to tell good from bad, right from wrong, beauty from ugliness." (31)

In the final third of his speech, Zhou Yang made the fullest official statement of support for post–Mao literature and literary freedom and presented another catalogue of "the main tasks of writers and artists" in the "new era." "We writers and artists," he said, though he can hardly be considered in either group, "must first of all emancipate our own minds" from many wrong ideas, including the "ultra–left trend of thought" of the Cultural Revolution era, "feudal and capitalist ideas," small producers' "narrow–mindedness," and all sorts of unspecified "idealistic and metaphysical concepts." (32) Such emancipation has definitely not gone too far, as critics of the Third Plenum line have asserted. On this point, he was very forceful:

> Certainly we must criticize and oppose all wrong ideas, anarchistic tendencies, extreme individualism, and bourgeois 'liberalization.' But the question now is not that we have gone too far in emancipating thought but that we have not gone far enough. There is still strong resistance and a lot of people's thinking is still ossified or semi–ossified. We can only give correct guidance to, not suppress, the emancipation of thought. Leaders in literary and art circles should begin by emancipating their thought before asking the writers and artists to do so. (32)

Furthermore, the "Double Hundred" policy is now written into the Constitution (1978) and it guarantees "the people freedom of scientific research and artistic creation." Henceforth, socialist culture and art will be developed "through the mass line, free competition, and free debate." (33)

The "main tasks" for writers and artists are many, but they are all subsumed under "the main task (of) depict(ing) the life and destiny of different kinds of people . . . as they work for modernization." In carrying out this task, writers should, "in the spirit of criticism and self–criticism, expose and criticize bureaucratic habits, the concept of feudal special privileges, the narrow–mindedness and conservatism of the small producer, all old ideas and habits that keep the people in a rut, and bourgeois, petty bourgeois, and anarchistic ideas that hold back social progress . . ." (33) At the same time, writers should rewrite Party history again so as to "portray the heroic deeds of the older generation of proletarian revolutionaries," and demonstrate once again "that the masses are the motive force in making history," not some god–like infallible leader. (33–34) To carry out these literary tasks it will also be necessary to "strengthen" Marxist literary theory both by taking Mao Zedong Thought "as a guide to action" and by having "the courage to revise and supplement" it to harmonize with the present situation. (35) The kind of people who can accomplish all of these tasks must be "daring trailblazers" that, Zhou concluded, China needs in the tens of thousands.(38)[24]

Aside from representing a dramatic public reversal of the draconian Cultural Revolution policies toward writers and artists, is there anything fundamentally new in either the theoretical or practical pronouncements of Deng and Zhou? If we recall the nature of Marxist literary theory in general, Zhou Yang's speech at the last such Congress in July 1960, and CCP literary policy since 1942; the answer must be no.

The two most important points Deng Xiaoping makes are that the chief function of literature is ideological propaganda for and against what the Party leadership is for or against at the present time and that external reality, as interpreted by external authority, is the "sole criterion" of literary and artistic quality. The presuppositions behind these statements are the standard Marxist ideas that literature, as part of the superstructure, is in dialectical relation to the economic base of society; that, therefore, some literary works are progressive while some are regressive; and, finally, that some external authority, namely the CCP, possesses a kind of cognitive privilege that enables it alone to tell the difference between such good and bad literature.[25] As usual, the list of things writers should do as a response to these theoretical ideas contains contradictions. For example, they should describe the essential quality of social relations, but they should not stir up social unrest or disturb the society's putative unity of purpose. They should describe "new socialist youth" and "popular enthusiasm" for socialism; but what if these two phenomena are non-existent? The role of the CCP also appears vague and contradictory. It should see that published writers "maintain a correct political orientation" while at the same time allowing complete artistic freedom to choose both subject matter and method of presentation. Is this not once again a case of (in Zhou Yang's 1960 formulation), "the integration of uniformity in political orientation and variety in artistic styles?"[26]

Zhou Yang's speech does indeed seem to reflect an attempt to return to the theoretical position of the years 1942-1966. Most importantly, the reflectionist theory of literature is reaffirmed and little room is left for other kinds of literature. For example, his praise for the post-Mao "wounded" or "exposé" literature is restrained by the assertion that "we" cannot, "of course," tolerate a "naturalistic" mode of presentation which would not make a "healthy" impression on the reader. Zhou's reaffirmation of the necessity to continue combining "revolutionary realism" with "revolutionary romanticism" means that writers are still expected to depict the "*future development*" of reality with the "*accuracy and foresight*" of the CCP and Marxism-Leninism-Mao Zedong Thought (27) and is still quite comparable to the Soviet policy of Socialist Realism as the "truthful, historically concrete representation of reality *in its revolutionary development*."[27] Related to this formulation is the outdated idea (tacitly affirmed by both Deng and Zhou) that form and content (theme) can be completely separated so that writers who are supposedly free to choose any method (form) of creation will all conform to the same pro-socialist, pro-Four Modernizations ideology (theme).[28] Or, as Zhou Yang said in 1960:[29]

> We have always held that letting a hundred flowers blossom means blossoming within the domain of socialism . . . Letting a hundred schools of thought contend means contending under the guidance of Marxism-Leninism, . . .

The "political needs of a given historical period," which both Deng and Zhou urged literature to serve, will of course continue to be decided in the PRC by the outcome of CCP leadership debates or struggles. The "given historical period" in which the Deng Xiaoping faction rose to supreme power and continued to call upon writers to criticize and expose all of the targets mentioned above lasted more or less until June 1981, but the scope of such artistic freedom to criticize was gradually narrowed by further leadership pronouncements throughout the year and a half following the Fourth Congress of Writers and Artists.

As a result perhaps of what seemed to be an open invitation by the Party leadership, the literature of 1979 and 1980 went beyond merely criticizing Lin Biao and the Gang of Four to a much more critical appraisal of contemporary social reality and the entire history of the first thirty years of the PRC. The style of most of these works is surprisingly realistic in the 19th century European or May Fourth sense of presenting the truth of one author's personal vision in contrast to the didactic precepts of Socialist Realism; and their themes are remarkably critical by virtue of their often harsh, satirical, or ironic exposure of the dark side of Chinese life. These themes include rural poverty and the often harsh treatment of the peasantry by rural CCP cadres; special privileges and venality of older "revolutionary cadres" who were attacked during the Cultural Revolution and are now trying to make up for their lost opportunities; extreme corruption and degeneracy in the officer corps of the People's Liberation Army, including the rape and ruination of young women and expropriation of public funds to build luxurious private homes; bureaucratic corruption so endemic among CCP economic cadres that virtually nothing can be produced without going through an incredible network of extra-legal bribery and gift-giving; outright embezzlement involving high level officials; moral corruption among a segment of the younger generation (often the children of high cadres) that has lost all semblance of idealism and all hope for the future of the nation; and the physical exhaustion of middle-aged intellectuals to the extent that heart attacks are as common for them at forty as they are for capitalist executives, and some intellectuals see no way out but to emigrate to the West.
By early 1980, the situation already seemed to the CCP Propaganda Bureau to be getting out of hand. Especially galling to the leadership was the great popularity of the play *What If I Really Were?*, a satirical attack on contemporary CCP bureaucratism and special privileges written in the summer of 1979 by Sha Yexin, Li Shoucheng, and Yao Mingde of the Shanghai People's Art Theatre, given forty-six restricted inner Party performances, and printed in a 10,000 copy run for inner Party reading only.[30] Most of the participants in a meeting of the Chinese Playwrights Association (4–10 November 1979) praised the play, while only a few criticized it for being too sympathetic towards a young man who pretends to be the son of a high-ranking

cadre in order to secure the privileges normally offered to such people in PRC society.

As head of the Propaganda Bureau, Hu Yaobang (soon to become Secretary General of the Party Secretariat and later Chairman of the Party) together with Zhou Yang called a Drama Forum from 23 January to 13 February 1980 on the subject of how to write correct plays. The highlight of the meeting came on 12 and 13 February when Hu Yaobang took the floor, admitted modestly that he did not know very much about theatrical affairs, and proceeded to deliver a 26,000 character, six–hour speech on just exactly how playwrights and all writers in general should, in his opinion (only his opinion – *yijian* – and not his instructions – *zhishi*) handle very nearly every conceivable artistic and literary situation.[31]

In Part One of his eight–part speech, Hu explained that the leadership had called this meeting because they felt that a "basic unified outlook" on many literary and artistic questions did not emerge after the Fourth Congress of Writers and Artists. In order to achieve such a unity of opinion, they decided that besides the issuing of Party Central documents it would also be a good idea to hold a discussion meeting and exchange opinions about issues of concern to everyone working in the literary and artistic fields. Although a diversity of opinions was a natural thing, dialectically speaking, it should eventually lead to a unity of thought – at least for a certain period of time.

In Part Two, Hu answered the question, 'How should we treat ourselves" in literature? Basing himself on Mao Zedong's famous distinction between two kinds of contradiction – those antagonistic contraditions between the enemy and ourselves and those non–antagonistic contradictions among the people[32] – Hu said that in literature and propaganda (axiomatically equated) some people and some works were making the twin mistakes of "taking counter–revolutionary elements who destroy socialism for heroes" and "taking our own people who have made mistakes to be irreconcilable enemies." (127) This vague remark could be made to apply to continued fictional criticism of opportunistic cadres who profited from the Cultural Revolution or "old revolutionary cadres" who are still making "mistakes" such as misusing their power.

After laying down this theoretical foundation derived from Mao Zedong Thought, Hu went on to give his opinions concerning the "correct" literary treatment of the CCP, Chinese society, the working people of China (including intellectuals as a small but important part of the working class), the People's Liberation Army, and Chairman Mao and Mao Zedong Thought. There were no surprises in his formulations. The CCP is the only leadership of the Chinese nation, without it there would have been no revolution and no new China and there would be no modernization in the future. No matter how many faults it may have (and he admitted many) it is still "great and loveable" and "we hope it will be treated correctly" in literature. (128) Our new Chinese society has many defects, but most of them are the result of the legacy of the old China and the machinations of Lin Biao and the Gang of Four. Of course, our Party has had mistaken policies, but you must always remember that "in one respect we are superior to anyone — we have abolished the system of exploitation" of man by man that exists in capitalist society. (128) For the sake of the many young people who do not understand how much better our new society is than the old society, you should reflect this fact in your literary works. "Propagandizing the fundamental difference between the systems of old and new China, is the revelation of historical truth." (128) Although Party policies on intellectuals have been mistaken "for a long time;" in redressing this wrong, writers must not forget the great majority of working people. Writers have the "responsibility" to present the lives of the toiling masses. The People's Liberation Army soldiers are "the most loveable people" and the "most reliable," and "literary works should show their important position." (128–129) Lin Biao and the Gang of Four distorted Mao Zedong Thought, "held Chairman Mao up as a god, venerated his works as a bible, and encouraged superstition." (129)[33] Nevertheless, Mao Zedong's positive contributions to Chinese history far outweigh his mistakes and Mao Thought will remain our indispensable guide leading us to the victory of modernization. Some comrades believe that the CCP faces a crisis of faith, self–confidence, and trust; but, although there has been a loss of prestige, the leadership is now engaged in a Party reform movement that will, in a few years, raise the Party's prestige to its highest level in history. In his conclusion to this section, Hu called upon PRC writers to write Socialist Realist literature. That is, he said that "literary works in the socialist era" must grasp and reflect "the essence of society", and he defined the "essence of society" (as always in Marxist literary theory) as "the progressive force that occupies the leading position in this new society of ours." (129)

In Part Three, Hu discussed the question of how to treat "the dark side" of PRC society. Quite simply, it should be treated by the ancient Chinese method of "praising the good and attacking the bad"; the "good" and the "bad" being readily discoverable by reference to Mao's theory of two forms of contradiction and the current Party leadership's interpretation of it (i.e., this speech). All major criminals such as "counter-revolutionary elements, destructive elements, killers, incendiaries, and traitors" should be exposed, attacked, and destroyed (by legal means) in literary works. All "backward tendencies among the people", such as "lack of organization and discipline, individualism, liberalism, refusal to study, lying, and so on," should also be exposed and educated out of existence in literature.

At this point Hu entered into a long theoretical discussion on how to handle "bureaucratism and special privileges". Basing himself on the 19th century Marxist-Leninist premise that all the state bureaucracies in capitalist countries have been established for the sole purpose of making and protecting the profits of the rich capitalists (and thus demonstrating his seeming lack of understanding of post-war welfare states in Europe and the Americas), he went on to argue that the nature of the socialist organs of state is fundamentally different — they are there only to "serve the people." Consequently literary works should definitely not imply that "bureaucratism" is a systematic problem in socialist China and much less should they imply the completely erroneous view that the CCP is some sort of specially privileged class.

Part Four contains some generalities about literary works "standing the test of time" which seem to imply that writers should not be too quick to criticize a current social evil because the real nature of the situation may not become apparent (through the working of the dialectic) for many years.

In Part Five, Hu further elaborated on Part Three through a discussion of the correct meaning of the slogans "interfere in life" and "write the truth." His position was as easy as one, two, three. One: if "interfere in life" means that writers take a "correct stance", analyse society correctly, criticize the old and encourage the new, "this is very good." Two: if it means departing from the Marxist world outlook, being negative about life, exaggerating the dark side, and lacking confidence in life, "this is simply an incorrect way of using literature to interfere in life." Three: if it means using literature to oppose the Party's correct line, "that is even more incorrect."

Reality is very complex and to write the truth writers must reflect this complexity by showing the "bright side" as well as the dark, though not perhaps in the same work. Even "tragedies" can be written, "but what we want to prevent is the writing of tragedies that just go on being tragic forever without any future, giving people a feeling of destruction . . . This kind of tragedy is not in accord with the development of history, is not realistic." (133) What Hu seems to be saying here is that writers can only write about a "tragedy" of the Cultural Revolution or the contemporary scene if they somehow make it clear that the situation has now changed or will soon change for the better. In short, they cannot write "tragedies" at all in the generally accepted sense of something unavoidable due to the nature of social reality, fate, or personal character.

In the conclusion of this section, after praising the literature of 1977, 1978, and 1979 as having "served a very good function, especially those works that greatly exposed Lin Biao and the Gang of Four," Hu finally discussed the play *What If I Really Were?*. Prefacing his remarks by saying that they were only part of mutual "discussion" and that he welcomed criticism, he went on to condemn the play for being insufficiently "mature", and for being "insufficiently realistic and insufficiently typical regarding the actual situation since the Third Plenum." This is especially apparent in its treatment of rusticated urban youth, represented by the protagonist Li Xiaozhang, who are presented as if they are willing to do almost anything to be transferred back to the cities. Furthermore, the problems of these urban youth are mistakenly portrayed as being "created solely by the unhealthy tendencies of the cadres." Finally, Lao Zhang, the old cadre who agrees to judge Li's case shows a too sympathetic attitude towards the young imposter and also appears in the unrealistic role of a *deus ex machina* (Hu's term is *jiushi zhu*, savior). Hu concluded that, although "we support the correct exposure and criticism of unhealthy tendencies among the Party and government cadres," unless this play is "conscientiously revised" it should not be shown to the general public. Hu said he believed that the author was hard at work revising the play.

Actually, as a result of Hu's "opinions" and because the authors declined to change it, *What If I Really Were?* has only been allowed to delight and instruct readers in Hong Kong, Taiwan, and among the international sinological community.[34]

The last three parts of Hu's speech deal with the "incomparably broad scope" of material for PRC literature — including how all of the Chinese people are working with one mind for the Four Modernizations, the sixty-year CCP led revolution, and Chinese modern history since 1840 and how it led to the glorious present — and the training of a "great literary and artistic army that dares to think, dares to act, and will not give in before a hundred trials and tribulations." The first thing they must do is to continue to "liberate their thinking" and the second thing is to continue to study and develop Marxist literary and artistic theory. Of special importance is the continued study of Chairman Mao's "brilliant" *Talks at the Yan'an Forum on Literature and Art* and their exposition by Premier Zhou Enlai. Hu then publicly asked Zhou Yang to write a textbook of

Marxist literary theory for use in high schools and universities.[35]

Before it was published nationally early in 1981, a number of writers took his call for criticisms seriously and spoke up against Hu Yaobang's speech as a deliberate attempt to stifle creativity and prohibit plays. Sha Yexin wrote that playwrights were now afraid to write for fear of being incorrect and directors didn't know what plays were suitable to present.[36] Bai Hua and Su Shuyang wrote a letter to a *People's Drama* forum on literature complaining that the high level meeting on *What If I Really Were?* had a chilling effect on play-wrights who are afraid of all high level meetings on literature.[37] The most devastating critique of Hu Yaobang's policy "suggestions" was issued under very moving circumstances and extended beyond the immediate situation to the entire question of CCP leadership in art and literature — it has become known as Zhao Dan's testament.

A Confucian aphorism says that, "When birds are about to die, their songs are melancholy; when men are about to die their words are good.[38] On his hospital bed shortly before his death, the 65-year old film star, Zhao Dan, concluding that there was nothing further the political authorities could do to him and that "now I am not afraid of anything," wrote the most far-reaching critique of CCP literary policy ever published in the PRC.[39] Prefacing his remarks by stating that even artists loyal to the CCP and its cause "will feel apprehensive" when the leadership calls meetings to "strengthen Party leadership," because they know that "each time this kind of 'strengthening' has meant an upheaval, wanton interference and even 'all-round dictatorship'." Calling on the CCP to carry out the Hundred Flowers policy, Zhao wrote that, "There is no need for the Party to exercise its leadership over how to write an article or perform a drama. Art and literature are the concern of the artists and writers themselves. If the Party gives too specific a leadership to art and literature, then art and literature will stagnate." In fact, art and literature have always stagnated under CCP leadership through which "some higher leaders, who are ignorant of cultural matters, have great powers" to create a situation in which "millions of art and literary workers have to follow behind them" with the result that "those works which are acclaimed in the art and literary fields are mostly nothing more than platitudes. Zhao even went so far as to state that in his opinion, "we had better not . . . take a certain article as our guiding thought" nor allow "our art and literary associations or groups [to] stipulate a certain ideology as the guiding principle," because "the vigor of an artist or writer — and his philosophical outlook — cannot be determined by a Party" or other

Party organizations. He concluded that "art and literature must be free from any restriction," and plaintively wondered out loud, "Will this have any effect?"

According to the generally authoritative Hong Kong monthly *Dongxiang (Trends)*, the CCP Propaganda Department concluded in the spring of 1981 that Zhao Dan's statement was an "anti-Party, anti-Socialist poison weed." Hu Yaobang's opinion prevailed and, as Sha Yexin wrote, "writing has come to a premature death."⁴⁰ The stage was then set for a new nationwide round of what Zhao Dan called "wanton interference" in art and literature — the Bai Hua Incident.

In April 1981, at the same time that the arrest of suspected dissidents was going on, Bai Hua earned the distinction of being the first officially published writer to be singled out by name for political censure. The opening shots were fired by the *People's Liberation Army Daily* in a series of letters, editorials, and articles by unnamed "special commentators" attacking Bai Hua's *Bitter Love* for openly repudiating the "Four Fundamental Principles," painting the CCP and the Chinese nation in completely negative terms, thus negating the value of socialism, and maliciously caricaturing Mao Zedong and Mao Zedong Thought.⁴¹ As the campaign against Bai Hua continued throughout April and May, it included a Peking Radio broadcast calling for criticism of *Bitter Love*, a *Red Flag* attack on Bai Hua's lack of patriotism, many "literary critical" articles on *Bitter Love* that echoed the *PLA Daily's* charges, and a mild rebuke to Bai Hua's critics from the *People's Daily*. In late May, Bai Hua was awarded a national poetry prize for a 1979 poem and the respected film critic Xia Yan spoke out on his behalf. Bai did not personally go to Peking to receive the award, but he was reported by the military commander of the Wuhan district to be in good health, both politically and physically, and hard at work on a revision of the *Bitter Love* film script. The incident was presumed closed by early June, and many hopeful observers thought the incident represented a victory for Deng Xiaoping's enlightened policy of permitting only friendly and constructive comradely criticism of writers. As with the play *What If I Really Were?*, the film version of *Bitter Love*, already completed under the direction of Peng Ning was not, however, allowed to be shown; and many less sanguine commentators believed that the Bai Hua Incident was only the usual first step in an overall campaign to suppress criticism of current CCP policy.⁴²

Subsequent events proved the less sanguine to be the more astute interpreters of CCP literary policy. Having reached a political compromise with their most adamant opponents by considerably downplaying their previously proposed party reform program — the so-called "*geng-shen* reforms"[43] — Deng Xiaoping's reform faction seemed to have gained primary control over the CCP power structure when Hu Yaobang was elected Chairman of the Central Committee, replacing Hua Guofeng, and Deng himself became Chairman of the Central Committee Military Commission or Commander-in-Chief of the PLA. These events took place at the Sixth Plenum of the 11th Central Committee held in Peking from 27 to 29 June.[44] Once the "principal contradiction" of 1977 to 1980 had been thus overcome, Deng and Hu then began in proper dialectical fashion to devote more attention to what had been only a "secondary contradiction" before — the continued attacks by writers like Bai Hua on the Cultural Revolution as symptomatic of serious problems in Chinese communism that have not yet been overcome, despite the rise of a new leadership.

In early August, Deng and Hu addressed a meeting of more than 300 provincial and regional Party secretaries and other propaganda, cultural, and educational leadership cadres to once again discuss the question of how to strengthen Party leadership over ideological work; that is, how to take firm control of all cultural life once more. The main target of their attacks were no longer the "Leftist" tendencies (Cultural Revolution Maoism), but the familiar "Rightist" tendencies to criticize socialism and the CCP leadership and to advocate "bourgeois liberalization." After complaining that things were so far out of hand that the CCP could no longer criticize anyone without being accused of using a big stick, Deng Xiaoping quoted Comrade Mao Zedong on the necessity for CCP members to practice sincere self-criticism; he then went on to attack "bourgeois liberalization" in the following manner:[45]

> "The essence of bourgeois liberalization is opposition to the Party leadership. Without Party leadership, there would be no socialist system. Both Party leadership and the socialist system should be improved, but bourgeois liberalization and anarchy are impermissible. We will adhere to the policy of 'letting a hundred flowers blossom and a hundred schools of thought contend,' and persist in handling contradictions among the people correctly. This will not be changed . . . this does not mean that no criticism and self-criticism should be made of bourgeois liberalization tendencies."

Hu Yaobang went on to elaborate on the need for criticism and self-criticism (in plain language: the Party criticizes you and you criticize yourself), using the campaign against Bai Hua and *Bitter Love* as an exemplum. He said that *Bitter Love* is not good for the people and socialism: "It is not an isolated matter. It represents a wrong tendency."[46] Any other writers who cared to follow Bai Hua had been given fair warning.

At the same time that Bai Hua and other supposed "liberals" were under attack, Zhou Yang, *The People's Daily*, *Wenyibao* (Literary Gazette) and others in cultural leadership positions also came under conservative attack for being soft on "liberalism." Falling into line with Hu's call for criticism and self-criticism, more than fifty leading cadres, writers, artists, and critics held another forum in Peking from 20 to 25 August to further discuss ways of strengthening the Party's leadership over all cultural activities. The major speakers were for the most part members of the literary gerontocracy, such as Zhou Yang, Chen Huangmei, Cao Yu, and so on, and they all criticized *Bitter Love* as an example of an "unhealthy tendency" toward "bourgeois liberalization" that would cause people, especially the young, to reject socialism and Party leadership. The statement of Chen Huangmei, a Vice-Minister of Culture, reflecting as it does a political criticism of literature entirely in keeping with Mao's *Yan'an Talks*, is particularly germane:[47]

> ". . . with the experience of the 'cultural revolution,' quite a number of writers, with irreproachable intentions, have sought to dig into the historical, social and ideological roots of the disaster. But there are some who doubt the Communist Party and socialism. They resort to bourgeois human feelings, humanism and human rights; eulogize the abstract dignity of humanity, the value of man, human freedom and the position of mankind, and even regard the persecution of the intellectuals as an objective law. This is a retrogressive phenomenon."[48]

The campaign against *Bitter Love* which, incidentally, the literary bureaucracy repeatedly insisted was not a Cultural Revolution style campaign (presumably because Bai Hua, unlike Wang Xizhi and others, never was in prison),[49] continued throughout the year, reaching its inevitable conclusion in December. On the seventh of September, the acting Minister of Culture, Zhou Weizhi, once more attacked *Bitter Love* in a speech delivered to the 20th Session of the Fifth National People's Congress Standing Committee. The following paragraph contains the main theses of the 1981–82 literary campaign:[50]

> "In literary and art circles, some people set the emancipation
> of the mind and the 'double hundred policy' against the four
> fundamental principles. Some even label the four funda-
> mental principles as straightjackets and four big sticks and
> certain people want to reject Party leadership. Some hold
> that creation is solely the self-expression of writers and
> artists; they deny the need to take the social effects of
> literary pieces into consideration. This reflects the fact that a
> small number of people in the art and literary world crave
> 'absolute freedom' and extreme individualistic 'rights,' that
> they want to get rid of Party leadership, depart from the
> socialist road and go in for bourgeois liberalization. The
> scenario *Bitter Love* is an example of this and so should be
> criticized seriously. But we should adopt an attitude of unity,
> help and education towards its author, Comrade Bai Hua."

All of these sentiments were once again given the highest official
expression during a most disappointing centennial celebration of the
birth of Lu Xun (1881-1936). Once again, as so many times before,
the past was made to serve the present and, with no apparent
realization of the egregious irony of the situation, Lu Xun was
presented by Chairman Hu Yaobang as the original spokesman for
literary policies deliberately designed to stifle all writers and artists
who might actually follow the true literary example of Lu Xun.[51]
Presenting a historical portrait of Lu Xun as a "true Marxist and
Communist" despite his failure to join the Party, Hu cited Lu Xun as
authority for the current policy of "literary criticism" being carried out
to (quoting Lu Xun — source not given) "root up the weeds and water
the flowers" and establish a proper "sense of right and wrong." Hu
then went on to call for continued (supposedly Lu Xun-like) criticism
of those "unhealthy, negative features" in contemporary literature and
art "that harm the people" and are a result of the fact that "some
comrades" (not mentioned by name) lack "Marxist scientific analysis
and appraisal" of contemporary life, "feel somewhat resentful" when
asked to revise their works, and "lack faith in the socialist system,"
putting their faith rather "in foreign or capitalist countries."
Despite considerable reluctance on the part of many writers and
even literary officials to participate wholeheartedly in the unpopular
campaign against Bai Hua, Tang Yin and Tang Dacheng were finally
commissioned to write an article in *Red Flag* summing up the

leadership's case against Bai Hua and *Bitter Love*. Entitled "On the
Mistaken Tendencies in *Bitter Love*,"[52] the article repeated and thus
gave official leadership sanction to all of the charges previously
levelled by the hard-line conservatives. Bai Hua was urged to accept
the Party's fraternal criticism, to reflect on his situation, and to correct
the mistakes in his thinking about the Cultural Revolution period and
the true nature of the CCP and its relation to the Chinese people.

In late November, Bai Hua caved in to the pressure of the national
campaign against him and wrote a letter of "self-examination" to the
PLA Daily and the *Wenyibao*.[53] Confessing that his lack of party spirit
and his individual pride had led him initially to reject the Party's
loving criticism, he admitted the correctness of virtually every criticism
levelled at him and his work from whatever quarter, accepting the
verdict that *Bitter Love* represents "an outstanding example of the
mistaken literary and artistic thinking of a few people today who turn
their backs on the Party leadership and the socialist road." In
extenuation, he could only plead ideological confusion and irresolution,
confessing that those "intellectuals represented in *Bitter Love* whose
emotional and spiritual attitudes are not sufficiently resolute" did in
fact represent his own contradictory and confused thoughts about the
chaotic Cultural Revolution decade, its present aftermath, and the
prospects for the future. He concluded by reaffirming the principles of
Mao's *Yan'an Talks*, thanking his attackers for their gentle manner and
helpful criticism, and promising to look more closely at the positive
aspects of the present era.

Once again, as has occurred so often in the forty years since the
Yan'an Forum, a cycle of repression-liberalization-repression had run
its course and, in order to prevent further liberalization, one writer and
his works have been singled out *pour encourager les autres*.[54]

Throughout 1982 the CCP Central Committee conducted a media
campaign in support of "socialist spiritual civilization." Typical of that
campaign was an article by an unnamed "commentator" which
appeared late in the year in *Red Flag* and was reprinted in *Beijing
Review*.[55] The article made the point that the content of material
civilization is the same for both capitalist and socialist societies and that
the practical knowledge achieved in capitalist societies in the course of
history can and should be used in the development of socialist material
civilization, but "socialist spiritual society" is very different from
capitalist spiritual society and is "a major aspect of its superiority."
This fact is due to "the elimination of the system of exploitation, public
ownership of the means of production," the planned economy, higher

labor productivity, greater productive development, and many other factors that are directly dependent on communist ideology as the core of "socialist spiritual civilization." (14) As a consequence, the most important element in the development of a "socialist spiritual civilization" is the ideological education of the population. On this point the article quoted Mao Zedong's "correct and profound ideas" that, "Political work is the life–blood of all economic work," and "Ideological work and political work are the guarantee for accomplishing economic work and technical work." (15, references not cited.)

   After citing the success story of the PRC years in the areas of "Marxist science and communist ideals" and the propagation of "new ethical and moral concepts" that constitute an important "practical demonstration of the superiority of the socialist system" over the capitalist system where the laboring masses are "victims of exploitation," "dire poverty," and "spiritual barbarism, degeneration and emptiness;" (16) the article went on to stress the role of the arts and sciences in providing "a spiritual motive force" and ensuring a "correct orientation of development . . . guided by communist ideology." There must be a "unity between ideological consciousness and knowledge and culture," and there is a particularly pressing "need to establish a Marxist world outlook and master scientific theories so as to put the people's political consciousness, ideals, and convictions on a scientific basis." "The fundamental aspect of ideological construction" in China today is, then, "strengthening the study of Marxist theory, raising its level and broadening its dissemination and education." (17) This is the task both of the Party itself and of the arts and sciences. Working under the slogan of "serving the people and socialism" and the Hundred Flowers policy, they should educate the people "to integrate and subordinate individual interests to the interests of the collective and the state" and "to resist the corruption of individualistic ideas characterized by the practice of seeking private gain at public expense and harming others to benefit oneself." (17,30) Finally, the article concluded that "the ideological construction of the Party is the pillar of spiritual civilization" as well as universalizing education in communist "ideals, morals, discipline, and the legal system among the people of the whole country." (30)

The legal system was revised once more the following month with
the adoption on 4 December 1982, after nearly a year of public debate,
of the fourth *Constitution of the People's Republic of China.*[56] The
Four Fundamental Principles are written into the Preamble:

> Under the leadership of the Communist Party of China (1)
> and the guidance of Marxism–Leninism and Mao Zedong
> Thought (2), the Chinese people of all nationalities will
> continue to adhere to the people's democratic dictatorship (3)
> and follow the socialist road (4), steadily improve socialist
> institutions, develop socialist democracy, improve the
> socialist legal system and work hard and self–reliantly to
> modernize . . .

Articles 22 and 23 outline the ways in which "the state promotes the
development of literature and art . . . that serve the people and
socialism," thus strengthening the building of "socialist spiritual
civilization." Articles 35 to 40 and 47 once more present a fundamental bill of rights including "freedom of speech, of the press, of
assembly, of association, of procession and of demonstration, of
religious belief, of person," of "personal dignity," of "private
correspondence," inviolability of the home, and "freedom to engage in
scientific research, literary, and artistic creation and other cultural
pursuits." This list of rights would seem to be somewhat broader than
those guaranteed in the 1978 Constitution if it were not for the
inclusion of a new Article 51 which would seem to explicitly undercut
them:

> The exercise by citizens of the People's Republic of China of
> their freedoms and rights may not infringe upon the interests
> of the state, of society and of the collective, or upon the
> lawful freedoms and rights of other citizens.

Article 52 also makes it the duty of citizens "to safeguard the unity of
the country and the unity of all its nationalities," and Article 54 makes
it the duty of citizens to "safeguard the security, honor, and interests of
the motherland," vague terms that will be subject to all of the problems
of interpretation mentioned above in connection with the third
Constitution.[57]

As a result of Party policies since the Drama Forum of early 1980,
the great wave of stridently critical realism with its open attacks on

contemporary social problems had subsided by 1982; but many fiction writers continued to examine personal individual problems not unrelated to the overall social situation though less obviously critical of the current regime and to employ what they regarded as modernist narrative techniques. At the same time many young poets, despite being attacked as "obscure" and even "nihilistic" by their elders, continued to experiment with the use of private symbolism and to advocate writing as a means of self–expression as much as social commentary. Indeed, many writers both young and old went on trying to produce works that emphasized technical artistry at least as much as, if never more than, thematic considerations.

Late in 1983, after Zhou Yang himself tentatively suggested the possibility that Marxist style (the "young Marx" of the *Philosophic and Economic Manuscripts*) "alienation" from political power, from labor, and from self and society might actually exist in contemporary Chinese society; a shakeup took place in inner Party propaganda offices and a short lived media campaign was carried out against such heretical ideas and others grouped together under the general rubric of "spiritual pollution," primarily refering to the pollution of China's revolutionary communist ideology by the importation of Western ideas and practices. These then included such items as "bourgeois individualism," writing as self–expression, modernist literary techniques, "bourgeois humanism" disguised incorrectly as "Marxist humanism," alienation, the profit motive, sexual promiscuity and many more.[58] A number of writers (Dai Houying for one), journalists (most notably Wang Ruoshui of the *People's Daily*), and propaganda specialists were publicly criticized and privately disciplined and some of them were under a cloud into 1984. The campaign was not pushed very vigorously by the Deng–Hu–Zhao leadership who were anxious not to alienate the intellectuals and professionals whose labors are regarded as the key to modernization and who are among the main consumers of contemporary literature. Many of the named writers even refused to write self–criticisms, though others, like Zhang Xiaotian, recanted their errors.

The literary situation as of autumn 1984 may be characterized as one of general stability under a paternalistic system of literary control in which a vast amount of generally unremarkable material was being published monthly or quarterly by more than thirty official literary journals. A few gifted writers consistently continued to turn out readable works, and now and again a particularly bright gem was spotted by alert readers, received national attention (often in direct inverse proportion to official criticism), and was eagerly sought out by readers and scholars of Chinese literature in Hong Kong and the broad world beyond.

Having surveyed the major policy changes and developments from late 1977 through the middle of 1984, we now begin our analyses of literature proper with an overall assessment of PRC literature by several of the best known writers themselves.

II. Literary Milieu:
Writers on Writing

Throughout the years 1978, 1979, and 1980, PRC writers spoke out very freely and forcefully to express their views regarding the current literary scene and literary policies, to present their evaluation of the literary output of the past thirty years, and to voice their hopes for the future of Chinese literature. Many debates took place concerning such topics as the nature of literary realism and the relation of literature to life,[1] the so–called "literature of the wounded",[2] whether it is a virtue to praise or to criticise Chinese society,[3] the relationship between democracy and literature,[4] and the role of humanism in contemporary literature.[5] Since many of these controversies and debates have been written about elsewhere,[6] in this chapter I would like to let the writers speak for themselves through a series of translated statements that add up to an overall evaluation of PRC literature and literary policies, and then draw a few conclusions of my own. The statements are translated from two literary discussion meetings, one large and one quite small, held in January and July of 1980.

The first meeting was convened by *Wenyibao* (Literary Gazette) and the Film Research Office of the Ministry of Culture to discuss the implications of a speech given by the eighty–year old script writer, film critic, and Vice–Minister of Culture, Xia Yan, to the Second Conference of Chinese Film Workers in which he asserted that a narrowly dogmatic interpretation of the slogans "the arts serve politics" and "the arts are subordinate to politics" resulted in a decline or even complete disappearance of artistic standards in China since 1949.

A *Wenyibao* reporter summarized Xia's speech and then initiated a discussion of the social function of literature and art with five well known writers: Li Zhun, Liang Xin, Bai Hua, Ye Nan, and Zhang Tianmin.[7]

Bai Hua was quite outspoken in support of the assertion that politics in command of literature more often produces useless propaganda rather than works of art. As he said:

> . . .A discussion meeting on the social function of the arts
> must first explore 'the relationship between art and politics;'
> that is the only way to go deeply into the problem. For
> many years now this problem has not been given a proper
> resolution and thus has caused a whole string of difficulties
> and losses for creativity. The typicalizing function of
> literature, individuality, subject matter, truthfulness . . . there
> isn't one of these points that isn't related to this problem.
>   Why has such a large problem never actually been given
> a satisfactory resolution? The real problem was that this
> question *seemed to have already* been decided (italics in
> original): 'you know without discussion, art naturally must
> serve politics,' 'politics is the soul!' The evil results of this
> sort of simplified and vague 'resolution' of this problem have
> gradually become apparent: for several years now moving
> characterizations in the literary realm have become fewer
> and fewer, even descriptions with the attractive force of life
> have become increasingly rare.
>   In reality the strength of literature resides in the
> forcefulness   of   its   characterizations;   the   writer's
> characterizations are the typicalization of people in real life.
> Characters in real life are persons of a definite society and
> they are limited by a definite political and historical period.
> A serious and responsible writer, however, will always
> (though perhaps sometimes unconsciously) create his char-
> acters according to the canons of realism, will often break
> through the political predjudices and pressures he has
> received from society in order to truly represent the
> tendencies of life itself, including political desires, moral
> concepts, and so on. The value of these (realist) works
> resides in this (true presentation of life).
>   Revolutionary politics can influence a writer's world view
> and help a writer to observe and analyse life, but politics
> should absolutely not 'overreach' a writer's world view, true
> knowledge, and clear perceptions of life in order to directly
> coerce a writer's work. For many years now the mistakes of
> our writers and critics have occured at precisely this point.
>   For many years now, the relationship between art and
> politics has been interpreted to mean that the arts must ex-
> plain current policy. In this way works of art have been very

rare, while works of shallow propaganda have increased apace. We may naturally reflect the influences and development in life of current policies or the political direction (revolutionary or reactionary) of any period of history. . .; but current policies and the political direction of any historical period and, consequently, the program of any political party or organization in society should not directly revise the appearance of life reflected in a literary work of art. I believe that this is a basic principle of literary realism, a basic principle that has been repeatedly proven throughout many years of practice. (29–30)

He went on to praise such works as Mao Dun's *Midnight*, Ba Jin's *Family*, and Lao She's *Rickshaw*:

These works had an incalculable political influence . . . on the lives of an entire generation. Yes, a political influence!

But he pointed out, none of them were written to explain any particular political policy or achieve any particular political goal. He then lamented the fact that after "liberation," due to "a mechanical interpretation of the relation between art and politics" [note that his critique here has expanded from the Cultural Revolution to the entire PRC period], these veteran writers no longer wrote good works and Chinese literature suffered 'an irrepairable loss'." (30)

Bai Hua continued his discussion by pointing out some of the ways in which PRC literature has been permeated with unreality and falsehood:

In the nineteen–fifties there was a saying that a certain writer had saved up a big supply of 'dried people' (*rengan*, punning on "dried bean curd", *dougan*); when he needed a certain character for a story, he would just take out so much 'dried people', soak it in 'water' (ink) for a while, and that was that. This is a joke, but it does explain just how absurd the understanding of some of our comrades toward the depiction of characters was: a character was never 'this individual,' but 'this class.' There was a definite formula for what middle peasants, poor peasants, or landlords should be like; under any circumstances they always had the same political attitude and behavior.

The force of art often resides in its individuality, but we often overlook this point and are used to using some political pre–conception to create a character. This is the degeneration of literature. (30)

Bai Hua went on to say that narrow political control of literature is counter productive because it results in poor quality literature that readers will not trust or believe. He called for a "correct Marxist–Leninist aesthetic" to examine the entire question of literary excellence. (31)

Li Zhun, a well known writer whose first story was chosen as a study guide for all workers in 1953,[8] continued the discussion first by confessing that he felt "ashamed before the people" for having written so few good works out of his large literary production of thirty years. At this, the reporter chimed in that the film audience "does not welcome" films based on a political concept. (31) Li then continued:

> . . .In our country, works of art on rural subjects receive the greatest vulgar political interference. I wrote more than ten filmscripts, but only three or four of them are worth showing again today, and that's just making do with what's available. The man hasn't died but the work is already dead; sometimes what's written early in the year dies by the end of the year. If things were still that way, I'd just as soon change professions, not work at this line, and not waste the country's money. All of these problems certainly make me feel bad,. .

Li then quoted Mao Dun's 1979 statement that "we are opposed to literature degenerating into the explanation of political slogans" as the first use of "degenerate" in thirty years of such literature and then went on to a revealing example of his own production of "command literature":

> . . .Some years ago when Henan was campaigning against right opportunism, the leadership directed me to write some– thing; it was a political assignment, three–in–one (a Cultural Revolution literary slogan), the leadership provided the thought, the peasants the life situation, and me the writing. When a writer has to rely on someone else to provide his thoughts, that's a shameful humiliation. At that time the

Anti-Rightist campaign had just begun. Because I had written a short story called "The Grey Tent," I had to criticize myself several times and I really was apprehensive. So I took on this assignment, wrote a play and, during the Cultural Revolution, that became one of my crimes.

What was the problem? It was serving a particular leadership element's political expression. Some people, in order to hold their position, have you write a play to make a political statement on behalf of one or a few individuals — that's how disgusting things were! And I dare to say, in the lower (party) ranks, such conditions still exist.

Liang Xin chimed in then: "In many places!" (31)

Li Zhun went on to call for freedom to think and write what one thinks, asserting that writers should think for themselves and that there is a lesson in the experience of the past 30 years:

> . . . If they don't give me the right to think independently, then I certainly won't be a writer. The lesson we've learned was too painful. If they let me write what I have seen for myself and believe to be true, even if I make mistakes, I'd be happy to criticize myself . . .

He then went on to criticize "campaign literature" made to order for CCP campaigns, as lifeless and repeated Mao Dun's statement about "degenerate" literature. His critique extended to pre-Cultural Revolution conditions:

> . . .I think that if we merely return to the conditions prevailing before the Cultural Revolution, we will still be unable to accomplish the mission that Comrade Deng Xiaoping outlined at this meeting 'to raise the scientific and cultural level of the entire nation and establish a socialist spiritual civilization of a high level'.

To do that, according to Li, the question of the relation between art and politics must be resolved:

> From the historical perspective, whenever the arts escaped from the position of bondservant, they developed and flourished greatly. The pre-Qin period was like that, the

Western Han had a period like that, and the High Tang was
even more so. (31–32)

Li then mentioned Cao Yu's plays, written in his late twenties, before 1949, as establishing the foundation for modern Chinese spoken
drama, and thus opened up the thorny question of why pre–1949
literature was better than post–liberation works and why the older established writers could no longer produce good works after 1949:

> He established a foundation, blazed a trail, but in the thirty
> years after liberation, he only wrote three plays and they
> were mostly written to support some particular political
> mission. According to his practice, experience, and talent, he
> could certainly have written many more good plays in thirty
> years, but he only wrote three. Why? This is something
> worth pondering deeply.

They didn't answer directly, but the previous discussion makes the
answer clear: political interference ruined literature and made it
impossible for many good writers to write. They went on to mention
Lao She, Ba Jin, and Liu Qing as examples of good writers producing
poor quality works after 1949 by trying to follow the political
guidelines.
Li Zhun continued:

> There are inumerable lessons! In the past some people
> would tell me my movies were better (more effective) than a
> political report. At the time I was very happy to hear that,
> but today I consider it a kind of sarcasm. A film is just a
> film. If a film substitutes for a political report, then it is
> merely didactic and formulaic! Besides its didactic function,
> a film also has an aesthetic and an entertainment function
> that a political report cannot replace. In the past we have
> considered all of the arts as merely a form of mobilization for
> war. (32)

Li then asserted that beauty and spiritual values had been denied in
CCP–dominated literature whose purpose was to keep the people
ignorant, but the April 5th Movement of 1976 demonstrated that many
young people had not been fooled.
Liang Xin agreed with Li Zhun about the painful lesson of the past
thirty years and blamed it on the CCP leadership's [Mao's] attempts to

restrict the arts to the narrow propaganda functions served during the War of Resistance: "But even today no leader has clearly stated that they cannot use those wartime propaganda team methods to direct the arts." (33)

Li Zhun and Liang Xin continued the discussion of politics in command of literature, asserting that audiences don't want to pay to see a film that gives them a political lesson and that the theme, thought, or message of a work of art should be artistically and unobtrusively worked into the entire work. They quoted Engels in support of this commonplace view. (33) At this point, Ye Nan took up the discussion and defended his idea of literary realism:

> The arts reflect life and, of course, cannot be divorced from human society. Works of art will have an influence on individuals and society, and in this regard we can say that the arts cannot be divorced from politics. In history, however, the arts often came into conflict with political blocs in society (including the church). When such conflict was acute, political methods were used to resolve them — for example 'literary persecution' or even execution. People were killed, but the arts were not completely killed off. We cannot allow literature and art to become an ornament in the emperor's crown. There have been works that obeyed certain individuals or turned their backs on the people, but they definitely will not last.
> Thus I believe, with regard to artistic creation, there are only two restrictions on writers and artists: (1) *social life* (history itself) and (2) the writer or artist's own *understanding* of the phenomena of objective reality, *emotions,* and *artistic sensibilities.* Because of this the great majority of artistic works that have been passed down throughout history have been the result of the writer or artist's fidelity to life (history).

Ye repeated the idea that by being faithful to real life observation, writers, even in "class society," often reflect a reality that goes beyond their own cognitive world view:

> . . .The question now is whether or not socialist literature and art, that is, Communist Party-led literature and art, follows radically different rules from literary and artistic creation

throughout history. I believe that it does not. The difference is that the Communist Party should be in complete accord with the interests of the people and the people's literature and art in complete accord with the interests of the Party. The problem is not really so simple, however: the policy direction carried out by the Party leadership may sometimes not be in accord with the actual objective situation and may betray the interests of the people, as in a mistaken Party line. Because of this fact, writers and artists should still only be limited by life (history) and their own *subjective world*. The problem is that in people's conception for a long time the idea that art serves politics has been interpreted to mean service to a particular Party leadership level or to a particular individual . . . this is the ruination of the arts!

Such a "vulgar understanding" of the relationship between art and politics has been very harmful:

Works of art should function in a broad area and need not be restricted by time or place. Our nation's excellent works of classical literature, for example, both at present and in the future continue to have a beneficient influence on the people's spirits. . . .

He then cited examples of made to order propaganda literature — Anti-Rightist and even currently popular anti-Gang of Four "literature of the wounded" — and stated that it will not last. "What superior works of literature and art rely on to endure a long time is the attractive force of artistic representation and brilliant thought."

After pointing out that thought devoid of artistry cannot make a work of art, Ye went on to lament the sad fact that, again because of the prevailing "vulgar understanding" of art and politics, writers, artists, and critics "did not dare to talk about beauty." Li Zhun and Bai Hua agreed, citing the example of Zhang Zhixin and her artistry.[9] Ye Nan then summed up:

Writers and artists are faithful to social life and the people. They should not be subservient to a certain individual's 'politics' and create false works of art. A writer who loses the people's heart will likewise be abandoned by the people! (33–35)

Zhang Tianmin stated his acceptance of the current slogan that the arts should serve socialism and "nourish new socialist people" in a broad general way, but he agreed that if the arts are limited to any particular political campaign they will fail as art, be of poor quality, and short-lived. Li Zhun then mentioned that time in Zhengzhou when 350,000 people came out to receive a model of a mango passed down by "the leader" (Mao).[10] Zhang Tianmin then mentioned that, of course, many pre-Cultural Revolution works also raised Mao to the level of a "Savior" and "Boddhisattva." Bai Hua then called for true literary criticism and not just the same old political criticism. The discussion then went back to the theme that the pre-liberation works of Cao Yu and others or premodern works like Cao Xueqin's *Dream of the Red Chamber* are better than anything produced since liberation precisely because of their conscious artistry and lack of political pre-conceptions.

Bai Hua, after once again vilifying the narrow political control of writers, asserted that:

> I believe a writer must stand on the high ground of history; must bear responsibility to the people; must bear responsibility to history. He definitely does not bear responsibility toward any one present event or any one particular authority.

To which Li Zhun added: "If you are still a writer."

Bai Hua went on to extend the discussion to the situation immediately after Hu Yaobang's speech at the Drama Forum mentioned above:

> Some leading comrades do not understand very clearly the writers' mission. As I said once before, 'the wind is blowing,' but we'll have to wait and see if it affects the climate [writers are being criticized, but not yet actually suppressed]. Some people asked me if these 'winds' will influence our creativity. I told them that the young writers would probably be greatly influenced; but we have suffered a great deal more, are pretty aware, and may be better off.

Li Zhun broke in to add:

> It will take courage! To break the artistic shackles might even require bloodshed!

Bai Hua agreed:

> Right, it will require courage. This problem still exists. All
> of these questions will require a number of theoretical essays
> to forcefully analyse and demonstrate their correctness. If
> we publish these ideas of ours now, some people may ask:
> how can those people think that way?

Li Zhun cut in again:

> This is a thirty year lesson of blood and tears.

Bai Hua concluded:

> An even greater problem today is that there are some
> comrades who, as soon as they achieve a leadership position,
> begin two policies: guarding themselves and checking to see
> if the arts and politics are close enough together. Can that
> way of managing the arts ever be a good one?

Zhang Tianmin then remarked:

> And the standard for handling this problem is generally
> vulgar, shortsighted, and even metaphysical.

Ye Nan put it more forcefully:

> There are some cadres in literary and art work who think of
> themselves as artistic experts. What are they experts at? It's
> only that they can point out what aspects of your work are
> poison.

The discussion concluded with an appeal by Zhang Tianmin and Li
Zhun for more attention to technical artistry, even in recent "literature
of the wounded" works of 1978 and 1979 that rightly criticize the
Cultural Revolution but in a less than satisfactory artistic manner.

The July 1980 discussion took place amid the picturesque
surroundings of Huangshan in Anhui Province. Convened by the
Anhui branch of the Chinese Writers Association and the editors of
Qingming and *Anhui Literature*, the theme of the meeting was
announced as "exploring the writer's responsibility on the road to the

Four Modernizations," the format was that of "mutual discussion" rather than set speeches, and the meeting was attended by thirty well known writers and critics.   The conference did not attract much attention in the national press; it was probably published in *Anhui Literature*, but the excerpts translated here are from the Hong Kong magazine *Qishi niandai (The Seventies)* whose editor received a copy from a friend in the PRC.   The remarks were prepared in written form from a tape recording and some of them are given anonymously as consensus opinions.[11]

Liu Binyan began the discussions with a statement of the difficulties writers have because their right of assembly is often infringed by rumors and harassment:

> People in our line of work should naturally have the opportunity to be together, but we writers have great difficulty meeting together even once. [First off it is difficult to find housing for guests in Peking.]
> Secondly, there are many rumors.   Last year before the National Congress of Writers and Artists, a number of younger writers invited Wang Meng, Deng Youmei, and myself to a meeting; afterwards some people spread the rumor that there was a literary salon in Peking with Zhang Jie as the hostess.(98)

At this point Liu's speech was cut off by angry exclamations about the evils and inaccuracies of rumors and the perfidy of those who spread them.   The topic of salons was forgotten until Li Zhun spoke up in his heavy Henan accent:

> . . . for a long time we writers have 'lived and died without associating' [quoting Lao Zi], not even meeting once in a whole lifetime; having no opportunity to meet friends through literature, having no opportunity to learn from one another, having no opportunity to mutually study and improve ourselves, we feel that we have improved too slowly — this situation should be changed!

He grew more animated as he went on:

> The way I see it there's nothing wrong with a literary salon!
> If someone says I'm forming a salon, then I'll feel extremely

honored because it's an expression of public praise! That's my attitude! As I see it China's salons are too few and don't really deserve to be called salons. As far as some characters are concerned, we have to meet them head on. If you say I've got a salon, even though I don't yet have a salon, then I'll just form a real salon! I only have a two room house; if I had more rooms, I would like to try to organize a genuine salon!

He went on to discuss the importance of literary salons or intellectual associations, such as the Tongcheng School, for the discussion and transmission of learning and scholarship, and then concluded:

... We should not be afraid of people saying we are forming a salon!(98)

Everyone agreed and applauded his statement, then the usually quiet Li Na spoke up:

... For the past ten years we have been frightened, no one dared to go to anyone else's home and writers did not dare to associate together. When we did occasionally meet, we wouldn't talk about anything meaningful; we didn't dare discuss politics and we didn't dare discuss literature — all we could do was chat about the weather. That was a most abnormal situation. Making friends through literature is a writer's right (*quanli*) and we should exercise that right. . . . Why shouldn't we form salons!? (99)

The discussion then moved on to the subject of the many thematic restrictions that still hamper writers and the critics demands for the production of ideological works, when Liu Binyan brought up the question of whether or not it is permissable to write about love in any guise other than "revolutionary love":

Many restrictions on artistic creation still exist today — unwritten restrictions. In writing about love, for example, can we only write about such extraordinarily correct love as that between Paul and Rita[12]? After Zhang Jie's story "Love Cannot be Forgotten" came out,[13] two critical articles mentioned the example of Paul and Rita as if only love like theirs was sacred and correct and could be written about. Aside from that type, any other kinds of love cannot be written about or can only be written about in a critical manner; otherwise it is unhealthy or the style is vulgar.

I cannot quite figure it out. Something that we really do not advocate but are hard put to say we do not allow and also something that exists objectively in contemporary life, something like the kind of love between those two people in Zhang Jie's story . . . Can we really write about it? Should we write about it or not? If an author does write about it, is it necessary to either affirm it or criticise it? Can we have only one of those two attitudes?

Liu did not answer his own string of rhetorical questions, but went on about current literary criticism:

Today's criticisms regularly have one major failing: They depart from real life to criticise literary works. . . . As essays those criticisms are logically coherent; but if you take a brief glance at real life, they just don't make sense — they [the content of the criticism and real life] are completely different things. (99)

Qin Zhaoyang agreed with Liu that literature should reflect real life and then pointed out that the Paul and Rita story takes place during a revolutionary war when there was naturally very little time for love and romance; but that was an "extraordinary period" and we must not expect only sacrificial revolutionary love in society today:

After Karl Marx's wife died, he couldn't go on writing his *Capital* and he died shortly after — how do we explain that? Do we mean to imply that *his* moral character was lower than Paul's?[14]

Feng Mu concluded this part of the discussion by saying that the theme of Zhang Jie's story was quite straightforward: "A marriage without love is an unhappy marriage. Thus she hopes that all families will be established on the basis of genuine love."

The editors then brought up the topic of popular songs, mentioning Li Guyi and Zhu Fengbo, female singers whose "beautiful, romantic, and pleasing" songs are extremely popular with the masses, but commenting that "what the masses love will always make some people unhappy. . . . How should we regard such a question?"

Liu Binyan commented ironically:

> Li Guyi's singing has become a veritable calamity that must be eliminated, but in reality it cannot be eliminated. The widespread popularity of Li Guyi's songs reflects a new need of the masses, and whatever the masses need and like cannot be suppressed by any authority, no matter how great. This is also something that cannot be replaced by anything else. (99)

The discussion then moved on to the popularity of Deng Lijun (Teresa Deng, a well known pop singer from Taiwan whose tapes were being smuggled into the PRC at the time) and one wag remarked that it should be accepted as part of the government's "united front" policy.

Then they went on to more serious matters. Early in 1980 the prestigious litery journal *Wenyibao* once again brought up the stale slogan of "social effects" under the cover of which Mao Zedong (following Qu Qiubai), Zhou Yang, and an army of lesser literary policemen turned all literary criticism in China into political screening of works for elements deemed to be socially "unhealthy" in their effects on society. When writers are urged to "pay attention" to the "social effects" of their works, they know that this is a call for ideological conformity, and those writers of conscience and courage react against it as best they can. According to the editors, a lively debate took place on this point in the first half of 1980, with "many comrades" improving the "thought" and "artistry" of their works, but there were also those who "took advantage" of the slogan to "wield a club" and wildly attack fellow writers in an unprincipled manner characteristic of the Cultural Revolution era.

Mao Shuyan commented:

> . . . it's very strange, but whenever some problem occurs in society today, the blame is always placed on the literary and art world [and recently shown Japanese and American films have been attacked for supporting murder, rape, and robbery] as if forbidding the showing of such films could eliminate crimes like murder, rape, and robbery from our society — this is really ridiculous! (100)

Some other (annonymous) comrades pointed out that:

There are now a number of unwritten yet real standards for dealing with the question of social effects. The first concerns praise or exposure. Whatever involves praise, no matter if it is true or false, its social effect is good. Whatever involves exposure, again with no regard for its truth or falsehood, its social effect is bad. The second involves the reflection of the past or the present. Whatever describes the past, including the Anti–Rightist Campaign and the ten years' calamity, is permissable. Whatever attacks contemporary social evils, is considered to have bad social effects. The third involves the Party or government rank of the object of description. Criticism of the common people or general, low level cadres is permissable; but criticism of the mistakes of individual high cadres is uniformly regarded as having bad social effects. Take the spoken drama *The Imposter* or the short story "Fei Tian" for example;[15] if these works had not exposed high ranking cadres, but only ordinary cadres or common characters, they probably would not have been singled out as having bad social effects. (100)

Qin Zhaoyang went on from there:

An extremely strange phenomenon has occured today with regard to social effects: those 'effects' that have already been created in society are then off limits to the arts. Once the arts deal with them, then it's a case of having a bad effect on society. Many things that have already become genuine 'effects' on society, things that the common people dislike the most, like seeking special privileges, bureaucratism, and so on, have all become the most tabooed subjects which we cannot touch. I believe we should not fear social problems, but we should be afraid of not daring to face social problems squarely. Refusing to face squarely objectively existing social problems will not work. The Cultural Revolution, as all the people saw it, was a very bloody affair. If literary works do not write about that, it's still an objective reality. Daring to bring up problems is the beginning of change and it gives hope to society. What will be the social effect of forbidding literary works to bring up and reflect problems? That can only cause people to believe that there is no hope

for change. Furthermore, we must trust the people, trust
that the people will absorb correct things from works of art.
To forbid works of art to reflect the realities of life is in
essence to be afraid of the people, afraid of reform. We
must not make one–sidedly harsh demands on works of art;
we should publicly praise those writers who dare to reveal
social contradictions and reprimand those people who
obstruct social progress. Works that are not written well
enough can be discussed, studied, and criticized, but should
not be clubbed to death (100)

Feng Mu, one of the first to bring up the slogan "social effects,"
admitted that some people had distorted the slogan in order to defend
themselves, club, and pin labels on others; but he refused to take
responsibility for these actions by people with whom he too was at
odds. He offered his interpretation of "social effects" in terms of the
general ideas or theme that the writer intends his work to convey to the
reader. He presented this authorial concern with social effects as the
equivalent of the "social function" of a work of art. His concept seems
almost theraputic:

> This social function has no other purpose than to raise the
> level of a person's mental world, to make a person's thinking
> more pure and clean, so that he can become a more beautiful
> person, a more upright person.

He concluded by asserting that any great writer whose thoughts are:

> always in tune with the people, in the process of creation
> cannot very well fail to consider the influence his works may
> produce in society; he should pay particular attention to the
> social function of his works. (100–101)

The editors initiated a new topic here by stating that ever since the
fall of the Gang of Four and the return of the Double Hundred policy:

> there has already begun to be some artistic democracy [but]
> everyone feels . . . there are still many problems. Despite all
> of the many directives of Party Central, there are still cases
> of coercive interference in literature and art. Some people
> are still accustomed to asserting their bureaucratic will and
> relying on administrative decrees to manage the arts. (101)

Liu Binyan then put the question as follows:

> There is one question that ought to be clearly discussed: What is bourgeois liberalization? What is a correct Double Hundred policy direction? If this question is not cleared up, then anyone who practices artistic creation must always be fearful and cautious. The people with clubs in their hands may start swinging those clubs at any time. I really don't understand: just what sort of liberalization do we have anyway?
>
> What is the main obstacle to literary creation? Because of differences in political opinions, in artistic principles, and in personal life experiences, there is no unity of opinion about just how far to go in the Double Hundred policy of relaxation. Some people believe we've already gone too far; actually, though, there are still very many things, like feudalistic paternalism in the family system, that have not been reflected in creative writing; or, let's say, have not been deeply reflected because the artistic quality of the works have not yet been good enough. Nevertheless, we rarely hear anyone say that the reflection of real life in our works is too narrow, the subject matter still not diversified enough, and that we should open up with all our courage and write even more penetratingly. What we hear is: 'You cannot do this! You cannot do that!' All we hear is censure and reprimands directed at the arts. Today it's as if there were a particular water course and some people are deeply afraid that we will spill out over the sides of that water course. It is, furthermore, a very narrow water course and it cannot accommodate today's literary and art circles. (101)

Zhang Jie then continued Liu's discussion by asking why it was that after "liberation" Chinese writers never produced any world class literary works or even came up to the pre-"liberation" level of Lu Xun, Ba Jin, and Lao She. Noting that it was not because writers had become ignorant, she answered her own question the way many people outside of the PRC have done for thirty years:

> I feel that the main reason is because the arts have been interfered with too much, regulated too much, so much that writers had nowhere to go creatively. Writers should enjoy ample creative freedom and freedom of speech, should have

the freedom to say 'no.' The Cultural Revolution stripped all of these away and forced us into the position of not being able to say 'no.' I think this is the greatest sort of tragedy! (101)[16]

According to the editors, the "participating comrades" then went on angrily and sadly to give many examples of the suppression of "artistic democracy":

In summing up, everyone agreed that very many problems still exist in the thorough implimentation of the Double Hundred policy and the establishment of true artistic democracy. Everyone expressed the feeling that we cannot simply sit by and wait, we cannot be unconcerned, but we must unite together in mutual support and carry on a resolute struggle to protect the writers' freedom to create and all other appropriate rights. (101)

Su Zhong then began a discussion of the greatest restriction on literature:

Today the greatest restriction on literary creation is the problem of truthfulness. Forbidding writers to write the truth about real life is the greatest restraining force today.

Why do some people engage in non–literary and non–artistic interference with literature and the arts? As I see it the main reason is that they do not trust the people and they do not trust writers and artists. This kind of lack of trust has reached a very serious level. In the eyes of some people, writers are alien creatures; they are all alien creatures who are always seeking ways to make socialism look bad. For this reason, they forbid us to write the truth. Whoever writes the truth will be interfered with.

Liu Binyan's "Between Men and Monsters" was the truth and is still regarded by some people as an 'anti–Party poisonous weed.'[17]

Bai Hua's "The Stars are Bright Tonight" was the truth, unlike so many past works that made war out to be child's play;[18] he described the true feelings of people in war, was censured for it, and had to go through a high level legal battle. The criticisms of "The Transfer" also hit upon this question — not being allowed to deal truthfully with real life.[19]

If a work touches on real life, then 'it's a reflection of the author's gloomy psychology,' or it's 'Black Curtain literature.' I've heard that criticism of "The Transfer" has already reched the level of a political question; that is, being 'dissatisfied with the situation *after* the smashing of the Gang of Four.' Is it a question of dissatisfaction with the general line of the Third Plenum or dissatisfaction with the things that are in defiance of that general line? There is no concrete analysis. What's wrong, after all, with the latter form of dissatisfaction? If a work contains deficiencies or mistakes, it can be criticised in the spirit of 'seeking truth from facts;' but simply labeling it without any analysis won't do. As a matter of fact, in real life problems like those in "The Transfer" are many times more serious than their reflection in that work!

From last winter through the first half of this year, all of those stale theories have returned: so-called 'write about the essential,' or 'what can be seen everywhere in life is not the equivalent of truthfullness'. . . all those clichés, they've all come back. If we draw a final conclusion from all of these theories it is simply that you're not allowed to write the truth about real life. (101)

Li Zhun then took up her argument and made a confession similar to what he said in January:

I owe a very big debt and that debt is that in the nineteen fifties I wrote several untruthful works. At that time I was too immature and full of enthusiasm; I only knew how to follow the political trend closely and suit the campaign — I did not think for myself. All of those works I wrote in opposition to 'women with bound feet' and 'right wing conservatives' during the collectivization period are unreadable today. Why? Because they're not truthful. This is a lesson that I will always remember. . . . [only truthful works are lasting] . . . It is still dangerous today to write the truth, but I am resolved 'to know that it may not be done, and to do it anyway. [quoting Mencius]' (102)

Tang Dacheng echoed Su and Li's sentiments:

> For a long time now it has been forbidden to write the
> truth, forbidden to truthfully reflect the people's lives, the
> people's loves and hates, forbidden for writers to base their
> works on their own observations and feelings about life and
> to express their own opinions. We could only write
> campaign literature or footnote literature. As a result we've
> been unable to produce true works. . . . this has been a tragic
> and shameful page in our nation's literary history. We must
> not under any circumstances ever again write lying literature
> or vainglorious literature.
> What has been the chief accomplishment of the past
> three years of putting down rebellion and restoring order?
> Seeking truth from facts. In the world of art this means
> restoring the tradition of revolutionary realism: that is to
> look at real life and to truthfully reflect real life. 'Truth' is
> the foundation, 'Truth' is the primary consideration − if
> there is no 'Truth,' then there is no discussing 'Goodness'
> and 'Beauty.' Truthfulness is the lifeblood of literature; it
> establishes the most fundamental moral character of
> literature. Why has the literary creativity of the last few
> years begun to gradually improve and flourish? It is because
> writers have dared to deal with the contradictions in society,
> have dared to reflect the true face of life. And this one point
> is the genuine hope of literature. . . . (102)

The editors then brought up the problem that "some people"
believe that "negative" works will have negative results, and Liu
Binyan commented that:

> After "Between Men and Monsters" was published, I
> received a large number of letters from readers. There was
> not one letter that said they felt more pessimism or despair
> after reading it, but there were many thousands of words
> offering materials, proposals, and suggestions for reforming
> society. And this demonstrates that readers take hope from
> reading the truth.

Bai Hua agreed with this assessment of popular support for the new
literature:

Very many people have written to me these past few years,
and, totalling them up briefly, I've found that only one of
five hundred disagreed with me and attacked me. The rest
of them all encouraged and supported me in speaking the
truth.

The editors then began a discussion of some of the writers' goals in
writing, stating first that:

. . . Everyone agreed (with the poet Han Han)'s statement
that our literature 'should make attacking feudalism one of
its most important missions.' Our country has a two to three
thousand year history of feudalistic rule and a feudalistic
mentality is deeply ingrained. After the victory of our
democratic revolution [CCP term for the period prior to 1949
and the "socialist transition"], opposition to feudalism was
not given its proper place. During the ten years' calamity
especially, when the poisonous remnants of feudalism were
allowed to proliferate and develop malignantly, our Party,
nation, race, and people suffered an unprecedented calimity.
Those poisonous remnants of feudalism are still present to
this day in our society, and they are especially serious within
the Communist Party itself in the form of a superstitious
belief in individual leaders, paternalistic rule, allowing only
one person's opinion, lifetime appointments of cadres,
bureaucratism, special privileges, etc, etc. They have already
become a serious obstacle to the accomplishment of the Four
Modernizations. Today we must make opposition to the
poisonous remnants of feudalism the most important
assignment on the ideological battle front, and our literature
and art naturally have an unshirkable responsibility in this
regard.
    And how do we oppose feudalism? Everyone agreed
that art must first of all *be* art. Reliance on simplistic
explanations is unacceptable and has no real strength. (102)

Deng Youmei then brought up the problem that the Cultural
Revolution had "twisted and warped people's souls," especially among
Chinese youth, and that modern literature should once again take up
Lu Xun's call to "cure the souls" and "create the souls" of this genera-
tion "to help them to become true and lofty human beings." (102)

Liu Zhen continued her thought:

> We communists should martial persuasive reasons to attract
> people to the concept of 'humanity'. We should take onto
> our bright banners all of humankind's beautiful morality!
> Human nature, human feelings, and humanism itself . . .
> should all be accepted! And they should be enhanced,
> glorified, and made even more perfect! We should not give
> them all to the bourgeoisie by default! (103)

Huang Zongjiang agreed:

> The proletariat should be most concerned with humanism,
> most concerned with human nature. Why do we say the
> Cultural Revolution was a holocaust, a great calamity?
> Speaking most fundamentally, because it destroyed human
> nature and advocated beastly nature, and it did not care
> about humanism but advocated beastiality. The fundamental
> aspect of today's re–establishment of order is to treat human
> beings like human beings. For this reason I believe that
> every humanistic concept should be appropriated and
> elevated by the proletariat!

Zhang Jie then went on to attack the Cultural Revolution for the
degredation of human nature and morality and called for literature to
"advocate human dignity . . . sympathy . . . and the beauty of human
nature." Qin Zhaoyang concluded by recalling that Lu Xun had
advocated humanism in his famous slogan of "save the children" from
a man–eating social system, thus "advocating human dignity cannot be
said to be bourgeois thought. . . . wouldn't that mean the proletariat
should not respect human beings? (103)

On the question of the present situation, the writers had sharply
divergent views. "The majority of comrades" were said to believe that
there was good reason to be "optimistic" and that the "overall situation
will not deteriorate" despite occasional attacks on individual writers
and works. "A few of the comrades," however, were reported to
believe that there was not that much reason for optimism and their
views were more fully spelled out:

There were three reasons [for their lack of optimism]:
     (1) In the three years since the smashing of the Gang of

Four, artistic democracy has really not been propagated to the extent that it should be. The small amount of artistic democracy that now exists might at any time — after some Party meeting or after the promulgation of some general order number such and such — be entirely swept away without leaving a trace. This is entirely conceivable!

(2) It is political power that functions in society, and literature has very little influence. Writers are frequently crushed as easily as one squashes an insect.

(3) In the ranks of literature and art there are a group of corrupt persons who only recognize power and not reason and who do everything in accordance with the wishes of the higher officials. This quite generally puts us in the position of being attacked both from within and without. (103)

Bai Hua agreed with the majority position of guarded optimism provided that writers believe in their own strength and the strength of "the people," who generally support the trend since the Third Plenum and oppose those who are trying to prevent reforms. Gao Xiaosheng offered the further opinion that the "club wielders" are pondering the situation too and taking a cautious attitude because, he implied, the highest leadership supports reform and relaxation of control and the "club wielders" are worried about losing their "black caps," the symbols of imperial office.

Bai Hua having mentioned the idea current among the general public that "writers have the most conscience" in society today, the meeting went on to discuss the need for writers to remain faithful to individual conscience and personal morality. After a final statement by Bai Hua on this point of conscience, the meeting went on to stress that both the expectations of Chinese readers and the desire to raise Chinese literature to a world class level demand that much more serious attention be given to improving the technical mastery and raising the artistic level of contemporary literature.

My summary of these two meetings concludes with this eloquent statement by the the much criticized author of *Bitter Love*:

Sometimes I think about a certain question: as a writer, should I be rejected by the people or should I let those in power reject me? I believe that when there is a contradiction between the two, I can only stand on the side of the people.

Because history is written by the people, and the history of literature is also written by the people. There are some works of literature that were rejected by the power holders during the author's lifetime but then became immortal classics after he died. Why was that? Because these works were recognized by the people. Therefore we must rely on our own conscience in writing, thinking all the time about the people, forever loyal to the people. (104)

If one were to sum up these for the most part dedicated Chinese Marxist CCP member writers' 1980 literary critical position, it would seem to ammount to the following far–reaching polemic. Ever since 1949, as a direct result of the Chinese Communist Party's narrow–minded and dictatorial policy of making literature and the arts serve politics in general and Party initiated policies and mass campaigns in particular, the artistic quality of modern Chinese literature has steadily declined. Literary works produced since 1949 are not so much artistic works of lasting value as propaganda pieces, of limited artistic value when written and of virtually no value today. The literature of this period is permeated with unreality, often describing characters, settings, and incidents that have only a tenuous relationship to the actual social life of the Chinese people at the time. More often than not, such literature was actually composed on order to whitewash some particularly bad social situation. The main reasons writers wrote such works that contradicted the evidence of their own senses was naive enthusiasm for the cause and fear — fear of being labeled ideologically heretical and punished accordingly by public disgrace, imprisonment, and even death. Those humanistic and individualistic left–wing writers who had achieved a high level of artistry in fiction and poetry and whose works were internationally known before 1949, were forced to abandon their craft altogether or to write political propaganda on the same dismal level as other works of "command literature" being turned out by younger writers. Even today, however, their works, composed, written and published in areas under Kuomintang (KMT, now romanized as Guomindang) control or in areas where the CCP was unable to organize literary control, are still far more readable than post–"liberation" works and have not been surpassed by any PRC writers in the past thirty years.

The CCP's literary and artistic policies, carried out from Mao Zedong's May 1942 *Yan'an Talks* through the increasingly repressive anti–intellectual and Anti–Rightist campaigns of the 1950's to the unprecedented catastrophe of the decade long Cultural Revolution, have also had other extremely harmful effects on Chinese life. Writers and other intellectuals have been deprived of their constitutionally guaranteed rights of free speech and assembly — meeting together they are regarded by the authorities as trying to form a political faction, much in the manner of the imperial court's distrust of scholarly associations. Their persons have been violated and they have been jailed and even killed on orders of government authorities acting in direct violation of Chinese law. They have been forced to write exclusively about class struggle, class friendship or comradeship only, disharmony and hatred in society, pitting Chinese people against Chinese people and ignoring or denying the universal human values of warmth, compassion, sympathy, kindness, romance, and love between the sexes. Such a deliberate exclusion of all humanistic values from modern Chinese literature since 1949 has contributed to a progressive dehumanization of personal, familial, and social relations among the Chinese people and a growing cynicism, confusion, and alienation among Chinese youth. Such a situation, if allowed to continue, will make it virtually impossible for China to become a socialist democracy with a high level of spiritual culture.

Although the situation regarding literary and artistic freedom has begun to improve since the fall of the Gang of Four, and especially since the Third Plenum of the CCP Central Committee of December 1978, the position of writers and artists in China today is still extremely precarious. Their freedom of expression is still subject to constant interference by bureaucratic literary authorities who have not yet begun to practice the "emancipation of the mind" themselves, are unwilling to allow others to be truly emancipated, and are extremely sensitive and resentful regarding the attempts of writers to represent truthfully the realities of social life in China today. Many writers are still afraid to write what they honestly think and feel, and those who do write according to their consciences do so only by mustering up great courage and with great trepidation. Such an intolerable situation is inimical to the creation of great literary and artistic works of universal and lasting significance in China, makes it impossible for modern Chinese literature and art to ever achieve world class status, and is an insult to the greatness of China's cultural heritage. The situation simply must imporve. Writers and artists are still at the mercy — now benevolent, but later, perhaps, tyrannical once again — of Party and government bureaucrats who judge their works solely on the basis of extrinsic political criteria and who have the sole power to prevent publication or other form of public presentation. Writers and artists must be given legal protection to pursue their respective crafts free from political pressure and the fear of punishment. Only in this way can they contribute to the creation of a truly human spiritual culture in China.

Comparing these writers' views with the official statements given in Chapter One, it would seem that, although there is general agreement that literature should play an ameliorative and educational role in Chinese society, literary values are in conflict with political values in the People's Republic today as writers and artists push for more freedom from political control in order to pursue their craft and present their own personal visions of reality. The outcome of this conflict and the protracted struggle that it will inevitably engender may have a decisive effect on the future development of any and all democratic freedoms in China. As John K. Fairbank observed in a penetrating historical survey of self-expression in China, ". . . political self-expression cannot easily be disentangled from self-expression in general because 'political' will usually include whatever people in power believe it includes. A poem that seems to criticize them becomes by that fact a political statement, whether so intended or not."[20] That may be true in all societies, but it becomes a dangerous political problem for writers, artists, and any other private citizens who wish to engage in self-expression when the "people in power" subjectively have a holistic mode of thinking and objectively are in command of a corporate order with totalistic aspirations by means of which they attempt, on principle, to control everything that people find meaningful in life. Under these conditions, which certainly exist in the PRC, the attempt of artists and writers to establish anything like the autonomy, integrity, and validity of artistic values *per se* can only be regarded as a threat to the entire system of political, economic, and social control maintained by the Communist Party of China. Let us briefly summarize these conflicting values.

The writers and artists represented in this chapter, most of whom regard themselves as Marxists and believe in the correctness of the Chinese Communist led revolution, are dedicated to artistic and humanistic values. They talk of the trinity of "Truth, Goodness, and Beauty" as primary values in both art and life. They are not opposed to didacticism in the arts, but they insist on the importance of an aesthetic and an entertainment function for the arts as well. Horace's famous dictum that the aim of literature is to delight *and* instruct would seem to be perfectly acceptable to them. They believe in the dignity and worth of the individual human being and they want to "treat human beings like human beings" in both literature and life. In literature this calls for honest characterizations of genuine individuals who are not simply "social class" stereotypes fashioned on the basis of some political formula. They also wish to express human warmth, friendship, family ties, compassion and sympathy (even for one's so-called "class enemies"), kindness, romance, tenderness, and love between the sexes. They wish, finally, to practice what they call literary and artistic "realism."

Their conception of literary "realism" is the most significant factor in the struggle for artistic freedom, and it comes into perennial conflict with the political power of the CCP. Literary realism, for these writers, is the "true representation of life" based on the writer's own individual vision, "world view, true knowledge, and clear perceptions," and it should be limited only by "the objective reality of social life (or human history)" and the individual writer's personal "subjective understanding of that reality," "genuine feelings," and "artistic sensibilities," including the skillful manipulation of the tools of his craft and the historical traditions and contemporary trends available to him. It should be judged, moreover, by other fellow writers on the basis of artistic criteria. The artistic products of such realism, according to these writers, are, of course, themselves products of human history, culturally limited by considerations of time, place, social class, education and so on; but they may nevertheless, and, in the case of the finest writers of true genius (they always mention Balzac, Tolstoy, Shakespeare, and Cao Xueqin among others as practicioners of "realism"), often do break through all such limitations in order to express universal human values (transcending social class) that have a profound influence on all subsequent human history, including literary history.

Such breakthroughs are, moreover, a normative value for these writers. Literary realism *should* break through all political, economic, and social limitations: in "class society" because the "ruling class" is unjust, and, most interestingly, in "socialist" societies like the PRC because the CCP leadership may sometimes be mistaken in its policies, may sometimes actually be working against the intertests of "the people" — there may actually be a "contradiction" between the CCP leadership and "the people." For this important reason, writers should be responsible first to "the people," for whom they bring hope for the reform of society and the imporovment of their lives. They should be responsible also to their own individual consciences, to the truth as they see it as individuals in society, and to world history. Only faithfulness to conscience and truth can establish the "fundamental

moral character" of literature. They should not be responsible to any
particular political party, party leader, or temporary political principle
that would compromise the above values.

By characterizing their favored mode of narrative, literary realism,
in this way, these writers are in effect demanding moral autonomy and
freedom for literature to expose *present* social evils even if those evils
exist at the highest levels of the Communist Party or government
leadership. They are once again asking for the kind of individual
freedom of literary and political expression that was denied to Ding
Ling, Xiao Jun, Hu Feng and many other dedicated revolutionary
writers in the past. Thus, whether they want to or not, writers who
advocate this brand of literary realism must inevitably come into
conflict with the values of the Communist Party of China that many of
them, as members, are sworn to uphold.

The Communist Party of China always contains many more or less
obvious factions, but as a whole it supports values that are political and
economic. Its primary value is to stay in power, to maintain its
political power. This is a primary value with all political parties, of
course, but it is much more important both individually and collectively
in a one party state where so much power and privilege adheres to
party membership and where there are so few "post–retirement"
benefits to be enjoyed. The CCP also stands for "modernization" —
the hundred year old dream of "wealth and power," of making China a
thoroughly modern nation with an advanced industry, agriculture,
science and technology, and military apparatus. The CCP also stands
for "socialist democracy," but maintains that it is equivalent to the
"dictatorship of the proletariat," which is in turn equivalent to the
"people's democratic dictatorship." The CCP is in favor of "socialist
legality," but makes it clear that its purpose is to strengthen state
power. In other words, they are in favor of a legal system but not of
the "rule of law." There are always some areas of life in which the
Party and powerful individuals in the Party are outside the reach of
that legal system. Many of these reforms, then, are designed to
enhance the power of the 4% of the Chinese people who are members
of the CCP to rule *in the name of* "the people." The CCP is in favor
of the "mass line" of "from the people to the people," but what comes
from the people are only suggestions and complaints (*shangfang,*
"going up to visit the government," and so on) without legal force,
while what goes to the people are political and economic orders and
directives backed up by the full legal force of the state. The CCP is
for "the emancipation of the mind," "seeking truth from facts," and
"practice" as "the sole criterion for testing truth;" but the potentially

liberating and democratizing force of these slogans is vitiated by a dogmatic insistence on Marxism–Leninism–Mao Zedong Thought and the Four Fundamental Principles (as interpreted by Party Central at any particular time) as the pre–established truth to be sought out by seeking, practicing, and emancipating. Finally, the CCP retains a belief in the necessity of "class struggle" as a final weapon in its battle against dissent. Anyone who resists the CCP may be legally defined as a non–person who is no longer a member of that Rousseauian abstraction "the people" and thus beyond the pale of any and all legal protections of human rights.

The CCP remains in favor of Mao Zedong's theory of "uniting with, educating, and remolding" writers, artists, and other intellectuals. In practice that involves "ideological work" or thought control. Under the revised slogan that literature and the arts should "serve socialism and the people," the CCP literary bureaucracy calls upon writers to support the Party by truthfully and realistically reflecting the "contradictions" in society from the Party's point of view, to "eulogize" the good "social effects" of the Party's current policies, to "expose" the bad "social effects" of those who obstruct those same policies, to create fictional models of "socialist new persons" for popular emulation, and to aid the Party in its never ending struggle against "ultra–democracy" and "ultra–individualism" (meaning, in our terms, democracy and individualism), "anarchism" (meaning spontaneous public demonstrations and protests against Party policies or social injustices), "small producers mentality" (meaning, I believe, individualistic peasant resistance to government policies), "bureaucracy" (meaning the actions of those officials who resist present leadership policies, not the systematic bureaucratic mismanagement and special privileges endemic in a one party government or management set up), and political deviance of both the "left" (Maoist, conservative) and the "right" (Young Democratic Group, or "bourgeois liberalism," of which anyone may find himself accused) as defined by the present leadership. This is certainly a heavy social responsibility that the CCP entrusts to writers and artists, but if they make "mistakes" the Party has already assured them that they will be "criticized, guided, and cared for" in a friendly and comradely manner such as we have already seen in Chapter One.

The conflict between the artistic and humanistic values of many writers, artists, and intellectuals and the political and economic values of the CCP can be expected to continue for a long time to come, and the outcome of such a conflict is uncertain. The history of this century provides numerous examples of dehumanizing assaults upon the dignity of the individual human being and the values of political democracy, most of them undertaken in the name of social revolution and material advance. By the same token, the United Nations General Assembly's Univeresal Declaration of Human Rights (1948) declares "equal and inalienable rights of all members of the human family" to be the foundation of "freedom, justice, and peace in the world." These sentiments, with which the PRC is now formally alligned, derive from the European Enlightenment and are embodied in one form or another in both the formal constitutions and the social practices of the democratic countries of the world. The Chinese people in general and Chinese intellectuals in particular have behind them a powerfully humanistic intellectual heritage which they have yet to fully appreciate and to combine with the now universally known fundamental principles of political democracy — popular sovereignty, spontaneous organization, and legal protection of the individual from the inordinate power of the state. Many Chinese intellectuals, including many of the humanistic Marxist writers whose words have appeared in this chapter, believe that their humanistic tradition and the democratic tradition of the West are quite compatable with both Marxism and socialism. As a modernizing Chinese intellectual community comes into increasing contact with world thought, including literary thought, I believe that they will also become increasingly aware of the extreme narrowness of the CCP's kind of Marxism and of the true values of political democracy. When the Chinese begin to combine the humanism of their own classical tradition with the modern forms of political democracy, then they will be genuinely living up to the Maoist slogan of "making the past serve the present and making things foreign serve China."

Having seen the theoretical importance attached by the writers themselves to the concept of literary realism, we now turn to an examination of some of Post–Mao neo–realist fiction in practice.

III. The Neo-Realist Critique of the Maoist Era

Most of the writers to be discussed in this chapter would agree with René Wellek's "disconcertingly trivial conclusion" concerning the definition of realism as a regulative idea. For most of them realism does indeed mean,[1]

> . . . 'the objective representation of contemporary social reality.' It claims to be all−inclusive in subject matter and aims to be objective in method, even though this objectivity is hardly ever achieved in practice. Realism is didactic, moralistic, reformist. Without always realizing the difference between description and prescription it tries to reconcile the two in the concept of 'type.' In some writers, but not all, realism becomes historistic: it grasps social reality as dynamic evolution.

Such a definition, especially fitting for the classics of the Eureopean nineteenth century, nevertheless seems most appropriate for the vast majority of the thousands of stories published in the PRC from Novembver 1977 through 1984. And yet the renaissance in China in the eighth decade of the twentieth century of a literary style largely superceded in Europe and elsewhere by a host of other narrative modes was greeted with tremendous enthusiasm among Chinese readers, followed shortly thereafter by an outpouring of anthologies and studies by scholars outside of China.[2]

Such enthusiasm is completely understandable when we consider the formidable list of literary taboos in effect during the Cultural Revolution decade *and before*: objective truth or common sense factuality (disparaged as "naturalism" or "critical realism"); psychological exploration and analysis of hidden motives (considered a "bourgeois" indulgence); human interest and humanism that detracted

attention from the "essential class relations" determining human behavior (increasingly subjective and prescriptive as class relations were
in Maoist ideology); love that did not serve interests of state or class
solidarity; "middle characters" uncertain of their ideological
committment; and spontaneous resistance to social injustice (even in a
historical context) — in short, any and all expressions of an individual
social vision of the way things are or the way things ought to be.[3] The
Chinese people had sufferred tremendously during that decade, but
their literature said nothing about the *felt reality* of their lives. The
neo-realist literature of the immediate post-Mao era (and especially
that of 1979 and 1980) was greeted with such enthusiasm, optimism,
and release of pent up emotions precisely because, to quote Wellek
again, it is a simple fact of modern Chinese literary history "that the
mere change to a depiction of contemporary social reality implied a
lesson of human pity, of social reformism and criticism, and often of
rejection and revulsion against society."[4] Rejection and revulsion
against the immediate past came first, followed by more sophisticated
attempts to identify the deeper causes of China's present malaise,
attempts that were prematurely thwarted just at the point where they
began to threaten the ideological power of the present Party leadership.

This chapter will present a brief survey of post-Mao neo-realist
fiction, introducing what I believe to be the most important themes
through a discussion of those works I find to be both artistically and
intellectually satisfying. With a few exceptions, I have confined myself
to short stories and middle length short stories (or novellas) published
in the officially controlled literary journals; but let us begin first with a
look at the popular publications (*minban kanwu*) of the brief "Peking
Spring" of 1978–79.These stories offer, perhaps, a glimps of what
might have been or might some day be if it were not for the fact that
(quoting Orwell) "collectively, the Party owned everything."[5]

An interesting and exciting result of the reversal of the verdict on
the Tiananmen Incident and the slogan of "emancipation of the mind"
was the rapid proliferation of over fifty popular publications growing
out of the wall poster campaign on Peking's "democracy wall" and
attempting to continue the spontaneous and critical aspects of the April
Fifth Movement. Primarily the work of students, derusticated
intellectual youth, and young workers, most of whom were former Red
Guards, rather than of well known writers; these publications
flourished during that brief time when the CCP hierarchy was too
preocupied with its internal conflicts and its bid for United States support to attempt to completely control literary and political expression.

At their inception, in fact, Deng Xiaoping, Hu Yaobang, and other members of the "reform faction" actively encouraged these youthful attacks on the Maoist conservatives combined with appeals for democratic reforms in China's governmental system.[6] They soon became a political liability, however, and by the fall of 1979 the majority of these journals and little magazines had been closed down. Aside from a reflex refusal of the CCP leadership to tolerate anything like genuinely spontaneous freedom of speech or unauthorized opposition to government policies, one other important reason for their suppression was that many of the editors of these publications — Wei Jingsheng, Fu Yuehua, and others — also attempted to organize spontaneous mass demonstrations and protests by unemployed youth and impoverished peasants. The Sino–Vietnamese border war of February and March 1979 provided Deng Xiaoping with the proper excuse to stir up an "adverse wind," and on March 16 he attacked those people whom he said were taking advantage of the situation to sell national secrets to foreigners.

His remarks were followed by a media campaign against those who were said to be currying favor with the foreigners by stating publicly that the Chinese people did not enjoy "human rights." Wei Jingsheng responded in his journal *Explorations* with an essay entitled "Do You Want Democracy or a New Tyranny."[7] He warned Chinese college students not to trust Deng Xiaoping, to watch what Deng did and not just listen to what he said. Three days later he was arrested and *Explorations* was closed down. He was eventually tried and convicted of selling secret intelligence — mostly just gossip that he had heard from the children of high Party cadres — and "counter–revolutionary crimes" and given a stiff fifteen year jail sentence. Liu Qing, another youth leader who originally took a more moderate stance on the question of direct political action, was subsequently arrested on various trumped up charges stemming from the fact that he released the very damning transcript of Wei Jingsheng's trial. He spent eight months in Peking jails and was then sent to the Lotus Flower Temple (Lianhua Si) prison in Shaanxi Province for three years of labor education. His prison memoir, smuggled out to be printed in Hong Kong and translated into English and French, is another classic document of the short lived democracy movement.[8] Most of the major popular publications were shut down by the authorities soon after Wei Jingsheng's arrest and those few that remained were finished off in April 1981 at the start of the campaign against Bai Hua.[9]

These unofficial publications raised a number of serious questions in a much more forceful manner than Party proclamations on "corrrecting mistakes" or even officially sanctioned neo-realist literature. *Explorations,* the most radically democratic of these journals, consistently raised the question of popular democracy — "the fifth modernization" Wei Jingsheng called it — as opposed to the dictatorship of the proletariat and democratic centralism.[10] The *April Fifth Forum* even published a lengthy theoretical article by Chen Erjin in which he compared the PRC to the USSR and Eastern European countries and came to the same conclusions about "proletarian revolution" leading to dictatorship, bureaucracy, and the domination of a "new class" as the Yugoslavian Milovan Djilas had some time ago. Besides calling for true freedom of speech and press, attempting to popularize the concept of human rights in China, and making some strong attacks on CCP bureaucratic privileges, corruption, and misuse of power, these journals also carried the strongest attacks on Mao Zedong and Maoism ever openly published in China. Wang Xizhe's "Mao Zedong and the Cultural Revolution" is, I believe, the most sophisticated theoretical analysis yet written by a democratic dissenter and a Marxist who wished to work for reform within the system. Many of Wang's ideas, as well as other ideas presented first in these popular publications, were later taken up in an ideologically safer manner by writers of officially sanctioned fiction, and a certain number of short stories that first appeared in popular publications were eventually published (sometimes with transparently cosmetic changes) in the standard official journals.[11]

The most important popular publication whose editors and writers atempted to avoid overtly political literature only to come very close to adumbrating a liberal view of the autonomy of literature and politics, and whose struggle to survive itself then became a political act leading to a Public Security Bureau order to cease publication in August 1980, was *Today.* From the time that it first appeared on 23 December 1978 as a big-character poster on the walls of the Ministry of Culture in Peking and elsewhere until being forced to shut down, *Today* published 29 short stories, 87 poems, and various other works by a number of very talented writers including Zhao Zhenkai (penames include Bei Dao, Ai Shan, and Shi Mo), Chen Maiping (Wan Zhi), Mang Ke, Shu Ting, and others.[12] They believe that literature should reflect the uniqueness of the individual human being; should present the author's individual vision of life; should express genuine emotions through the beauty and artistry of skillfully employed images, metaphors, and symbols; and, above all, should be autonomous and free from the direct restraints of politics. Summing up their credo, two of their members wrote:[13]

> There is always a contradiction between the pragmatic values
> of politics and the non–pragmatic function of literature as an
> expression of the emotions and feelings of an individual.
> Politics in an authoritarian system is centralized, while the
> emotions of people sought and portrayed in literature are
> myriad. Writers should be entitled to express their own
> feelings and thoughts in their own ways.

The imprisonment of Wei Jingsheng, Wang Xizhe and other overtly
political dissenters and the suppression of the very limited circulation
popular publications had a chilling effect on those young people who
in 1978 and 1979 wished to go beyond the confines of PRC politics and
literary practice. Some of the writers of the popular publications,
however — like Zhao Zhenkai and Shu Ting — went on to join the
resurgent older experienced writers who expanded the range of critical
and realistic fiction appearing in officially regulated journals to an
unprecedented extent in 1979 and 1980. Before it flourished during
those two remarkable years, however, neo–realist fiction began with
the "literature of the wounded" of 1977 and 1978.

What, then, was the "literature of the wounded?" Was it the heart
rending cry of "the people" bursting forth out of the depths of their
hitherto unexpressed pain and anguish? Was it an angry denunciation
by "the people" against their jailors and persecuters? Was it the
collective revelation of the Chinese stigmata designed to lead to a
shock of recognition and discovery (*anagnorisis*) or a collective
purgation and purification (*catharsis*)? Or was it only a politically
motivated attempt to take advantage of popular hatred of the Gang of
Four in order to shift the entire blame for the unspeakable horror of
the previous decade on to them and thus preserve the sacred image of
Chairman Mao and his epigones? And finally, was it good art?
   The answer to all but the last question is an affirmative one.
Consider the reported audience reaction to a public reading of the fol-
lowing "poem" at a recital on the theme of "Learning from the Martyr
Zhang Zhixin."

   The wind says
   Forget her
   I have buried the crime with dust!
   The rain says
   Forget her
   I have cleansed the humiliation with tears!

> . . .
> Only a tiny blade of grass still singing . . .
> She
> Was shot to death . . .

"Waves of sobbing in the audience."

> I am ashamed that I
> A Communist Party member
> Am no better than a tiny blade of grass
> Who lets her blood flow into its arteries . . .

"As if whipped accross the heart, the audience shuddered, then broke into a hurricane of applause that went on and on."[14] The same kind of reader response greeted both Liu Xinwu's "The Class Teacher" — the first anti–Gang of Four story, published in *People's Literature* in November 1977 — and Lu Xinhua's "The Wound" — the story that gave the movement its name, published, after several rejections, in the *Literary Daily* (*Wenhuibao* of Shanghai) on 11 August 1978.

Marian Galik has analysed several of these works in relation to the *topoi* of "re–encounter" or "return" and "scars," tracing those motifs all the way back to the *Shi jīng* (*Book of Songs*) and the famous nineteenth chapter of Homer's *Odyssey*. He has amply demonstrated that the scars (both physical and psychological) function as collective stigmata and identifying marks setting apart the victims of the Gang of Four terror from their diabolic persecutors.[15]

As with the popular publications, at their inception and for a longer period of time, the "literature of the wounded" was supported by the post–Mao Party leadership of both the "whatever faction" (the Maoists) led by Hua Guofeng and the emerging "reform faction" led eventually by Deng Xiaoping.[16] As Galik and many others have pointed out, the "literature of the wounded" met the political and ideological demands of the 1977–78 leadership more than "the adequate and justified needs of the literary and artistic development of Chinese literature."[17] That is to say, in terms of literary excellence, the literature of 1977–78 was indeed "wounded literature," in many respects indistinguishable from that of the Cultural Revolution era except that the roles assigned to "good guys" and "bad guys" had been reversed. As bad art these stories hold only historical interest for us today, and that primarily because they gave us our first officially approved picture of the Cultural Revolution nightmare. An examination of the stories in the officially sponsored, hastily prepared, and, unfortunately, very poorly translated and printed volume *The Wounded: New Stories of the Cultural Revolution 77–78* (translated by Geremie Barmé and Bennet Lee and published by the PRC's Joint Publishing Company in Hong Kong in May 1979)[18] should provide a sufficient demonstration of their artlessness.

Liu Xinwu's story, here rendered as "Class Counsellor," is both the first and the archetypal "wounded" story. The characters are typical stereotypes. Zhang Junshi, the school teacher, is a selfless, wise, dedicated good cadre who is always right and always patiently working to educate Chinese youth in the correct way to live in accordance with the *current* Party policies, the precepts of the Marxist–Leninist classics, and the works of Chairman Mao. Shi Hong is a "progressive" young member of the Youth League Propaganda Committee who dares to wear pretty clothes and has inherited from her cadre father and school teacher mother a passion for reading the Marxist classics as well as Mao Dun, Goethe, and Tang poetry. Xie Huimin, the Youth League Branch Secretary, is a typical "reactionary" (meaning a blind follower of the Gang of Four) whose mind is completely controlled by Party propaganda and who cannot make the slightest move unless it is in response to a newspaper directive. The story revolves around the question of what attitude to take towards Song Baoqi, a confessed juvenile delinquent and victim of the Gang of Four society, who had been roaming with a street gang before his detention.

Although the main interest of the story is the discovery by teacher Zhang of the identical spiritual impoverishment of both the "criminal element" Song Baoqi and the perfect Party product Xie Huimin, in the denouement Zhang decides that he will give Xie Huimin the leftist classic *The Gadfly* by Ethel Boole Voynich that Song Baoqi had stolen and that Xie had assumed without reading to be "obscene." In this way he encourages her to approach all of life's major questions on the basis of "genuine" Marxism–Leninism–Mao Zedong Thought. The last paragraph contains the obligatory flower fragrance wafting by on a spring breeze while the stars in the sky smile down on teacher Zhang's beautiful vision. Almost everything about the story seems uninspiring as literature, but as a factual report of life in the PRC it was immediately recognized as the truth by hundreds of young readers all over the nation who wrote to *People's Literature* describing themselves as either a Xie Huimin or a Song Baoqi.[19]

The single most important artistic achievement of Lu Xinhua's story "The Wound" was the invention of its title, *shanghen*, "scar traces," which provided a powerful symbol for an entire generation whose minds and bodies carry the mental and physical scars of life in the PRC

since at least 1958. Here at last are individuals who hurt and bleed and
cry out as they fall upon the thorns of life. Aside from its shocking
revelation of the alienation of family ties, friendship, and love in favor
of loyalty to the Gang of Four (and Chairman Mao, not yet
mentioned); the most striking feature of this confessional story of a
young woman who in June 1969 disowns her "reactionary" mother
because her being attacked by the Cultural Revolution "was like an
ugly scar on her clean and fair complection,"[20] is that after viewing her
mother's scarred and wounded corpse she shows no signs of remorse
for her cruel treatment of her mother.[21] Rather, as in so many other
stories of 1977–78, she vows never to forget who was responsible — the
Gang of Four *only* — and rededicates her life to the Party and its
present cause, after which she feels a surge of resolution as she strides
off under the bright lights (typical PRC literary cliché) of Nanking
Road.

Although Lu Xinhua wrote his story of spiritual tragedy under the
influence of his Fudan University classroom reading of Lu Xun's
famous story "The New Year's Sacrifice" (*Zhufu*), he is unable to
probe to the heart of darkness in Chinese society nor to the root cause
of the spiritual tragedy. Unlike Lu Xun, he cannot (at least not in
print) suspend judgement,[22] nor can he avoid going along with the two
basic characteristics of the "literature of the wounded": criticism of the
Gang of Four *alone* and loyalty to the *current* Party leadership.

There is nothing of artistic interest in the rest of the stories in *The
Wounded*. Kong Jiesheng's "Marriage" reaffirms the startling
proposition that love is related to happiness just as Liu Xinwu's later
"A Place for Love" reaffirms Ba Jin's 1930s discovery that "love is not
a crime" by asserting that, "to deny the place of love in the life of a
revolutionary is itself revisionist and decadent."[23] Yang Wenzhi's "Ah,
Books!" asserts that Chairman Hua now allows the Chinese people to
buy books like Victor Hugo's *Les Miserables* that were once burned in
heaps during the Cultural Revolution. Wang Yaping praises the
policeman's "Sacred Duty" to uphold the law, while Lu Wenfu and
Wang Meng remind the Chinese people that "Dedication" to science,
the Party, and the nation is "Something Most Precious." Finally, Liu
Xinwu's "Awake, My Brother" deals with the problem of a young
worker's disillusionment and drift into nihilism by having him won
over by a new style Party Secretary who is "on the level" and out to
undo the evil done by the Gang of Four. It is not that most of these
ideas did not represent a necessary and welcome advance over the
themes of pre–November 1977 literature — indeed they did, and they
reflected the changes in Chinese society at the time as well — but the

"literature of the wounded" was still primarily tendentious, artificial yet artless, and a far cry from the canons of critical realism.

Although many stories of poor quality and dubious thematic interest continued the *shanghen* style into 1979, after the Third Plenum of December 1978 older established writers began to publish stories that discussed the wounds of the past in a somewhat more artistic manner. Ru Zhijuan's "A Narrow Path Through the Grasslands," for example, though still containing obviously model and minatory figures, relates a young woman's experiences in the oilfields during the years immediately before and after the fall of the Gang of Four.[24] Besides demonstrating the prescriptive class nature of PRC society that is ever so subtly suggested by terms such as *chadui* ("live and work in a production team"), *choudiao* ("transfer"), and *fapei* ("be assigned"), indicating an ascending order of desirability from a Rightist or Rightist's child, through an ordinary youth, to a high cadre's child; a natural symbolism is employed throughout in which the desolate grassland stands for China itself and the narrow path stands for both the tortuous road of recent history and the uncertain future choices open to a young woman searching for love and meaning in her life. At the story's end we can be fairly certain that she will not follow the callous reinstated cadre's son south with his lilacs (symbols of his special treatment), but we are not informed as to just exactly what she does intend to do other than take some time to ponder the lessons she has just learned on the grasslands

Considered as a *shanghen* story by Galik, the Liaoning writer Jin He's "Re–encounter" actually marks a complete transition to the critical neo–realism of 1979–80.[25] A fine irony is maintained throughout this story of re–encounter between a reinstated Party Secretary enthusiastically in charge of the 1977 campaign to "thoroughly search out theives, assaulters, and vandals" of the Cultural Revolution and a young worker accused of killing one student and crippling another worker in a violent 1967 Red Guard confrontation the primary purpose of which was to protect this same Party Secretary.

The irony is based upon conflicting definitions of the words crime and criminal. It begins when Party Secretary Zhu Chunxin forcefully asserts that "violent criminals like this owe a debt of blood and should be punished severely." It continues when the interrogator, Chief Li, insists that the accused, Ye Hui, is hiding something and that "no leading cadre would let you get violent!," and is reiterated during Zhu's painful recollection of the fight Ye Hui's Red Guards waged for his protection during which a rival faction member shouted out that "Zhu

Chunxin stirs up the masses! He causes violence and bloodshed!.
He's going to get everything he deserves.!" The supreme irony is
made explicit when, after a harrowing meeting with the young man's
mother, who believes her son will be executed for his crimes
committed in the name of defending "Chairman Mao's revolutionary
line," a guilt ridden Secretary Zhu goes to the jail for one last private
meeting with Ye Hui. He tries to tell him, repeating current Party
propaganda, that, "Lots of people, myself included, made various kinds
of mistakes during the Cultural Revolution . . . (but) we must all learn
from experience, and raise our consciousness . . . (and) look at it as
education . . .;" but Ye Hui interrupts him with a laugh:

> But your mistakes and mine took different forms, and so did
> our 'education!' In your case, you can clearly and boldly
> blame everything on your harassment by Lin Biao and the
> Gang of Four; but in my case, I must confess to following
> Lin Biao and the Gang of Four, and to subverting the
> Cultural Revolution! (242)

Ye Hui then demonstrates an abundance of moral courage, though
perhaps a lack of good sense, when he brushes aside Zhu Chunxin's
offer to take full responsibility, insists on taking whatever punishment
he receives "because I did actually commit a crime," and implies that
Zhu Chunxin, whose lack of moral courage is demonstrated throughout
the story, is still the best kind of leading cadre the CCP has to offer.
Zhu is visably shaken when Chief Li orders the "criminal offender"
back to his cell. He "shuddered violently, and his face turned pale (as)
two words kept reverberating in his mind: 'criminal. . .offender. . .'"
(243) If Zhu Chunxin stands for the CCP and Ye Hui for the Red
Guards, then the author leaves little doubt in the readers mind as to
who has committed the greater crime. The same civilized morality that
demands that Ye Hui pay for the crime of murder also demands that
the CCP do more than merely acknowledge their "mistakes" and
announce that they have learned a great historical "lesson."

At the same time that official publications and older established
writers were beginning to probe more deeply into the causes and
consequences of China's post–Mao malaise and to write in a more
realistic style, many younger writers active in the "democracy
movement" were at work creating a more consciously artistic and more
pessimistic literature that went beyond both the didacticism of the
"literature of the wounded" and the politically acceptable early 1979

neo–realist works which continued to portray good cadres who work
for "the people" and support the present Party line. The most talented
among them were the *Today* group and their works became known
collectively as the "literature of the ruins" from the title of a story that
appeared in the first issue of *Today*.[26]

"On the Ruins," by Shi Mo (Zhao Zhenkai), tells the story of a
Peking history professor, Wang Qi, who has decided to hang himself
after being ordered to go to a Cultural Revolution mass denunciation
meeting. He walks out on the ruins of the Yuan Ming Yuan (the
so–called Summer Palace, once one of the architectural wonders of the
world, built by the Kangxi Emperor in 1709 and destroyed by French
and English troops in the autumn of 1890) with a rope in his pocket.
On the ruins he meets a five or six year old girl who matter of factly
tells him the story of how her father was beaten to death because he
stole some pumpkins from his production brigade. In the face of the
greater suffering of the common people, this western educated
intellectual decides not to take his own life:

> Night descended quietly. He sat there in the darkness for
> a long time.
> Suddenly he stood up quickly and walked off in the di-
> rection the little girl had disappeared in without even
> glancing back.
> The rope just swayed there in the wind. (77)

"On the Ruins" may be read as a brief meditation on time and on
Chinese history as well as one man's realization of the need to go on
living. At first the narrator presents Wang Qi trying to escape from
human time (history). After all, "Does time still have any meaning for
him today?" He has become an enemy of the people, his daughter has
left home and publicly broken off relations with him, his old college
classmate has committed suicide, and his wife is dead. All he has left
of time are his memories, an old photograph of his family, and his
resolve to escape. Then he comes face to face with Chinese history —
the ruins of the Summer Palace which Shi Mo evokes in an almost
poetic prose seldom encountered in PRC writing:

> . . . In front of him, on the hill directly opposite, was an
> expanse of stones — the ruins of the Yuan Ming Yuan. How
> did he happen to walk here? It was completely unconscious.
> No. Consciousness is in the unconscious. Perhaps there was
> some sort of mysterious attraction that pulled him into this

magnetic field like a small metal chip.

. . .

Standing before him was Chinese history — several decades, several hundreds, even several thousands of years of history: those countless arrogances and rebellions, lecheries and injustices; those rivers of fresh blood and mountains of white bones; those luxurious yet cold, still pools, palaces, and tombs; those troops of thousands of men and horse flashing accross the vast canopy of Heaven; that broad axe dripping with blood on the executioner's block; that sundial whose shadow moves accross the smooth stone slab; those thread-bound ancient books piled high in dark dust sealed rooms; the long drawn out drum beat of the slow midnight watches... ... made up this vast wasteland of ruins. (72-73)

China after a hundred years of chaotic historical changes — a wasted ruin of human history.

Amid these symbols of national history, Wang Qi can only recall the history of his own past happinesses — taking pictures with his daughter, the scent of his wife's breath on his face — and sorrows — desertion and death. Even the word death itself, that he speaks aloud in various tones of voice, seems empty and completely meaningless. Then his self-pitying reveries are shattered by a little girl who tells him "without the slightest trace of emotion":

'My dad's dead, the sixth of last month he was beaten to death by Er-leng and Shuan-zhu from north of our village.'
'Why?'
'My dad stole the Production Brigade's pumpkins.'
He walked over, put his arms around the child, impulsively pressed his cheek to the little girl's startled face while drop after large drop of tears overflowed his eyes. It was the first time in many months that he had cried. Salty, acrid tears rolled down his cheeks, down the corners of his mouth, and down into the shirt pocket with the photograph of his daughter. (76)

After the little girl runs away in fright, he decides to go on living. Why? That the author does not directly tell us is a small thing, perhaps, but it is a great artistic advance in PRC literature. Perhaps because he feels that one more death in Chinese history can have no particular meaning. Perhaps because he realizes the inherent egotism of his planned suicide. Or perhaps, like the writers of ruins literature, he wants to go on and bear witness to the suffering of the Chinese people on the ruins of recent history. At any rate the "message" of this well written story is not made explicit and room is left for multiple interpretation.[27]

Another "ruins" story that deals with the tragic irony of twentieth century Chinese history is Wan Zhi (Chen Maiping)'s "Open Terrain," the symbolism of which presents modern China as a "darkling plain where ignorant armies clash by night." A nameless old man with a shovel, almost an image of the Grim Reaper himself, is working the night shift on a construction project to build a factory with American assistance on an abandoned battlefield where the KMT, despite that same American assistance, was defeated by the CCP in the Civil War some thirty years earlier. He stands before the abandoned pill boxes from which, as a KMT officer, he had urged his young troops on to a last ditch resistance and sees that,

> This is a graveyard where the war and many men's worthless lives are buried .
> . . . The pill boxes arranged one by one in a row, the open terrain has become a graveyard. He looked at them, they were the past, the past was death, and death, too, was like his memory. (114)

The main question the story asks through the musings of this former leader of the losing side in China's "Revolutionary Civil War" is what was it all for? Was it just Fate that determined who won and was buried in glory under a heroes monument and who lost and remained buried in shame in this shallow grave marked only by a bombed out row of pill boxes?

> Perhaps it was 'him' who pressed the buttons. 'He' was only Fate. 'He' was the voice that softly urged him on! His life seemed to have been drawn in a circle by 'him,' starting from a certain point and returning again to that same point. In the past he came here in an American army truck and built pill boxes; today, although he didn't arrive in an American army truck, he did come to build an American—equiped factory and to tear down those same pill boxes. (115)

The question is too much for him to answer as he sifts through
"those insubstantial things" that are the parched bones of the young
men who died under his command. All he can do is pose further
questions:

> . . . None of them can ever exist again, but why did they
> die? And when was the value of their lives lost? No, he
> cannot answer. He once urged them on and reprimanded
> them. Why had he done so? Today he doesn't even under-
> stand it himself.
>
> He committed a crime, but why was that? Because he too
> easily trusted the foreigners? Or was it Fate? Or was it his
> own ignorance? (118)

Whatever the ultimate answer, whatever the ultimate significance of
the Civil War and the thirty years that followed it, after all those years
of suffering and "self reliance," one thing is for certain: on that open
terrain down the hill from the heroes graves and directly on top of the
losers graves a modernized American–equiped factory will be "very
quickly" erected.

An American–equiped factory built over the unmarked graves of
Chinese youth of thirty years ago — an ironic symbol of New China
that Mao Zedong would hardly have recognized as his legacy. Not
since Xiao Jun was reprimanded for his insistence that the Civil War
was unnecessary has such a heretical statement been so forcefully
made.

Taking their inspiration from post–war German writers like
Heinrich Böll,[28] the youthful creators of the "literature of the ruins"
questioned the meaning of the recent past in a manner completely
devoid of political slogans or even recognizable support for current
Party policies, however enlightened. Had they been allowed to
continue publishing, it is hardly likely that their works would have
contributed to the Four Modernizations; but they might have gone
some distance in the direction of the modernization of Chinese
literature.

The achievements of some of the neo–realist writers of 1979–81
were also quite impressive in their depiction of a world of reality completely at variance with all of the vast corpus of PRC literature since
1949, with the exception of a few "poison weeds" published during the
brief Hundred Flowers period of 1956–57. These works went far
beyond the Hundred Flowers works, however, to present a veritable

popular history of the PRC since at least 1957 and to call into question most of the accepted CCP versions of those events. In the following section, I want to examine a number of these stories concerning the Great Leap Forward, and the themes of violence, poverty, cruelty, and persecution of the intellectuals during the Cultural Revolution.[29]

Another story by the veteran writer Ru Zhijuan, "A Mis–edited Story," was greeted as a major breakthrough due to its use of scenic montage rather than linear time structure and of a single thematically significant dream sequence.[30] Such breakthroughs, however, represent only a tentative return to techniques quite common during the pre–communist era of modern Chinese literature, and the main interest of this story is still in the contrast between the selfless Yan'an cadre and guerrilla leader, Lao Gan, and what he becomes as a loyal Party Secretary during the Great Leap Forward. During the Anti–Japanese War and the Revolutionary Civil War, Lao Gan would always leave some food for the peasants who risked their lives to protect him; but during the Great Leap Forward he bleeds the peasants dry by insisting that they can produce the outrageous sum of 16,000 catties of grain per *mou* of land and cutting down a beautiful stand of pear trees in order to "take grain as the leading element."

Lao Shou, the peasant who supported Lao Gan throughout the war years, becomes a "right deviationist" due to his stubborn refusal to falsify production figures and cut down the pear trees he has tended since the last time he gave up all of his jujube trees to provide firewood for the PLA fighters during the Anti–Japanese War. In the dream sequence of the penultimate section, Lao Shou seeks out the Lao Gan of old who has now, as a member of "the party in power," become a tyrant and a burden to the people who made his victory possible. He is ironically awakened from that dream by another piece of Great Leap foolishness when his grandson shouts out that "our Brigade has smelted some steel!" That is, they have produced some of the vast ammount of "backyard steel" that turned out to be a total waste of labor and materials.

The story quite rightly ends there, thus realistically implying that virtually all of the 1958–78 rural policies were mistaken and that it is a pipe dream to expect the post–Cultural Revolution CCP to suddenly be re–embued with the legendary Yan'an spirit. The editors of *People's Literature* added a note saying that Lao Gan and Lao Shou met again in January 1979 and are now hard at work on the realization of their youthful ideals. It is often the case that a neo–realist story is published with just such a protective ending tacked on by either the author or the editors.

The most moving story of rural poverty from the Great Leap to the Cultural Revolution is, I believe, the young writer Shi Tiesheng's basically apolitical story "Blacky."[31] In it a "good dog" is employed as a powerful symbol for the entire Chinese people, or at least for the peasantry. The first person narrator is a young man who, having already decided to commit suicide, goes back to see his rural home one more time. We are informed at the outset that it all happened in that "past era," but no specific time is given. Arriving home he learns that his family home (a typical Shaanxi cave dwelling) had been given to a certain Zhang Shan, son of Zhang Shiyou, after his father died; but it is now abandoned because Zhang Shan was taken away by the authorities and his family was forced by hunger to become vagrants in the time honored fashion of famine stricken peasants throughout Chinese history. Only the dog Blacky — a "good dog" says a ten year old boy who feeds him — is left behind loyally guarding the door and allowing no one to enter Zhang Shan's house.

When the summer rains come, the usual floods are exacerbated by the recent deforestation and everyone is reduced to a semistarvation diet of chaff while expecting another famine year. All other scraps being reserved for the pigs, Blacky is reduced to eating human excrement; but she doesn't seem to mind. "Oh Blacky," exclaims the narrator, "it's really hard; seems like only a willingness to suffer repeated hardships can make you a good dog."

Blacky is then driven by elemental "emotional needs" — seen as a "vague hope" by the narrator — to seek a mate. When she returns home pregnant and gives birth to a litter of pups, her struggle for survival becomes grim indeed. She begins to fight with the other hungry dogs and she begins her moral decline: she starts to steal. Ashamed of it at first, later she loses the civilized emotion of shame and quite impassively accepts the narrator's protective punishment after which she goes right on stealing to survive. She even catches a badger, but the effort is exhausting. Meanwhile the poverty of the human beings around her deepens daily:

> The little pups ate more every day, Blacky's teats were dry again, and once again she dragged her emaciated body around everywhere seeking food.
>
> It was late autumn, the crops had all been harvested, the fields were quite bare, and Blacky found absolutely nothing.
>
> It was a famine year, the summer floods had destroyed the wheat, the autumn grain yield was practically nil, every

family was boiling thin rice gruel and steaming coarse dumplings. Blacky found absolutely nothing.

Having licked the trough until it shown brightly, the old sow could only grunt with hunger.

Human excrement was hard to find . . .

The little pups were barking and crying. They were not yet able to forage for themselves. (30–31)

At this point Blacky commits an unpardonable offense. She steals a lamb from the sheepfold and is immediately discovered. The denouement is swift and certain, but Shi Tiesheng's description of the event makes it abundantly clear that this "good dog" is a symbol of the Chinese people:

The little pups yellped shrilly, Blacky jumped into the willow basket, licking this one and that one. 'There's nothing to be afraid of; after a while you will all go out with human beings and you must be good dogs.' The look in Blacky's eyes was so calm and good–natured.

When the people slipped the rope around her neck, Blacky stretched her neck out joyfully. She thought it was a special prize; an extra special honor for being a good dog – didn't that fat city dog who could jump through rings of fire have a beautiful chain collar around his neck?

But the rope was pulled tight. As Blacky ran along with the man pulling the rope, she seemed to be somewhat surprised: why was the rope becoming tighter and tighter?

Blacky gradually felt that something was amiss: so many strangers were loitering by the door to her cave dwelling and sitting on the windowsill of her 'sacred alter.'[32] She let out a shrill warning yelp.

The man pulling the rope threw the free end over a tree branch and pulled it hard. Blacky thought this joke was really being carried too far and she let out another shrill yelp of protest.

But the people didn't stop pulling; several of them pulled all at once. Blacky began to feel choked; but before she had time to realize what had happened, her body was already hanging in the air.

The look in Blacky's eyes in that last second left a deep impression on me – she looked so perplexed, so terrified, and so unjustly wronged. (31)

During the Great Leap and the Cultural Revolution (that "era now past"), the Chinese people "joyfully" followed their master's orders and before they "had time to realize what had happened" ("to awaken," *xingwu*) their master turned out to be the hangman. Shi Tiesheng concludes his story with the optimistic authorial comment that he can now write about those days without fear of reprisal because "humanity has won out over that dark era," but, in the fashion of a dedicated realist writer, he adds "in order to defeat it we must first recognize it." (31)

Qiao Shi's story "Providing a Meal" brings the theme of rural poverty during the Cultural Revolution right up to 1979 and boldly implies the complete failure of the revolution in the countryside. Narrated through the recollections of an old peasant woman, San Ma (Third Mother), it is a very sad story that illustrates not only the lack of material progress in the countryside but also the arrogant and parasitic relationship of many CCP rural cadres to the peasantry since the Great Leap Forward. The title is a sardonic reminder that China's rural population has been expected not only to feed her urban masses and their "vanguard" Party but also to hand in their meagre surplus to finance industrialization.

In 1979 San Ma is informed by her Production Brigade Leader that she is going to be visited by the local Party Committee Secretary. She protests that she has no flour noodles (a rare and expensive item) and is very anxious about the Brigade Leader's suggestion that she just cook some mixed grain porridge, the standard fare of poor peasants in that area. She then recalls two contrasting occasions when she cooked dinner for two different leading cadres. Their contrasting attitudes to that very mixed grain porridge, a palpable symbol of rural poverty, caries the main theme of the story.

The first time was in the 1950s during the land reform drive. Brigade Leader Chen came to her home then dressed in the PLA uniform of a Yan'an cadre and acted accordingly. When he realized that these hungry peasants had prepared some special noodles made of flour for him, a delicacy San Ma's own daughter had not eaten for some time, he took his bowl over to the hungry girl and held it while she eagerly devoured its contents; then he served himself from the family pot of mixed grain porridge and proceeded to deliver a lecture against the peasants making any special sacrifices for Communist Party cadres, concluding that "we are Communist cadres, not KMT enforcers." From that time on, "in San Ma's heart and mind, Brigade Leader Chen was a yardstick to measure and evaluate Communist cadres.[33]

On another very different occasion in 1975 when the local peasants were "in such bad straights they couldn't use their cooking pots" and "were not allowed to discuss how much to share among themselves, but only allowed to talk of their contribution to the country and the collective," Party Secretary Hou, nicknamed the "True Dragon Heir" (the emperor's heir apparent) and having a reputation for insisting on a fine banquet when he honored the local residents with his presence at table, decided to come to their house for dinner. San Ma wanted to buy some special provisions for him, but her husband, Li Santian, naively insisted that Hou could eat what they ate every day. He boldly but mistakenly asserted:

> Isn't Secretary Hou a Communist Party cadre? He's not a tiger from the mountains or a god from the temple.[34] He should take the bitter with the sweet along with us poor, lower, and middle peasants. (25)

San Ma takes her husband's advice with disastrous consequences. Qiao Shi's ironic use of CCP slogans to describe the way Secretary Hou "entered deeply into the life of the people" is masterful:

> Secretary Hou overcame very great difficulties and hard ships and, with an incomparably perserverent revolutionary spirit, the heroic attitude of 'not being afraid of hardship and not fearing death,' and an indefatigable fighting effort, finished eating that bowl of mixed grain porridge, put down the bowl, stood up and left without saying a word. (27)

Secretary Hou did not wait long to take his revenge for that insulting bowl of porridge. At a meeting of the Peasant Committee to estimate the grain harvest and set state purchasing quotas, he deliberately overestimated the quotas in order to goad Li Santian, a committee member, into protesting that the peasants would starve if they sold that much grain to the state. Hou then flew into a rage, accused Li of being a "Rightist," hauled him before the entire village, explained that his class status had "metamorphosed" and that he was rightly the target of the revolutionary masses. After her husband's misfortune, San Ma concluded that theirs was still a world where only money and power count and they would do better to ingratiate themselves with the leadership like some other favored villagers did by purchasing special meats and wines when the cadres came for dinner.

The story ends on a note of resignation when the 1979 Committee Secretary turns out to be none other than Brigade Leader Chen, the ideal Yan'an to land reform cadre, now an old man himself and tired out from the things he's suffered since the 1950s. When San Ma asks him why his hair is already white, the following poignant conversation ensues:

> 'Ran into calamities, floods, and droughts.' Old Chen answered her as he took another spoonful of dumplings.
>   'Well, did your hair run into a flood or a drought?'
>   Old Chen laughed too as he replied, 'Floods *and* droughts, I had 'em all, and also an attack of locusts. We're lucky that they didn't pick us completely clean!' Then his expression became very serious again and he went on, 'Otherwise, how could I be eating your porridge today? This is the good fortune that those calamites brought us.'
>   San Ma could see the flesh quivering on Old Chen's face, his eyes radiating a kind of sad yet angry glow, and his mouth holding back bitter pain; all as if there was something gnawing at his heart.
>   Then he said, 'If our poor peasants are supposed to consider it their glory to be poor forever, then why did we make the revolution?' (30)

Old Chen, a revolutionary for over forty years, is so agitated that he drops his chopsticks; but he does not go on to answer his own question. After he leaves, San Ma feels very uneasy and falls to wishing nostalgically that her husband was still alive to see Old Chen eat a bowl of mixed grain porridge with them once again. "That would be so fine!"

Although not as artfully crafted as "Blacky," this story movingly evokes the plight of the Chinese peasants at the hands of the rural cadres during the Cultural Revolution, expressing in simple human terms — eating mixed grain porridge for thirty years — the meaning of statistics such as those broadcast by the New China News Agency early in the same year that while the population of China had increased by 300 million from 1957 to 1977 the acreage of arable land was reduced by 100 million *mou* and the average per capita food grain distribution was less in 1977 than in 1957.[35] There is a certain factual weakness in the story, however, in that the comparison is between a 1950s Yan'an style model cadre and a 1975 authoritarian and parasitic cadre who is presumably loyal to the Gang of Four, while Mao Zedong is not mentioned. This is not too significant, though, since all of Qiao's readers know that the Great Leap and the Cultural Revolution were masterminded by Mao against the opposition of Peng Dehuai, Liu Shaoqi, and many others. When it was written, however, Liu had not yet been rehabilitated nor was it safe yet to directly attack the policies of the Great Helmsman in officially published fiction.

Two months before Jin He's "Re–encounter" the subject of Cultural Revolution violence was given its first stark yet almost lyrical treatment in Zheng Yi's story "Maple."[36] A first person narrative related by a Mr. Wang, a college art teacher, this tale of love and death and Maoist fanaticism is built on a single extended metaphor in which the blood red maple leaves stand for the Red Guard youth of China who fell like dead leaves spilling their rich, red blood in the factional battles of autumn 1967. As an artist, Wang loves to paint the maple trees in their autumn glory, but the battle trenches and mortar craters that stud the campus ruin the scenery. Captured by one Red Guard faction while reconnoitering for another, Wang is intentionally realeased by a former student, Lu Danfeng ("red maple"), after she gives him a pair of intertwined maple leaves and a note for her boyfriend, Li Qiangang (changed to Honggang, "red steel") who is a member of a rival Red Guard faction. The main action then ensues as Wang hides in a college classroom and witnesses a bloody battle during which many are killed and wounded on both sides for the glory of "defending Chairman Mao's revolutionary line" according to Jiang Qing's September fifth directive to "attack with words and defend with weapons."
The climax comes when Danfeng's faction is trapped on the roof of a classroom and she is confronted by Honggang. He begs her to "come to her senses" and she pleads with him to "turn his guns around" and attack his own mistaken faction. She reviles him, cries out, "The Jingangshan troops can never be annihilated! Communism is irresistible! Vow to defend to the death Chairman Mao's revolutionary line! Vow to defend Chairman Mao until death! Vow to defend Lin ... ...," and leaps to her death falling like an autumn leaf from the nearby maple trees. The bold statement that Chairman Mao and Lin Biao were intimately linked, a simple fact of history, was something new in neo–realist fiction and also an object of criticism from Maoist diehards. In the next passage, the metaphoric identification of these fallen youth and the maple leaves is quite transparent:

She lay there, lay there quietly on a bed of maple leaves
blasted down by the recent firing. An evening breeze blew
down a few red autumn maples (*rudan,* "like *dan,*" like Dan
feng as well as "like red"), scattered them over her body
bursting with youth, scattered them over her pale cheeks.
Only then did I remember the letter and the maple leaves
she had given me for Li Honggang and I hurriedly took them
out of my pocket only to discover that the letter was still
basically intact but the maple leaves had already been
crushed beyond recognition. (427–428)

In the denouement, the official lies about the Red Guard's
involvement in the Cultural Revolution are shown to have begun in
1969 when Li Honggang is himself executed on the ironic charge of
pushing Lu Danfeng to her death in 1967. On that day, Wang did not
attend the public execution, but only went for a walk along a tree lined
road where "the maple trees were red again, like burst after burst of
leaping flames, the fire red crowns of the trees were as red as blood
just spurting from an open wound, thick and brightly flowing. . . . . .
(431)

In his introduction to a recent anthology of Chinese short fiction
from the 1920s, 30s, and 40s, C.T. Hsia remarks that "the abiding
question is not why people are so ridiculous or stupid . . ., but why
people are so unkind and cruel."[37] Cruelty on a vast scale was an
everyday feature of the Cultural Revolution decade and thus it forms
the theme of many neo–realist stories. One in particular, Zhu Lin's
"The Web," takes us back into a world of rural China not so
sardonically depicted since Lu Xun's "The New Year's Sacrifice" of
1924.[38] Lu Xun could have easily and sadly recognized the people
standing in their doorways "watching with relish" as the woman they
nicknamed "Toughie" for her ability to endure her husband's many
beatings is forced to parade the streets beating a gong and shouting out
that she is a thief, "the sound of the gong stirring their appetites." He
would know them as the same people who "went away satisfied,
exchanging comments" after listening to Xianglin Sao's tragic story of
how her son was eaten by a wolf.[39]
     The story rises to a powerful symbolic ending in which the
protagonist dies of sheer exhaustion after watching a spider (the CCP)
build a web (life in the PRC) into which an unsuspecting fly
(herself/the Chinese people) falls:[40]

The spider scuttled over to the little green fly and sprang on it, forcing itself down on the fly's body and chewing it greedily.

Gradually the spider's stomach swelled, and the fly became an empty shell hanging from the web.

One, another, a third . . . the empty shells of innumerable small flies hung from the web. No wonder the spider's stomach swelled ever larger; no wonder it looked like a carefree boddhisatva leisurely controlling everything in the world.

Despite this easily decoded symbolic ending, the critical theme of the story is as old as the *Shi jing* poem "Big Rat" and the "Robber Zhih" chapter of the *Zhuang zi.*[41] The story asks the questions, "what is really stealing?" and "who are the real thieves?", through a series of incidents in the tragic life of the protagonist from the 1950s to the 1970s, all taking place after "liberation." As a child in the 1950s her father spanks her for eating one stalk of "communal" sorghum to teach her that "a person shouldn't steal," but when they are all fleeing the famine of 1960 she is shocked to realize that the raw sweet potato her father gives her is stolen (the word goes unspoken when her father shouts at her to "Eat it!"). At sixteen her parents force her to marry a lazy, good–for–nothing fellow named Rainy who steals from the villagers and then publicly beats her so that everyone believes she is a thief, but before that a hundred pound bag of rice that Rainy gives her parents for the trip home is "confiscated" (legally stolen) by the market supervisor, thus insuring her parents' death on the road. Her child's grain allotment is also legally stolen — withheld — because she is not able to bribe the Production Team Leader. Sent out at night by Rainy to steal beans, she is surprised to discover Team Leader Lai stealing large sacks of grain. He glares at her "firm young breasts" and steals her honor and self–respect with a brutal rape.

After his promotion, she often sees Party Secretary Lai taking big baskets full of fresh duck eggs while her own daughter is starving for lack of even one egg a day. "They were for himself, and to offer to his superiors, commune and county officials;" and the question of whether or not he was "stealing" never occurred to her. Finally, Secretary Lai catches her stealing a few scoops of duck–feed barely for her starving daughter and decides to fine her two hundred catties of grain. Suddenly she reminds him of all the things he has taken from the communal stores: ". . . isn't that stealing too? What you've stolen is too much to be counted. If you say I'm a petty thief, then you're a big thief!"[42] Secretary Lai then beats her and orders her "to parade through the streets as an example to the masses," reminding us once again of a Lu Xun story, "A Public Example." Zhu Lin's relentless examination of the meaning of the word *tou*, "stealing," leaves little doubt in the reader's mind as to who the real thieves are and it is to her credit that she does not pretend that the situation has been changed overnight due to the new Party leadership.

Since all classes in Chinese society suffered greatly during the Cultural Revolution, it may seem unreasonable to attempt to specify which class suffered the most; but one rather small yet very important group of people has always received the first shock of every ideological campaign since 1942: the intellectuals. And their story was seldom told until after the death of the Great Helmsman whose resentment against and distrust of intellectuals persisted ever since their alleged mistreatment of him when he worked in the Peking University Library during the May Fourth Era. That is why Shen Rong's 1980 novella "Reaching Middle Age" became an immediate critical and popular success.[43]

For over thirty years after the Yan'an Forum on Literature and Art, Ding Ling was repeatedly attacked for her story entitled "In the Hospital" describing the rude awakening of an idealistic young nurse, Lu Ping, when faced with the intrenched ignorance, insensitivity, filth, and bureaucratic mismanagement of a CCP administered hospital in the Yan'an base area.[44] It is a measure of the new leadership's willingness to try to win over and improve the lives of the intellectuals, now regarded as the leading element in China's modernization drive, that Shen Rong's story was awarded *People's Literature*'s first prize for novellas.[45] The story itself provides a measure of just how harsh have been the lives of even the most dedicated intellectual followers of the Maoist slogan "serve the people."

Dr. Lu Wenting is certainly the fictional daughter of nurse Lu Ping, but her life is much harder. After graduation from medical school, she gladly accepts a four-year internship during which she is not allowed to leave the hospital. Married to a metallurgist, Fu Jiajie, after a lyrical courtship and with two children to take care of, as an ophthalmologist she often sees seventeen patients a morning and performs several operations daily. She never receives a promotion nor a raise in her 56.50 RMB (about $28 US) per month salary during all the eighteen years she works in the hospital without ever missing a single day. Her family of four lives in a twelve square meter room with but one desk that she and her husband can only study on at night after the children have gone to bed. Not surprisingly, like so many of China's middle aged intellectuals and like PRC society as a whole, she is physically and spiritually exhausted. That exhaustion is compared to metal fatigue in a metaphorical statement made by her husband:[46]

> Metals also suffer from fatigue. First they develop microscopic fatigue cracks, later these gradually expand, and when they reach a certain point, the metal simply collapses and breaks off . . . (232)

Lu Wenting collapses with a heart attack after performing her third successful operation in one day and her total fatigue is reflected in the fact that all of her dim reveries of past happinesses when "life and love were good" cannot overcome her powerful desire to rest in the peace of death. Her spiritual exhaustion is also shown in some very well written "streams of semi–consciousness" such as the following:

> In her semi–conscious state, Dr. Lu felt herself walking down a long endless road.
>
> It was not a tortuous mountain trail, which, although very dangerous and difficult to ascend, nevertheless inspires one's spirit of adventure with its many twists and turns. Nor was it a small footpath between the paddyfields, which, though narrow and hard to walk on, neverthelsss is surrounded by the fragrance of the young plants that gladdened one's heart and spirit. It was an impassable sandpit, a quagmire, and an endless wasteland. As far as the eye could see, there was no trace of human life, only deathly silence. Oh! What a difficult road to travel; what an exhausting road!
>
> Lie down and rest! The sand is warm and the mud is soft. Let the great earth warm your icy cold body and the spring rays carress your tired bones. She seemed to hear the God of Death softly whisper her name out of the darkness:
>
> 'Rest in peace, Dr. Lu!'
>
> Oh, how wonderful it would be to rest this way for eternity, with no more thoughts, worries, sorrows, or fatigue. (197–198)

She cannot die, however, not because of her husband's love and poetry reading at her bedside nor her child's pneumonia (that did not make her miss even a minute of work); but because of her patients whose eyes keep surrounding her in her reveries. The most unsatisfactory thing about this story as a work of art, is that a month and a half after her best friend leaves for America, Lu Wenting, "leaning on her husband's shoulder, slowly makes her way step by step toward the gate. . . to welcome the sunlight and the cold wind." (286) Evidently she must continue to walk down that "long endless road." When Shen Rong was in Vancouver, I asked her if some editor had perhaps suggested that she end the story this way on an up-beat rather than with the more powerful and more reasonable death of Lu Wenting, and she replied in the negative. She said she felt that a "person" like Lu Wenting "deserved to live." Her answer, based as it is on extra-literary considerations, is a fitting commentary on many post-Mao neo-realist writers' concept of the relationship between life and art.

In a literary context where the boundaries between life and art are often very hazy even in the minds of creative writers themselves, it will hardly seem remarkable to find superior craftsmanship or artistry in works of nonfiction dealing with the theme of intellectual persecution during the Cultural Revolution. Such is the case with two very different memoirs by two also very different veteran writers. One is Ba Jin's characteristically highly emotional and moving short piece about the death of his wife, "Remembering Xiao Shan" and the other is playwright Yang Jiang's sophisticated, subtle work of powerful understatement, *Six Chapters of a Cadre School Life*.[47]

Ba Jin's short essay testifies to the cruelty of the Cultural Revolution treatment of one of China's best loved writers and to the strength he derived from his wife's unflagging protection and support. For those intellectuals who survived the ordeal, her words to him provide a meaningful slogan: "Endurance is our victory." But she herself was unable to stand the years of harassment. As Ba Jin laments:

> What crime had she ever committed? She too had been locked in a 'cowshed,' had borne a little sign reading 'cow devil,' and had swept the streets! What for, really? The reason was very simple: she was my wife. She was ill and could not receive medical care; this too, all because she was my wife. I tried everything, but not until three weeks before she died — relying on 'going through the back door' — was she finally able to enter a hospital; but the cancer cells had metastasized, bowel cancer had become liver cancer. (114)

It cannot, perhaps, be proven that stress causes cancer; but the incessant personal attacks of those days that made even "one quiet peaceful night of family living" an impossible luxury certainly took their toll on Xiao Shan as "spiritually she was tossed back and forth like a football." As Ba Jin sadly recalls, "I watched her waste away day by day, watched the spark of her life gradually being extinguished, and I felt so sick at heart!" (117–118)

Her only regret, she confided to Ba Jin before she died, was that "I won't be able to see you liberated." That is to see his "case" decided. Eleven months after her death a six man committee headed by Wang Hongwen himself decided that his problem was one of non–antagonistic "contradiction among the people" and he was once more made a member of "the people" by Party prescription. From then on Ba Jin has lived with Xiao Shan's crematory urn in their bedroom "where I can feel that she is still with me. . . . Then when I close my eyes for eternity, please mingle my ashes with hers." (128,131)

As Howard Goldblatt points out in his introduction, Yang Jiang's *Six Chapters* touches on a number of themes such as the distrust and resentment of the peasants for China's urban intellectuals, the tremendous human waste involved in this effort to "remold" the intellectuals, the poverty of the Chinese countryside, and the mutual devotion of this sexagenarian Chinese couple (Yang Jiang's husband being the well known scholar and writer Qian Zhongshu). More important than the "overall sense of disappointment, frustration, and skepticism" that Goldblatt rightly senses in the work, I believe, is the sometimes subtle, sometimes gently ironic, and sometimes open state-ment of the complete failure and foolishness of this misguided Cultural Revolution effort – and, by implication, of all of those ideological efforts since 1942 – to fundamentally transform human nature to make it fit the Maoist communist mold. She not only "reaffirms the endurance of humanity" but also predicts the ultimate victory of universal human nature over any ideological system that is not in conformity with it.

An ironic example of this theme is presented in her discussion of the ubiquitous "study sessions" the intellectuals of the Chinese Academy of Science were forced to endure before being given their chance to go to a cadre school:

Virtually all we did . . . was to participate in study sessions,
until even the 'laborer–teachers' who were 're–educating' us

were fed up with the situation. One young 'laborer–teacher,'
who was twenty–two or twenty–three years old, grumbled: 'I
work all day long in front of a blast furnace tempering steel
without feeling the least bit tired, but after sitting here all
day, not only do I get a sore butt, but I'm beat to my socks.'
Obviously, tempering people (*lianren*) is more exhausting
work than tempering steel, and being a teacher (literally,
sitting on a cold bench) isn't all it's cracked up to be. (12–13)

This theme is strongly affirmed in the final segment, though in a
tongue in cheek apologetic manner. At one point, Yang Jiang asks
herself why just before "Liberation, when so many people had been
fleeing the country in alarm; ... hadn't we chosen to leave?" She then
gives the answer that best applies to the great majority of China's
intellectual elite:

We had simply been unwilling to abandon the mother land,
... it was all tied up in the concept of 'we' or 'us.' And even
though we had never met the billion other people who made
up this 'we,' this 'us,' we were still part of the same body —
we all shared a common lot and were closely bound up with
one another. We were all indispensable parts of a whole.
(41)

So much for the Marxist concept of "class struggle," which is never
directly mentioned in the work. She then goes on to scold herself for
thinking so much about reuniting her own family after getting out of
the cadre school:

... I couldn't see beyond the well–being of my own family.
Since Liberation, after having been through the fire and
crucible of reform, I'm afraid that I was worse off than at the
very beginning. (41)

Finally, in the penultimate paragraph of the work, she ironically
sums up the "lesson" she has learned from her participation in this vast
experiment in human transformation and tempering:

I now understood something more clearly than ever: after
undergoing more than ten years of reform, plus two years at
the cadre school, not only had I not reached the plateau of
progressive thinking that everyone sought. I was nearly as

selfish now as I had been in the beginning. I was still the
same old me. (43)

Having completed this rather lengthy survey of neo–realist fiction
directly related to the Cultural Revolution, I would like to round out
this chapter with an examination of a few of the best stories on the
subjects of rural life, factory work, bureaucratic corruption and CCP
special privileges that extend the neo–realist depiction of PRC life up
to the truly contemporary social reality of the 1980s.

In the realm of rural fiction, long the dominant vehicle for direct
ideological propaganda, Gao Xiaosheng, a former "Rightist" sent down
to the Jiangsu countryside from 1958 to 1979, emerged as a realistic
alternative to the then disgraced Cultural Revolution romanticist Hao
Ran and a worthy successor to the popular 1950s writer Zhao Shuli.
As a practitioner of the persistence of traditional forms Gao is the
equal of both of them, but as a writer of critical neo–realist fiction he
surpasses both of them.[48] Despite his prolific output, however, his one
and only masterpiece remains the 1979 story "Li Shunda Builds a
House".[49] A detailed account of one poor peasant's unrelenting
thirty–year struggle to build a simple three room house for his family,
a struggle whose main antagonist is the CCP and its various
misdirected rural policies aimed at transforming the countryside; this
story goes much further than Qiao Shi's above mentioned work in its
implicit criticism of the entire post–land reform system as the major
cause of China's continuing rural poverty.
As Leo Ou–fan Lee has pointed out, this story is based on a
structural irony. Through the use of aphorisms, folk sayings, puns, and
other traditional storyteller's narrative devices a naive hero is created
and his simple minded acceptence of utopian Party propaganda and
naive comments on recent history establish a powerful irony of point of
view when "the knowing reader . . . penetrates to, and shares, the
implicit point of view of the authorial presence behind the naive
persona."[50] Indeed, Li Shunda becomes an allegorical counterpoint and
corrective to Mao Zedong's Foolish Old Man who tried to move a
mountain with only primitive methods and thus bequeathed to his
son's a legacy of backbreaking toil without end — the Chinese labors of
Sisyphus.
Derided by skeptical friends for his "lofty goal" of building a house
in the 1950s, Li replies that "it certainly can't be as hard as the Foolish
Old Man moving the mountain."[51](142) After all, as a "good follower,"

he has complete faith in the Communist Party. "He obeyed Chairman Mao, followed the Communist Party, resolutely carried things through and practiced them in everyday life. Whatever any Party member said to him he considered it an order." (43)

His simple honesty and naive trust in the Party's ever changing policies are actually the main reasons why he never manages to build even his simple "two–room, one–story" dream house. He is almost ready to start when the Great Leap Forward claims all of his building materials and after ten years of communism he is left with an unoccupied pig pen to live in. He saves up enough cash once again by 1966; then, when he foolishly gives it to a Cultural Revolution "rebel," it's gone again, and he himself is sent to jail where he "studies construction" since the jail is the best built house he's ever lived in after twenty years of communism. We are assured that Li will be able to build his house in the post–Mao era, but he'll have to bribe various factory, transportation, and construction supply workers with packs of cigarettes in order to complete his task.

Neither Gao Xiaosheng nor his fictional character Li Shunda can rightly be accused of being anti–socialist, but their story's metaphorical meaning is undoubtedly that socialism in China — whatever it might be — has definitely not been built yet and cannot be built on the basis of the utopian slogans and ill–advised mass campaigns of the past thirty years. Something very close to this thesis can be seen as the motivating force behind Chen Yun and Zhao Ziyang's economic reforms in the countryside. Those reforms seem to be quite successful to date and their success has been the theme of a number of Gao Xiaosheng's later stories featuring the rather sympathetic country bumpkin Chen Huansheng.[52] In his role as enthusiast for current policies, however necessary and beneficial, unfortunately Gao Xiaosheng has not yet crafted another story that achieves the allegorical heights of "Li Shunda Builds a House."

Factory fiction, once a world of "new socialist men" and women, model workers who live only for production and demand nothing more than the spiritual reward that comes with the knowledge that they are building socialism,[53] has also changed greatly in the post–Mao era. The man most responsible for the change is the genuine "worker–writer" Jiang Zilong, author of a series of stories that realistically describe and satirize bureaucratic mismanagement and abuse of power in the PRC industrial system while at the same time creating "new socialist men" of the post–Maoist type who point the way out of the current mess by supporting currently popular economic reform policies. His most famous story, "Manager Qiao Assumes Office" received the most votes in *People's Literature*'s 1979 reader preference poll as well as winning first prize from the National Short Story Prize Committee, and his own favorite story, "The Foundation" has been translated in two recent English anthologies.[54] Although very critical of the economic mess in the PRC today, Jiang has never been attacked by the Party's literary critics.

"Manager Qiao Assumes Office" and its sequel "More About Manager Qiao"[55] present a detailed and panoramic picture of bureaucratic mismanagement, production bottlenecks, workers' grievances, and inner Party factionalism in a large electrical machine factory while offering complete support for an almost perfect embodiment of the dedicated post–Mao reformist type of Factory Manager. Qiao Guangpu, a loyal Party member, an overseas student in the USSR in the fifties, and a pre–Cultural Revolution Factory Manager who spent time in a "cow barn," volunteers to step down from his safe post as Company Executive to take on the difficult job of Manager in a factory that is two and one half years behind in meeting its production quotas. He is willing to accept "military discipline" if he fails and his only condition for taking the post is that he be allowed to take along his old friend, Shi Gan, another victim of the Cultural Revolution, to be the factory Party Committee Secretary. Thus, he will take care of the economic management and his friend will handle the political problems, such as workers gripes, damaged egoes, and so on. He has the full support of his superior, Huo Dadao, Chairman of the Electrical Machine Department, who promises to go to bat for him with the higher bureaucrats at Party Central.

The stories are narrated in an extremely realistic fashion reminiscent of Mao Dun's *Midnight*, as personal conflicts and complex infighting are seen to revolve around Manager Qiao's attempts to reform factory management and poor work habits in order to increase production. The basic problems of PRC industry are described with sociological accuracy and seen to be the following: loss of work spirit among formerly dedicated cadres who suffered during the Cultural Revolution; lack of proper training, sloppy work habits, poor discipline, low morale, and no enthusiasm among the workers, especially the younger ones (one young man had worked on a lathe for six years, didn't even know how to oil it properly, and couldn't care less); lackadaisical to nonexistent supervision and virtually no quality control resulting in an astronomical rate of product defectiveness; factionalism among the workers, who are split into three conflicting age groups: the older pre–Cultural Revolution workers, the Cultural Revolution rebel workers, and the youngest post–Cultural Revolution workers; and factionalism among Party leaders along similar lines, with old line pre–Cultural Revolution bureaucratic opportunists pitted against ex–rebel cadres who are shown to be particularly able and idealistic Party workers who still want to accomplish something and make the system work.

In the course of many complex maneuvers, Qiao tries to balance all of these competing forces while putting through a set of measures that demonstrate Jiang Zilong's intimate knowledge of and support for nearly the entire package of Chen Yun and Zhao Ziyang's economic reforms. The first set of reforms is designed to increase production and includes the following items: proficiency testing for everyone, including the management (of course, Qiao passes and the former manager fails miserably); differential material incentives for more productive workers; creation of a Factory Service Brigade to handle maintainance work and staffed by those workers who fail the proficiency tests; and the provision of new child care facilities and dormitories for the workers. The second set of reforms is designed to increase sales and profits and includes the training of "sales experts" to handle both national and international sales and distribution; expansion of "product propaganda," good old fashioned capitalistic advertising to gain product recognition; setting up of local sales offices throughout the country; and the establishment of national and international "sales intelligence offices" to learn all about foreign companies, foreign technology, and how to deal with foreign capitalists.

Besides the many problems involved in winning over the workers to this new way of doing things and preventing bureaucratic sabotage behind his back on the part of the former management who do not want him to succeed, Qiao's main economic problem is the maintainance of an internal supply of materials necessary for continued high speed production. Certainly the most interesting and revealing aspect of these stories is the matter of fact way in which Jiang describes these material supply and transportation problems being solved by an enthusiastic and highly pragmatic ex–Cultural Revolution rebel cadre, Chi Wangbei, through the skillful manipulation of an extremely complex web of personal and bureaucratic connections (*guanxi*) among other factory heads, small town railroad station operators, railroad transport teams, and local Party hacks of all sorts and sizes. We might say that everything is handled by Chi on the basis of the "Asiatic mode of production": you grease my palm and I'll grease yours. Manager Qiao, as a good Marxist moralist, does not approve of Chi's resort to this Balzacean web of personal and financial relationships; but Chi assures him that at this stage of Chinese history his method is the only viable way to get the job done. And, most importantly, he does keep the supplies coming in. As Deng Xiaoping might say, it may not be a red method but it is a method that gets results. In the end Qiao's reforms are seen to be succeeding, but many other problems remain to be solved before China's industries can be run on the basis of anything approaching the rationality and scientific organization that generally prevail in capitalist corporations. That Jiang Zilong's stories, even when they concern relative successes, leave the reader with a feeling for the many problems still remaining is an indication that as a social realist he is more accurate than Gao Xiaosheng. As a writer, however, neither of them can really compare to the early Mao Dun whose sociological accuracy was blended with a fine sense of psychological characterization that make novels like *Midnight* and stories like "Spring Silkworms" better than anything Jiang or Gao have yet accomplished.

Manager Qiao is really too good to be true, his characterization is accomplished without the slightest suggestion of irony, and his popularity with the urban reading public is no doubt due to their ex- treme desire to see such a man carry out such policies in real life. In the character of Chi Wangbei Jiang seems to be suggesting that Marxist moralism, hurculean dedication, and perfect planning are not necessarily the only ingredients required for successful industrial man- agement. In this imperfect world, the ability to use the real system of human interactions is perhaps just as essential as a thorough grasp of Marxist economic theories. The story of another quite different factory manager seems to drive home this point even more strongly.

In my estimation Jiang Zilong's finest story is, then, "A Factory Secretary's Diary" and it involves the same irony of point of view and ironic comment on the discrepancy between ideology and practice that we saw in "Li Shunda Builds a House," only this time it is achieved through the creation of an unreliable narrator.[56] Factory Secretary, Wei Jixiang, a self–professed "square peg in a round hole" with no enthusiasm for his present position due to over exposure to the petty factionalism of the top management of a small chemical factory, makes a day by day report on the activities of a new style pro–worker, pro–bonus, pro–profit manager, Jin Fengchi, whose unorthodox style of work and hard drinking lifestyle he professes to dislike. In the course of the story, however, the reader's admiration for Manager Jin increases apace as we see him outdoing even Manager Qiao's assistant, Chi Wangbei, in his ability to manipulate the complex real world of *guanxi* in the interests of his workers and their individual enterprise.

As he tells Secretary Wei:

> . . . I must say you're a bit of a stick-in-the mud. Tell you
> what, in capitalist countries, money counts, but in our
> country, it's your connections. That's something I've learned
> through experience. This certainly won't change in the next
> three to five years. Ours is a small factory and we've no big
> cadres. That means we've neither power nor position. If
> you don't have good connections and don't butter people up,
> you can do nothing. (43–44/227)[57]

Wei responds, playing it safe: "An amazing theory! I could not decide
if he was admirable or despicable."

The main action of the story takes place when Secretary Jin wangles
a 100 RMB bonus for his workers on December 31, 1979 and insits on
dividing it up immediately against the objections of the ideologically
orthodox and thus conservative factory Party Secretary, Liu, who
doesn't want to give away so much of the state's money. Ironically,
Liu, characterized as a "good man," is opposing a September 1979
Central Committee policy. As Jin argues, "The higher–ups keep
changing their minds. Who can predict the new rule next year?"
(51/236) Things have to be decided fast in the interest of the workers.
On January 3, 1980, Wei records, all 1979 bonuses are in fact frozen.

As a result of his actions on the workers' behalf, Manager Jin is
elected to be a delegate to the People's Congress with only three votes
cast against him. In a doubly ironic surprise ending, one of those very
satisfying short story endings one rarely encounters in PRC fiction,
narrator Wei records that Manager Jin did not vote for himself, but
rather for the ideologically more correct practitioner of socialist
morality, Party Secretary Liu. He explains himself as follows:

> 'It's true,' he said, tossing down his drink. Now the liquor
> had really gone to his head. 'I know you must think that I'm
> as slick as a snake. But I wasn't born like that. The longer
> you muddle along in this society, the smarter you become.
> After a few slips and falls even you'd wise up. The more
> complex the society, the sharper the people. Liu's a good
> man, but he didn't get as many votes as I. How can good
> men like him cope in the future? If I'd listened to Liu and
> run the factory in a rigid way, production would have
> dropped. I'd have offended the workers and there'd be no
> profit. The state and our leaders wouldn't have been happy

about it. Don't think I'm glad because I've got the most votes. On the contrary, I feel very bad. I knew Liu wouldn't vote for me, but I voted for him... ...' (53/239)

Jiang Zilong cleverly lays on one final layer of irony by having narrator Wei conclude thus:

I deeply regretted that I'd voted in his favor. Though he got the most votes, he is not of the calibre of a people's delegate. You mean to say Jin Fengchi is the most qualified candidate for people's delegate today?
I'm certain that he'll lose the next election. (53/239)[58]

We are not to believe it. Jiang Zilong has mastered the art of irony in this story, enhancing the reader's estimation of Manager Jin without ever once recording a complimentary remark about him, not even from his own mouth. While seemingly favoring ideological purity over practical self-interest, he has actually spoken up in an ironic mode in favor of universal human nature in the form of the workers' natural desire to share in the fruits of their labors.

Not only bureaucratic mismanagement, but the moral corruption, abuse of power, and special privileges of the Communist Party (including the hitherto sacrosanct People's Liberation Army) viewed by many as a new "privileged class" became one of the dominant themes of PRC fiction in 1979 and 1980. In many of the most controversial stories — most of them represented in the anthologies mentioned at the beginning of this chapter — not even one Party cadre is portrayed as upright and decent. After Hu Yaobang's speech at the Drama Forum in early 1980, however, most of the critical stories have a Party cadre as a "positive character" (although he may admit his past "mistakes" and shortcomings) who is intended to be regarded as the "type" of the present Party leader.

Although the abuses they delineate are shocking enough, even to those of us who have always known that "absolute power corrupts absolutely," and their publication was greeted with widespread popular enthusiasm; few of them are rereadable as literature. Artistically the finest work remains the play that Hu Yaobang was justifiably anxious to prevent being performed in public: *What If I Really Were?*[59]

As Edward Gunn pointed out, this story of an educated youth, Li Xiaozhang, who impersonates the son of a high ranking cadre in the Party Central Commission for Inspecting Discipline in order to have

himself transferred back to the city from the state farm he has been
sent down to, represents an "extreme of experimentation" for PRC
literature in the post–Mao era.[60] Such experimentation includes the
presentation of morally flawed characters as protagonist, settings
involving high ranking elite cadres, the use of some techniques derived
from Western modernism, and an ironic undercutting of accepted Party
interpretations of reality. *What If I Really Were*? also combines the
themes of the generation gap, the contrast between urban comfort and
rural squalor, moral corruption in both Party and society in general,
and the Party as a privileged class, all "in a setting so permeated with
cynicism (that) the use of conventional socialist rhetoric to define or
prescribe is viewed as ridiculous."[61]

The all pervasive skepticism regarding Party rhetoric is brought out
forcefully in the following conversation between Bureau of Culture
Chief, Sun, and his daughter, Juanjuan, whom Li Xiaozhang's pregnant
girlfriend has asked to plead her case:[62]

> JUANJUAN: Minghua has a boyfriend still on the farm.
> They've known each other for years now, and they want to
> get married. Only her father won't agree to it and he won't
> give his consent unless her boyfriend is transferred back to
> the city. Dad, poor Minghua is really desperate. You've got
> to figure something out for her.
>
> SUN: You're her classmate, so you should go to work on
> her father's ideology. Tell her father that such thinking is
> incorrect. In our country there's no such thing as high or
> low status. Any job, whether on a farm or in a factory,
> serves the people and has a bright future.
>
> JUANJUAN: Spoken like a simpleton. *You* go say that!
> Who listens to that babble nowadays?

At the end of the sixth scene Li Xiaozhang admits his guilt when
confronted by Zhang Lao, but he argues that he would not have gotten
anywhere if it had not been for that "insatiable" group of people
pampering him and seeking special favors from him because of who
they thought he was. Zhang Lao asks who "they" are and Li shows
him the evidence he's collected to protect himself:[63]

> See for yourself. This is Managing Director Zhao's; he
> wants a larger house. This is Bureau Chief Sun's; he wants
> his son–in–law transferred back from the northeast. This
> was written by Director Qian herself yesterday for me to give

to you personally, asking for your support in pulling strings for her and Secretary Wu to join an overseas delegation. They all wanted favors from me, but whom could *I* turn to? And they all tried to charm me so that I would help them solve their problems, but who was there to solve mine?

In the courtroom scene that makes up the epilogue wherein "our beloved and faithful audience" is urged to "express their own opinions on the fairness of the court's verdict," Li brushes aside the question of whether he has committed a "crime" (*zui*) by acknowledging that he "was wrong" (*cuo*):[64]

I was wrong to be a fake. If I really were the son of Zhang Senior or another leader, then everything I've done would be completely legal.

He then goes on to express his ironic appreciation to all those people mentioned above who treated him so kindly.

Finally Zhang Lao, who has agreed to defend Li, tries to re–establish a proper moral climate in the Party and society through the reassertion of socialist rhetoric. He argues that Li Xiaozhang is also a victim of Lin Biao and the Gang of Four, who "completely destroyed our campaign to send youth to the countryside and made these young people cynical," and that all of the respectable Party cadres who collaborated with the supposed son of a high cadre did so "from habits that are rooted in a feudalistic, privilege–oriented mentality." In light of the rectification campaign proclaimed at the Twelfth Congress of the CCP in September 1982 and still going on at this writing, Zhang Lao's final remarks may be seen as prophetic:[65]

I am really afraid for our cadre system, which, having survived the Gang of Four, may be brought to ruin by its own corruption.

Beware, comrades, or else — though some of you may now be sitting in this court of law — in the court of Party discipline you will just as surely be standing in the dock of the accused!

Zhang Lao's rhetoric is really not the last word because the audience has been asked to make the final judgement. As we have seen, however, they were never given that opportunity. We may feel that Zhang Lao's words, blaming the corruption of his contemporaries on the feudal past instead of on the fact that the Party is almost the only avenue for advancement in PRC society, are already sufficient to support the stated aims of the current Party reform movement being directed from Party Central. If we thought so we would be overlooking the fact that many members of the audience might feel, like Sun Juanjuan, that these pious platitudes have now lost all efficacy. Certainly the Politburo or the Propaganda Department feared that the latter result was more likely. Thus Hu Yaobang announced that the play did not accurately reflect the "essence" of the relationships said to exist between the Party and "the people" in Chinese society at the time and that its performance would have the "unhealthy" social effect of causing people to sympathize "with a character who is unworthy of sympathy."[66]

One final question this play, and indeed the bulk of the neo–realist fiction we've just surveyed, leaves in this reader's mind is not a literary but a socio–political one. How can a situation in which membership in a single self–regulating political party offers the only access to power and privilege in society ever result in anything more promising than alternating periods of abuse of power followed by moralistic campaigns against those abuses conducted by some of the very people who are themselves tainted by those abuses? Only future historical develop–ments can answer such a question in the Chinese context. It is, however, of the greatest significance that the "didactic, moralistic, and reformist" neo–realist fiction of the post–Mao era leads us to ponder such social questions; this fact, more than any other considerations of artistic merit alone, accounts for its great popularity and importance both to its intended Chinese readership and to students of modern Chinese literature and society.

The tradition of realist fiction in modern China stems from a combination of the serious concern for society and principled demand for social justice that is characteristic of the finest products of traditional Chinese literature and the more individualistic humanitarianism of predominantly nineteenth century European literature. It flourished during the period from 1917 to 1949 and had a profound influence on the modern Chinese mind. Under the influence of a narrow–minded Maoist interpretation of the function of literature in society it lost its critical edge and became the handmaiden of the Party. The works discussed in this chapter are ample proof that the tradition did not die. Chinese writers consider themselves intellectuals and are so regarded by society in general. As intellectuals they feel a serious responsibility to comment on and influence society. We may be certain that whenever they are given the chance they will continue to conscienciously explore all of the problematic areas of contemporary Chinese society. Those of us living outside of the PRC may continue to criticize their style of writing for not going beyond the social realism of the great nineteenth century novels to what Erich Heller calls "the other realism" which abandons the primacy of external phenomena in favor of the perceiving consciousness and in which style is itself a primary indicator of theme.[67] At the same time, however, being fully aware of the difficult and uncertain conditions under which they labor, we can only admire them for their moral courage and their humanity.

IV. Ironies of History in the Reportage Fiction of Liu Binyan

> The Revolution against the enemies
> of the Revolution is epic;
> The Revolution against the partisans
> of the Revolution is tragic.
> —Carlos Fuentes[1]

"The stories you are about to read are true; only the names have been changed to protect the guilty. Any resemblance to persons living or dead is purely intentional." Liu Binyan is not Costa–Gavras, his artistic freedom is much more limited, and, thus he never penned such a deliberately ironic epigram to any of his fictionalized reports; but he did write at the end of his most celebrated work, "Between Men and Monsters," that, "for reasons the reader can understand," he had changed some of the characters' names. Later on he wrote that he had done so in hopes that those who were guilty of involvement in Wang Shouxin's criminal network would recognize themselves and reform.[2] Such obvious didacticism is not the technical method of the ironist; and Liu Binyan, a Party member and a roving reporter for the *People's Daily* whose works consist primarily of "fictionalized reportage" or "special features," would probably not characterize his literary technique or style as that of conscious irony. He attempts to write with journalistic objectivity and respect for the truth of social reality as he sees it and does not deliberately attempt to achieve that "suppression of all explicit moral judgements [and] dispassionate construction" leading to a kind of fabling "without moralizing" which is regarded as the essence of the ironist's style.[3] Liu considers himself rather to be a realist writing in the tradition of nineteenth century European realism and the modern Chinese tradition of social criticism.[4]

In what sense then do I intend to speak of irony in relation to Liu Binyan's carefully realistic reportage? In a historical sense by applying a number of commonly accepted insights from professor Northrop Frye in a manner slightly different from their original exposition. In his well known "theory of modes," Frye describes the chronologically most recent and currently most common mode of "most serious fiction" in Europe as being written in "the ironic mode" which has grown out of "the low mimetic mode of most comedy and of realistic fiction." In realistic fiction, such as Liu Binyan writes, "the hero is one of us" and is "superior neither to other men nor to his environment." He may, however, sometimes triumph over both; otherwise he could hardly be called a "hero." On the other hand, in the ironic mode the protagonist is "inferior in *power* or intelligence to ourselves, so that we have the sense of looking down on a scene of *bondage, frustration, or absurdity*. . . [and] . . . this is still true when the reader feels that he is or might be in the same situation, as the situation is being *judged by the norms of a greater freedom*."[5] The concept of greater power or greater freedom, personal or political, possessed by the reader (outside of the PRC) is crucial to my understanding of irony, tragic irony, in Liu Binyan's works as well as in his real life thoughts and actions. Fully cognizant of the fact that neither personal nor political freedom is absolute in any society, I hope that I shall not be accused of making invidious comparisons if I state at the outset that we have more of both than Liu Binyan, not to mention the average citizen of the People's Republic.

As Frye points out, in tragic irony, the hero "is only somebody who gets isolated from his society" and its central principle is that "whatever exceptional happens to the hero should be causally out of line with his character" and not due to any Aristotelian tragic flaw (*hamartia*) or pathetic obsession.[6] The perspective of ironic tragedy, from the reader's point of view — from our point of view when we read Liu Binyan's stories — is indeed, as Frye puts it, "attained by putting the characters in a state of *lower freedom* than the audience."[7] It is not that Liu Binyan has deliberately put his characters in "a state of lower freedom than the audience" in order to achieve an effect of tragic irony; judging the events realistically presented to us "by the norms of a greater freedom," however, we cannot help viewing his protagonists, ordinary citizens of the republic, as quite similar to Frye's typical or random victims or scapegoats who are neither wholly innocent like Christ nor wholly guilty like Prometheus, but rather "innocent in the sense that what happens to [them] is far greater than anything [they] have done to provoke" *and* "guilty in the sense that [they are] member[s] of a guilty society, or living in a world where such injustices are an inescapable part of existence."[8]

Judging the events related in them "by the norms of a greater freedom" we may read Liu Binyan's works and consider the fates of his characters and himself their creator as examples of the many ironies of history that became increasingly tragic during the first thirty years of the People's Republic of China. We may even be tempted to assert that Frye's "ironic mode" seems to have become a way of life for millions of PRC citizens in their day to day dealings with the Party and the State that governs them; and this seems especially true for intellectuals and writers like Liu Binyan. They seem to have been forced by circumstances to adopt the role of the Aristotelian *eiron*: "the man who deprecates himself . . . [and who] makes himself invulnerable [or at least tries to, by] appearing to be less than [he] is" in order to defeat or escape harm from the much more powerful Party–supported *alazon* or "imposter, someone who pretends or tries to be something more than he is."[9] In political meetings and campaigns as well as in the writing of literature, even as a political assignment, they often adopt the "technique of *saying* as little as possible and *meaning* as much as possible" or "a pattern of words that turns away from direct statement of its own obvious meaning."[10] We have already encountered examples of this in Liu Binyan's questions about the correct way to write about love; questions that no one answers, the mere raising of which is enough to make a powerful statement to the reader or audience who is used to the technique.

Liu Binyan generally makes direct statements, and yet, from the point of view just described and from the perspective of history, we cannot but interpret his statements and the events they present as parts of a greater pattern of tragic ironies of history. Having answered the theoretical question of what I mean by irony in relation to Liu Binyan's fictionalized reportage, I shall now sketch out what seem to me to be the three most tragic ironies of PRC history to date and then examine how they are amply reflected both in Liu's works and in what he himself has suffered for writing those works.

As the neo–realist critique of the Maoist era demonstrates, the major tragic historical irony since Mao Zedong proclaimed the founding of the People's Republic would seem to be that whenever Chairman Mao himself – the man who promised the Chinese people a "new democracy," socialism *and* modernization, and liberation from poverty, oppression, and ignorance – was most firmly in control of the nation's political and economic development; those were the very periods when the Chinese people of all social classes, but especially the peasants and workers in whose interests he claimed to act, suffered the greatest hardships. A concomitant pattern of irony developed in which it was precisely the most idealistic followers of Chairman Mao's utopian ideals who invariably suffered most from his Machiavellian betrayal of those ideals in practice. This was true, for example, of Communist Party writers like Liu Binyan who most enthusiastically supported the Chairman in his call for an attack on Party bureaucracy during the Hundred Flowers Movement and ended up ironically among the prime targets of the Anti-Rightist Campaign. It was true as well for the many poor and ignorant peasants who suffered further impoverishment even to the point of mass starvation after faithfully cutting down all of their trees and handing up all of their worldly goods including even their cooking pots during that disastrous plunge backward into economic chaos ironically styled the Great Leap Forward. Finally, it was also true of the most idealistic young Red Guard elements who naively believed that Chairman Mao shared their hatred of the CCP bureaucracy and genuinely intended for them to overthrow it and establish Paris Commune style organs of popular democracy; those of them who were not physically annihilated by Lin Biao's PLA forces acting under Chairman Mao's direct orders were sent down to the countryside to languish for a decade, their talents and abilities completely wasted.

The second tragic historical irony would seem to be that the Chinese Communist Party, whose members sacrificed so much in thirty years of struggle, the goal of which was to liberate the Chinese masses from rural gentry despotism, urban dictatorship, warlord depredations, and grinding poverty, had, by the end of its first decade in power, established a dictatorship with an aspiration to control the everyday life of the Chinese people that went far beyond the aspirations or abilities of traditional autocrats like Qin Shihuang, Zhu Yuanzhang, or Qianlong. The Party had replaced *both* the rural gentry *and* the imperial bureaucracy to become a new "privileged class." They had also pretty well exhausted the resevoir of good feeling among the Chinese people who had embraced their rule in the 1950s after so many years of war and chaos. The peasants feared them as a result of the Great Leap Forward and its aftermath; the students, teachers, and intellectuals feared them as a result of the Anti-Rightist Campaign and the general repression of culture; and the workers disliked their oppressive style of industrial management. This irony was made tragically complete when the chief results of the Cultural Revolution turned out to be the direct dictatorship of a deified Chairman Mao and the creation of the most ruthless, corrupt, opportunistic, know-nothing

Maoist Party apparatus, a Maoist Communist Party that operated like nothing so much as a Mafia style gang, in "feudal fascist" fashion as it is styled today.[11] In periods of chaos traditional China has always been plagued by bandits and gangsters. From 1969 to 1976, however, ganster–like figures operated from the yamen and were a scourge on the populace at least as rapacious as any ruling group in Chinese history.

What may be regarded as the final irony has not yet developed to such tragic dimensions as the previous two. Hopefully it never will. At any rate, it is an ominous trend that Liu Binyan and all of the writers mentioned in this book have to contend with. It is the fact that, like the Soviet de–Stalinizer Khrushchev and Brezhnev after him, the immediate post–Mao leaders of the drive to overcome China's disastrous Maoist legacy were themselves deeply implicated in the historical decisions that led to the two major ironies just discussed, and they continue to imploy Maoist methods of alternate relaxation and repression, cajolement and coercion and Maoist rhetoric to explain those methods. Some of them are more committed to relaxation and more open to change while others among them regard the current relaxation as having already gone too far. All of them share the primary concerns of economic development — "modernization" — and maintainance of Party control. They continue to call upon writers and artist to support the Four Modernizations and obey the Four Fundamental Principles of Party leadership, socialist road, dictatorship of the proletariat, and Marxism–Leninism–Mao Zedong Thought, imprison independent activists like Wei Jingsheng and Wang Xizhe who call for a fifth democratic modernizatioin, and harass writers and artists like Bai Hua and company who make a film that puts the major blame for China's present plight onto the overall Chinese Communist Party system and its superstitious belief in those same Four Fundamental Principles. They believe that "emancipation of the mind" means acceptance of the present Party line — the "Resolution" of the Sixth Plenum of the Eleventh Central Committee — as dogma and that the main purpose of a "socialist legal system" is to firmly es-tablish party–state control as it existed during the first seventeen years of the People's Republic.[12] Remembering the last ten terrible years of Maoist rule, the Chinese people certainly feel that Deng Xiaoping has led them up out of the fires or Hell and onto the steep slopes of Purgatory where they may at least hope for future salvation through hard work; but, unlike Dante and his faithful guide Aenaes, the present leaders of the CCP are either unable or unwilling to look the Devil (Mao's ghost) coldly in the face and repudiate him and all he stands

for. They keep His Thoughts ever in their hearts and continue to wear
proudly the insignia of His Party. One cannot, therefore, predict what
further ironies may be visited upon the Chinese people by the future
epigones of the Party that Mao built.[13]

Shortly before and during the first phase of the Hundred Flowers
Movement of 1956, Liu Binyan published three pieces of reportage
fiction in support of Chairman Mao and Premier Zhou's call for
criticism of the Party's bureaucratic and autocratic style of work. In all
three of these stories — "On the Bridge Constructioin Site" (April),
"An Inside Story," Part One (June) and Part Two (October) — Liu
criticized a local Party organization on the basis of what he believed to
be Mao's ideal of a good communist. To do so he employed a standard method of communist fiction: contrasting a character "type" who
lives up to those ideals in every way with a number of bureaucratic
leadership "types" of the sort that such periodical campaigns were
always aimed at. What set these stories off from previous Chinese
Communist works of "Socialist Realism" was their failure to arrive at a
simple solution and an optimistic conclusion.

In "On the Bridge Construction Site," a young work leader, the
engineer Zeng Gang, is contrasted with an older middle level cadre, Lo
Lizheng, the Brigade Leader on a very important bridge construction
project. Lo typifies all the defects of Chinese Communist industrial
management. His work crews labor under a model of bureaucratic
inefficiency, requiring orders from the boss before they proceed to the
smallest tasks. They generally loaf around at the beginning of every
month and then have to work like demons during the last week to meet
their production quotas. In this they follow Lo's typical planning
procedure which involves three basic points: set an artificially low
production target, exceed the target every time by "going all out" at the
last minute, and receive merit rewards for "overproduction." In the
mean time, the work regularly involves underutilization of capacity and
a carefully calculated waste of manpower and resources. Lo lives in
fear of being investigated by Party Central, while at the same time he
does his best to alienate the workers under him through his arrogant
manner and insistence on making all the decisions and issuing com-
mands which are by definition "correct" even when they disregard the
workers' practical suggestions and the elementary laws of physics — in
the case of one cutting operation in which 75% of the finished products
are substandard due to a management error. Personally, Lo is tired
and apathetic about his work and he prefers to enjoy himself out
hunting in the company jeep or tinkering around repairing his friends'

wristwatches. His credo is quite simple and he expresses it frankly:

> I often wonder: with correct Party leadership, what else do
> we need? . . . Just one principle: don't make any mistakes!
> Make no mistakes — that's victory! Just this one principle,
> but it's hard to carry out . . .(56)

Zeng Gang, in keeping with Liu's Maoist idealism, is everything Lo
is not. He is an efficient planner who devises work methods that save
thousands of dollars. He is decisive, quick witted, resolute, and even
brave; willing to take risks to experiment with new engineering
methods. He works alongside the men on difficult tasks and expresses
great concern for their well being — eating and sleeping with the
workers, he comes to learn that "pysical labor is not easy" and that
national development is "squeezed out of the blood and sweat of the
workers."(33) He is not averse to urging the workers on to make
greater efforts, however, because he believes that the workers want to
follow Chairman Mao's admonition to struggle against "conservatives"
and "bureaucrats" and make more superhuman efforts to speed up
industrial production.(63) He wants to do what any good Communist
Party member and industrial leader is supposed to do: improve the
material well being of the people as rapidly as possible.

A crisis comes in the spring of 1955 when the swelling Yellow River
waters threaten to ruin the bridge construction project. Lo Lizhen's
"crisis management" style is to take no initiative in order to make no
mistakes and thus bear no responsibility for whatever happens. He
therefore wastes valuable time in a vain effort to "ask for instructions"
from the Provincial Engineering Bureau with the result that the
uncompleted section of bridge and all of the equipment under his control are washed away in the flood. His call finally goes through,
however, and his final remarks on the whole incident are, "What luck,
what luck! My call finally got through — no matter what happened, I
asked for instructions . . ."(58) Zeng Gang's performance in this crisis
is nothing short of heroic. He mobilizes his men to risk their lives
working round the clock; keeps the water pumps working full blast to
stave off the flood while he personally supervises the work; refuses
direct orders from his superiors to dismantle the work scaffolding and
wait for "directions"from higher up; and thus saves a major section of
the bridge from the flood waters.

Irony number two wins out, however, in the denouement. When
the reporter–narrator returns to the construction site the following
spring, he finds the workmen busy trying to salvage the equipment and

materials that had been under water all winter as a result of Lo Lizhen's bungling. Asking about Zeng Gang, he learns that he was transferred (demoted actually) from the site to a much less important type of work shortly after the success of his heroic efforts to save the bridge. The local Party Secretary had found him guilty of "arrogance and self satisfaction," not to mention taking individual initiative in disregard of the express directions of his superiors at Party Central. Lo Lizheng is still firmly in charge, however, and has learned all of the new slogans about combating "conservatism" and "bourgeois thinking" in management. The reporter–narrator is left standing in the early spring cold watching the workers clean up the mess and wondering to himself: "Spring breeze, when will you ever blow into the manager's office."(69)

"An Inside Story" is a much longer piece concerning an honest and humane young non–communist reporter, Huang Jiaying, and her struggle against the bureaucratic apathy, callousness, and corruption of the Party leaders running a local newspaper. The title comes form the fact that many of her critical investigative stories about local conditions are not published. Liu Binyan was on the editorial board of *Zhongguo Qingnian* (Chinese Youth) at the time and probably wrote from personal experience in describing her situation:

> For some time now quite a few of Huang Jiaying's reports had become "internal news," typed up, printed, and sent around to a few departments or to specially commissioned writers outside the paper for use as reference material. Later on she got wise and learned to dull the sharpness of her critique in order to get her stories into the paper. At least that would be better than having them end up "in the files" of a small number of organizational departments.(72)

Just like Zeng Gang (and Liu Binyan himself), Huang Jiaying believes in Party Central, believes that the Central Committee and the Provincial Party Committees want to improve the lot of the Chinese people; but she is disturbed by many of the things she sees "down below" in the organizations and work places at the subprefectural level. She even thinks of writing a letter to Party Central to inform them of the "bureaucratic and formalistic tendencies she has seen and of the demands of the working masses," but she never has enough information to prove her points and she believes the leadership is probably already "studying" those problems.[14] At the age of twenty–five she has not yet been admitted into the Party precisely because of her

reputation for writing reports containing too much disturbing truth
about such things as the miserable working conditions of the miners
and their resentment of the Party leadership's insistence on their
participation in interminable after hours discussion meetings. When
she learns that the miners only have time for four hours sleep a night,
she is extremely dissatisfied with the newspaper's failure to report on
these and other deplorable conditions and she tries to do something
about it.

Unlike Zeng Gang, Huang Jiaying has an ally in Cao Mengfei, a
twenty–nine year old editor in the Industrial Department of the paper.
He too is dissatisfied with the paper's failure to report on the
deplorable conditions of unemployment and underutilization of
manpower due to faulty personnel policies and a lack of coordination
between the many levels of bureaucracy involved. He even goes so far
as to propose what would seem like the simplest solution to the problem: freedom of movement for industrial workers, an option that has
never been allowed even to this day.

The main representative of the Party bureaucracy is the Chief
Editor, Chen Lidong, an old cadre with twenty years of revolutionary
experience who believes that the young cadres who joined the Party
after 1949 do not know how to do anything. He has no personal
interests, works only for the good of the Party, and with the support of
the local Party Secretary, runs the paper as a one man operation,
requiring the assistant editors of all departments to obtain his personal
approval before taking any editorial action. As one colleague describes
him, "his greatest asset is that he will never make any big mistakes."
(124) He has two problems, however: his editors and reporters are
apathetic because they are allowed no initiative, and the working
people do not like his paper because it is full of empty Party rhetoric
and is not responsive to their real needs. As the omniscient narrator
puts it:

> The readers of the *New Light Daily* could not understand
> why the paper was so full of slogans and orders like 'forge
> ahead vigorously,' 'resolutely persevere,' and 'actively
> respond,' while stories concerning the lives of the masses
> themselves, their demands and their suggestions, were so
> pitifully scarce. (123)

A few pages on, the narrator provides an explicit answer:

Is it really only Chen Lidong himself who is responsible for
the poor performance of the paper? Who on the Provincial
Committee ever told Chen Lidong to be concerned with the
masses or to run his paper for the good of the the masses?
(125)

As a result of Huang Jiaying's courageous support of the mine
workers' demands and of a drastic decline in the paper's circulation
when the Provincial Party Committee stops subsidizing the workers'
subscriptions, several of the other reporters and junior editors are won
over to push for reforms. One in particular, Ma Wenyuan, a typical
"middle character" and Chen Lidong's Production Assistant, is
transformed from an apathetic and timid yes-man into an enthusiastic
activist who dares to stand up to the boss and dreams of being able to
use the paper to support the cause of the common people. Even Chen
Lidong himself is partially won over, admitting that his thinking has
been too one-sided, agreeing to give his subordinates more room for
initiative, and, in a final surprise reversal, supporting Huang Jiaying for
admission to the Party.

Irony number two prevails again in the end, however, and this
courageous young woman who is truly dedicated to the Party's stated
mission of "serving the proletariat," is rejected for Party membership;
her application is postponed due to her lack of the requisite respect for
"leadership, organization, and discipline." That is, for taking the
workers' side in a dispute with the Party leadership. As her former
boyfriend gloats after the meeting:

Leadership, organization, and discipline are the most basic
elements after all, the most fundamental and the most
reliable; even if you overemphasize them a little, you won't
get into any trouble. Democracy and freedom are always
related to the individual and if you're the least bit careless
you'll end up with extremism — bourgeois or petty bourgeois
thinking . . . (146)

One may well imagine that such a person would do quite well in the
coming Anti-Rightist Campaign, but people like Huang Jiaying, Zeng
Gang, and their creator could never seem to learn the art of
"concealing one's own opinions in order to enter the Party" and
"refusing to support the interests of the Party [which they regarded as

supporting the interests of the working masses] in order to enter the Party."(112)

Ironies number one and two both combined to silence Liu Binyan for twenty–one years after these three valiant attempts to help Chairman Mao and Premier Zhou reform the Communist Party bureaucracy they had created. As usual it was Mao himself who opened the way for the Party's counterattacks on his most dedicated followers. Ten days after the 8 June 1957 editorial in the *People's Daily* signaled the end of the Hundred Flowers Movement, Mao's previously unpublished Februrary 27 speech appeared in the same paper in a greatly revised form including the famous "six criteria" which effectively transformed Liu Binyan's fragrant flowers into poisonous weeds. The Party's literary bureaucracy soon condemned Liu's stories, especially "An Inside Story," as "bourgeois" and he was "exposed" as a mouthpiece of the "bourgeois rightists" within the Party.[15] As he related to Lee Yee in 1982, Liu himself was utterly shocked to discover that he, a Party loyalist since his youth in Harbin, had been branded a Rightist for writing stories in support of Chairman Mao's policies. Even a "loyalist letter" (*xiaozhong xin*) that he had written but never sent to Chairman Mao was used as evidence of his alledged Rightist sympathies.[16]

From 1958 to 1960 Liu was sent down to live among the peasants and he tried to reform himself in accord with the leadership's ideas, but, ironically, this first hand experience of the effects of the Great Leap Forward only served to confirm his earlier critique.[17] By 1962 he had decided to give up writing as an altogether hopeless profession, but he still kept some diaries which were taken from his unlocked desk by a female comrade, secretely copied, and later used as evidence against him when he was once again classified as a "Rightist" in 1965, a scant two months after his original "Rightist" cap had been removed. In all of the years from 1958 to 1979, he and his family lived a normal life for only those two brief months.[18]

In 1979, after twenty–one years of silence, Liu Binyan burst upon the literary scene with one of the most powerful indictments of the Maoist Party system ever to appear in a government approved publication. More reportage than fiction, this long narrative, entitled "Between Men and Monsters," takes us into the nightmare world of the Cultural Revolution decade when Maoist demons preyed upon the men and women of China in an unprecedented manner. The story is well worth recalling in some detail.

This story of the rise to power of the leftist Wang Shouxin and the building of her illegal economic empire, begins with the fall of a reformist Party Secretary who had been sent to Bin County in Heilongjiang Province to try to overcome some of the many difficulties left over from the three years of economic hardship caused by the Great Leap Forward and to settle some of the many unjust cases left over from the Anti-Rightist Campaign. Just after he succeeds in righting the wrongs done to the people by the Party in the late 1950s, he is removed from the political stage by a Red Guard "rebel faction" in November 1966, and a leftist Political Commissar of the People's Liberation Army takes power as the arbiter of the fate of Bin County's 500,000 people. Political Commissar Yang soon becomes the great benefactor of Wang Shouxin.

Wang Shouxin, a woman of forty-nine, energetic, ambitious, and uneducated, begins as the Coal Company Paymaster. During the Cultural Revolution storm, she is rejected by both the students and the older cadres of the Commercial Department; but she finds instant support from Political Commissar Yang and an old ex-bandit named Zhang. Together they set up a "struggle group" within the Coal Company in order to "rebel" against the older management cadres. Their only opposition is led by a very poor, very honest, very hard working employee named Liu Changchun, who is, unfortunately, not even well liked by the older cadres because he works too hard on his own "private plot" every night after finishing his shift at the Coal Company. Through his initial introduction of these characters Liu Binyan has very clearly delineated the way in which Chinese society was fragmented as a result of Maoist ideology, thus setting the stage for the destructive social conflicts of the Cultural Revolution decade.

At a "discussion meeting" carefully orchestrated by the PLA, a decision is taken to follow Political Commissar Yang and make "revolution" to sweep away all "bull monsters and snake demons," class enemies taking the "capitalist road." A number of "struggle meetings" follow in which Liu Changchun and his group are discredited and he is branded an "anti-PLA counter-revolutionary" because of his "Rightist" ideology of "seizing on production and suppressing revolution," that is, working hard to improve material conditions in the countryside without the proper Maoist regard for "social transformation," or ideological purity. Liu tries to resist his accusers on the basis of Point 16 of the "Sixteen Points" issued by the Central Committee on 8 August 1966 which called for both "cultural revolution" and increased production, but such documents carry no weight in Bin County where the PLA rules by force alone.[19]

From that time on, everything that Liu Binyan believes the Chinese Communist Party ought to stand for is "turned upside down." Basing himself on the support of Chairman Mao, PLA Political Commissar Yang puts Mao's famous "barrel of a gun" thesis into operation and assumes all the power and privileges of a Mafia capo. He forces the previously reluctant commercial cadres to admit Wang Shouxin into the Commercial Department, ordering her "election" as Assistant Director of the Commercial Revolutionary Committee. At last she tastes real power, and Liu Binyan's description of the meaning of power in the PRC is quite forceful:

> Running here and there with Political Commisar Yang since the 'rebellion,' for the first time in her life she tasted the flavor of holding power in this society of ours: so many people obeying just one person, praising you and flattering you, giving you both material benefits *and* honor! It was many times more respectable than the highest ideal of her youth — to be married to a KMT police officer or a landlord! (155)

Yang then further orders her "election" into the Party in September 1969, after the Ninth Congress at which the quintessential Maoist Central Committee was chosen by delegates "elected" in exactly the same manner, and in the same month that Zhang Zhixin was arrested by the dictatorship.[20]

The rest of the story reads like a combination of *The Godfather*, *Catch 22*, and an exposé in *The Progressive* as it chronicles the ten year growth of Wang Shouxin's organized crime network and its support at every level of the Maoist Communist Party. As both Manager and Party Branch Secretary of the Coal Company, renamed the Fuel Company — "all of it belonged to her; everyone had to obey her instructions" (157) — she organizes a hierarchical system of fuel distribution based on the value of the gifts of wine, food, medicines, and services coming in to her personally from the various economic units being supplied. She suborns her son's commission of rape and punishes the unwilling victim's father by cutting off his fuel oil. She charges high level cadres 40 RMB per day, a month's salary for a worker, for the use of the collective's vehicles to gather their own firewood. She trades on her political and economic power as the number one Maoist in the county to exchange political support for favors of all kinds from strategically placed cadres in every department. She establishes a private school for the children of high cadres who are "sent down" to the countryside, promising to protect them and promote them into the universities in exchange for favors such as a 100,000 RMB tax break; thus she wins the loyal support of an ever widening circle of both present and future leadership cadres. Finally, through a complex scheme of false bookeeping, she embezzles great sums of public money to finance her ever growing commercial empire. Liu Binyan comments satirically, with "militant irony" as Frye would say:

> Compared to capitalist exchange, this sort of 'socialist' exchange certainly demonstrated a very great 'superiority': neither side in the exchange had to possess any capital, put up any personal property as security, nor risk the slightest danger of failure or bankruptcy; and they both profited on the deal.
>
> [In the end] the Party's political cadres themselves were gradually transformed into parasites who devoured the people's flesh and blood and blighted the socialist system like an infestation of canker-worms . . .(162)

The Maoist Communist Party becomes "her Party": described by Liu Binyan as an underworld style organizational network. Virtually the entire local County Party organization is corrupt and they are backed by various Party leaders at the provincial level and even higher. This powerful Party apparatus, unrestrained by any form of law or even code of ethics, aids Wang Shouxin in every way as her illegal economic enterprises expand like those of Milo Minderbinder in Joseph Heller's *Catch 22.* And virtually no one dares or even desires to work against her. Letters of accusation from rural communes that she has defrauded are simply ignored by all of the County Party Secretaries sent down from Harbin during the entire ten year period. Liu Binyan would seem to indict the entire Maoist Party system when he writes:

> With only one single exception, the ten Party members [promoted by Wang Shouxin] were all 'hard working and obedient.' Obedient to whom? Wang Shouxin of course. According to the logic that following closely the Party Secretary is following closely the Party and protecting the Party Secretary is protecting the Party, what sort of mistake were they making anyway?
>
> In short, Wang Shouxin had a reliable rear guard in the Fuel Company. In the organs of the County Party

Committee and Revolutionary Committee she had over
thirty 'rebel faction' brothers busily protecting her at all
times. She received nothing but confidence and praise from
the County Standing Committee and the Party Secretary.
What did Wang Shouxin lack? Her enterprises reached the
height of prosperity. (173)

Although Wang Shouxin managed to amass a personal fortune of
over 400,000 RMB, her crimes were finally exposed by a few brave
"little people" at considerable risk, investigated and punished by the
central authorities after the Third Plenum of December 1978, albeit
against the persistent opposition of the entire Party leadership of
Heilongjiang Province. Thus "Between Men and Monsters" provides a
picture of the situation in China at least until 1979 and the early 1980s.
Government investigators and reporters like Liu himself have to
proceed in a manner similar to police campaigns against organized
crime in the U.S. and Europe. Witnesses are regularly intimidated by
the local authorities and afraid to cooperate with outside investigators.
Very few want to give evidence of what everyone knows, and with
good reason. After the central authorities and reporters leave the
province and return to Peking, they will be left to the tender mercies of
the all powerful local Party apparatus. Liu makes it very clear that
these local leadership cadres own the people's money and their lives
and that the distinction between legal and illegal activities simply does
not exist in their minds. Their word is law because they are the "rebel
faction" of Chairman Mao, the Politburo, and the Central Committee
of the Party Mao reorganized in 1969 on the ruins of Red Guard destruction. They perpetuate "relationships of naked power and
privilege" through a feudalistic code of warm "brotherly loyalty,
reciprocal benevolence, friendships, and family connections." (188,
193)
   They do in fact take revenge against local residents who dare to
cooperate with the "outsiders" in their investigation. When Liu
Binyan was writing "Between Men and Monsters" in the fall of 1979,
they were still in power and he was not at all optimistic about the
prospects for their removal. Thus he concluded his remarkable story
with the following warning:

The case of Wang Shouxin's embezzlement was uncovered
and this was no doubt a result of the great political changes
that have taken place in China since the smashing of the
'Gang of Four;' but how much change has there been in the

social conditions that made possible the existence and development of a Wang Shouxin? Are there not still large and
small Wang Shouxins in every corner who continue to
devour the substance of socialism and corrupt the body of
the Party without receiving any punishment from the
dictatorship of the proletariat? People, be on you guard!
Now is not the time for shouts of victory . . .(205)

A lawless and corrupt world where "men" toil under the reign of
seemingly insatiable "demons" whose naked force is thinly vailed
behind an all pervasive and irresistable network of familial and
feudalistic connections cemented by confessions of faith in the Great
Helmsman — the Cultural Revolution world of Maoism *in extremis.*
At this point we might want to ask, does this gloomy picture apply to
all of China, or does Bin County perhaps represent only an isolated
case? The answer would seem to be found in the readers' response to
"Between Men and Monsters." Liu Binyan received letters from
readers in every province of China except Tibet, and they are in
universal agreement that the conditions described in Bin County are
also present in their own provinces. Liu read one of these hundreds of
letters from a worker to the Fourth National Congress of Writers and
Artists; it is worth quoting at some length:

> I don't know how it happened, but while I was reading
> your "Between Men and Monsters," I actually squeezed the
> tea cup I was holding with such force that it shattered. The
> pieces of broken glass cut a deep gash in the palm of my
> hand, but I didn't even feel any pain; the stimulation of it
> actually made me feel a kind of elation . . .
>   The network that you describe in Bin County is not really
> limited to Bin County, and the various kinds of people in Bin
> County are not really the exclusive products of Bin County.
> To put it frankly: the Bin County network is the epitome of
> our entire nation and it is the obstacle that our 'Four
> Modernizations' must overcome. This is our most urgent
> task.
>   After we got off work, I read your "Between Men and
> Monsters" aloud with feelings of great excitement to the
> fourteen workers on our shift. Among them there were
> women with children, busy young people, and older workers
> who were exhausted and needed rest; but not one of them
> left during the entire three hour reading. In fact, many more

people joined us . . .

I have been asked by these workers to express our
congratulations to you. What we mean is that we hope our
comrade Liu Binyan will continue to speak the truth on our
behalf because we never want to hear all those lies and
falsehoods again . . .

After complaining about the workers' poverty, many families not
having enough money to make it through the month, and the
mendacity of "happy songs" in praise of the system, the letter
continues:

When some people heard that I was reading "Between
Men and Monsters," they called in the Party Branch
Secretary of our shop. What a coincidence! He came in just
as I was reading, 'The Communist Party controls everything;
the only thing that it does not control is the Communist Party
itself.' That Party Secretary furiously grabbed the magazine
out of my hand, thumbed through it until he came to the
cover [i.e., until he saw that it was the prestigious *People's
Literature*], tossed it back to me, and stormed angrily out of
the room. As you can see, there are still many people who
do not like your writing.

The letter concludes with a touching offer to help Liu Binyan if he
should ever be in trouble:

Just remember we are your firm support. We do not
know you, but if you look us up, we will definitely protect
you and take care of you, because you are singing out the
song that is in all of our hearts. (21–22)

Many similar letters from workers, commune members, and cadres
asked Liu to come to their locale and investigate some deplorable
situation there.[21] Throughout 1980 and at least to the middle of 1981,
Liu did continue to travel around China, lecturing at colleges and
universities, attending literary meetings, investigating local situations,
and writing. He wrote that he enjoyed the greatest freedom to create
in his entire life, urged his readers to have faith in the political line of
the Third Plenum of December 1978 and the sincerity of the
Deng–Hu–Zhao leadership's determination to reform the Party and
eliminate the abuses of the past, and continued to depict the aftermath

of the Maoist decade in several long pieces of reportage fiction.[22] Ironically enough, one of the stories that Liu wrote at this time, entitled "The Warning," resulted itself in a stern warning to him and his publishers at *Zuopin* (Works) monthly and necessitated his writing an apologetic letter to high cultural authorities.[23] Having been unable to do so in 1981 due to illness, Liu visited the United States in 1982 and spent several weeks at the well known University of Iowa's International Writers' Workshop.

None of his later works are as striking as "Between Men and Monsters," but they all depict the same dark world of Chinese life at the local level throughout the Cultural Revolution decade and its continuation into the present. I shall discuss briefly two of his most representative pieces published one year apart and offering an extended treatment of the same theme in both an industrial and an agricultural setting.

"A Man and His Shadow," written in June 1980, is the only one of Liu's stories the title of which reveals a strategy of conscious literary irony; but that irony dissolves when Liu finishes up with a full page of explicit editorial comment. At any rate, our two ironies are fully demonstrated in this biography of Zheng Benzhong, a young man who does everything in his power to live up to the Maoist inspired ideal of a selflessly dedicated industrial worker whose only desire is to build a socialist industrial society. For twenty-two years, from 1957 to 1979, he heroically performs every feat that a good Maoist is supposed to: he works longer and harder than anyone else; is daringly innovative in devising new techniques to increase production; solves a number of technical problems with the most rudimentary materials; risks his life as Team Leader on the most dangerous tasks in order to protect the safety of his fellow workers; is modest and unassuming; never asks for bonuses or overtime; and often works around the clock for nothing.

The central irony in all this, however, is that he is not a Maoist "red and expert" cadre. Officially he is a "Rightist!" He is labeled a "Rightist student" in 1957–58 while taking his degree at a Chengdu Technical Academy. Although a Party Committee decides to remove his "Rightist cap" after he graduates, his dossier (described as "a paper folder containing your background, your social status, the proof that *you* even exist")[24] is misplaced and the Party authorities, jealous and suspicious of his student status, treat him as a criminal from that time on. A series of factory managers, Party Secretaries and other industrial cadres oppose him at every turn throughout his twenty-two year struggle to live up to Chairman Mao's image of proletarian virtue.[25] As the leadership becomes increasingly Maoist, the persecution and mistreatment worsens despite the fact that he is the only worker who actually fulfills the Maoist slogans on the industrial front. The Maoist industrial cadres who possess only political and ideological qualifications take advantage of his technical abilities and give him all the most difficult tasks while at the same time refusing to remove his "Rightist cap" out of fear of losing their status as wardens of what seems to be a vast industrial prison system. (254–255)

Zheng Benzhong's "Rightist cap" is finally removed for good after the Third Plenum of December 1978, but the factories he has worked in so well are still left with corrupt managers and dispirited workers. As the reporter–narrator describes the situation at that time, "the only thing those factory leaders are concerned with is to organize a faction and grab more power for themselves . . . The workers are powerless. Aware of many corrupt practices, they are angry but don't dare speak out; apprehensive about the future of their factory, they have no heart to work hard." (244) Liu concludes his report with an appeal that individual Chinese be judged on the basis of their actual performance and not on the basis of an ideological shadow identity. In that way men like Zheng Benzhong would be highly valued for their many beneficial contributions to society.(257)

"Wind and Rain," written from March to May and published in June 1981 in *People's Literature*, tells a story almost identical to Zheng Benzhong's concerning a language teacher turned amateur scientist and poet, Jin Xin, and his life–long struggle to help the peasants of northern Liaoning Province overcome their crushing poverty. He too may be considered a model of Maoist virtue. Although somewhat crotchety and stubborn, traits that sometimes alienate even his admirers, he has tremendous sympathy for the impoverished peasants who eke out a bare living growing potatoes. He is intrigued when an old peasant tells him about a superior seed potato that the local people have to travel north at great expense to purchase from sharp dealers who often cheat them and that often produces atrophied potatoes anyway when planted in local soils. Asked by the old peasant why he, a "person of culture," doesn't think of a better way to grow potatoes, he decides to dedicate his life to the task.

He turns himself into a true "people's scientist." For years he skips meals to save money for books on potatoes. He reads all the available literature, mostly Russian, on the science of potato growing and the causes of atrophy in potatoes. He conducts many practical experiments on seed potatoes under the most trying circumstances, literally snatching the potatoes away from his hungry children during the famine years that follow the Great Leap Forward. At last he discovers what all the Russian scientists could not: the secret of potato atrophy lies in not allowing the seed potatoes to sprout more than once before planting. Just as he makes this momentous discovery, the Cultural Revolution comes to the countryside and his "secret" scientific experiments are attacked as an unhealthy example of "bourgeois individualism" by the Maoist "rebels" who take over the County Party Committee.

From this point on, although he doggedly perseveres in his experiments whenever possible, Jin is repeatedly opposed and mistreated by the Maoist authorities. Having been branded a "Rightist element" because of his class status as a "stinking intellectual," he is severely beaten in 1970 for his stubborn refusal to confess that his activities are criminal. As a result of the beating, he suffers a stroke and is bedridden with partial paralysis; but he writes a report on his seventeen years of potato experiments. From 1972 to 1975, Jin chooses an old peasant to use his new potato planting method and the old man harvests a bumper crop and begins to make a profit and have enough to eat for the first time in his life. In September 1975, however, he is given his reward by a Maoist Party Secretary who claps him in jail for traveling without proper papers and then parades him through the streets as a "stinking intellectual." Jin responds by cursing the Party Secretary as a "stumbling block to the building of socialism." At that point, his long-suffering wife, who has herself spent a some time in a May Seventh Cadre School and suffered greatly on his account, locks him out of their house in a rain storm. He wanders around in the wind and rain and falls down faint in a local schoolyard.

After the fall of the Gang of Four, Jin is joined by a number of patriotic and thoughtful people, both young and old, who offer voluntary support to his potato research. He even begins to receive some support from various Party officials, but still has to struggle mightily against opponents of the Third Plenum line right up to the time the reporter-narrator interviews him in 1980. An Agricultural Research Department official helps him to legally procure land to conduct his experiments, but most local Party officials pay no attention to his successes. A reformist Propaganda Officer inspects Jin's potato fields firsthand and starts to publicize his work, but other officials refuse to grant Jin freedom of movement to investigate potato planting in other areas. An amateur writer writes an open letter to Deng Xiaoping about Jin and his work, but several papers refuse to print it. Finally Jin is discovered by the *Guangming ribao* and his work becomes front page news early in 1979. His troubles are not over, however, even though he gains official recognition. Many powerful individuals continue to try to discredit his research, and he does his own case little good by his understandable distrust of all government experts and officials, an attitude of mind brought about by his bitter experiences during the Great Leap Forward and the Cultural Revolution. Jin's story ends with his complete vindication when an Inner Mongolian Party Secretary helps him to put his methods into practice on a large scale and threatens to expose any conservative Maoists opponents for obstruction of the economic program of the Third Plenum. Jin himself remains at Peking University where he is continuing his potato experiments as part of his lifelong struggle to eliminate poverty in rural China. "In the final analysis," the reporter-narrator writes, "our nation's poverty is the main source of all the virulent abuses in politics and thought."[26]

In a brief discussion of "Between Men and Monsters" at the Iowa Conference on Chinese Literature in 1980, Leo Ou-fan Lee suggested that we should not approach Liu Binyan's works armed with all the standard critical assumptions of modern western literary criticism. Boldly embracing the "intentional fallacy," he asserted that Liu's primary concern for "sociology" rather than "literature" constitutes prima facie evidence for the correctness of such an idea.[27] Liu Binyan himself has offered support for this line of reasoning on several occasions. In a celebrated speech at the Fourth National Congress of Writers and Artists, he made a very strong appeal for the reinstitution of "sociology" (shehuixue, by which I believe he meant all of the "social sciences" practiced in the west and not merely the discipline of sociology as understood in North American universities) as a valid intellectual approach to China's present crisis, citing the example of the Soviet Union since 1956 and the anomalous situation that foreign scholars understand more about the problems facing contemporary Chinese society — population, employment, juvenile crime, bureaucratism — than the Chinese themselves do. "In short," he said, "we are facing a vast unknown world!" (19) Eight months later in an open letter to an unnamed comrade, Liu described "reportage literature" as a genre that combines fact and fiction in order to teach "the people" about social reality. He wrote:[28]

> Reportage literature is a species of marginal literature
> that is intermediate between journalism and literature,
> science and literature, and politics and literature. From the

point of view of form, it offers much more freedom, its structure does not have to be so compact and well-organized, and it can encompass a rather free blend of factual events, fictional images, and thought.

. . . The literary style of our newspapers is somewhat monotonous, being primarily confined to news reports and editorial articles. The kinds of essays that present some fictional images, emotions, and local color and that offer original thinking and personalized language are rather too infrequent. That sort of writing is, I suppose, just what is meant by reportage literature.

Liu Binyan writes, then, with a "heavy sense of mission": to "help [his] readers recognize this era — the era of peaceful construction — [and] its demands on the individual, . . . to recognize both the society in which we live and various different types of individuals, including the position we find ourselves in today and the demands that this era makes upon us."[29]

Thus cognizant of Liu Binyan's explicit purpose in creating his own Chinese version of what has been known for some time in North America as the "new journalism" or "the literature of fact" as exemplified in the works of such eccentric personalities and powerful stylists as Truman Capote, Norman Mailer, and Tom Wolfe;[30] it may seem captious of me to belittle the artistic merits of works of fictionalized reportage written at considerable personal risk for the laudable purpose of exposing a spate of egregious social evils. Liu Binyan himself has, however, participated on numerous occassions in critical discussions aimed at raising modern Chinese literature to world class levels of excellence, and thus I feel justified in commenting briefly on his works in terms of some of the most rudimentary elements of literature: plot, characterization, setting, style, and theme.

In terms of plot, characterization, setting, and style, Liu's works remain artistically primitive. With the partial exception of "On the Bridge Construction Site," his works have no *plot* in the artistic sense of a structure of events deliberately presented in a certain order to achieve a particular effect. They consist rather of chronological *stories* related from the first-person point of view by a reporter-narrator, a structural device that seems increasingly unnecessary as his post-1978 works approach the level of pure reportage. Liu's characters are sometimes quite striking, as in the case of Wang Shouxin and Jin Xin, or, just as often, rather unbelievable, as in the case of Zeng Gang and

Zheng Benzhong. What is individually striking about them is not developed and they are difficult to believe in (to accept, even though we
know from the outset that they are actually based on real people)
precisely because they are universally characterized through the
depiction of their overt behavior only. Their motivations are simply
assumed without any attempt being made to convey a sense of
psychological depth or understanding. This is perhaps consistent with
the formality of the reporter–observer–narrator, but it certainly does
not live up to Liu's promise to provide "fictional images, emotions, and
local color," and it does nothing to give his readers a sense of why just
these particular characters do these particular things whether for good
or for ill. A major change takes place over time in the "world" of
these reports – the presentation of "scenes of bondage, frustration, or
absurdity" becomes increasingly dominated by the sacred Person and
Thoughts of Chairman Mao – but there is no change in the method of
depicting setting or atmosphere; the physical background of the stories
adds nothing to their artistry and has no thematic role to play. Liu's
style throughout is pedestrian and colloquial in keeping with the
Maoist ideal of worker–peasant–soldier literature, and, although there
is some "local color" in the dialogue sometimes, there are no powerful
metaphors, symbols, or other technical devices to lift the narrative
above the level of journalism and into the realm of art. With the exception of "Between Men and Monsters," most of the other works
reviewed here are too lengthy, repetitive, and tedious to read. This is
especially unfortunate because the events related in them are in themselves extremely moving and of the utmost significance for an understanding of the qualilty of life in the PRC today and for some time to
come. The primary reason for this poor stylistic showing is, I believe,
that these works were edited and published in a literary milieu in
which literary criticism as artistic criticism hardly exists and what
passes for literary criticism is in fact merely political and ideological
criticism of the "correctness" or "incorrectness" of the ideas presented
in any published writing.

We come then to the element of theme, and it is here in the realm
of ideas that Liu Binyan's works excell and that he reaches the limits
imposed by irony number three described above. One major theme
seems to run through all of Liu's published works up to this writing:
the terrible harm done to the Chinese people and nation by both the
ideology and organization of the Chinese Communist Party in its most
purely Maoist manifestations. At great personal risk and despite the
imposition of humiliating punishments, Liu has consistently and
courageously exposed the hypocrisy, cruelty, corruption, and

dehumanization inherent in the Maoist communist economic, political, and social system from the point of view of his own belief in a correct type of Marxism–Leninism that that system has so far seemed to him to distort.[31]

In the process, he has provided his readers with overwhelming first hand evidence for a critique of the Chinese Communist system as a whole, despite the fact that, as a loyal follower of that Party and its ideology, he does not make such a public critique. The inescapable conclusion of that critique, it seems to this reader, is that the number one obstacle to the "modernization" of China — by which is meant at the least both industrialization with social justice and democratization with legal protection of individual civil rights vis–a–vis state power — has been and continues to be the organization of its political, economic, social, and cultural systems on the basis of a very narrowly conceived and carried out Marxist–Leninist–Maoist ideology.

What other available models does Liu Binyan have? After his courageous critique, after his bold assertion that "the Communist Party controls everything; the only thing that it does not control is the Communist Party itself;" what alternative can he offer? What kind of "original thinking" can he engage in? The moment we ask these questions, we seem to come full circle, arriving back at Frye's "ironic mode" from which vantage point we see Liu Binyan as unfortunately "inferior in *power*," in "a state of *lower freedom*," and caught up in frequent "scenes of *bondage, frustration,* and [even] *absurdity*." It would seem very unfair at this point to criticise him for the lack of new ideological alternatives in his writings, for his continued faith in the present Deng–Hu–Zhao leadership (which, as far as we know, may represent the absolute limit of "liberalization" possible in the PRC today), for his failure to attack or even to mention in any way their authoritarian and undemocratic actions, and, finally, for his continued alliegence to Marxism–Leninism (especially since he conceives of it quite differently than the Maoist diehards against whom he contends). All of these things may be intellectual weaknesses, but for now they must be forgiven. Liu Binyan has read Georg Lukács and even Kurt Vonnegut, but he is still severely restricted in his access to intellectual resources. He praises Tolstoy and Balzac, but there is scarcely any way that he can take an imaginatively fresh look at the "human comedy" and create anew his own personal philosophy of human history; even if he did, he could not have it published in his own country and he would be extremely unlikely to want it published anywhere else. For Liu Binyan and many other revolutionaries of his age, gradual reform of the social system seems to be the only viable alternative.

In closing, the difficulty of his situation may be suggested by a statement he made in September 1980 in answer to "leftist" inspired rumors that he was in serious political trouble for writing "Between Men and Monsters."[32]

> These comrades [who were alarmed by the leftist rumors] were overly anxious, but such a reaction has its reasons: If these rumors were believable and a person could be easily locked up, interrogated in isolation, or deported solely because he wrote an essay or gave a speech (even one containing serious mistakes), would not Party Central's policies of promoting democracy, liberating thinking, and strengthening the legal system become nothing more than empty promises?

Knowing as we do that some persons — Wei Jingsheng, Liu Qing, Wang Xizhe, and others — have been "easily locked up, interrogated in isolation," and deprived of the rights written into the constitution of the PRC (though not deported) "solely because [they] wrote an essay or gave a speech;" we may conclude that the final irony of this study is that Liu Binyan continues to believe that the present leadership's policies of "promoting democracy, liberating thinking, and strengthening the legal system" are not "empty promises." His faith in Marxism–Leninism as a viable ideology for China, if interpreted and applied correctly, seems to remain unshaken and he continues to write articles exposing current social evils as best he can under the prevailing political restraints which he assures us are the most liberal he has ever worked under. He is undoubtedly an honest man willing to risk much in order to promote his ideal of Marxism with a human face and to contend against the opposition of Maoist and feudalistic "demons" who threaten to turn the clock back on China's quest for a more humane and livable society. At this delicate point in Chinese history when the country is once again beginning to open up to the trememdous variety of worldwide intellectual, social, and literary thought, we can only admire Liu Binyan for what he has done so far, for maintaining his honesty and integrity as a powerful critic of past and present abuses of power on the part of the government and Party he still serves.[33]

V. Resurgent Humanism in Bai Hua's *Bitter Love*[1]

We have already discussed the Bai Hua Incident as the result of a shift toward more rigid political control of the arts by the Deng Xiaoping–Hu Yaobang Party leadership in 1981. Before we make an extended literary critical analysis of *Bitter Love* (*Kulian*) to see just what sort of literary expression represents such an "unhealthy tendency" that it threatens the leadership of the CCP and socialism itself, it might be well to review briefly Bai Hua's life, literary career, and views on the function of literature. In doing so we will see that he owes his entire life education to the CCP and its socialist system. He has never had any opportunity to seriously study "bourgeois liberalism" from anything but the CCP's Marxist–Leninist viewpoint. From some scattered remarks about "America" in *Bitter Love*, we may assume that he, quite naturally, has very little accurate information about life in the Western democracies.

Born in 1930 in Henan Province, the son of a patriotic merchant who was buried alive by the Japanese invaders, Bai Hua left high school in 1947 to follow Liu Bocheng and Deng Xiaoping's guerrilla army in its southern campaign. He was later transferred to Yunnan Province where he served under General He Long, whom he greatly admired. He served in the PLA as a propaganda cadre until 1957, as a result of attacks by the magazine *Changjiang wenyi*, he was purged in the Anti–Rightist Campaign. Taken into custody in 1958, he was sentenced to several years of forced labor before being given a post as editor in a Shanghai film studio where he met and married the actress Wang Bei.

Before 1957, Bai Hua had written a number of short stories, collections of poetry and a popular film script on the standard worker, peasant, soldier themes of praise for the New China. Not being allowed to write for twenty years, but gaining considerable first hand experience of and deepening sympathy for the suffering of the Chinese people in the years after the debacle of the Great Leap Forward and

during the catastrophe of the Cultural Revolution, he immediately
became one of the most outspoken and critical writers after 1977. His
many poems, short stories, and film scripts attempt to explore the
underlying causes of China's contemporary crisis and to expose the
corruption at the heart of much of Chinese life today, especially in the
higher echelons of the Communist Party itself. Asked to speak at the
Fourth National Congress of Writers and Artists in 1979, he frankly
admitted that many writers were still afraid of Party repression and
boldly called for literary breakthroughs to explore all of the previously
forbidden areas of Chinese life with critical realism and artistic
excellence.[2]

We have already seen many of Bai Hua's ideas on the function of
literature in Chapter Two above and we know that he is committed to
the use of literature for the amelioration of society. Before the Bai
Hua Incident, he made public several other ideas that are relevant to
the composition of *Bitter Love*. In a formulation similar to Hu
Yaobang's, he asserted, from the point of view of a putatively correct
Marxism–Leninism, that the Gang of Four had distorted this
"scientific ideology" into an imposed "religious ideology" and "deified
a revolutionary leader by means of authoritarian government and mass
movements" which "the majority of people did not dare to oppose."[3]
Answering the question, "What are you trying to do?" he replied that
he was attempting to restore the faith.[4]

> We are trying to renew the people's faith in socialist
> revolution. We are trying to help the people be aware of
> China's present situation, as well as the difficulties and
> promises that await us on the road ahead.

In another well known speech on the question of the relationship
between literature and politics, he expanded on his previous views
concerning literary realism in two significant ways. First of all, he
stated that writers often understand "the people" better than policy
makers do:[5]

> In comparison with those who formulate policies, writers
> who struggle and live with the masses are very likely to to
> have a better understanding of the masses' attitudes toward
> current policies, whether or not these policies are in accord
> with life's objective laws.

After this statement that would seem to imply that individual writers may well understand the Chinese people's needs and desires better than the CCP theor? theoreticians — the kind of ideas that were considered "bourgeois individualism" in the case of Ding Ling and others — Bai Hua then went on to quote Marx, Engels, Stalin, and finally Goethe on the need for the expression of individual truth in realist writings in order to accomplish the goal of becoming "engineers of the human soul:"[6]

> This appellation encompasses our goal, which is to beautify and perfect mankind's soul. We praise what is true, good, and beautiful in life, and expose what is false, evil, and ugly. We courageously struggle and diligently labor because we have a lofty goal. And precisely because we have this lofty goal, we cannot confine literature to a thing which must serve politics.

Bai Hua's aim in writing *Bitter Love*, then was to present "real life at its most frightening and its most beautiful"[7] in order to further the humanistic project of the perfection of the human soul.

European humanism we may recall developed during the Renaissance from a combination of the Greek and Roman values of *Paideia, pietas*, and culture — the qualities that distinguish human beings from animals or beasts — and the Medieval emphasis on human frailty and transcience — the limitations of human beings when compared with divinity. For Renaissance humanists, man was defined as the one being on earth that is both autonomous and finite; their humanism was both profoundly rational and deeply moral. As Erwin Panofsky put it in a celebrated definition, humanism "is not so much a movement as an attitude which can be defined as the conviction of the dignity of man, based on both the insistence on human values (rationality and freedom) and the acceptance of human limitations (fallibility and frailty); from this, two postulates result — responsibility and tolerance."[8] Western humanistic values include, then, human dignity and freedom, which were eventually elaborated into the concept of the inviolability of the individual and the legalization of human rights vis-à-vis the state; rationality and tolerance in the philosophical, religious, and political spheres, which were eventually elaborated into political democracy and religious ecumenicalism; and the recognition of human frailty and fallibility — the inevitability of illness, decay, and death, the possibility of error, and the persistence of evil — with their necessary corollary of individual responsibility or accountability before God and man and law.

Chinese or Confucian rational humanism with its belief in man as an autonomous being capable of rational moral choice, was first developed by Confucius and his followers and is epitomized in the word *ren* (usually translated as "humanity," "benevolence," or even "Goodness") which may be conceived of as "an all-inclusive moral virtue as well as the highest moral attainment that a man can achieve in life by human effort."[9] Furthermore, Confucian *ren* (etymologically from *ren* "man, human being") is an intrinsic element — the single most important element — of human nature and "a natural resource of human nature" that "entails a notion of uninterrupted dynamic process of moral life."[10] In other words, it is a "natural moral faculty that is the seed of (all) moral growth."[11] As further developed by Mencius, autonomous moral cultivation, the cultivation of *ren*, becomes both a rational and a religious commitment based on the "belief that moral discourse possesses a charismatic appeal to the inner calling of human life;"[12] that, as Socrates believed, virtue is its own reward; and that in cultivating *ren* and practicing moral virtue man is attempting to govern and perfect his nature in accordance with the precepts or principles of a rational universe — subsumed under the Chinese concept of Heaven.[13]

Although Confucianists often regarded the cultivation of *ren* as an end in itself — especially when the government of the state was particularly corrupt and immoral — Confucian humanism always enjoined its followers to engage in rational moral endeavor in a social context in which the traditional norms of social and ritual conduct (*li* in Chinese) were presupposed; however, since *ren* is an end and *li* only a means, *ren* is regarded as morally superior to *li* and human beings always have the rational ability and the social duty to make autonomous moral judgments concerning the rightness or justice of social rules or customs. In the Chinese context, this notion of the primacy of *ren* can be seen as a functional equivalent to the Western idea that organized society (including the state, the guardian of *li*) exists for the benefit of the individual human being and not the other way around. There is thus a "creative tension" between *ren* and *li* that operates throughout Chinese history as a theoretical framework for the independent moral judgment of individuals concerning the rightness or justice of the exercise of state power.[14] In spite of the fact that this creative tension often "disintegrates on the practical level" because "no viable norm for change is provided in classical Confucianism,"[15] this provision of moral autonomy in Confucian ideology has been the inspiration for principled and courageous criticism of tyrannical and immoral government throughout Chinese history. Many high-minded

Confucian intellectuals and men of action, whose deeds have been recorded both in the official histories and popular fiction, have opposed themselves between a bad government and the people on the basis of their concept of *ren* and its Mencian extention to "benevolent government" (*renzheng*); in the process, they have defended individual human dignity against the tyrannical impositions of state or collective power. Given the economic and political conditions of traditional tional Chinese society, of course, these humanistic individuals were often unable to protect the majority of the Chinese populace from government exactions, but that unfortunate fact no more detracts from the value of their moral striving than, for example, the existence of social injustice in Athens invalidates Socrates' rational moral striving for justice and goodness in human life.

Chinese humanism, then, shares with its Western counterpart the supreme value of human dignity within the confines of a rational universe. It also shares the values of rationality and tolerance (a religious tolerance often considerably greater than in the Christian West) and the recognition of human frailty and fallibility; although the Chinese never made sin and guilt the essence of human nature, they were well aware of the persistent danger of evil, and thus of the necessity of stressing individual moral responsibility. As we have seen, the value of individual freedom of choice was present in Confucianism, despite the fact that political freedom in the liberal democratic sense and legal protection of human rights vis-à-vis the state were always more subordinate to the interests of the group.

In its published form, *Bitter Love* is a "film-poem," a long rambling narrative, sometimes poetic, that was later used as a filmscript, no doubt with considerable modification to introduce dialogue and so on. It begins in the summer of 1976 and proceeds, like so much anti-Cultural Revolution fiction, by means of flashbacks. The plot structure is complicated, but the story can be easily summarized. Ling Chenguang ("cold-morning-light"), a folk artist and patriotic student was forced to escape from China because he participated in anti-Japanese demonstrations. He is taken on a ship to "America" (*meizhou*, presumably the United States) where he becomes a very successful artist, but he gives up his fame and fortune after 1949 in order to return with his wife, Lü Niang, to work for the New China. His wife gives birth to their daughter while still on board ship but within sight of the five-star flag of the PRC flying above a lighthouse on the Chinese coast, and they name the girl Xingxing (Star). Also on board the ship returning to China is a well-known overseas Chinese poet Xie Qiushan and his wife, Yun Ying who seems to be suffering from tuberculosis.

They are very happy during the 1950's and early 1960's, but when the Cultural Revolution breaks out, Ling is attacked as a Rightist and his family is forced to live in a "dark little room." Xingxing marries an overseas Chinese and leaves China in the early 1970's despite her father's protest that she should stay for love of their "ancestral homeland" (*zuguo*), During the anti-Gang of Four demonstration in Tiananmen Square on 5 April 1976, Ling is photographed by police agents as he hangs a huge poster "Qu Yuan Questions Heaven." He then has to flee into the marshes where he lives like a "primitive man," eating uncooked fish and grains. There he meets a seventy-four year old former history professor, Feng Hansheng who is also in hiding because of his love of honest history. Ling expresses a desire to paint the beautiful landscape round about and Feng offers to go and "borrow" some artist's materials for him. When Feng returns later than expected, bringing some other people with him to tell Ling that he can come back now because the Gang of Four are gone, Ling thinks that he has been betrayed, runs ever higher up into the hills, and finally freezes to death in the snow. His last act on earth is to trace a huge question mark in the snow and then lie down in the place below it where the period would be.

Although my primary purpose in this chapter is to point out Bai Hua's remarkable expression of humanist values through his skillful employment of symbolism to depict the tragedy of a patriotic artist-intellectual, I should first point out a number artistic defects in *Bitter Love*, considered either as a "film-poem" or an actual cinema performance. The primary defects are melodramatic over-reliance on coincidence and deficient or implausible characterization. For example, Ling Chenguang just happens to meet Chen Juanjuan and her parents waiting in line to go on board ship in Shanghai; he is rescued a second time by Lü Niang when he is being chased by the Shanghai authorities; and Lü Niang, already mysteriously married to Ling, turns up in "America" poorly dressed and without even the price of admission to an art show. How in the world did she get there And what happened to her father? Except for Ling himself, none of the other characters are very fully developed. Feng Hansheng, a seventy-four year old ex-professor of history, plays a rather incongruous role. It is hard to believe that such an old man would be able to steal (he calls it "borrowing" - a bit of out of place humor for such a serious film) all of the things that he comes up with, including a full complement of artists's paraphernalia. Ling Chenguang's eating raw fish and uncooked grains is also unnecessarily melodramatic in view of the fact that later on, in the company of Feng Hansheng, he makes a fire to cook chicken, smokes a pipe, and even enjoys a few cups of wine. It may be argued that all of these quickly passing scenes serve to advance the plot but, in the absence of very fine directing, there would be a real danger of an otherwise very moving film degenerating into hopeless melodrama. Indeed, the Taiwan version of *Bitter Love*, was just such an unfortunate production that had a most incongruous effect on the viewer.

Finally, Bai Hua's humanistic warning against the Maoist theogony is extremely important; however, part of its force is vitiated by his overly shrill insistence that "man makes himself." This sort of *hubris*, although characteristic of the positivistic streak in European thought since the Enlightenment, turns its back on the profoundly humane and humanistic influence of all higher religions, including Buddhism, and betrays more than a little influence of the vulgar Marxism of Chairman Mao. Buddhism, though it often degenerated to the level of harmful superstition due to human weakness and lack of knowledge in a hostile world, never advocated mass violence; neither did Confucian philosophy condone mass warfare and killing (Mencius was very embarrassed at once having advised in favor of a military campaign); and philosophical Daoism (Taoism), especially Lao Zi and Zhuang Zi, are notoriously pacifistic. The traditional Chinese intelligentsia's persistent emphasis on social harmony corresponding to cosmic harmony no doubt often served many men of dubious integrity as a convenient cloak to hide social injustice, but it was then and still is a rational and moral social ideal that stands in sharp contrast to the unending strife implied in the Maoist doctrine of "permanent revolution" or the workaday communist ideal of ceaseless "class struggle."

Before analyzing Bai Hua's expression of many of these humanistic values, I want to discuss the use of the rhetorical technique of irony in *Bitter Love*. Besides traditional Chinese techniques of allusion and symbolism, the most commonly used technical device in *Bitter Love* is the familiar Shakespearean and Chinese poetic technique of scenic juxtaposition (which would no doubt appear as montage in the film) in order to establish thematic contrast or identity. A stark contrast between 1976 and the past is established simply by constantly changing back and forth from Ling's hiding place in the rushes to various scenes, such as his happy childhood days playing hooky and learning folk arts from indigent sculptors and painters; stealing magnolias from a Chan Buddhist Temple and meeting the old abbot Hungyi; the purity of young love with a childhood sweetheart, Chen Juanjuan; and episodes of family happiness in the 1950's. A contrast is also made between Ling's comfortable life in America where he has a car, a summer house, a stereo set, and a black maid, and the mistreatment, poverty, and squalor he has to endure during the Cultural Revolution decade. This contrast is not made, as Bai Hua's critics charged, in order to express envy of the capitalists or to make the Chinese nation look bad — but to point out how much the protagonist was willing to give up because of his great love for China and the terrible way artists and intellectuals were treated by the Maoist dictatorship. Another contrast that occurs throughout is that between the beauty of the Chinese landscape and the sordid ugliness of people's lives under the oppressive Maoist dictatorship of the Gang of Four. Finally, a symbolic contrast is made between past and present when the "homeland" changes from the "lighthouse" of 1950 to the "dark little room" of the Cultural Revolution. Incidentally, a "dark little room" is where innumerable intellectuals were forced to live during the Cultural Revolution. For example, Ai Qing and his wife lived in a hole in the ground; Ba Jin and Xiao Shan were locked in a toilet; the assistant director of the Shanghai Conservatory of Music was confined for 14 months in a closet under a stairway where the toilets were flushed into a septic tank, his legs swelled due to lack of oxygen, and he suffered other forms of physical abuse, but he was lucky — he survived, while ten of the teachers under his direction committed suicide.[16]

Identity is also established in several places by this technique of scenic montage: an ironic identity between the Nationalist (KMT) and Japanese tyrannies and the Maoist tyranny of the Gang of Four. Once while Ling is being chased and shot at by police agents in 1976, he recalls an identical scene of escape from KMT agents after a workers' protest in the 1930's; the two scenes switch back and forth several times in order to establish an unmistakable equivalence. Just as Ling was forced to leave China in the 1940's during the Japanese occupation, his daughter is forced to escape from an unlivable situation, unlivable at least for her, in the New China of the 1970's. Xingxing's decision to leave is an even more powerful critique of the regime because she, who was named after the flag, the very symbol of the nation, chooses to leave of her own free will and against her father's wishes. Despite the fact that she has never lived anywhere other than the PRC, she cannot share her father's intransigent patriotism. When Ling is told that he has been photographed and must leave Peking in April 1976, he is utterly "dumbfounded;" even after the Cultural Revolution, he cannot believe that he still has to flee from the police as he did under the reactionaries and foreign imperialists.

The irony of the Maoist betrayal of the Chinese people's hopes is present throughout *Bitter Love*, but especially in relation to the overseas Chinese poet Xie Qiushan and his wife Yun Ying. On the ship returning to China in 1950, when Yun Ying is questioned out her health, she answers hopefully that "everything will be all right" as soon as they reach their "homeland." Her condition is seen to improve quite a bit during the the early 1950s, but during the Cultural Revolution she becomes very ill again and finally dies alone in a May Seventh Cadre School where she has been sent away from her husband so that her "reform through labor" may be accomplished more quickly. Her words, "everything will be all right," ring out in Xie Qiushan's ears when he learns of her death from a letter that has been casually tossed in on the floor of his broken-down apartment. Xie Qiushan had earlier bewailed the Maoist betrayal of communist ideals in an ironic poem he recited to the Lings and some other friends in their "dark little room" when he and Yun Ying came to say good-bye before leaving for the Cadre Schools.

> Since we are comrades, comrades-in-arms, compatriots,
> Why must you lay traps for us?
> Since you plan to put us in chains,
> Why must you always be smiling?
> Since you plan to stab us in the back,
> Why must you first embrace us?
> You seal up our mouths with tape,
> But we fill our minds with questions!
> True comrades, comrades-in-arms, compatriots!
> Why not shine on each other like the stars in the sky?

The stark simplicity of this poem on the betrayal of brotherhood immediately calls to mind Cao Zhi's (192-232) famous "Seven Step Poem" that his brother Cao Pi, Emperor Wen of Wei, forced him to write:[17]

> Boil the beans to make a soup;
> Strain the pulse to clear the broth.
> Under the cauldron the beanstalks burn;
> In the cauldron the beans cry out:

"We're all born of the same roots —
Why so eager to torment us?"

The ironic contrasts and identities established in *Bitter Love* appear
all the more meaningful when we recall that the author, Bai Hua, was
once a true believer in Maoist communism and a "good child of
Chairman Mao." Indeed, in his prize winning poem, "Spring Tide is
in Sight," (*People's Daily*, 17 March 1979), written two months before
Bitter Love, he shows himself still to be a loyal son of the Communist
Party. Unlike his fictional protagonist, Bai Hua did not sit out the
Communist revolution in America, but risked his life travelling with
the PLA throughout that period and was himself full of romantic
enthusiasm, ardent faith, and boundless hope for New China under
communism ("How naive and romantic I was in those days,").[18] As
with his friend Liu Binyan it was his experiences among the common
people in the factories and the rural areas — truly living among the
people who were suffering under the Maoist regime — that caused him
to express his indignation and protest against tyranny in the literature
of exposure. These experiences convinced him, as so many Europeans
had been convinced about Stalin long ago, that Chairman Mao was a
"god that failed."

In the first and last two lines of "Spring Tide is in Sight," Bai Hua
metaphorically announced his reason for writing once more after
twenty years of enforced silence: "I want to be a drop of water in the
spring rain cracking open the hard ice, / like a hot tear of joy
sprinkling down on the flowers waiting to bloom." He also allusively
announced his intentions in writing *Bitter Love* by quoting a famous
line from the *Li sao* of Qu Yuan, the archetype of the man of integrity,
patriotic official, and writer–intellectual alienated from an unjust and
foolish ruler:[19]

Long, long is the road and far, far the journey:
I shall seek high and low in my steadfast quest.

His intentions are to embark on a long quest for truth, to explore the
Cultural Revolution in order to find out what went wrong, and then to
present his findings in the form of a long, impassioned, and sometimes
allegorical poem, all in the tradition of the patriotic loyalist Qu Yuan.
Specifically, he intends to explore the evils visited on the Chinese
people by the Maoist theogony, especially the debasement of human
nature, the denial of human dignity, and the trampling down of human

rights by the dictatorship.

Bai Hua's reassertion of humane values is brought out even more clearly in the second of three allusions to Qu Yuan. After young Ling Chenguang is caught stealing magnolias from the garden of a Chan Temple in order to paint them, the old abbot Hungyi agrees to prepare some calligraphy for him in exchange for his paintings. The scroll Hungyi writes for him is another line from the *Li sao*:[20]

> This too is what my heart delights in;
> Though I die nine deaths, I shall have no regrets.

"This" in the *Li sao* refers to the fragrant flowers mentioned in the line directly preceding and used allegorically throughout the poem for the humanistic moral virtues of honesty and integrity as well as the combined artistic values of truth, goodness, and beauty. In *Bitter Love* there is also a parallel reference to the magnolias that young Chenguang had painted so beautifully, and thus the use of this Qu Yuan line in this context may be confidently taken to embrace by allusion all of the meanings included in the original.

Bai Hua's final reference to Qu Yuan involves an even more direct identification of his artist protagonist Ling Chenguang with the writer who was fearlessly loyal to his country and his principles in the face of great personal danger from an evil ruling group. As mentioned above, during the April Fifth Incident of 1976 — a spontaneous mass protest against the Gang of Four and the Maoist vilification of Premier Zhou Enlai — Ling Chenguang hung up a huge scroll bearing the words "Qu Yuan questions Heaven." This phrase can be taken to refer not only to Qu Yuan questioning the supernatural powers as he did in the *Li sao* in search of guidance for the moral and political conduct of human life but also to the work "Heavenly Questions" (*Tianwen*), traditionally attributed to Qu Yuan. In either case, use of this allusion involves one of the main themes of *Bitter Love*: rejection of the facile assertion that the Cultural Revolution decade was the fault of the Gang of Four alone. In the *Li sao*, Qu Yuan specifically attacks King Huai of Chu for his venality and foolishness in accepting the advice of flatterers, slanderers, and opportunists rather than that of good men who put the interests of the people and the nation first. King Huai's mistaken policies led to his own death and to the downfall of the Chu state, thus vindicating Qu Yuan's predictions. The allegorical reference to Mao Zedong as the real cause of all the suffering of the Cultural Revolution is quite transparent: Ling Chenguang, like many other participants in the April Fifth Movement, is asking: "what about Mao's role in the

Cultural Revolution?" The *Tianwen* reference further supports this
interpretation. David Hawkes accepts the explanation of the often
cryptic work as a book of riddles intended to challenge conventionally
accepted views by asking rhetorical questions. For example, "Shen
Sheng hanged himself by the neck. What crime was he guilty of?"
Everyone who read these lines knew that Shen Sheng was forced by his
wicked stepmother to hang himself even though he was innocent of
any crime, and that his ghost returned to threaten the state with destruction because his body had not been properly buried.[21] Ling
Chenguang's (Bai Hua's) question is: "what crimes were Premier Zhou,
the people, and old Party cadres guilty of that they should suffer so at
the hands of Mao Zedong and the Gang of Four?"[22] We may not agree
as regards Premier Zhou and the Party, but Bai Hua, like so many
others, certainly believes that the spirit of Premier Zhou is a better
guide for the future than the ghost of Chairman Mao. As he wrote in
"Spring Tide is in Sight": "The whole Party should learn from
Comrade Zhou Enlai who gave his all /And took nothing from the
people but plain tea and simple food".

After his epigraphic allusion to Qu Yuan, Bai Hua immediately
presents his readers and the film audience with two powerfully
humanistic visual images. In the lead–in before the title, one lone
goose, tired yet proud and flying with great difficulty, appears first on
the screen, soon to be joined by several others until the entire screen is
filled with geese flying through the blue sky in a formation resembling
the Chinese character for "human being" (*ren*) while a "proud" voice
sings the film's theme song softly in the background:

> Aaaaa . . .
> Singing joyfully of their dignified course,
> We trace a human figure as we soar swiftly across the sky.
> Ever so beautiful!
> The most noble image between Heaven and Earth.
>
> Aaaaa . . .
> Singing joyfully of their everlasting hope,
> We trace a human figure as we sing loudly across the sky.
> Ever so brilliant!
> The brightest star in the Silver Galaxy.
>
> Aaaaa . . .
> Singing joyfully of their dark suffering,
> We trace a human figure as we advance steadily across

the sky.
Ever so splendid!
The strongest character in the universe.

In classical Chinese literature, flying geese are a conventional symbol of the weary traveller's yearning for home and family and the exiled official's longing for his homeland. In *Bitter Love*, Bai Hua extends the meaning of this conventional symbol from the patriotic love of country or the personal love of family, both Confucian values of long standing and both present in the context of *Bitter Love*, to symbolize also the values of human dignity, freedom, and struggle against oppression. The geese flying in the formation of the character for "human being" appear nine times in the course of the film–poem, each time immediately when the protagonists are in dire straits, and each time as an inspiration to them to continue to struggle.[23] Thus Bai Hua links up traditional Confucian values of Chinese culturalism — the individual's loyalty to his own people and culture — with more characteristically European values of individual freedom and struggle against tyranny. Like *Bitter Love* in its entirety, the theme music that always accompanies the geese reminds us repeatedly of the greatness of the individual human being struggling to maintain his or her dignity in the face of overwhelming evil and adversity.

The second visually powerful image of humanity, which Bai Hau has chosen to be both the first and the last thing seen on the screen, is a single solitary reed: "a reed standing straight up, though buffeted by fierce winds. A reed, ceaselessly shaken, but standing resolutely erect, silhouetted against the vast blue sky . . ." The reed stands here for the pliable yet tenacious quality of resistance on the part of the Chinese people to the Maoist assaults on their human dignity as well as the resistance of the humanistic values of Chinese national culture to the crude reductionism of Maoism with its many years of "rectification" (*zhengfeng*) movements, thought–remolding campaigns, Chinese Gulags, and "adverse winds" (*nifeng*) of many kinds that culminated in the mass hysteria and government encouraged sadism of the Cultural Revolution. Such resistance is, of course, from a position of weakness and human frailty — the reed is often bent in the wind — that only serves to further highlight the Chinese peoples's courageous assertion of individual moral autonomy and human dignity.

Furthermore, when considered in conjunction with the Qu Yuan quest for truth motif as well as Feng Hansheng's love of honest history (which is, of course, what *Bitter Love* as a whole represents: truth in literature and history), Bai Hua's reed takes on the qualities of one of

the most famous metaphors for human rationality and dignity in
Western intellectual history: Pascal's "thinking reed." Certainly Bai
Hua would agree with the sentiments expressed in Pascal's famous
Thoughts number 347:[24]

> Man is but a reed, the most feeble thing in nature; but he
> is a thinking reed. It is not necessary for the whole universe
> to take up arms to crush him: a puff of smoke, a drop of
> water, is enough to kill him.
>   But even if the universe should crush him, man would
> still be more noble than that which killed him, because he
> knows that he dies and he realizes the advantage that the
> universe has over him: the universe knows nothing of this.
>   All our dignity, then, consists in thought. Upon this we
> must depend, not on space and time which we cannot fill.
> Let us labor then to think well: this is the foundation of
> morality.

These sentiments of a Christian moralist closely parallel the Mencian
thesis that the ability for and the practice of humanistic moral thinking
make up the "slight difference" that separates humanity from the
brutes. Both Mencius and Pascal believed this "heart/mind that can
think" (Mencius) or this "mathematical" and "intuitive" mind (Pascal)
to be Heaven-sent or God-given, and thus a precious possession, the
use of which for the moral betterment of mankind constitutes the
highest spiritual element of man's calling on earth.[25]

We have seen that Bai Hua's intention in writing *Bitter Love* was to
explore the causes of the Cultural Revolution and that he insisted on
going beyond the facile official explanation that Lin Biao and the Gang
of Four were alone responsible for the tragic events of 1966 to 1976.
More than a year before the Communist Party of China began to
seriously reassess Chairman Mao's role as the initiator and leading
force behind the Cultural Revolution,[26] Bai Hua, employing the
allegorical method of Qu Yuan that his opening epigraph had prepared
us for, had shown quite plainly that he held Mao Zedong and the
Maoist theogony to be mainly responsible for the ten years of
catastrophe just past. As with the use of the geese, the reed, and other
thematic scenes, the key allegorical scene is repeated twice with added
details the second time. When Ling Chenguang was a child visiting
the Chan Temple near his home, he once asked the old abbot Hungyi,
"Why is this Buddha statue so Black?" The old abbot replied

solemnly, "The incense smoke of many good men and pious women has blackened it." "What?" young Chenguang asked incredulously, and the abbot continued, "You find that strange? My child, in the dusty world of men there are many affairs whose end results are often the opposite of their good intentions." Little Chenguang walked away without fully understanding the abbot's words. A perceptive reader sees the point already, but Bai Hua repeats it later with even greater force.

Feng Hansheng and Ling Chenguang are talking one evening when Feng shouts out an apostrophe to his Chinese "homeland" (*zuguo*): ". . . so beautiful and the people so good; to suffer great hardship for you; even to die for you! It's worth it all!" Ling Chenguang agrees with him and then recalls that childhood scene again. ". . .He saw the Temple (*miaotang*),[27] resplendent in gold and azure, and heard the sonorous beating of the drums . . . He went into the main hall, so deep and dark, with incense smoke wafting all around . . . The great tall Buddha statue was no longer golden, but had turned black.

> Chenguang stared at the Buddha statue. From offscreen came his own childhood voice:
> 'Why is this Buddha statue so black?'
> The old abbot's solemn voice echoed through the great hall:
> 'The incense smoke of many good and pious people has blackened it.'
> 'What?'
> 'You find that strange my child! In the dusty world of men there are many affairs whose final results are completely opposite from their good intentions!'

The scene ends with a close-up of Ling Chenguang's "uncomprehending expression," and is immediately followed this time by an all-too-familiar scene of Maoist madness during the Cultural Revolution:

> Ling Chenguang is absentmindedly walking along a Peking street, moving just like in a dream and looking for all the world as if there was no one around him . . . The entire street is crowded with people waving the *Recorded Sayings of Chairman Mao.* Fixed on every face is a devout, naive, and fanatical expression . . .

   The technique of scenic juxtaposition or montage greatly facilitates the allegorical identification of the Maoist theogony of the Cultural Revolution with what is for Bai Hua no doubt the "feudalistic superstition" of Chinese Buddhism. We can outline the allegory as follows:

Buddhism .... Maoism (not necessarily Socialism or
                           Communism)
The Buddha .... Chairman Mao
The "good and pious people"
or The Sangha .... The Red Guards
The Dharma (Law) .... The "Little Red Book," or
                           The Selected Works of Mao Zedong

No doubt we should then think of Lin Biao, Jiang Qing, Zhang Chunqiao, Wang Hongwen, and Yao Wenyuan as the various Boddhisattvas of the dark age just past. After this scene, the rest of the flashbacks all refer to events during the Cultural Revolution which are justly portrayed as the direct result of the cult of Mao Zedong as it was employed by Mao himself, Lin Biao, and the Gang of Four. The result of the deification of one man was that the Chinese people were forced to live for over a decade both physically and spiritually in the "dark little room" of the dictatorship of the Cultural Revolution where, as Ling Xingxing complained to her father, "there's no window, there's no light, there's no air . . . we can't even see the sky . . ." Bai Hua intends then a warning that the deification of any single leader will inevitably lead to tyranny and should never be allowed to happen again. In the context of 1979, he was supporting the principle of collective leadership promoted by Deng Xiaoping's "reform faction" within the Chinese Communist Party against the Maoist die–hards, represented at the time, by Hua Guofeng.
   Having thus broached the most important problem of what Saint Paul called "the spirit of evil in things heavenly,"[28] Bai Hua does not pursue the matter any further nor make any deeper analysis of this particularly sensitive issue in *Bitter Love*.[29] Instead, he goes on to extole the dignity of humanistic struggle against such evil. After Ling Chenguang has labored through the night to paint a window looking out on a bright spring landscape on the dingy walls of their "dark little room" — a window bringing light being an obvious image for the humanizing force of art[30] — a choric voice offscreen makes explicit the theme of human creativity through struggle:

Human beings will always survive, always work, and always
do battle! If there is no window, then let us simply paint on
a window; and if it is too cold and dark, let us simply paint in
the spring–time! The world was not created by God, but by
human beings!

This last sentiment of radical secular humanism echoes an earlier poem
that Xie Qiushan recited somewhat ambiguously just at the moment of
their arrival in New China and the birth of Ling Xingxing:

God did not really create humanity,
Yet He has received the praises and prostrations of
    humanity for nearly two thousand years!
There are still numberless magnificent churches
Whose bells have not ceased ringing for two thousand years.
The Creator of humanity is actually humanity itself;
Humanity creates itself — including God.
In order to create, we endure agonies as boundless as the sea,
While the good fortum we enjoy is as small as a single drop
of clear water.

Like Hu Feng before him, Bai Hua offers his readers the dignity of
humanity's Promethean struggle to create a better world in spite of the
inhumane powers of darkness arrayed against them. On the ruins of
the old China, build a new China; on the ruins of the Cultural
Revolution betrayal of that first vision of a new China, build another
new China. One is reminded of Goethe's lament for the age, ironically
chanted by a chorus of invisible spirits — "juniors of my faction,"
according to Mephistopheles.[31]

Woe, woe!
You have shattered it,
This lovely world,
With mighty fists.
It reels, it collapses!
A demigod has smashed it
Utterly!

A lament that is immediately followed by the admonition:

Build it again,
Build it again in your breast!

Let a new way of life
Begin
With vision abounding
And new song resounding
To welcome it in!

Human dignity, the worth of the individual, truth or rationality, the goodness of human nature, and artistic beauty are all aspects of Bai Hua's vision of everyday struggle to create a better life that are repeatedly af firmed through the actions of the main characters in *Bitter Love*. Truth is affirmed in Feng Hansheng's love of honest history as well as in Mr. Chen (Juanjuan's father)'s dedication to science and learning ("our house has many books") and his frustrated desire to use his expertise for the good of the Chinese people. The importance of art and beauty is reiterated in several scenes. When the artist protagonist first appears, we are assured that he is "our friend" and his art is seen to have deep roots in the folk arts of China — it comes from the people and he uses it for the people. Art is a window bringing light and beauty to human life (Ling Chenguang painting a window on the "dark little room") as well as knowledge and inspiration [Mrs. Chen (Juanjuan's mother) playing Chopin's Polonaises]. The values of human kindness, friendship, and love — without any regard for social class background — are brought out very forcefully. Feng Hansheng and the One-armed General risk danger on the strength of their friendship for Ling Chenguang, while Chen Juanjuan gives him a carving knife as a token of friendship and Lü Niang and her father rescue him from a Nationalist army press gang as an example of simple human kindness. Chen Juanjuan, Lü Niang, Ling Chenguang, and Ling Xingxing all experience romantic love and cherish it even though it also brings them sadness — Juanjuan because she misses her chance to marry Chenguang, Xingxing because she has to leave her parents and her country behind in order to live abroad with her husband, and Lü Niang because she has to watch helplessly while her husband suffers during the Cultural Revolution — in every case, a sadness that is occasioned by national calamities beyond their control. Finally, family happiness, so cruelly disrupted during the Cultural Revolution decade,[32] is affirmed through the loving relationship between Lü Niang and Ling Chenguang, most movingly depicted in the scene where they dance quietly together while their daughter falls asleep in a chair just after Ling Chenguang returns home from being beaten by Red Guards on his birthday.

Bertrand Russell once remarked that patriotism is perhaps the most destructive emotion in the twentieth century, a liberal sentiment that very few Chinese intellectuals would agree with. He was thinking, of course, of the kind of blind love of country and race (or nation) that was almost everywhere in Europe, and in Japan as well, mobilized by powerful ruling groups into the blind obedience to governments that was a particularly unsavory feature of the nationalistic and racist madness of two world wars and that in many places today is still being fired up by demagogues of all political persuasions in order to mobilize support for their power politics and effectively tively silence any sober opposition. This sort of patriotism very soon degenerates into the worship of the State, the Government, the Party, or the One Great Leader; generally progressing in that order. Just such an idea of patriotism has generally been promoted by the CCP.

Now that such blind faith (indeed, any faith) in the State and the Party are at an all time low, the CCP has been campaigning almost daily in the media as well as in the schools, offices, and factories for a new birth of patriotism. As an example of their brand of patriotism, "Article One" of the *Rules for University Students in the Capital* states, "Ardently love the Chinese Communist Party, ardently love the socialist homeland, ardently love the people."[33] The highest expression of patriotism in the PRC today, according to the leadership, is to love the Communist Party. Criticism of the Party *per se* — criticism that is not authorized by one or more high level Party factions during a so-called "line struggle" — is automatically regarded as unpatriotic and possibly treasonous, depending on the need for conformity felt by the leadership at any particular time.[34] It was precisely on the basis of this equation of patriotism with love of (and obedience to) the Communist Party that the anonymous commentator for the PLA Daily accused Bai Hua and *Bitter Love* of being unpatriotic. If one accepts their definition of patriotism as love of the CCP, then their argument is irrefutable. *Bitter Love*, unlike "Spring Tide is in Sight" with its encomium to our great "mother" the CCP, was not intended to and even more certainly does not flatter the virtues of the CCP. But I believe it can be shown to be a profoundly patriotic work nevertheless.[35]

The patriotism thematically reflected in *Bitter Love* from the first to the last scene is patriotism in a humanistic mode that is in complete accord with all of the humanistic values previously discussed. It is first of all a profound love for the Chinese people — the human beings that together constitute the Chinese nation — in all the dignity of their work, their striving to create a better life, and their suffering. This

love of the Chinese people entails an impassioned appeal to the
government that the people be treated with the dignity and respect due
to all human beings without regard for social class background, that
they be given the necessary freedom to think and to create without
unjust interference on the part of the state or the Party authorities, that
they be allowed to exercise their rationality and employ their
hard–earned knowledge for the benefit of the whole nation, and that
they be allowed to enjoy the warmth and security of friendships and
family life. Secondly, it is a deeply felt love for the natural beauty of
China, an artist's appreciation and passion for the sheer physical
beauty of the legendary Chinese landscape. Finally, both of these
aspects taken together – love of the Chinese people and the Chinese
landscape – contribute to a deeply felt respect for national cultural
values (Chinese values) in contrast to the physically and spiritually
destructive anti–traditionalism of the Cultural Revolution.

The first scene after the title is an aerial view of the Chinese land
scape, a "boundless landscape, our great ancestral homeland (*zuguo*),
loving and kind like our mother's breasts . . ." The clouds, mountains,
and rivers pass by before our eyes until we see "a painter" whom the
narrator assures us will become our "friend" because he is an ardent
lover of the Chinese homeland and people. He is painting, "humble
and small" before the homeland; he is totally absorbed in and
identified with the "wonderful natural scene" of the homeland, ever
changing before his loving and observant gaze. The scene ends with a
close–up of his "cautiously reserved yet deeply serious eyes" as the
author invites us to view the Chinese homeland through the eyes of
this patriotic artist.

Ling Chenguang's entire life is motivated by and is an expression of
that humanistic patriotism described above, and it is no doubt in some
ways an autobiographical account of Bai Hua's own experiences as well
as the experiences of a whole generation of Chinese intellectuals,
writers, and artists. He is born in rural China and learns the folk arts
of China from impoverished artists. He loves the natural beauty of the
Chinese landscape. He used his artistic talents in support of the
workers of China against both the corrupt Nationalist government and
the Japanese imperialist invaders. He refuses a chance to leave his
homeland in the 1930's and travel abroad with Chen Juanjuan and her
family, thus sacrificing a chance for romantic love and a comfortable
life overseas in favor of patriotic struggle at home. He is forced to
leave under protest when he is locked in the cabin of a ship by sailors
who fear his discovery by enemy patrol boats. In America, he becomes
an artistic success by painting only Chinese people and Chinese

landscapes; and, while there, he keeps up with news about New China. As a result of his strident insistence on being allowed to return to China in 1950, we are told that all of his property is confiscated by the local government (one of the many implausible events in *Bitter Love* that in itself also reflects Bai Hua's "patriotic" ignorance of western democracies) and he has to work as a scrub hand to earn his passage back to China on a French liner. Nevertheless, he is full of "hope" and "confidence" in the future of New China, and even names his first born child after the national flag of the People's Republic. He is perfectly content and happy painting the glories of his homeland in the 1950's (Bai Hua does not allude in any way to purges of writers and artists from 1942 to 1957), and even after the horrors of the Cultural Revolution, he agrees with Feng Hansheng's assertion that any suffering endured for the sake of the homeland is worth it. He disagrees with his daughter's decision to leave China; and when Chen Juanjuan comes to see him in his "dark little room," he tells her that he has no regrets whatsoever about not going abroad with her in the 1930's or about returning to China in the 1950's. Finally, he is motivated by the most high–minded and courageous sort of patriotism when he participates in the April Fifth demonstration against the Gang of Four and even dares to question the role of Chairman Mao himself. Even after the Cultural Revolution, he is still "dumbfounded" and cannot believe that he has to hide from the government of New China just as he hid from the KMT and the Japanese before.

As with his very careful and deliberate use of *miaotang*, an older term referring specifically to the Chinese imperial court and thus associating the Maoist theogony with "feudalistic superstition;" in one of the most significant and moving scenes in *Bitter Love*, Bai Hua's choice of words once again demonstrates to the careful reader that his patriotism is love of the Chinese people and homeland, not the state, government, or any political party. Throughout the film–poem, the word *zuguo* (literally, "ancestral country") is consistently and repeated- ly used to refer to China. There is only one significant departure from this usage: the celebrated scene where Ling Xingxing suddenly announces to her father, after some months of secret planning during which time she has received her mother's approval, that she is marrying an overseas Chinese and going abroad to live. She seeks her father's blessing, but it is not forthcoming:

> Chenguang was cold and shaking all over:
> 'I cannot allow my daughter to leave my homeland
> (*zuguo*); I travelled a dark road for half my life in order to

return to our homeland . . .' He did not seem to have the
strength to go on talking.

'Papa!' Xingxing screwed up her courage: I'm going with
my husband. I love him and he loves me. I know you; I
know you too well, Papa! You love this nation (*guojia*) of
ours; bitterly regret leaving this nation. But does this nation
love you?!'

Her words were like a clap of thunder. Chenguang's
body reeled back and he quickly steadied himself against the
wall. He was powerless to answer her question. His small
studio was fearfully quiet . . .

Guojia, now used generally for both "nation" considered as a
geopolitical unit and the "government" or the "state" (understood in
the PRC to mean the Communist Party), is a term that in traditional
times was used to designate the imperial house, the Son of Heaven
himself, and the imperial court, as well as the country which, in theory,
was regarded as belonging to the emperor. *Zuguo*, in contrast,
originally meant the *guo* or "feudal state" where one's *zu*, "ancestors",
were first enfeoffed; later it came to be used by Chinese living outside
of China to refer to their "native land." In using *guojia* just this once
and in this highly emotional context, Bai Hua is clearly questioning the
government's, that is, the Communist Party's treatment of patriotic
intellectuals, writers, and artists like Ling Chenguang (and himself)
whose only desire is to live a decent life and benefit the Chinese
people — the true Chinese nation — through their work. And he is
specifically questioning the Party's treatment of intellectuals from 1958
to 1977. From his poem "Spring Tide is in Sight", we know that Bai
Hua himself was a strong supporter of Deng Xiaoping's proposed party
reforms in 1979 when he wrote *Bitter Love*, but at the same time he
knew from bitter experience that such reforms might never actually
come to pass.

The final scenes of *Bitter Love* are an eloquent testimony to Bai
Hua's humanistic patriotism. They also leave the reader–viewer with
what has unfortunately turned out to be a prophetic question mark. It
is easy to understand why the Maoist conservatives, and even Deng
Xiaoping himself, did not want the film to be shown. The scene is
worth rendering in toto: the rescue workers are trying to locate Ling
Chenguang to give him the happy news of the fall of the Gang of
Four.

A helicopter hovers slowly overhead . . .

Looking down with a bird's eye view of the rushes and hills . . .

On the snow–covered fields, a black question mark . . .

The helicopter gradually descends . . .

The question mark grows larger and larger: an enormously large question mark, it was the very last journey of Ling Chenguang's life; he used his last remaining strength to trace the figure (?) in the clean white snow. The period under the question mark was Ling Chenguang's already frozen body.

Chenguang lay curled up on the snow–covered field with his hands stretched out as far as possible toward the sky. At the end, he did not have the strength to raise his arms very high, but we can see that he had made a great effort to do so . . . His eyes are not closed; they are open, open and unmoving . . .

The scene once more (as at the beginning) looks out over a panorama of the Chinese, landscape: the rivers and streams flow on and the roads criss–cross back and forth . . .

Ling Chenguang's passionate monologue can be heard off screen:

'If this were only an artist's canvas, only some artist's pigments, only some shadows and sketches, some lines dreamed up out of an artist's idle fancy; then we could tear it up, paint it over, or throw it away; but unfortunately, it is our homeland!

Our blood is flowing in her rivers and streams. Our childhood dreams still remain in her forest woodlands. There are hundreds and thousands of roads criss–crossing her vast surface, and on all of those roads we have all suffered many hardships and cast off numberless pairs of worn out shoes. But from all of that we have earned a sacred right — the right to exclaim:

My native land! I love you!'

A flock of geese fly slowly by in the 'human being' formation. The character for 'human being' fills Heaven and Earth . . . growing gradually more distant, the image finally disappears at the edge of the horizon . . .

A proud voice sings softly:

'Aaaaa . . .
Singing joyfully of their dignified course,
We trace a human figure as we soar swiftly
          across the sky.
Ever so beautiful!
The most noble image between Heaven and
          Earth!

A single solitary reed, fluttering in the wind, stands up,
resolute and straight . . .

Bitter Love concludes with an "enormously large question mark,"
thus ending the patriotic protagonist's life of unrequited love for his
homeland with the Qu Yuan motif of silently questioning Heaven as a
last refuge from an unjust human predicament. In the immediate
context of Ling Chenguang's flight and death, his question refers
specifically to three promises (the CCP's promises of 1977) proffered
by his friends coming to inform him of the fall of the Gang of Four.
Xie Qiushan shouts out, in a hoarse voice, as he scrambles up the hill
after his friend, trying to assure him that the demons are no longer in
charge of China:[36]

Old friend! These are not the ghostly fires of hell! This is
the light of humanity approaching you, old friend! Not
demons, but human beings! It's us!

Feng Hansheng also tries to reassure him that honest history is now
acceptable again:

Chenguang old friend! My draft history (A "true history" of
the Cultural Revolution, the Communist Party, or what, we
are never told. — tr.) has finally been published . . . Old
friend! Come out and see: we've survived into an age that
can face history squarely!

Finally, the One–armed General who helped him escape from
Peking—presumably the sort of exemplary officer Bai Hua portrayed in
his short story "A Bundle of Letters" — answers Xingxing's question in
the affirmative (echoing the Party's stated position on intellectuals at

the time):[37]

> Come . . . out . . .! The homeland needs you! The
> homeland . . . loves you! loves you!

Xingxing has already returned home to look for her father, and his
wife is there too; but she does not shout out any promises of a brighter
tomorrow. Perhaps she has seen her husband suffer too much to make
such assertions on behalf of the new leadership. At any rate, it is a
tribute to Bai Hua's courage and integrity that he does not end with the
usual celebration of the new order and optimistic assurances that
everything is going to be all right in a new era of "unity and stability."
Rather the scene ends with the five of them in tears as the snow stops
falling, the clouds drift away, and dawn breaks through slowly in the
eastern sky. The dawn breaks not, as in a Cultural Revolution story, to
herald the victory of the class struggle, but rather to permit the ironic
discovery of Ling Chenguang's "enormously large question mark."

In his celebrated novel, *Bread and Wine*, Ignazio Silone's
protagonist and alter ego, the revolutionary saint Pietro Spina is asked
by the Stalinist Comintern to take a political position completely at
variance with his most deeply held personal convictions. The penalty
for refusal is certain expulsion from the Italian Communist Party. A
good friend of his offers the comradely advice not to be headstrong.
Pietro replies:[38]

> Let 'em leave me alone! They can't expect the impossible
> from me. I can't sacrifice to the party the reasons which led
> me to join it.

But, his friend insists, "Leaving the party means abandoning the idea."
"That's false thinking," concludes Pietro. "It'd be like putting the
Church before Christ." For Bai Hua, the Italian's fear of putting the
Church before Christ becomes his fear of the CCP leadership putting
the Party before "the people." We have already seen what Bai Hua
said about that in 1979, but in 1981 the showing of *Bitter Love* was
prevented by the Party and Bai Hua, whose "Party spirit" (*dangxin*) is
apparently very strong, accepted the Party's criticisms of his work.
Perhaps he felt that the Party and the people were once again united or
perhaps he simply had to give in to overwhelming pressure. At any
rate, *Bitter Love* is only one of a great number of literary and artistic
works produced in the early 1980's that stress the resurgent humanistic

values outlined above in opposition to the stultifying theories of Mao Zedong's *Yan'an Talks*.[39]

Let us now turn to a controversial novel that even more openly expresses the theme of "humanistic Marxism" in the PRC.

VI. Chinese Marxist Humanism: Dai Houying's Novel *Ren a, ren!*

Over 300 novels have been published in the PRC since 1978. The majority of them concern historical topics and conform to the general criteria laid down by Hu Yaobang in his 1980 speech at the Drama Forum discussed in Chapter One above. Only a few of them would seem to merit serious study, and in this chapter I am going to discuss what I feel to be the most significant, albeit flawed and ultimately failed, attempt to write a serious psychological novel in the PRC since at least the early 1950's.[1]

Written from May to August 1980 and first published in November 1981, this novel by Dai Houying, a woman and a teacher of literary criticism went into its fourth printing in April 1982 and was extremely popular with Chinese readers.[2] Not surprisingly, it also became very controversial. In late 1981 and early 1982, meetings were convened in Canton to criticise and discuss the work and a spate of critical articles appeared in the Shanghai and Canton papers. As usual, critical opinion concentrated on the characters and ideas or "ideological content" of the novel and gave only perfunctory treatment to the work's "technical innovations." Opinions were divided, however, on the overall merit of the work and this seemed to reflect the general situation on the "artistic and literary front" at the time. Some critics were extremely favorable, considering the main characters to be near perfect examples of the fictional creation of "socialist new people" who work for "progressive change," possess "inner beauty" of spirit, and a "heavy sense of responsibility" for the future of the nation. Other critics, perhaps the majority, lauded the work's "exploration" of ideas but complained that the author comes to the "mistaken" conclusion that Marxism can be reconciled with humanism and that love and an end to class struggle can reform the world.[3] In the meantime, readers continued to buy up every new printing and the book remained virtually unavailable in Chinese bookstores.

In a manner similar to Soviet literature during the two post–Stalin thaws of 1953–54 and 1956, *Ren a, ren!* is a novel of character and ideas that explores the sense of individual responsibility, the relation of the individual to history, and the fate of individual human nature in a mass state.[4] Individual moral character and the inner world of Chinese urban intellectuals is the subject matter of *Ren a, ren!* and its major theme is the reaffirmation of human dignity and worth after twenty years of Maoist rule in China. It is also a semi–autobiographical confession of mistaken historical judgement, blind faith, cowardice and betrayal, loss of faith and consequent emptiness, painful reawakening, and the gradual reassertion of an individual's right to independent thought. In a Postface the author confesses that she was a believer in the necessity of class struggle and the denial of humanism whose eyes were only gradually opened during the reign of the Gang of Four. After their downfall, she began to reflect on everything that she had thought and done and came to the conclusion that the denial of humanism in Chinese Marxism was a grave error. She then resolved to write a novel putting forth her ideas. "One character writ large suddenly appeared before my eyes: 'humanity!' A song that had been cast aside and forgotten for so long tripped off of my tongue: human nature, human feelings, humanism!" (353)

The major "technical innovations" hailed by the critics remind us that in PRC literature, as in the USSR, the rediscovery of the wheel is a common and repetitive occurrence. This is not to say, however, that the exploration of what the author considers modernist narrative techniques from twentieth century Western fiction — stream–of–consciousness, dream sequences, symbols, and allegorical names — should not be greatly encouraged. It definitely should be both praised and encouraged, especially when the explorer is someone like Dai Houying who quite obviously has something extremely important to say. The entire corpus of Chinese fiction during the communist era is, with rare exceptions, devoid of such artful use of narrative techniques as those just mentioned in which the form of beautifully metaphorical language is employed to explore and define "values in an area of experience which, for the first time *then*, are being given."[5] Devoid of the beauty of language, it is equally devoid of that individual vision of life that was often found in modern Chinese fiction from 1917 to 1949 and that is ordinarily expected of all serious writing. Armed with dialectical materialism and suffering from an "illusion of full knowledge," Chinese writers of the last thirty years have not been allowed to, in Pasternak's words, "cease to recognize reality" and thus arrive at newly created names — art — for the categories and visions that arise from the passionate engagement of the individual mind with the visible universe.[6]

Dai Houying's technical explorations are largely unsuccessful, being vitiated in nearly every case by what might be called a residual didacticism born of years of reading and teaching worker–peasant–soldier fiction and by a wholly understandable urgency to make her humanistic ideas known to her compatriots. Unlike Western modernist writers whose techniques she urges her fellow writers to explore, she has no confidence that her readers' intellectual capacities will be sufficient to derive a meaningful interpretation of her metaphors, symbols, dream sequences, allegorical devices, and other forms of figurative language. Judging from the storm in a teacup that has raged over the so–called "obscure poetry" of Gu Cheng, Bei Dao and Shu Ting — poetry that employs metaphor and symbol — she may have good reason to doubt some of her readers' perspicacity, at least the conservative critics who defend literary purity against any "metaphysical residue" which they can neither understand nor permit.[7]

In the course of the novel one or another of the characters reveals the true meaning of nearly every possibly ambiguous figurative usage that might give rise to multiple interpretation and lively intellectual debate. Zhao Zhenhuan discovers and announces the meaning of his opening dream of swimming upstream in pursuit of an illusive young woman: the young woman is not his ex–wife, Sun Yue, but their daughter Hanhan. He then exclaims through his tears of joy, "I have recovered my soul, and it is you!" (2, 350) You Ruoshui's Dickensian name is explicated for us when his wife shows him a cartoon some students put up in the college library. The caption reads, "Why is he called flows (*you*) like (*ruo*) water (*shui*)?" Underneath is a picture of a man with the letter "A" for a head swimming mightily between the closely packed rocks of a stream. (321) You Ruoshui's boss, the College Party Secretary, is named Xi Liu which means "creek flow." Only the name of his son, Xi Wang, a homophone for "hope" is mercifully not explained in the usual manner. The male protagonist He Jingfu's long–stemmed pipe is a most powerful symbol of humanity and figures prominantly in the finest bit of writing in the novel, but its symbolic significance is explicitly mentioned several times. The heart symbolism of Sun Yue's "very strange dream" in chapter 14 is transparent enough, it is He Jingfu's heart and by sharing it with him she is enabled to fly away and escape the crowd wildly clammering for her blood (175–183); in a conversation with He Jingfu sometime later,

he tells her that he would gladly tear his heart out of his breast and
show it to anyone who would like to see it. (308) The whole incident is
lifted from Lin Daiyu's fearful dream in chapter 82 of the *Dream of
the Red Chamber* and thus readily accessible to almost any literate
Chinese.[8] A good deal of familiar Chinese Marxist style literary
criticism occurs throughout the novel, as when Zhang Lizao,
nicknamed "the writer," sends Sun Yue a letter urging honesty and
fairness in fiction and commenting that, "Everyone (of their college
classmates) is a type. Everyone's experience could be made into a
novel." (186) or when He Jingfu sums up a group discussion with the
comment that, "all together we are a reflection of our era, its good and
bad points, its brightness and its darkness, its past and its future."
(340)

Lengthy titles given to the novel's four parts also point clearly to
both their subject matter and theme, thus establishing a readily
understandable structural framework:

> Every human being has a history stored up in his mind
> and it is active in many diverse ways.
> Every heart is searching for its home and each one has its
> own particular requirements.
> This sort of thing happens every day: two hearts make
> contact, sparks fly, and a mutual resonance begins.
> This kind of weather must be regarded as normal: sunrise
> in the east, rain in the west; you think it will not clear up and
> yet it is clearing. (1,77,185,275)

The real interest of the novel lies in the depiction of the inner lives
of the characters, their reactions to the terrible and confusing events of
the past twenty–three years, their loves and hates, hopes and fears, and
expectations for their individual lives and the future of the nation. In
her depiction of the characters' inner lives, Dai Houying tells us that
she employs "some of the representational methods of
'stream–of–consciousness,' such as [the depiction of] the characters'
feelings and emotions, fantasies, thought associations, and dream
states" that she has "assimilated" from her studies of the "modernist
school" of Western fiction.[9] Although she does not, strictly speaking,
employ the technique of the "stream–of–consciousness" or "interior
monologue" as it is generally employed in Western fiction, she does,
nevertheless, create a number of mutually distinguishable individuals
each one having his own particular view of the ideas and events that
pass in review during the course of the novel. There is nothing at all

Joycean or even Woolfish about her diction and syntax, none of her sentences are ungrammatical or lacking in logical order, and her prose style is almost never poetic or ambiguous; but she does succeed in presenting the inner workings of her characters' minds in a manner quite unusual for modern Chinese fiction in the communist era. Rather than saying that she employs the "stream–of–consciousness" method, unpoetically and therefore unsuccessfully, it might be better to say that she follows a recipe similar to that described by Ilya Ehrenburg, which I quote here with obvious substitution of names:[10]

> Let us suppose that the novel deals with Zhang San, the reader's next–door neighbor. Neither Zhang San's appearance nor his everyday life is a secret to the reader. The reader has often seen Zhang San, heard him speak at meetings of the Party committee, perhaps even dropped in on him from time to time. Yet Zhang San remains unfamiliar and undiscovered territory to him. If the writer is able to show what this distant neighbor is thinking about, how he bears grief, how he works, loves and makes mistakes, the reader will feel enriched by reading this novel; he has come to know Zhang San and therefore has become better accquainted with himself.

The most important thing that the readers of *Ren a, ren!* come to know about the characters depicted therein are their intellectual confessions and affirmations, confessions and affirmations that have found an enthusiastic readership and that perhaps represent an honest reflection of the spiritual life of many PRC intellectuals in the 1980s.

Xi Liu, Secretary of the C–City College Party Committee, is the only member of the older generation who has nothing to confess and only stale orthodoxy to affirm. He is the antagonist of the novel, an old cadre toppled from power during the Cultural Revolution decade whose attitude toward history is summed up in two brief epigramatic statements — his credo, frankly revealed to Sun Yue: "In the past I made important contributions; for ten years I suffered; now I have power," (17) and his silent complaint: "History has still got a hold of me and won't let go. It's given me a rebellious son and there's not a thing I can do about it!" (63) Both his inner and outer lives are almost wholly concerned, however, with trying to do something about it, to stop the flow of history that seems to him to be leading the CCP and the nation away from ideological orthodoxy and towards the twin evils of "revisionism" and "bourgeois liberalism." It is all the fault of intellectuals like He Jingfu who refuse to abandon metaphysical speculation about human nature and humanism.

Believing (with Mao) that the essence of Marxism is class struggle, he is adamantly opposed to its corruption by Utopian ideas about universal human nature, humanism, and love. In debates on these issues with his son, Xi Wang, however, his knowledge of Marxism is shown to be wholly derived from Communist Party propaganda tracts and ever–changing party directives which it is his duty to obey without question. When Xi Wang quotes Engels concerning the "animal nature" of mankind, Xi Liu angrily forbids him to "slander" Engels. Xi Wang then exultantly points out the page reference in the *Complete Works of Marx and Engels* and sneers, "Ha, ha! You are so busy upholding the principles of Marxism, that you don't even have the time to read Marx." (66) Although he angrily maintains his position against his son's more educated and idealistic arguments, Xi Liu silently reflects to himself that he has not actually read very widely in the classics of Marxism–Leninism; that he does not care to tire himself out trying to understand the problem of human nature from a Marxist perspective; that class struggle as the key policy was always good enough for him; and, finally, that those people in leadership positions who *have read* all of Marx, Engels, Lenin, and Stalin (he does not mention Mao), still say one thing today and something else tomorrow. "What's the use of reading so many books anyway?" (67) Considering the "tortuous road" (CCP term) that Chinese Communist Party ideology has taken during the "twelve line struggles," it is hard not to sympathize with a man of such obviously mediocre intellectual capacities forced to keep up with the vagaries of the dialectic.

In fact, Sun Yue, his loyal supporter in 1957 who fell with him in 1966, and He Jingfu, the man they helped to ruin in 1957, both sympathize with him. Sun Yue recalls that he once possessed many good qualities, such as intelligence, ability, and closeness to the masses; but that now only the vulgar and repellant side of his character remains and "he is only concerned about his own power and position." (17) He Jingfu admits that he was once a very valuable person, but remarks that now his only value is to "let people see how a Communist Party member can degenerate into a person of vulgar interests, petrified thinking, and narrow–mindedness." (23) Since no other explanation of his degeneration is offered, the reader may conclude that the Communist Party, by placing a premium on every type of conformism, cowardice, and opportunism,[11] has made him what he is today.

In refutation of those critics mentioned above who, as late as 1982, continued to assert that he is a poorly delineated character and unrepresentative of the majority of CCP Secretaries, it is only fair to point out that Xi Liu quite accurately anticipated the cultural–ideological position of the emerging Deng–Hu–Zhao leadership a full eight months before the Bai Hua Incident. At first he is not sufficiently subtle, to be sure, when he insists that a new Anti–Rightist Campaign is the only way to handle intellectuals who go on "blooming and contending" in a manner harmful to the interests of the proletariate and its vanguard. (78) Later on he catches up with the emerging slogan, however, when he asserts that, "Letting a hundred flowers bloom and a hundred schools of thought contend is a resolutely proletarian policy which definitely cannot permit bourgeois liberalism." (283) His final outburst of exasperation against Xi Wang's defense of humanism, though effective as satire, may be taken as an expression of the personal frustration of all those Communist Party leaders who encounter at every step "the opposition that the strangeness of man raises:"[12]

> Ai! Humanism, humanism! It's been criticized so many times, but people still want to talk about humanism. Every one living and loving together completely equal, without resorting to class struggle whenever required. They certainly paint a beautiful picture!
> If I don't strike out and attack (*dou*) others, they're going to attack me. People, oh People! People are always the same! If we attack them all the time, we still cannot reform them; but if we don't attack them, they're even worse! (286)

As in the cases of the withdrawal of the film *Bitter Love* in 1981 and the recall of the magazine *Huacheng* (no. 1, 1982) containing Yu Lojin's confessional exposé "A Spring Fairytale," Xi Liu's views prevail in a meeting of the College Party Committee and he successfully prevents the publication of He Jingfu's book, *Marxism and Humanism*, despite the fact that it had been accepted for publication and in violation of constitutional guarantees of freedom of speech and publication.[13] No less an authority than Hu Yaobang himself would seem to agree with my estimation that Xi Liu is a most representative "type" within the CCP today when he says:[14]

> Many basic Party organizations are paralysed. The leaders are abusing their power. They are disrupting Party

discipline. They work in closed factions. Many are corrupt .
. . We should not exaggerate these difficulties, but we should
not be afraid to reveal the dark sides of the Party.

The characterization of You Ruoshui, Xi Liu's lackey, certainly
does tend toward Dickensian caricature; but even he may be regarded
as representative of all sorts of lower level functionaries and literary
hacks who write reports and speeches for local Party Secretaries.
When his wife angrily informs him that the teachers and students in
the college library are "all outraged about the wrong being done to He
Jingfu" by Xi Liu's "unjust" suppression of his book, she asks him, "Is
that a brain or a fatty tumor you're carrying around on your
shoulders?" (320) He doesn't answer and she storms out of the house
without preparing his lunch, but his inner thoughts reveal his utter
cynicism and pessimism:

> What am I carrying on my shoulders? I can't say for sure
> myself. At any rate, its mission is not to produce thoughts.
> Life is already hard enough without having any thoughts. If
> I had any thoughts, wouldn't it be even more difficult? He
> Jingfu has thoughts; so what about it? The teachers and
> students are all so outraged on his behalf! It's not worth a
> fart! Justice or injustice does not depend on talk, it depends
> on power! If you don't have power, you have to settle for
> injustice. Whoever wants to be outraged by injustice, can
> just go on being outraged forever! (320)

In keeping with this philosophy, he has developed his own method
to protect himself from responsibility. "The method I use to handle
these leaders," he reflects to himself, "is always the same: turn my
spearpoint around and attack them." (317) Whenever his "mistakes"
are pointed out by a rising faction within the highest Party leadership,
he is always ready to attack his former benefactor in the faction falling
from power. This is perhaps an ideal way for a lower-level cadre to
protect himself during factional disputes among the top leaders, and
You Ruoshui, like millions of other cadres, used it very effectively to
rise in the ranks by attacking old cadres like Xi Liu during the early
days of the Cultural Revolution. In 1980 he is using the same method
to attack the Gang of Four in an essay entitled "Survival after
Calamity," but he is also keeping an eye open for any hint that Xi Liu
is about to lose his power or prestige again due to his opposition to the
Third Plenum (December 1978) policy of "liberation of thinking."

The one thing he will never do is to think for himself, and his nightmare in which Xi Liu's head grows on his shoulders and speaks for him is an accurate psychological portrait of this ventriloquist's dummy.

Cynicism, pessimism, and apathy are not confined to completely negative characters like Xi Liu and You Ruoshui. Xu Hengzhong, once an idealistic "rebel" against Xi Liu and other such Party bureaucrats in 1966, and Li Yining, a middle school teacher and confidant of Sun Yue, seem to represent a great number of intellectuals who have lost their original ideals as a result of their historical experiences in the past twenty years. Xu Hengzhong, whose ironic name means "promised eternal loyalty," once believed in the ideals of communism enough to attack Xi Liu during both the Hundred Flowers Campaign and in the first year of the Cultural Revolution, but his experiences both under the Gang of Four and after their downfall have caused him to embrace a thoroughly cynical view of human history: "All history can be reduced to one word — purge. In the past I purged other people and now other people are purging me. I see through it all now." (37) He believes that ideals such as those of Sun Yue and He Jingfu are nothing more than "idle fantasies" (199), that "you always lose if you pick a fight with someone who has power," because, even though the papers are full of propaganda about a socialist legal system, "in C–City College Xi Liu's word is the law;" (331) and he repeatedly quotes Su Qin's (Warring States period) sardonic wisdom as his credo: "Alas, the parents of a poor man do not love him as a son, but all the friends and relatives of a rich man fear him. How can anyone born into this world not pay his respects to power, privilege, riches, and status?" (38)[15] He would like to do something decent in life, but he feels dispirited and powerless.

Although he cannot bring himself to tell him to his face the first time he meets him, he does finally confess the whole story behind his 1957 wall poster attacking He Jingfu to Sun Yue. He became an "Anti–Rightist hero" at that time very much against his own convictions. Burdened by a guilty conscience, he is even a little too harsh on himself, describing his actions as motivated by "selfishness" and "foolishness" when in fact his story demonstrates that he was actually motivated by fear. He had just scratched his own signature of support off of Jingfu's wall poster attacking Xi Liu, when he was stopped by the chief editor of the college paper carrying a camera. Thus compromised, he agreed to the use of his name to attack Jingfu. The poster that he copied over and put up was actually written by the

chief editor under Xi Liu's direction. By just such historical
inevitabilities, are cowards made into heroes in the PRC. Xu further
confesses that from then on he understood how to be a political
opportunist. He entered the Party, stayed at college when others were
rusticated, had his name in the paper, and became a celebrity. When
the Cultural Revolution came along, he became a "rebel" after the son
of a high cadre told him that Liu Shaoqi was beyond saving. Sun Yue
thinks to herself that everyone who lived through those years
understands perfectly now that we were all "acting out a tragedy in a
comic mode and a comedy in a tragic mode, never certain whom we
should curse or whom we should pity." (115–116) After all of these
experiences, Xu Hengzhong is resigned to living without a goal or
making "just living" his only goal. (336)

Li Yi–ning, whose ironic name means "suited to peace," has
learned from her many unhappy experiences to be completely
apathetic and lead a completely private life. She sympathizes with Sun
Yue, but she believes that Sun is a "sucker" for communist propaganda
who deludes herself into thinking that "the people" need her. She
herself is a middle school politics teacher who is resigned to "a life that
has neither wind and waves nor color and fragrance," completely
lacking in romance, and she is totally apathetic politically: "I regard my
political textbooks the same way I regard a crochet manual or a
cookbook. They're all practical reference books. So I can be quite
unmoved by them. But you (Sun Yue), you're much too foolish!"
(19) After relating her tragic story of romantic and marital unhappiness
in the New China, an old story of arranged marriages, parents ruining
their children's lives, and a husband betraying his wife for political
reasons; she says that she is now satisfied with the simple security of a
marriage to a man much younger and of a much lower cultural level
than she whose simple human goodness was untouched by communist
political propaganda. In their life together, "revolutionary struggle" is
now carried out for "material needs" and consumer goods have replaced so–called communist "spiritual" values.

When Sun Yue sadly admits that she would have been one of her
persecutors due to her faith in CCP policies, Li Yi–ning urges her not
to feel so much regret for the past. After all, "Everything you
originally thought was an illusion, was impossible; it is only natural
that nothing was achieved, so what's there to regret?" (145) When her
daughter comes home and joins the conversation, we see the result of
Li Yi–ning's style of education. She too admonishes Sun Yue,
"Auntie, let me teach you something: don't think about anything; don't

think about anything; don't bother about anyone else's affairs; it's enough just to take good care of your own affairs. When you get old, retire, go to the park and practice *taijiquan* (gentle spirit–building exercises), buy yourself some white *mu' er* (edible gelatin–like fungus) and make a nice sweet soup. How about it?" (146)

As for the many problems facing the Chinese people, Li Yi–ning and Xu Hengzhong both agree that they will never be solved. As she says, "I have seen through China's situation completely. Things will never be put right. The Chinese people's slave nature is too deeply rooted and their inertia is too heavy." (335) Even if there is some reason for hope in the present situation, she is too tired: "But I cannot fly anymore. What is required now is protracted, unflagging, plain ordinary hard struggle and work." (337) She is only an ordinary person with few expectations of life. Her character may well be representative of the vast majority of Chinese people who hope for nothing more than peace and quiet, the absence of political campaigns and disturbances, and a slow but steady rise in their standard of living.

The younger generation is represented by two characters who, taken together, delineate a spectrum from the impatient to the vulnerable. Xi Wang, the "rebellious son" of Party Secretary Xi Liu whose name is an obvious homonym for "hope," is an impatient member of the "thinking generation," a very forceful social critic, and a natural ally of idealistic intellectuals of the older generation such as He Jingfu and Sun Yue. A young man in his early twenties, he has nothing to confess and a great deal to affirm. He is opposed to the "feudalistic" practices of his father and other high cadres — decision by executive fiat, nepotism, and special privileges — and in favor of independent think- ing, respect for the individual, humanism, and popular democracy. Arguing with his father about the suppression of Xu Hengzhong's article critical of the Gang of Four's literary policies, he asks pointedly, "What policy are you following? When will you ever learn that the power the people give you is not just to harrass others and even less to exact your personal revenge?" (68) He urges Sun Han to think for herself and to maintain her self respect in the face of social pressure. He becomes a spokesman for He Jingfu's humanism when he reads out long passages from He's book in the course of an argument with his father. After he learns of the College Party Committee's decision to stop publication of Jingfu's book, he is furious. Meeting Sun Yue, who is just then on her way to inform Jingfu of the decision, he angrily informs her that, "My father is going to prevent the publication of *Marxism and Humanism* in the name of the C–City College Party

Committee. He doesn't want to do anything himself, doesn't even know how to do anything, and he won't let anyone else do anything either. He's a stumbling block to the liberation of thinking, but he is still very proud of himself! He probably thinks that being able to trip up other people is quite a professional skill." (303) When Sun Yue asks him how he would have handled the situation, he immediately calls for a democratic procedure. "I think the whole thing should be brought out in the open to let all of the students and teachers in the school discuss it. They could also write letters to the newspaper office." (306)

Xi Wang's impatience is demonstrated in his debate with He Jingfu about the pace of social reform in China, in his overall evaluation of the idealistic older generation, and in his final resort to action after the College Party Committee's decision on Jingfu's book. Jingfu argues in favor of taking "a historical attitude," working for gradual reform, and Xi Wang responds, "But who is going to bear the heavy burden of history? The next generation . . . The actual situation today is that my generation, and Hanhan's generation as well, are all sharing our parents' hardships . . . But does the older generation have a sympathetic understanding of my generation?" (252) He wants more action to push toward the resolution of "contradictions" in society. "Perhaps I cannot wait until that day when everything is realized in practice!," he concludes with a sigh. (254) In the course of the conversation mentioned above, he tells Sun Yue that the students are very appreciative of the efforts of He Jingfu and herself, but they do not believe they will be effective. He then contrasts their two generations thus, "But we are not like you, always looking before and behind, hesitant and indecisive. China has a tremendous pile of problems. Going along so slowly, it's going to take forever! Isn't your burden too heavy? We hope very much that you will throw away your burden . . ." (306, elipses in original). This is a remarkably ambiguous statement, one of the few times when the reader is free to speculate. What burden does he mean? Their fear, their obedient "party spirit" of following orders or "democratic centralism," the ideology of Marxism–Leninism–Mao Zedong Thought, or the Chinese Communist Party itself? Dangerous thoughts these, and better for us to speculate thus than PRC readers or critics. Finally, after telling You Ruoshui that the current of science and democracy (echo of May Fourth youth) is unstoppable, Xi Wang takes direct independent action by putting up an illegal wall poster on the Chinese Department bulletin board. Entitled "The rule of law is not personal rule — thoughts about our freedom of publication in light of the thwarting of professor He's attempt to publish a book," he not only describes the entire incident from first to last, but also mentions Xi Liu and the College Party Committee members by name. In the character of just such a young person, Dai Houying and many others of her generation lodge their chief hope for China's future.[16]

The fifteen-year-old Sun Han, who wonders in confusion "Why does history first hang a millstone around my neck?," (241) is, like all of her generation, vulnerable. She is vulnerable not because of her altogether natural desire to see her parents reconciled or to know her father and not think of him as an "evil man," but vulnerable because she and her generation are the object of tremendous pressure towards conformity on the part of the educational system and the Communist Youth League that she eventually joins in spite of her assertion that she intends to remain independent of politics. The contrast between her and Xi Wang and the pressures of the educational system are both brought out dramatically in the following dialogue. Xi Wang tells her, "Uncle He is a man of character. Character, understand? . . . Uncle He's character is that he has his own independent understanding of things and his own attitude toward life . . . he respects human worth. He has a strong sense of self respect, self love, and self confidence." Poor Hanhan replies that, "The teacher told us that it is individualism, to have too strong a sense of self respect!" Xi Wang enthusiastically admonishes her, "Ai ya, little Hanhan! Without self respect a person falls to the level of an animal. You don't understand these things now, but anyway you can learn many things from a person like Uncle He, things that you can't learn from anyone else. He never speaks without sincerity and never feeds you a lot of useless and exaggerated platitudes." (123-123)

On 20 December 1982, the Eleventh National Congress of the Chinese Communist Youth League (CYL) was attended by 1,900 delegates representing the organization's 48 million members. After brief welcoming speeches by Hu Yaobang, Deng Xiaoping and others, Hu Qili, Member of the Secretariat of the CCP Central Committee delivered the keynote address. He made two basic points. The Communist Party must arouse the consciousness of the youth of China "to lead the Chinese revolution and construction to victory." Chinese youth "must follow the leadership of the Communist Party and the guidance of Marxism-Leninism, be one with the people and firmly keep to the correct political orientation in order to be useful in revolution and construction." Wang Zhaoguo, a forty-one year old "youth" recently elected First Secretary of the CYL Central

Committee, then delivered a work report calling on the youth of China
to "unite and march towards the brilliant future of socialist modern
ization."[17] Since its post–Mao restoration, the CYL has recruited 26
million new members of which 2.7 million "outstanding members"
have entered the CCP. Although their primary goal is now defined as
the completion of the Four Modernizations and youth of intellectual
origin are greatly encouraged to join, the control of the hearts and
minds of China's youth is the main purpose of the CYL and the
situation is much the same as that described by Czeslaw Milosz for
Poland in the 1950's:[18]

> Everything, thus, takes us back to the question of mastery
> over the mind. Every possible opportunity for education and
> advancement is offered to the more energetic and active
> individuals among the workers. The new, incredibly
> extensive bureaucracy is recruited from among the young
> people of working–class origin. The road before them is
> open, open but guarded: their thinking must be based on the
> firm principles of dialectical materialism. Schools, theaters,
> films, painting, literature, and the press all shape their think-
> ing.
>   We should also call attention to a new institution, the
> 'club,' whose significance is comparable to that of the chapel
> in the middle ages. It exists in every factory, every school,
> every office. On its walls hang portraits of Party leaders
> draped with red bunting. Every few days, meetings follow-
> ing pre–arranged agendas take place, meetings that are as
> potent as religious rites.

When the self–proclaimed "independent non–party person"
Comrade Sun Han enters the Communist Youth League, she comes
home and asks her mother to "supervise and control" her because her
classmates say that her "thinking" is unstable and her emotions given
to sudden highs and lows in response to newspaper reports about
"good people and good things" and personal experiences of "bad
people and bad things." (238) Sun Yue then reflects that when she
entered the CYL at fourteen, her feelings were always stable, and she
asks herself if that was not the reason that she was "blindly optimistic,
woefully ignorant, slow to react, and insensitive and unfeeling."
Having learned a bitter lesson about the harmful effects of being
"supervised and controlled" from outside and giving up her
individuality and right to think independently, she "did not agree to

take on such supervisory authority." (239) When Hanhan then asks her the most important question with regard to Chinese youth today, "Mama, will my generation turn out like yours? . . . Take such a tortuous road?," she answers with a suggestion of doubt, "I hope not," (*Buhui ba*) and silently vows to herself not to give her child the sort of mindless education that she had. Sun Han is certainly vulnerable to social pressures, but perhaps she can maintain herself as a member of the "thinking generation" through the salutary influence of Xi Wang, Uncle He, and her mother.

The most interesting and important characters in the novel are Sun Yue and He Jingfu, but between them like a "two sided mirror" (as Sun Yue once thinks to herself) for twenty years is Zhao Zhenhuan, Sun Han's father. His character is not particularly well developed and his inner life is of no great interest. His function in the novel is primarily that of offering Sun Yue a choice and pushing her toward it and himself acting as an exemplum of the theme of reform and reconciliation. He divorced Sun Yūe while she was in prison during the Cultural Revolution and married a beautiful worker with proletarian political clout and a questionable moral background. The novel begins with his regrets and resolution to seek Sun Yue's forgiveness and his actions constitute the novel's minimal plot line. He writes a letter to Sun Yue confessing his sins and asking for forgiveness and a chance to make things up to her and their daughter, he goes to C–City and accepts the criticisms of his former classmates in order to regain his sense of identity and integrity, he writes a similar letter to Hanhan, he refuses to cooperate with a corrupt chief editor on the provincial paper where he works, and finally Sun Yue forgives him and addresses him as "classmate" again while rejecting his offer of marital reconciliation and agreeing to send Hanhan to visit him during her next vacation from school. He is overcome with the mixed emotions of joy and sadness, recognizes that, "I lost what I deserved to lose and recovered what I deserved to recover," (341) and, having gone through a kind of purgation, ends with a baptism of tears and rebirth to a new life and a new chance to be a decent person. "Bidding a smiling farewell to the past is something that only happens on the stage" he says to himself, "but I want to say good–bye to the past with my tears." (349)

Sun Yue, a thinly veiled self portrait, is the most skillfully achieved characterization. Presented in all her mental anguish, she is a striking example of someone who willingly became a "captive mind," submitted to all of the pathetic adjustments of her feminine instincts and personal interests to the jealous demands of ideology and organization, and is now hesitantly struggling gling toward freedom and individuality.[19] An emotionally romantic young woman, she was strongly influenced by the humanitarian strain in 18th and 19th century "bourgeois" literature with its passionate advocacy of liberation for the oppressed masses and its assertion of individual demands for love and happiness, but, under the relentless pressure for conformity built up during the Anti–Rightist Campaign, she gave all that up when she "gave her heart to the Party," rejected He Jingfu's profession of love (even though she loved and admired him above all others at the time), joined Xi Liu and the rest in attacking Jingfu as a "Rightist" in 1957, and was duly praised for having learned a lesson in class struggle. Thinking back now, she bitterly regrets her sacrifice of happiness for the sake of the Party and class struggle: ". . . what a sacrifice! I closed my eyes and locked up my heart in the face of all of the temptations to happiness." (109) At that time, she blindly embraced Chinese Marxism as a new faith that offered a utopian vision of the future, but now she has lost her innocent faith and is in great fear of losing all of her ideals or even going insane: "Once a pious nun discovers that God is her own creation, will she not go insane?" (110)

"Today," Sun tells Li Yi–ning, "I have discovered that so many things that I used to regard as natural occurances were in fact tragedies, silent tragedies;" (144) and she feels nothing but guilt and shame for her part in the creation of those tragedies. She wants to accept responsibility for her personal involvement in the historical tragedies of the past twenty years, understand why such terrible things could happen, and do something to make up for her past mistakes and expiate her guilt; but she feels exhausted, lacks courage, is hesitant and afraid, knows that "there is more than one 'self' in every person's heart," (84) but is torn between following her old false "self" represented by Xi Liu and his kind of Communist Party or her newly emerging "self," her true self, represented by He Jingfu and the ideals she shares with him. Her inner struggle provides the main tension and suspense of the novel and is demonstrated by a series of contrasts between her thoughts and her actions through which we see her real life actions increasingly approaching but never actually matching her true inner aspirations and beliefs.

The first striking contrast is the long dream mentioned above, a transparent piece of Freudian wish fulfillment in the course of which she picks up He Jingfu's heart (a symbol for his humanism) on the street, swallows it, becoming symbolically united with him; discovers that the unknown "him" (Xi Liu, Marxism without humanism?) she has lived with for so long has no heart; rejects "him," and is rejuvenated while "he" becomes magically immobilized; and finally manages to fly out of reach of all of "his" followers who are chasing her with knives poised to cut out her new heart. The dream ends with an overwhelming sense of cosmic ataraxy:

> My heart was filled with joy, my feet bounded up into the sky, and I flew up lightly and effortlessly. My heart seemed to glow even brighter in my chest. I thought to myself: I'm going to become a tiny satellite and wander around this vast universe for a spell. Some day I shall descend to earth in some remote spot just like that shooting star that He Jingfu saw at the Great Wall. The universe will be eternally infinite and the great earth will be eternally tranquil . . . (183, elipsis in original)

Very shortly after this illuminating dream which should have made her true inner needs perfectly clear, however, Sun Yue rejects, for the second time in her life, the one thing in the world she most desires. When He Jingfu declares his twenty year love, she tells him that she does not want to live with him because of her guilt, shame, and fear:

> I feel like I owe you a debt. A debtor and a bill collector cannot possibly love each other equally. . . . I've thought about it over and over and the conclusion is that I cannot marry you. My self respect will not allow it.
> I can't fool myself; I love you, I love you very much. So many times I have called out to you in my dreams. So many times I have painted a mental picture of what it would be like to live together with you; but then, just at that time, another picture appears: I am being attacked by other people out of misunderstanding and scorn, being liquidated by history itself. . . . . .
> Now there is only one road left before me: to live alone.
> (224–225, second elipsis in original)

A little later, she rationalizes her self repression by means of the romantic non sequitur that the highest form of love is unrealized love. She looks longingly out the window, yearning for Jingfu's embrace, and thinks to herself:

I want so much to run to you and tell you: 'I'm going to bury
my love for you forever in the bottom of my heart.' Jingfu,
love buried in the bottom of one's heart is the freest kind of
love. It is liberated from all formalism, and marriage is
nothing more than the formalistic union of a man and a
woman. (272)

One need hardly add that such unrealised romantic love is also free of
all normal human responsibility and potentiality for joy or sadness,
success or failure.

The most poignant and penetratingly depicted contrast is that between Sun Yue's romantic humanist interpretation of *The Tempest* and
the moral she derives from it and her dismal self denial and betrayal of
her own ideals in the face of Xi Liu's opposition to the publication of
He Jingfu's *Marxism and Humanism*. After a brief discussion with
Hanhan about good and evil in human nature; Sun Yue realizes that
Jingfu has given up his courting, feels a terrible sense of regret, and
engages herself in an extended internal dialogue in which she reaffirms
her lost ideals and rededicates herself to a life of positive creation.
One of the two high points of the novel, the passage deserves extensive
quotation:

Life is simply life. All the fascination of life is in the
fact that it is always replete with contradictions, always
turbulent and uncertain. It swallows up the human soul
(*linghun*) and it disciplines the human spirit. Now I have
tasted many of life's bitter herbs and from all that bitterness
I've come to savor a certain sweetness.
Have you read Shakespeare's *Tempest*? All of that great
artist's philosophy is contained in it. Shakespeare saw that
life is replete with the struggle between beauty and ugliness
and good and evil, and so he created both spirits that
symbolize beauty and goodness and monsters that symbolize
ugliness and evil. But his greatest creation was that magician
who could control everything in both the natural and the
human worlds. He is a symbol of the perfect human being.
In his control over beauty and ugliness he demonstrates
human strength and confidence. He can raise a great storm
at sea and wreck a great ship carrying a prince. He can also
cause the wind and waves to be still in an instant and bring
all of the beauty of the natural world together at his side.

He is the master of history, controls the present, and creates the future. He raises up the good and punishes the wicked, puts an end to hatred, and sows the seeds of love.

In short, this character tells people: human beings are the masters of everything. This thought is the crystallization of Shakespeare's entire life of seeking and exploring. Anyone who has not searched and explored in that way cannot understand this sort of thought.

But I do understand. Because I have searched; I have passionately searched. And in searching, I have fallen down repeatedly. Thus, I have learned how to think deeply.

The God of Fate looks so big and powerful that he can toy with all kinds of people in the palm of his hand. Ever so many surpassingly clever and powerfully influential personages have been made fools of by Him. In the past this phenomenon has driven many people into the depths of despair, into self–negation and the negation of humanity; but is not the true cause of this condition to be found precisely in the fact that we lacked conscious awareness, self–respect, and self–confidence Was it not precisely because we unconditionally surrendered everything we had to the will of Fate? What if we regain our conscious awareness, self–respect, and self–confidence? What if we take back all of the rights that we gave away? Then we could master Fate. . .

I know that suffering, like all other emotions, can be sublimated; sublimated into art, philosophy, and faith. Although I lost the love of my youth, still it was not a complete loss. The glowing hot embers still remain and are enough to warm me, enough to light my road into the future.

Jingfu (she imagines talking to him), you said once before that a person should not just wait, but should actively create. That was absolutely right. Now I only want to create, to create together with you. I have lived, I have thought deeply, now I should reap the harvest. It does not matter whether the harvest is one of weeds or of brambles, at least it will be our personal creation, a creation of our hearts and blood. . . . As long as one breath remains, just so long shall I keep on making demands upon life! Jingfu, since life has squeezed us so much, why shouldn't we squeeze something out of life now (269–271)

Such an interpretation of *The Tempest* could hardly be made, perhaps, outside of the world view of Chinese "romantic–revolutionary" literary criticism in which all of world literature has to be justified as "progressive" and "realistic" and a preparation for the inevitable triumph of Marxism–Leninism and proletarian communism. In a rather naive fashion, more in tune with May Fourth romanticism than European Marxism, Sun (Dai) makes Shakespeare out to be, like Mao Zedong, a believer in the Faustian–Promethean triumph of human beings over both material nature — earth, air, fire, and water that the industrial revolution has "conquered" only to suffer its revenge in the form of unprecedented ecological disaster — and their own inner nature — the dark recesses where "the heart of darkness" dwells, ever ready to burst forth in world wars, Nazi and Stalinist holocausts, and Cultur al Revolutions of unspeakable cruelty and destruction. Blithly ignoring the facts that Prospero's magic is the result of supernatural intervention akin to Zhuge Liang's popular Daoist magic in the *Romance of the Three Kingdoms (Sanguo yanyi)*, that Prospero is more an archetype of Goethe than of Faust — a creative imagination that brings into being on the dramatic stage a world of cosmic and moral order that is never quite realized in human life — and that behind Shakespeare's romantic "fairy tale with unusually lifelike characters"[20] there is a profoundly religious vision of spiritual redemption, reconciliation, and rebirth achieved through suffering and purgation;[21] Sun (Dai)'s interpretation seems to be reducible to a slogan of radical secular humanism: man makes himself. Her resolve to overcome her despair and fear (especially fear of "the God of Fate," a symbol that in this historical context one might read as the Chinese Communist Party itself) and to go on to a new life of artistic and intellectual creation is completely commendable; unfortunately this resolve is no sooner made than repudiated in action.

In a chapter entitled, "Who could have imagined that such a thing would actually happen?," the answer to which would seem to be anyone who had lived in the PRC since 1957 or been a member of the CCP since 1942; Sun Yue recalls in her mind her dismal performance at a meeting of the College Party Committee called by Xi Liu to prevent the publication of He Jingfu's book. In ironic contrast to her stirring resolution to take back her conscious awareness, self–respect, and self–confidence, she fails to make a strong defence of He Jingfu's position for fear that her comrades will say that she is supporting him for purely personal reasons and will then dredge up all of the old stale gossip about their private lives. Although she does speak up for the book's publication in accord with the Third Plenum line of "blooming and contending," she loses control of her emotions and vitiates her argument by trying to explain her personal feelings for He Jingfu. We can certainly sympathize with her when she reflects to herself that "private life" has become a dirty word in the PRC:

> If I did not force myself to hold it in, I would probably burst out crying! During these past years, due to the extension of class struggle into every area, we no longer have any private life any more. As soon as someone mentions the word 'private life,' everyone immediately has the impression of something 'shameful.' Everyone believes he has the right to interfere in anyone else's private life, not to mention the Party Organization. (298)

Her feeble support of He Jingfu's constitutionally guaranteed right to publish is of no avail. Only one other person speaks up strongly for him, while You Ruoshui, Xi Liu's wife, and the Propaganda Director speak against him and the majority of the committee members just keep their mouths shut and wait for Xi Liu to tell them what he wants. The majority decides that the manuscript should be returned to He Jingfu for extensive revision, and that Sun Yue in her capacity as General Secretary of the Chinese Literature Department Party Committee should "do extensive and thorough thought work" — propaganda in favor of a position she does not believe in — on He Jingfu and their students. This is the policy of "democratic centralism" in action and she is bound by the Party Constitution to obey.

Sun Yue goes to He Jingfu's house and, after her discussion with Xi Wang mentioned above and another long talk with Jingfu about freedom of thought, she gives him an ideologically correct but factually false report of the meeting. Seemingly oblivious of the fact that the Party has done nothing of the kind, she tells him that "the Party Committee has studied the opinions and the reactions of the masses, and come to the conclusion that your book is unsuitable able for publication if it is not revised. . . ."[22] We hope that you can understand that this is a form of loving care for you and that you will voluntarily take back the manuscript." (312) Jingfu's unspoken reaction to her performance is right on the mark. He thinks to himself, "It was just like listening to a phonograph record. The diction was terse and precise, the enunciation was crisp and clear, but the emotional tone was confused. I suppose that is a habit she has developed from acting as a cadre for many years. Or perhaps it is a kind of talent? Anyway, I don't like it." (312) As Czeslaw Milosz wrote of his Polish comrades in the 1950's, "After long acquaintance with his role, a man grows into it so closely that he can no longer differentiate his true self from the self he simulates, so that even the most intimate of individuals speak to each other in Party slogans."[23]

This remarkable speech of Sun Yue's is a perfect example of the confused state of her mind as she tries desperately to remain a good cadre in spite of her conviction that the Party Committee is wrong. It is in ironic contrast to her indignant contempt for the bulk of Committee members who only follow Xi Liu's wishes (297), to her dream of flying and creating, and to her Promethean interpretation of *The Tempest*. Indeed, it seems a complete violation of everything that she claims to believe in and yet it is spoken voluntarily without resort to coercion. As a "captive mind" struggling to be free, she seems to be losing the struggle and that is precisely because she still believes in Marxism–Leninism and "democratic centralism", doctrines that in practice require a person to freely relinquish his most precious possession, the one thing that distinguishes him as a human being (as much of the symbolism and argument of this novel points out) and separates him from the uncivilized animals — his ability and his right to think for himself, to make moral and intellectual judgements on the basis of his own personal evaluation of truth and right.

Sun Yue goes on to tell He Jingfu, "I support your point of view. You should know that," thus admitting that she is deliberately acting against her own better judgement. Jingfu is not surprised by the news. As he says, "it is unreasonable, but it could be expected; it happens almost every day," What hurts him, however, is that it is done in violation of both CCP discipline and national law. As he silently reflects:

> I am hurt, nevertheless; extremely pained because I heard ever so clearly that this is a decision of a College Party Committee, but according to Party discipline and national law, this sort of decision making should not even occur at all! I don't like to see our Party Organization making decisions in this fashion. They are clearly depriving a Party member of his democratic rights and yet they say it is a form of loving care! . . . Why do they have to lie? Why do they have to cheat? And all in the name of the Party Committee? What we need is to be open and aboveboard, to face each other sincerely. Even if they beat me or cursed me, it would be

better than this disingenuous profession of 'loving care!'
(313)

In the denouement, Sun Yue finally decides to marry He Jingfu and
they are optimistic that the higher levels of the Party Committee on
Discipline will investigate Xi Liu, learn the truth, and support the
publication of Jingfu's book. Judging from the Bai Hua and Yu Lojin
Incidents of 1981 and 1982, such optimism seems premature; but
intellectuals like those represented by Sun Yue and He Jingfu will
probably continue to struggle for their ideals against both their own
inner doubts and the forces that oppose them.

The character of He Jingfu combines all of the intellectual themes
of the novel. He is the ideal type of the man of the future, one who
will redeem history and lead China to salvation. As he says, "I collect
and treasure history in order to present it to the future. I am travelling
toward the future now, but the road is still very long." (24) He is also
a romantic wanderer, a Chinese Don Quixote, a lover and a patriot
forever questing after the illusive romantic trilogy of Truth, Beauty,
and Goodness and convinced that he has found them in the philosophy
of humanistic Marxism, in the one true love of his life, and within the
depths of universal human nature. His thoughts and his actions
combine to present the themes of humanism, independent thought,
love and romance, forgiveness, reconciliation, and self–sacrifice.

What does He Jingfu's humanism consist of in intellectual terms?
Above all it is respect for the worth and dignity of the individual
human personality and defense of independent ideas and opinions.
From the following extended passage, read out loud by Xi Wang from
the book *Marxism and Humanism*, we can see that He Jingfu's
humanism requires a radical change in the Chinese national character
and method of governance:[24]

> We must respect human beings, respect individual
> human personality, nourish and strengthen human dignity.
> I believe that in our society today, human self–respect is
> not too strong, but actually too weak. Several thousand years
> of the feudal system have gradually trained us to become a
> certain kind of person: unused to thinking about the worth of
> a human being, unable to form independent opinions about
> life, uninclined toward developing independent personal
> character. It would almost seem that the value of a person's
> existence does not reside in the degree to which he can

contribute *this* to society, but rather in the degree to which
he can meld himself with or subordinate himself to *that*, that
is to dissolve his individual character in the general character
the group. (italics in original)

How monotonous life would be, however, if human
beings had no individual character! And how slow–paced
would be the progress of society! Fortunately there are
always a few people in history who are not satisfied with this
state of affairs and who are not to be impeded by various
outmoded concepts. They are able to emerge from the
general mass, rise above the common run, and become fresh,
new, individual, and powerful characters. They are the first
to call out the message that is in most people's hearts, to lead
forth a vast army, and to push history forward.

Just think, were not all revolutionaries of every age
people like that? Do these people not win our respect
precisely because, under the historical conditions prevailing
in their day, they actualized human worth to the utmost
degree? For this reason, we give unlimited praise to
individual character We want to shout out to all of our
friends: Let us nourish individual character! (281)

This thoroughly romantic peroration on the role of individual
genius in human history would seem to go far beyond the historical
materialism of classical Marxism; but, as the following passage
demonstrates, it is intended to be a restoration of Marxism in
contradistinction to so–called "bourgeois humanism:"

Friends, do not be so quick to worry. I admit that I have
drawn nourishment from bourgeois humanism, but I want to
return the bourgeois label to you. Bourgeois humanism only
affirms and actualizes the individual character of the
minority and demands that the majority sacrifice themselves
for the sake of the minority and live an inhuman life. This
kind of humanism is a sham. There is another kind of
humanism, however, and that is Marxist humanism: it desires
to liberate all mankind and wants every person to become a
free and independent entity. Read for yourselves this
passage from Marx and Engels: '. . .while in communist
society, where nobody has one exclusive sphere of activity
but each can become accomplished in any branch he wishes,
society regulates the general production and thus makes it

possible for me to do one thing today and another thing tomorrow, to hunt in the morning, fish in the afternoon, rear cattle in the evening, criticise after dinner, just as I have a mind, without ever becoming hunter, fisherman, shepherd or critic.' What an enchanting world! In such a world every person becomes his own master. Friends, do you not believe that Marxism contains within it the most thoroughgoing and revolutionary form of humanism? Do you not believe that in order to achieve that ideal world of communism we must destroy every remnant of feudalism that oppresses the human being's original nature and smothers the human being's individual character? Do you mean to say you believe that feudal dictatorship is eternally suitable for us? That it is warm and comforting like spring and difficult to part with? (282–283)

There is an unintended but profound irony in He Jingfu's enthusiastic quotation of this famous burst of unbridled utopianism from Marx's *German Ideology* (1845/46), the most frequently quoted of all scriptural slogans during the Great Leap Forward, the movement that brought about the suicide of his uncle and the death by slow starvation of his father, mother, and younger brother.[25]

Despite all of Jingfu's sanctimonious rejection of a preposterous charicature of "bourgeois humanism"[26] and well chosen quotations from the Marxist classics, Xi Liu supports You Ruoshui's conclusions, which can all be traced back to Mao Zedong's *Yan'an Talks*, that He Jingfu's humanism is mistaken on four major counts:

One: he opposes the theory of class struggle and advocates class reconciliation. Two: he advocates abstract freedom, equality, and love and actually wants us to love the enemy. Three: he advocates abstract human nature and human feelings and opposes carrying out class analysis of people. Four: he advocates individualism and liberation of individual personality. (280)

Throughout 1981 and 1982, Xi Liu's position gradually gained ground until it became the basis of the present ideological line on art and literature and the class struggle.[27]

The most interesting and significant thing about He Jingfu's humanism, I believe, is not so much its intellectual formulation, which leaves much to be desired; but rather its true origin in He Jingfu's life. Where then, according to Dai Houying's characterization, does his humanism come from? Although Marx, Engels, Lenin, and Chernyshevsky are mentioned in passing; the true well–springs of He Jingfu's humanism are presented as coming from predominantly traditional Chinese sources: his grandmother's peasant wisdom, his teacher's exposition, in typical non–Marxist May Fourth style, of Victor Hugo, his father's simple goodness and dignity, and his faith in the inherent goodness of the Chinese people he met during several years of rustication and wandering.

He Jingfu relates the first awakening of his humanism (to Xu Hengzhong) in the course of his "Romantic Story." He has been wandering around aimlessly, working at odd jobs, carrying with him only the *Complete Works of Marx and Engels* and the *Dream of the Red Chamber* (*Hong–lou–meng*), and has come to the conclusion that his assertion of the primacy of human sympathy over class struggle in 1957 was not wrong after all. At the age of thirty, standing in a barren road, without even an identity card or a ration ticket, sociological proof of his existence, he catches sight of a shooting star and meditates to himself on the meaning of human worth:

> I thought to myself: If I die now as far as human history is concerned I would be just like that shooting star in relation to the universe — without sound or breath. But I am not really a shooting star. I'm a human being. A human being who has feelings, friends and relatives, love, and hate.
>
> I thought back then to my grandmother who used to tell me about the stars and the Milky Way.
>
> 'Everyone has a pearl of dew on his head and every one has his own particular good fortune,' Grandma often said to me while pointing at the stars in the sky. She told me that human beings are just like the stars in the sky — they each have their own place and their own right to live. The stars hang in the sky without anyone holding them up, and a human being can live in the world without anyone supporting him. 'The stars in the sky shimmer and the dew on the earth shines.' That was the earliest philosophy I ever learned. (47–48)

His first philosophy, then, was the folk wisdom of a hard working and independent minded Chinese peasant.

When He Jingfu visits Sun Yue and discovers that she is translating Victor Hugo's last novel, *Quatrevingt-Treize* (1873), he recalls that a middle school literature teacher, who was later persecuted for his advocacy of the "bourgeois humanitarianism" of Victor Hugo, had urged him to read it and that it had a profound influence on him. Both the author and the novel itself are of great significance as historical and literary allusions supporting the theme of humanism put forth in *Ren a, ren!* Victor Hugo was the son of a Napoleonic general and a woman of Vendée peasant stock. He believed that the French Revolution would bring human liberation and not the Terror and the Napoleonic Empire that actually resulted and thus he gradually shifted his allegience from Bonaparte and King Louis Philippe to democracy. Exiled for violent opposition to Napoleon III in 1851, he did not return to Paris until 1870 when he was hailed as a heroic prophet. *Quatrevingt-Treize* is a long historical novel about the terrible year of 1793 which witnessed both La Terreur and the beginning of the bloody Guerre de Vendée. The war between the Royalist peasants led by nobles and priests and the Republicans led by General Hoche lasted for three years, involved extreme cruelty, and resulted in great devastation of the countryside. The themes of Hugo's novel, however, are human justice, self-sacrifice, and charity toward a valiant enemy. Consequently, he permits the Royalist Marquis de Lantenac to rescue three children from a burning house in violation of his own troops' strategy; Gauvain, his nephew and opposite number on the Republican side, to arrange for his escape from jail and take his place at the guillotine; and Cimourdan, the judge who decides in favor of Gauvain's execution, to commit a remorseful suicide. The words of Hugo's letter to Edgar Quinet would seem to sum up quite well the theme of Dai Houying's novel as well:[28]

Comme vous et avec vous, je veux dégager la révolution de l'horreur dont on a crû lui faire une force; dans ce livre je la fais dominer par l'innocence; je tâche de jeter sur ce chiffre effrayant, *93*, un rayon apaisant; je veux que le progrés continue de faire loi, et cesse de fair peur.

The most important and most beautifully described origin of He Jingfu's humanism is the example of his father's goodness and dignity in the face of death. Believing that Sun Yue may be lost to him forever because of Zhao Zhenhuan's return and Hanhan's innocent desire for her parents to be reconciled, Jingfu closes himself up in his room, looks at the long-stemmed pipe his father left him and the new

tobacco pouch Sun Yue made for it. He weeps as he recalls to himself
the symbolic significance of these two objects:

> The two people that I love most in my entire life — my
> father and her — together left me a souvenir, this
> long–stemmed pipe with its tobacco pouch. Can that be
> mere coincidence?
> From now on, this long–stemmed pipe will be even more
> precious to me. Looking at it I can see two hearts, one is that
> of a peasant and the other that of a student. These two
> hearts are so different! And yet they are both full of love;
> they both tremble and grow with pain and suffering; and
> they both know lofty sentiments and self–sacrifice. (260)

He then recalls how, before the revolution, his father's younger brother
and his father had almost drowned themselves in a river near their
home because they could not bear their hunger, but the water was too
cold and they climbed out. His uncle later joined the revolution and
became a cadre, but finally he was actually driven to suicide by
drowning when he dared to defend the local peasants against the
Party's Great Leap Forward policies. He was branded a
"counter–revolutionary" for sending a letter to Party Central exposing
the county Party Committee's practice of reporting falsely inflated
grain production figures while the peasants were starving. On the way
back from his "trial," he broke loose and threw himself into the river.
His body was dredged up onto the shore and made the object of a
"struggle session" in which all of the local peasants including his
relatives were forced to take part, a pit was dug, and the Party leaders
had his body thrown in while exprsssly forbidding his friends and
relatives to conduct a funeral or give him a coffin. Jingfu and his
father sneaked back in the night, dug up his uncle's body, put it in a
box, and gave it a proper burial.

As Jingfu says to himself, his father's thinking could never be made
to include the concept of "class struggle," especially since under the
communist government a person's class status could change by
prescription at any time even in the course of a matter of days. Thus
"class struggle" was aimed at him and "gave him the opportunity to
fully demonstrate the unadorned simplicity, nobility, and beauty of his
soul. That soul of his provided me with an uncommon nourishment. I
drank of my father's milk . . . . . ." (263, elipsis in original)

During the Great Leap Forward and the ensuing famine, Jingfu and
his father, mother, and younger brother and sister gradually starved.

His mother and younger brother died first, his father and sister could only lie in bed, and he had barely enough strength to go out every day and dig up edible roots with his hands and crush dried leaves into ersatz tobacco for his father's long–stemmed pipe. "If only my heart, my blood, my love, could be transformed into tobacco," he thought. (264) Then one day when he came home, his father called him over to his bedside, looked at him from head to toes with tears streaming down his cheeks, and told him:

> 'There is still half a peck of potatoes in the little crock. I always put them aside. I can die now, but you cannot die. If you die now, who will ever know for sure what kind of a human being you are? Then there's your uncle. . . . you must go find your Auntie . . . your sister's grown up . . .'
>
> He did not finish, and he had not smoked the pipe. I knelt down by the side of the bed and did not get up for a long time . . .
>
> I picked up the pipe that had fallen to the ground. I inhaled my first mouthful of 'smoke,' smoke made from burning the leaves of the scholar tree. My father left it to me . . . (264)

Then, after this remarkably symbolic scene with its almost religious ceremony of "passing on the incense smoke" (*chuan xianghuo*), in this case bitter smoke rather than fragrant, Jingfu recalls a time several years later:

> My uncle and I had already been rehabilitated. My Auntie had returned home with her son and her daughter who was born during the calamity. 'If your father was still alive . . .' my Auntie started out like that many times and I always replied, 'He would certainly feel consoled.' I believe that my father's soul in Heaven (*zai tian zhi ling*) must certainly feel comforted because he never thought about himself. But father, how could I not keep you in my heart?
>
> Whenever I pick up that long–stemmed pipe, I think of you. I drink your milk from that pipe, father's milk. Mother's milk was made from blood and father's milk was also made from blood. Mother's milk was stored in her breasts and father's milk was carried in his heart. (264–265)

Jingfu's humanism, then, was learned at his grandmother's knee, reinforced by his teacher's example, and sanctified by his father's blood. His book is dedicated to his father's memory with the hope that the Chinese people will never again suffer the beastialities perpetrated in the name of class struggle:

> I commemorate my father, mourn for my father. My funeral oration is written in the draft of my book, *Marxism and Humanism*. To carry on class struggle in order to eliminate class exploitation and oppression is necessary, honorable, and glorious. To falsely create classes, divide the people, and break up families for the sake of drumming up 'class struggle,' is ruthless and absurd. The former liberates the people, the latter injures them. The former truly considers the people to be 'human beings,' the latter only regards the people as walking and talking tools. (265)

Tools, men like the legendary Lei Feng whose only desire in life was to be a screw, do not think for themselves; but Confucius said, "A gentleman (meaning a true man) does not act as a tool." (*Analects*, II. 12), and He Jingfu agrees. Admitting that he "blindly" entered the CCP at the age of eighteen (43), his years of wandering among the common people and actually studying the classics of Marxism–Leninism have led him to doubt the official orthodoxy and to believe in liberation of the mind and independent thought. He is glad that Sun Yue is suffering mental anguish, because it means there is still hope for her. As he tells her, "Sun Yue, if a person's thoughts were never confused in his whole life, that would only mean that he had never seriously lived or thought. Or else he was mentally retarded." (165) Such skepticism, he believes, is the first step toward the true liberation of the mind and freedom.

He Jingfu believes that he is very fortunate to be alive after the Cultural Revolution calamity, that his search for truth is the source of spiritual freedom, and that he now has the courage to "endure enerything" in order to maintain his independence of thought. In another conversation with Sun Yue, he quotes the Chinese proverb, "If you do not die in a great calamity, you must have good fortune in your later life," and she asks him what he means by "good fortune:"

> It is freedom, spiritual freedom. We are no longer superstitious, no longer following blindly, no longer

> immature and impetuous. Isn't that good fortune? And
> besides that, we are much more thick skinned than we used
> to be. (310)

Sun Yue laughs, but he goes on to explain that "thick skin" is a much
better defense of one's true "self-respect and character" than the usual
"hypocritical" way of saving "face":

> One of the results of our trials is that we have become
> thick skinned and no longer fear the loss of face when we are
> criticized and struggled against. And that can strengthen our
> courage and resolve to hold fast to the truth.
> You want to criticize me? Be my guest! Going to put a
> sign around my neck? Oh? No sign? You're not even
> going to take away my salary? That's much too easy! What
> great good fortune! Ha, ha, ha! (311)

The human body can be forced by tyranny to perform many hated
tasks, but the human mind is not that easily destroyed. If the body is
not utterly destroyed, the mind will persist in its perverse practice of
thinking for itself. In the same way human nature will cause a man to
fall in love and to think of his love as a goddess in spite of every
precaution the state takes against such unproductive foolishness. He
Jingfu falls in love with Sun Yue when they perform together in a
popular anti-Japanese play, "Put Down Your Whip," but he confines
his romantic protestations to his diary and, after the diary is made the
object of public ridicule and he learns of Sun Yue's marriage to Zhao
Zhenhuan, Jingfu becomes, "a wanderer, in love with a woman who
really doesn't love him, who is already married, and who can never
know about his love anyway." (26) A self-styled Don Quixote, Jingfu
never abandons his romantic love for Sun Yue; but he does come to
see her not as a goddess or a Dulcinea but as a kindred soul struggling
with all of the problems that beset Chinese intellectuals today. In the
end, his loyalty is rewarded and he wins his true love's heart and hand.
The future, a better future than China has ever known, just might
belong to them; but they will have to struggle together for it.

In keeping with the promise of a wedding to come, the final theme
that He Jingfu embodies is the trilogy of forgiveness, reconciliation,
and self sacrifice. He forgives Xu Hengzhong even before he learns
that Xu was forced into writing that 1957 wall poster against him. He

forgives Zhao Zhenhuan for his cruelty and insensitivity, urges Sun Yue to forgive him too, and feels a responsibility to help him to become a good person again. He even forgives the Communist Party despite all of the suffering their policies have caused him, his family, and the Chinese people. Through the symbol of his father's long–stemmed pipe, he demonstrates his belief in reconciliation be- tween "classes" in Chinese society, uniting the students (the intellectuals) and the peasants and workers as was the case during the May Fourth period. The spirit of self–sacrifice is apparent in his kindness to Hanhan and his willingness to step aside and allow Zhao Zhenhuan to plead for a reconciliation with Sun Yue as well as in his resolution to "endure everything" for the sake of truth and to struggle for a better future for the Chinese people.

One Western critic has suggested that He Jingfu may be compared to Prince Myshkin in Dostoyevsky's *The Idiot* (1869).[29] Myshkin is, of course, a far more complex and enigmatic character than He Jingfu or any other character in Chinese fiction since 1949, but there are a num- ber of striking parallels. Myshkin returns to St. Petersburg from a sanitarium in Switzerland where he has been treated for epilepsy; He Jingfu returns to C–City College after years of wandering in the Chinese hinterland "treating" his blind faith in Maoism with a dose of Marxist–Leninist rationalism, Chinese literature (we never really find out what he learned from the *Dream of the Red Chamber* nor why he carried China's greatest novel with him), and objective experience. Myshkin has a noble desire to save Nastassya Filipovna who is living under the protection of a man she does not love (compare the mysterious "he" in Sun Yue's dream); He Jingfu has a noble desire to save Sun Yue who has been living under the protection of a doctrine she does not understand. Dostoyevsky considers Myshkin to be a model for the salvation of Russia, and Dai Houying seems to believe that intellectuals like He Jingfu represent the future salvation of China. Myshkin alone remains unembittered and always kind–hearted in the face of the sordidness and shamelessness of the other characters' lives; He Jingfu alone remains unembittered, never pessimistic, and steadfastly idealistic despite the unprecedented violence and cruelty of Chinese life from 1957 to 1977. Myshkin is the victim of an extortion attempt, proves his innocence, then offers money to the guilty party in a Christ–like gesture of compassion; He Jingfu is the victim of political repression, is rehabilitated, and offers continued fealty to the Party and the doctrine that killed his mother, father, sister, and uncle and brought unimaginable misery to the Chinese people. Myshkin is filled with compassion and forgiveness for Rogozhin after the murder of

Nastassya, and, in the denouement, is sent back to the sanitarium suffering from incurable epilepsy, and does not even hear Madame Yepanchin say "It's time to be reasonable."[30] Finally He Jingfu is full of compassion and forgiveness for everyone, believes that Marxism is the highest form of humanism, and, in the denouement, is optimistic that the Party will help him publish his book on humanistic Marxism.

In conclusion we can say that *Ren a, ren!* is technically flawed in that the author fails to integrate her humanistic message into an artistically achieved form. She is too concerned to re–educate her readers in her newly discovered Marxist humanism and thus, despite the employment of "modernist" techniques derived from English literature of fifty years ago, ideology is still uppermost in her mind as she creates her semi–autobiographical fiction. At the same time, she deserves praise for her use of the first person narrative mode through–out in order to highlight the individual human being and, to emphasize individual human dignity and worth, to delineate moral character and to present inner conflicts and a confused struggle for psychological growth and independence of mind. The putatively Marxist ideology of radical secular humanism[31] seems to me, however, to be an insufficiently sharp tool to probe the depths of the human mind. Inspiring Dai Houying (Liu Binyan and Bai Hua as well) to re–emphasize the goodness and worth of the individual in an oppressively collectivist society, at the same time this ideology seems to blind them to, or at least severely inhibit them from probing the genuine evil that springs from human nature and seems to require more than a merely secular humanistic explanation in terms of materialistic determinism. As a consequence, I feel that books like *Ren a, ren!*, although they represent the re–awakening awakening of the highest form of idealism among PRC writers and intellectuals, have only just begun to depict the moral landscape of the chaotic years from 1957 to 1977. Perhaps only a generation of writers younger than Dai Houying can reach beyond the boundaries of Marxist ideology (humanistic or not) and realist poetics to probe deeper into the psychological depths of the individual and produce something closer to the poetry of prose.

VII. Beyond Realism: Neo-Romantic Fiction of the Post-Mao "Thinking Generation"

Before discussing some recent neo–romantic fiction, it might be well to review briefly the history of romanticism in modern China. To do so we need to begin with the European experience. European Romanticism as an all pervasive "mood" has had a tremendous influence on modern world culture and as a specifically literary movement has been the subject of lively critical debate throughout this century.[1] René Wellek long ago demonstrated the unity of Romanticism throughout Europe as "a closely coherent body of thought and feeling" in which the major writers shared "the same conceptions of poetry and of the workings and nature of the poetic imagination, the same conception of nature and its relation to man, and basically the same poetic style, with a use of imagery, symbolism and myth which is clearly distinct from that of eighteenth–century neoclassicism."[2] Aside from Wellek's three criteria of "imagination for the view of poetry, nature for the view of the world, and symbol and myth for poetic style,"[3] several other criteria of Romanticism must be recalled here for their impact on modern Chinese literature. Chief among these are the belief that poetry represents the spontaneous ex-pression of personal emotions; that literature is a form of self–expression and even prophecy; that the poet (writer) is a visionary prophet who sees more deeply than others, knows the shape of the future, and has a responsibility to enlighten mankind; and the optimistic belief that human development is limitless and all human beings have a limitless aspiration toward an infinite good. An iconoclastic belief in revolutionary political ideas of human rights and social justice derived from the French Revolution led to the presentation of fictional (often autobiographical) protagonists who are non–conformists and rebels of the Promethean type. Enthusiasm for and idealization of first the "noble savage" and then the peasant led to the serious treatment of lowly subjects in common language.

The other side of heroic Promethean individualism and self-assertion was Wertherian romantic melancholy and longing for love, for something permanent in a world of increasingly rapid change, for a piece of Eternity. Finally there was the endless quest for Truth, Goodness, and Beauty that alone gave meaning to life.[4]

There is a sentimental-erotic tradition in Chinese poetry, drama, and 43 narrative that begins with the *Chu ci* in the fourth to third century B.C., includes the poetry of Li Shangyin (812–858), Du Mu (803–852), and Li Yu (937–978), as well as dramas like the *Western Chamber (Xixiang ji)* and the *Peony Pavilion (Mudan ting)*, and China's greatest novel, the *Dream of the Red Chamber*. As expounded by C.T. Hsia, that tradition primarily lyricized the negative feelings of loneliness, melancholy, grief and despair and celebrated the martyrdom of unfulfilled lovers who are imbued with the capacities for love and sorrow, possess literary talent, and are caught up in the destructiveness of love gone mad or poisonous love. It is a "death-oriented" tradition of unfulfilled love, and traditional Chinese readers "always preferred the more lyrically intense scenes descriptive of the hero or heroine in a state of love's deprivation."[5] Through the intervention of Western literary models beginning with Lin Shu's translation of Dumas fils' *La Dame aux camélias* and Western ideas of dynamism beginning with Yan Fu's translations of Huxley and Spencer, the Chinese sentimental-erotic tradition expanded into an analogue of European Romanticism.

In Leo Ou-fan Lee's characterization of *The Romantic Generation of Modern Chinese Writers*,[6] we can see many of the criteria of European Romanticism transmitted to and transformed in China. The concept of literature as spontaneous self-expression — consonant as it seemed with the venerable Chinese concept of *shi yan zhi*[7] — led to an outpouring of autobiographical and confessional literature notable for its stress on spontaneity, intensity, subjectivity of personal emotions and celebration of the individual self. Both the individual psyche and the world of nature were explored as aspects of a passionate search for Truth, Goodness, and Beauty which were believed to culminate in the spiritual ecstacy of romantic love extolled as the height of both joy and suffering, honesty and sincerity, defiance of philistine conventions, emancipation and self-consciousness.

The modern Chinese literary intelligentsia, mostly of bourgeois or gentry background, were determined to use literature as an iconoclastic weapon to destroy the moribund values and customs of China's feudal past and to introduce what they believed to be (sometimes with little real understanding) standing) dynamically new and better values such as those of Western science, democracy, socialism, and communism. The European concept of poet as prophet reappeared in the guise of the Chinese writer (*wenren*) as a modern day prophet of a better future with a sense of mission to save the Chinese nation and make it rich and powerful through the liberation of the individual and a release of Faustian–Promethean energy and dynamism. Their ultimate goal was often a vaguely defined Utopia that would involve the total rebirth of a new people and the emancipation and happiness of all mankind. In the end, many of them turned to Marxism as a species of romantic religious faith that was accepted *in toto* through conversion experiences such as those of Guo Moruo and Qu Qiubai. Where the original European romantics attempted to merge with nature, the romantic young Chinese writers extolled a "mythified proletariat" and passionately attempted to merge with the masses and thus overcome their intolerably melancholy feeling of being "superfluous men."[8]

During the Anti–Japanese War, such romanticism died a natural death in the occupied areas and was replaced by the resurgence of a more traditionally influenced drama, essay, and anti–romantic narrative literature which was regarded, however, as an "unwelcome muse" after the establishment of the People's Republic; while the highly individualistic and idealistic spirit of the leftist romantics turned revolutionaries was either voluntarily abandoned (Guo Moruo and He Qifang) or forcibly subordinated to the demands of Communist Party discipline (Wang Shiwei, Xiao Jun, Ding Ling, Feng Xuefeng, and Ai Qing).[9]

During the entire Maoist era, from the Yan'an Forum on Art and Literature of 1942 until at least a year after Mao Zedong's death in September 1976, (with the brief exception of a few works of "critical realism" during the Hundred Flowers Movement of 1956 which earned their authors many years of enforced silence),[10] the literature of the People's Republic was gradually drained of almost all of the criteria of either European Romanticism or its Chinese analogue of the May Fourth era. Under various rubrics such as Socialist Realism, Revolutionary Realism, and Revolutionary Romanticism, PRC literature became an instrument of mass education in the Party's approved vision of reality — past, present, and future. For over thirty years we have witnessed the paradoxical spectacle of a putatively realistic narrative style that made a theoretical fetishism out of mimesis (the reflectionist theory of literature, or literature as imitation of the life of "the people") being employed in the composition of predominately illustrative or allegorical plots and the creation of model and minatory characters — villains, heroes, and heroines — closer to the intellectually vacuous esthetic types of "pure romance" than to the characters of either the realistic or romantic narrative traditions of nineteenth–century Europe or May Fourth China.[11]

The Cultural Revolution decade completed the eclipse of the May Fourth tradition, banishing even the residual "particle of art" that sometimes justified the search for quality in the Western study of the first seventeen years of PRC literature.[12] Gone were not only the individual personal vision of reality, autobiographical and confessional literature, but also all spontaneous expression of either joy or sorrow in a non–political context, personal intensity, subjectivity of personal emotions, interest in nature in its own right and exploration of romantic love without reference to the concepts of class and class struggle. What was left was only the counterfeit romanticism of heroic labor campaigns and the transformation of the countryside (Hao Ran's *The Golden Road*), patriotic celebrations of the war years (*Taking Tiger Mountain by Strategy* and other revolutionary Peking operas), and deification rites of Chairman Mao such as the operatic extravaganza *The East is Red*. By 1977 Chinese literature had reached one of the lowest points of its entire three thousand year history.

Although the primary interest of Western students of post–Mao literary phenomena has been focused on the resurgence of the realistic short fiction of social criticism discussed in chapter three, in the rest of this chapter I would like to explore the predominantly romantic elements in five middle length narratives (50–80 pages) by five young and previously unknown writers, writers who seem to me to represent what has come to be popularly known as the post–Mao "thinking generation." The sixth generation of modern Chinese intellectuals, the Cultural Revolution generation, they have been well described by the intellectual historian Li Zehou:[13]

> In their quest, they have rejected models of classical harmony and classical realism. They have forsaken conventional modes of expressing feelings. Have they not been wrenched by incomprehensible circumstances, by the decade of chaos they went through? Deceived by society, by all kinds of cruel schemes, they have experienced rebellion, search for power, factional strife, armed struggle, physical

labor, unemployment, crime. Every conceivable kind of hardship has shattered, tattered their souls. Politically outraged, emotionally wounded, intellectually doubt–ridden, they are reflective, full of feeling in their approach to the contemporary situation. They may be pessimistic, hesitant about the future, unable to grasp any prospect with certainty. They lack confidence, yet are grappling to comprehend. In extreme uncertainty, they remain hopeful. Commemorating the sorrows of their lost youth, they, nonetheless, quest for, experiment with truth. Haltingly, hobbling, they march on, . . . Their complex, confused thoughts and feelings have been poured into the stories, essays, paintings, poems of the last few years. Are these beautiful? They are the heartfelt outpouring of countless bitter experiences. But, I think, that their tattered souls will ultimately heal.. Beauty may yet achieve a new manifestation in their future.

Although insufficient as evidence for a new "romantic generation" in the May Fourth sense, these works do seem to demonstrate the reemergence of a significant number of the literary criteria characteristic both of European Romanticism and its Chinese analogue. Briefly, these works are all autobiographical and even sometimes confessional in nature,[14] they all involve a species of romantic melancholy and longing, a strong re–assertion of the individual self, an idealistic personal quest for Truth, Goodness, and Beauty, the concept of literature and art as a powerful form of self–expression, exposition of the value of love, and a renewed interest in external nature and natural imagery for the expression of human thoughts and emotions.

Since none of these works is currently available in English translation, let me first briefly introduce them in chronological order.[15] "Open Love Letters," by Qin Fan (the pen name of Mr. and Mrs. Jin Guantao), was first written in March 1972 and circulated in manuscript and mimeograph copies among educated youth for many dangerous years before its second draft of September 1979 was published in *Shiyue* (no. 1, 1980). It consists of a series of passionate letters, not all of them about love in the narrow sense, exchanged between four rusticated intellectual youth in which they pour out their feelings, thoughts, hopes and fears concerning everything from love and personal happiness to science, philosophy, and the fate of the nation. "A Winter Fairytale" (*Dangdai*, no. 3, 1980) is Yu Lojin's autobiographical account of her first divorce and a lyrical testament to the heroic greatness of her martyred brother Yu Loke, who was executed on March 5, 1970 for his opposition to the Chinese Communist policy of inheritance of class status. "A Spring Fairytale," published in a subsequently confiscated edition of *Huacheng* (no. 1, 1982), is the fifth draft revision of Yu Lojin's confessional revelation of the events surrounding her second divorce, her affair (romantic but non–sexual) with a 58 year old high ranking literary cadre in Peking, and the sordid affairs of her father and her entire family from the Anti–Rightist Campaign to the present. "When Sunset Clouds Disappear" (*Shiyue*, no. 1, 1981) is Li Ping's autobiographical account of the loss of love between the Red Guard son of a victorious PLA general and the unfortunate granddaughter of a defeated KMT officer. It also contains a realistic review of the Revolutionary Civil War and a romantic ascent of Mount Tai in search of Truth, Goodness, and Beauty. Zhang Kangkang's novella "Aurora Borealis" (*Shouhuo*, no. 3, 1981) is the story of a young woman's inner struggle to free herself from an unwanted engagement and her quest for life's spiritual meaning in an increasingly materialistic society.

As a result of their personal experiences during the Cultural Revolution era, some overtly political and some — betrayal by sweethearts or trusted friends — indirectly influenced by politics, all of our protagonists suffer from deep feelings of alienation and melancholy. The four main writers of "Open Love Letters" describe themselves as feeling lonely and isolated, misunderstood by and estranged from the philistine society around them, desolate, empty, and full of grief. In "Winter Fairytale," Yu Lojin describes herself as feeling so lonely, helpless, and a prey to melancholy when the young man for whom she has ended a loveless marriage of convenience refuses to marry her, that she finally understands Heine's ironic comments about love and even believes that Werther's suicide for love "was not an impossibility!" (103) She doesn't believe she'll ever be happy again and resolves to live only for her brother's spirit and to tell his true story (107). Nanshan, the heroine of "Sunset Clouds," experiences a tragic sense of injustice from childhood on due to her unequal treatment as a "class enemy" and therefore an outsider (105), and Li Huaiping, the male protagonist, suffers from a melancholy sense of loss (so many things "disappeared," *xiaoshi*, during the Cultural Revolution that the word reoccurs repeatedly) throughout the telling of his tale. Chen Qinqin, the heroine of "Aurora Borealis," is profoundly alienated from her fiancé and his young friends who are so easily pleased by China's new consumerism; feels lonely, isolated, and

depressed in the urban factory environment which compares
unfavorably with the comraderie that existed among rusticated youth in
the countryside (17), and she wonders why she always feels so
dispondent and at a loss (29,33,37).

The other side of this melancholy is a deeply felt longing for something more in life that these young protagonists know simply must
exist. Chen Qinqin yearns for "something" she cannot describe but
knows must exist (11), is always hoping for something unusual to
happen (17), and longing for something to move her the way the
idealistic youth she's read about in novels of the fifties were stirred by
the chance to realize their ideals in practice (29–30). She wants another kind of life, one that has more meaning than mere consumer satisfaction or factory routine (56). In the end she is attracted to the
protagonist Zeng Chu and his friends because she shares his belief that
the chief question is how to make life more rational and more
meaningful and that "only in the midst of our quest for justice and
truth will we discover authenticity, goodness and beauty." (50) Li
Huaiping also longs for many things. He longs to be a part of
Nanshan's loving and understanding family (104) and even more to
believe in something that can give meaning to life like Nanshan's new
found Christian faith (109). As a dialectical materialist he cannot understand or accept either Nanshan's or the wise old monk's religious
faith, but he envies the calmness and confidence it seems to give them
and he longs for deeper understanding (120). He is greatly impressed
by a three way discussion between Nanshan, the old monk, and a
foreign tourist concerning the history and nature of human civilization,
religion, and the meaning of life (129). These are the things about
which he has hitherto known all the answers and has only recently
begun to passionately pose the questions. Although he feels that these
questions are ultimately unanswerable, he cannot help yearning for
understanding. Lao Jiu, the chief male protagonist of "Open Love
Letters," has the same intellectual passion and the same determination
to make of his entire life a quest for Truth, Goodness, and Beauty.

Our young autobiographical protagonists' melancholy does not lead
to nihilistic despair, resignation, nor even less to cynical opportunism,
three common attitudes held by many other youthful characters in
these stories; but their longing for something better and their faith that
it must exist lead them to a powerful reassertion of the claims of
individual self. Such reassertion is manifested primarily in the
projection of a Promethean image of the young intellectual, in

inconoclastic rebellion against social convention, in active struggle for personal freedom and happiness, and in confessional writing as a form of self–vindication.

In their letters to Zhenzhen, the young woman whose youthful passion they wish to arrouse for the cause of science and national salvation, Lao Jiu and his friends project a highly romanticized view of the future role in Chinese society of young intellectuals, scientists, and artists imbued with lofty sentiments, fearlessly and resolutely seeking the light of knowledge (Promethean fire, 60) that alone can bring wealth and power to the Chinese nation (11,13). They have faith that only science can save the nation (48) and in their vision young scientists replace the poets of European Romanticism and the May Fourth writers as heroic prophets of a better future and warriors for Truth, Goodness, and Beauty (50–51). They even see themselves as replacing the older generation of communist revolutionaries who completed the physical revolution but cannot accomplish the real revolution in think- ing that will liberate the Chinese mind from the shackles of traditional feudalistic modes of thinking (57–59). Armed with scientific theory based on empirical observation ("practice"), they see themselves engaged in a Promethean struggle both with the forces of nature and the philistine society around them (62–63), and they are confident of victory even if it requires twenty to thirty years of struggle (58). As Lao Jiu writes:

> humanity's magnificent spirit of struggle can never be stopped. . . . Why should we rely on the age? We should rather let the age rely on us. The future belongs to our younger generation! (61)

Lao Jiu's iconoclastic rebellion against social convention takes the form of passive resistance to the Party's call for class struggle, refusal to participate in the factional struggles whipped up in college during the violent phase of the Cultural Revolution (19, 50–51), and opposition to the philistine moralism of corrupt social climbers like Tong Ru and Zhenzhen's sermonizing elder brother. He writes:

> I oppose and despise all those people who deprive young people of their time, life, love, and cherished desires . . . . I look down on the vulgarity of the moralists . . . and I care even less about public opinion and reputation. I respect feelings, true feelings from the depths of the human heart. (19)

Paralleling Lao Jiu's ideological iconoclasm is the direct action of the fictional characters Zhenzhen and Chen Qinqin and the real life Yu Lojin in freeing themselves from loveless relationships and struggling for individual happiness. After much soul searching, Zhenzhen and Qinqin both inform their fiancés — whom they recognize as having done them no real wrong and having no major fault other than passive acceptance of the status quo of 1970 and 1980 respectively — that they cannot marry them for the purely personal reason that they simply do not love them. Qinqin is particularly courageous in that she takes full responsibility for her actions and refuses to be a willing commodity despite the combined pressure of both sets of parents who believe that they have contracted the still normal form of arranged marriage (29,45, 55–56). In "Winter Fairytale," Yu Lojin asks for a divorce from the peasant husband she married for her parents's sake in 1971 and gives up her son (born of a wedding night rape — the only sexual relations in three years of marriage) in order to seek a kind of love and marriage that would lead to personal self–fulfillment and a life of sentiment. She suffers much pain and guilt and hopes at the time that she will never have to divorce again, but she chooses for herself because she has never loved her husband and refuses to go on living without the comfort of real love (99–102). Out of respect for her parents, she also keeps a great deal of her story private until their adverse reaction and a public campaign against her after her second divorce lead her to publish "Spring Fairytale."

All of these five pieces assert the rights of individual persons in opposition to social convention, but only Yu Lojin's much maligned "Spring Fairytale" matches the confessional heights, though not the literary brilliance, of such celebrated May Fourth stories as Yu Dafu's "Sinking" or Ding Ling's "The Diary of Miss Sophia."[16] Despite the fact that the names have been changed to protect the very few innocent people who appear in it, this work is nothing less than Yu Lojin's personal *J'Accuse* and an attempt to set the record straight and defend herself before the bar of public opinion after having become the naive victim of a combination of her own romantic fantasies and yearnings for love, an unconscionable philanderer, and a Communist Party morality campaign in the press (142,195,198). She herself believes it is immoral to publish someone else's intimate letters, but, in view of his public attacks on her, it seemed the only way to exonerate herself. Involving as it did the unsavory behavior of a high ranking cadre, her story was quickly banned by the authorities and probably failed to save her reputation except among the most liberal minded of urban youth.[17]

The use of autobiographical or even confessional writing as a form of individual self–assertion is further supported by the theory, most fully expounded in "Open Love Letters" but implicit in the other pieces, that art and literature are vehicles of personal self–expression and independent vision. Lao Xiemer and Lao Jiu repeatedly urge their wandering artist friend, Lao Ga, to be the courageous and independent creator of an art to match the age. As Lao Xiemer puts it:

> You should become a resolute and original artist! Don't forget that you are living in the seventh decade of the twentieth century. Our age does not like either philistine 'artists' making up 'revolutionary music' and 'revolutionary dances' according to a formula or vulgar songsters humming their touching little tunes. A soft heart cannot contain the epic changes that are taking place in the world today. You are an artist of our new age — you should be a bright torch and a sharp sword! (34)

Lao Jiu also encourages him to have courage and struggle to become "a true artist — rhapsodist of the feelings of the age." (19)

Lao Ga vows that he will "hold back my hot bitter tears and paint the picture of our present arduous struggle and our future joy in victory." (18) Confident that, "The bitter cold night rain must pass. /Most certainly to be followed by . . . / The radiant enchantment of the sun," he vows to continue his artistic wanderings with a "new song" in his heart. (67)

The high idealism of our young writers has been touched upon already, but the degree to which they remain dedicated to the virtues of Truth, Goodness , and Beauty in an age of cruelty, opportunism, and cynicism is quite remarkable. Although these concepts seem to be thematically inseperable in their works and each is believed to be present in the other two; we sense that Goodness is chiefly manifested in love (and friendship), Beauty in Nature, and that Truth — both the objective truth of facts and the subjective truth of feelings — is something they are all trying to present above all in their writings. The value of Truth is expressed most fully in the "Open Love Letters" of our young scientists.

Zhenzhen is a highly romantic young woman who begins "to pursue the values of Truth, Goodness, and Beauty which are quite without deception, to seek the harmony of the soul, and to look for a spiritual realm of lofty morality" (16) just before the Cultural Revolution breaks

out. Her experiences during the next few years cause her to despair of
the possibility of ever seeing her ideals manifested in actual human life
(30). She is eventually won back to the all important struggle by the
friendship of the artist Lao Ga and the love letters of the scientist Lao
Jiu who paints a passionate picture of the value of Truth.

Human life for Lao Jiu is a passionate and courageous search for
Truth (60–63) and Truth is a sharp sword (43) that can cut through the
repressive "mind forged manacles" of feudal modes of thought as well
as a bright light (50) that can lead mankind toward a better future.
Truth is freedom and human liberation itself (23, 48, 62,) and the
search for Truth requires the passionate commitment of a person's
"reason, will, and emotions."[18] This passionate longing to know the
truth about human life and the physical world is a primary aspect of
human nature intimately related to mankind's quest for Goodness and
Beauty and culminating in the best and most beautiful of human
emotions— love. As Lao Xiemer writes to Lao Jiu:

> From the point of view of philosophy, Truth, Goodness, and
> Beauty are rather shallow; but in love they are resplendent,
> and this is because it is only in ideal love that we find
> genuine Goodness and Beauty. (14)

A major theme of all five of these stories is the quest for romantic
love, a subject that was totally ignored in officially sanctioned Cultural
Revolution fiction but has become a regular part of most PRC fiction
since 1979.[19] In "Open Love Letters" the quest for love is completely
successful and in "Aurora Borealis" we can be confident that it
ultimately will be, while both "Winter Fairytale" and "Spring
Fairytale" are confessions of the same author's failure to find real love,
and "Sunset Clouds" records the stillbirth of love due to political circumstances. Despite these differences in outcome, the presentation of
romantic love as a key to personal fulfillment, as a basic human need
and a right, and the delineation of the meaning of love are similar
throughout each story.

"Open Love Letters" is preceded by an epigraphic quotation from
Oedipus[20] to the effect that, "Zeus sent down the fire of life, /Whose
lingering flames are still slowly burning," (4) and Lao Jiu's ecstatic
hyperbole, "Zhenzhen, our sacred love is the lightning of life," (63)
seems to leave little doubt that love is the fire of life. Elsewhere Lao
Jiu writes that, "Love is a keen edged precious sword glinting like a
rainbow with the blood of countless men. And my own blood shines

there too! It's all so wonderful!" (22) These two young people who
have never met and know each other only through letters come to love
each other out of the depths of a basic human need so often thwarted
in those days. As Lao Jiu writes to Lao Xiemer (in a manner
reminiscent of Yu Dafu's autobiographical protagonist in "Sinking"), ".
. . I suffer for my ideals. I'm not a computer or an automaton. I'm a
living human being. I need to love the person I love and to receive her
love also." (8) And Zhenzhen writes to him in the same manner, "I
believe that I need an ideal person to come and love me and I also
need to offer my own love unselfishly to him." (25)

   Love for the writers of "Open Love Letters" is not only a need and
a right but also a gift from God, a legacy from the development of
human civilization (36), a spiritual force that illuminates every other
aspect of human life (36), and a passion that motivates reason, thought
(50,37), the quest for Truth (60), and the great enterprise of one's life
work (21). As Lao Jiu writes, "human passion was never the natural
development of thought; on the contrary, great thoughts always came
from passion." (37) A truly human being "should have a passionate
love for Truth and dedication to great enterprise (60)." Such passion
and dedication constitute the most important basis for love and the
reconciliation between reason and passion, love and work, that gives
meaning to life. Lao Jiu probably speaks for many intellectual youths
of his generation when he writes:

> My love is completely merged with my work. I cannot
> distinguish between loving my work and loving my lover.
> Someone who passionately loves me, must certainly love my
> ideals and my work; and someone who loves my ideals and
> work will certainly become the person that I love. . . .
> Because loving such a person is simply loving one's own
> ideals, simply loving the great enterprise that we are
> struggling for.(21)

   In her two "fairytales" (romantic dreams of love betrayed), Yu
Lojin reveals herself as an almost hopeless romantic who falls instantly
in love first with a "pale young scholar" who cowardly refuses to marry
her and, several years later, with a high ranking cadre old enough to be
her father who enjoys her romantic attentions while secretly
orchestrating a public attack on her moral character. Having entered
into two loveless marriages of convenience, once with a peasant who
frequently beat her and once with a worker who had absolutely no
sympathy for her needs or understanding of her writing; her romantic

fantasies, though sometimes childish, are perfectly understandable.

On her first wedding night, after a humiliating marriage to a young peasant contracted in order to enable her "Rightist" parents to escape political persecution in Peking, she dreams of being given a little time to fall in love with her husband:

> He would tenderly embrace me, caress my hair, look at me with love, and treat me like a pitiful little child. He should comfort me like that; his hardships are much fewer than mine. Within that silent love, in that exchange of emotions, I would feel deep satisfaction, sweetness, and happiness. All the pain and unhappiness in my heart would disappear. . . (91)

What happens next is a frightening, disgusting, and insulting rape that leaves her feeling "like a fish that has just been gutted" and wondering "why has life given me so much suffering?" (91) For the next three years she uses a pair of scissors to protect herself from her husband's brutish sexuality.

After her second marriage, contracted this time to secure an apartment and a census registration for her entire family (172), she continues to dream of what it would be like to be married to someone who really knows how to love her. In bed, the only time her husband shows any "romantic" interest in her, or at the movies, she fantacizes about how her "imaginary lover/husband" would treat her:

> Oh, How wonderful it would be if only I had a lover/ husband like that! He would be so pleased when I kissed him in broad daylight; it would be everything he always wanted, his greatest happiness. And I would feel so grateful to him for not being so vulgar at night. It would be so wonderful! (146)

All this "degenerate woman," as the Peking press called her (212), really wants from love and marriage is a modicum of romance, tenderness, demonstrative affection, mutual respect and understanding. And she is extremely honest and moral, telling both of her husbands straight out that she never loved them — something they cannot really comprehend because they have no idea of romantic love — and insisting on going through two painful and humiliating divorces so that she can be free to marry for love. She feels that it is equally as immoral to continue inflicting mutual pain and unhappiness in a loveless marriage as it is to carry on an affair with a married man, and it is her insistence on marriage that most terrifies the hypocritical higher cadre she unfortunately becomes infatuated with.

Chen Qinqin is just as unhappy as Yu Lojin about the prospect of marrying someone with whom she has no romantic involvement and she also offers an interesting description of the meaning of love in a woman's life. On two occasions she recalls what a very wise "big sister," a third year university student from Peking, told her when they worked together on a rural commune in the Northeast:

> A life without love is incomplete, and love is simply finding your own 'self' in your love partner; it is making a higher demand on yourself, a better kind of longing and a haven. Setting up a family is easy, but love, well, it's very hard to find; and, for that reason, it's unlimited . . . A young woman who has never loved before is powerless to describe the image of her future lover or husband. Even a woman who has been loved many times cannot provide any formula for love. It is nothing less than the marvelously perfect correspondence of two spirits (hearts and souls, *xinling*), the embodiment of your own soaring emotions through the person of another living human being. (30, 41)

In her search for such a self–fulfilling love, Qinqin breaks off her engagement with the blameless but philistine young third class carpenter, Fu Yunxiang; rejects the possibility of loving a nihilistic and selfish young student like Fei Yuan who is afraid to advise her in her moment of crisis because it might harm his chances to study in Japan if anyone found out that he had advised an engaged woman to break it off; and seeks out the altruistic, optimistic, enthusiastic young intellectual and worker Zeng Chu, a participant in the April Fifth Movement and an idealistic believer in economic and political reform. Zeng Chu assures her that it may be a long time coming but the magnificently beautiful and mysterious northern lights (the aurora borealis) will be seen again in China (60). And that brings us to our final topic — the renewed interest in nature and the use of natural imagery to express human thoughts and feelings.

Artistically the most refreshing and enjoyable aspect of these five works is the extensive descriptions of external nature and the thematic and structural use of natural metaphors and symbols to express the

characters' thoughts and feelings about central human problems. It is
perhaps not surprising that these rusticated intellectual urban youth
(both the fictional characters and the authors themselves) might turn to
a contemplation of the beauties of the Chinese countryside for solace
and inspiration at a time when the human world appeared both cruel
and chaotic.

In one of her early letters to Lao Jiu, Zhenzhen provides an
emotional description of how the wonders of nature sustained her
when she was under constant attack in the summer of 1967. She
"broke out of her cage on a quest for freedom," took a five day train
trip to Chengdu, and a lengthy truck ride up winding mountain roads
to a small town called Ma'erkang. In the foothills, "a gust of warm
wind gently caressed my skin" . . . and "the miracles of nature unfolded
before my eyes." (9) The entire hill is covered with red azaleas
blooming "passionately and proudly." "Nature was smiling at me,
spring was smiling at me; could I possibly not smile too?" (10) When
the truck reaches the snow capped mountains and the landscape turns
bleak, her mood turns dark again until suddenly she spies a solitary
yellow flower. "Just then, in the midst of this world of ice and snow, I
happened to discover a small yellow flower. My heart leaped up
again: a flower! Such an indomitable life force!" (10) She then
apostrophizes the flower:

> How beautiful, a miracle of nature! You nameless yellow
> flower, growing here on this high mountain top with wind
> and snow howling all about; you are so resolute, courageous,
> and beautiful, so proud and utterly contemptuous of your
> cold cruel environment! (10)

As a young woman trapped in the cold cruel environment of the
Cultural Revolution, Zhenzhen's identification with the flower and her
employment of it as an inspiring symbol of resistance in adversity are
quite transparent. They remind one of the the inspiring symbolism of
the pine, the bamboo, and the plum blossom of classical Chinese
poetry.

The next morning, sunrise viewed from a bridge over a mountain
torrent sends her into an ecstatic meditation:

> The vast flood of emotions pent up in my heart needed to be
> liberated by that lofty mountain sunrise. . . . Oh, what a
> woundrously beautiful scene it was! The snow covered
> mountain top glistened with a myriad mythical hues of

> fabulously beautiful gemstones set sparkling by the soft clear reflections of the morning rays. . . . Tears burst the dam of my eyelids with an audible rush and the resplendency of that mysterious light was even more enchanting viewed through the mist of my tears. Was it not the shimmering light of an ideal world (*lixiang shijie*) . . . Only this snowy mountain peak, bright, lofty, and pure, could bring about the sublimation of my emotions and express my fantasies, and my hope! . . . A passionate longing to scale the heights of that mystical peak seized ahold of me . . . caused my spirit to be transported into a state of self–transcendence and emotional non–attachment, simultaneously blinded and totally aware. (10–11)

Such transports induced by the beauties of nature yield once more to the harshness of social reality, but when "recollected in tranquillity" by "that inward eye which is the bliss of solitude" (Wordsworth), they continue to provide our young protagonists with the inner strength to endure their daily hardships.

In "Winter Fairytale" Yu Lojin describes herself as receiving the same feelings of solace from nature when she spends three years (1967–70) on a "labor reform" farm:

> Nature did not admit that we were criminals. We dug fish ponds, planted wet rice, orchards, and vegetable gardens. . . did everything. We made demands on nature and at the same time enjoyed the happiness that nature gave us – at every sunrise, every sunset, every time the colors of the four seasons shown forth splendidly before my eyes, I felt so full of gladness at such indescribable beauty! I made a great many landscape sketches, intending to show them to my older brother to make him happy. (73)

She further describes the beauties of the countryside as inspiring in her the will to go on living:

> On the farm, whenever I saw that beautiful scenery, I felt that I was still alive, that I still had expectations from life . . . It really was quite beautiful there close to Bohai, the sky was deep blue and clean, the air fresh, and the clouds so lovely; as I sketched those scenes I felt it was a great pleasure. (73)

Throughout "Winter Fairytale," nature is employed as a direct indicator of Yu Lojin's emotions. Heaven sends tears of rain when her home is raided by the Red Guards (67), the night stars make her dream of freedom (78), and the stillness of an early spring evening provides the perfect mood setting for the passionate expression of love (97–98); but natural imagery is used most powerfully when she imagines that her executed brother's titanic spirit returns in a storm to match the storm of her emotions and to protest her being married off by her father to a peasant:[21]

> It was about to rain! Black clouds rolled up closer and rain fell in buckets. Lightning flashed overhead, shaking the vault of Heaven with the sound. A thunderbolt towered upright like a long silver dragon before crashing right into our little courtyard — only a couple of yards from our front door! We hurriedly closed the door and hid in the back of the house.
>
> 'Love and freedom! These are the two things everyone wants!'
>
> In the sound of the rushing rain and the violent roaring of the crashing thunder, I seemed to hear elder brother's angry and indignant scolding. . .
>
> 'Please don't scold me, elder brother! please don't denounce me through the crashing thunder!'
>
> I didn't really think of myself. . .
>
> All my feelings of sadness, pain, and despair became one confused mass with the sound of the rain and thunder. (84)

After she pleads with her elder brother's spirit embodied in the storm, crying out that, "I don't have the courage to act like you [and refuse to sell herself in marrage]! How else can our whole family survive?" (84); the storm gradually subsides, the rain stops, and she feels emotionally relieved as she steps outside and breathes in the fresh air. Then she notices the clouds scudding away:

> After the rain, the clouds flew quickly past in such a great hurry! I envied that rack of clouds — they were hurrying so quickly into the distance!
>
> The clouds were flying fast, moving forward, leaving with no regard for anything. . . Suddenly I had a sad realization: that is elder brother contemptuously moving on, moving on contemptuously! (84–85)[22]

In "When Sunset Clouds Disappear," nature is invoked in a number of ways, the most obvious of which is as a structural device that highlights the thematic content of the piece. Each of the four sections is given the title of the season of the year that matches its content, the first three parts employing conventional symbolism and the last part serving as an apparent reversal of a traditional Chinese symbol that turns out, on reflection, to be an even more poignant statement of the poetic tradition.

Part One, "Spring," describes the protagonist, Li Huaiping's youthful dream of love and romance with Nanshan as well as refering to his father's dream of building a New China from 1950 to 1966. Part Two, "Summer," describes another kind of romantic frenzy when young people's blood boiled with the moral fervor of a Children's Crusade and collective hate and fear covered the land from 1966 to 1969. Such was the nightmare experience of the Cultural Revolution that followed hard upon the youthful dreams of spring, and that was when Li Huaiping's Red Guard group raided the home of Nanshan's ex–KMT grandfather giving rise to shame and guilt that neither of them can ever forget. Summer is followed not by Autumn but by a "Winter" of discontent, as Part Three describes the years from 1970 to 1978 when both the dreams of spring and summer were blasted by the cold winds of the Cultural Revolution aftermath: rustication, political indoctrination, work, boredom, depression, and loss of ideological illusions. "There is a harmony in autumn," wrote Shelley, "and a luster in its sky, / Which through the summer is not heard / As if it could not be, as if it had not been!;"[23] Part Four, "Autumn," coming after "Winter" and describing the present day (1980) meeting of Li Huaiping and Nanshan, fourteen years after that terrible night in 1966, is ostensibly an attempt to turn away from the traditional poetic symbolism of autumn–equals–sadness and to affirm rather the agricultural meaning of autumn (akin to Shelley's autumn– equals–personal maturity theme) as a time of harvest.

After Li Huaiping hesitantly profers his proposal to become Nanshan's "lifetime companion," she rejects him and delivers a long lecture on the stages of life and human history, concluding that youth is the time for love (she's thirty–one) and they have missed it; but the loss of love is not, as Li so romantically insists, the loss of the most important thing in life. No. With stoic resolution she tells him that now is the time to work and reap a rich harvest from their life experiences and that work, without romantic love, will impart meaning to their lives. After having said all that though, and just before they part forever, her behavior ironically undercuts everything she has just said. She tells him to keep the book of English literature (an obviously romantic love token) that she loaned him on that dreamlike morning when they met just months before the Cultural Revolution. Watching her disappear into the distance after listening to her "not really totally understood words," Li Huaiping reflects that, "my every memory and all the dreams and yearnings of my youth also followed her into the distance. Right, the past is gone forever. Beginning today our field of vision should be turned toward a broader future." (134)

It seems to me that, despite the obvious attempt to convey a message similar to Wordsworth's famous "splendor in the grass" passage,[24] the discerning reader is nevertheless left here with the most melancholy prospect of a life of work without love which all the more poignantly reaffirms the traditional autumnal sadness of classical Chinese poetry. This post–Cultural Revolution fictional denouement seems strikingly similar also to the vision of hope that almost equals despair which M.H. Abrams discerned in the writings of Wordsworth and Shelley after the failure of the French Revolution to result in the expected regeneration of the human race. The young romantic writers of the post–Cultural Revolution era have already "suffer[ed] woes which Hope thinks infinite" and yet they doggedly continue "to hope till Hope creates / From its own wreck the thing it contemplates."[25]

During his ascent of one of China's holiest mountains, Mount Tai in Shandong Province, Li Huaiping meets a wise old man named Nanyue – a seventy–seven year old Chan Buddhist monk who seems to have just stepped out of a Tang dynasty *chuanqi* tale – and the contemplation of Nature's wonders becomes the occasion for a Socratic dialogue on the necessity of science , art, and religion in human life and civilization. Li and the old monk discuss science and philosophy in general terms on their way up the mountain, with Li taking the position that science is the only valid way to discover truth and the old monk arguing that science is limited in the kinds of knowledge it can supply and can never really supplant philosophy and religion.[26] When they reach a scenic overlook known as the Cloud Cutting Sword, Li witnesses the seldom seen phenomenon of a cloud front being cut in twain by the force of the wind pushing the clouds up against the towering sword–like peak. Despite his belief in science and disbelief in miracles of any sort, he is sore amazed and hard put to imagine what "mysterious power" so easily cuts the clouds assunder. (116–117) When the old monk rather prosaically explains the mysterious occurance as the result of a weather front, Li questions him about his, to Li, incomprehensibly persistent belief in religion. The old monk does not try to directly refute Li's dialectical materialist inspired atheism, but waits for a further opportunity to draw him out.

The opportunity comes when they reach the highest peak and Li becomes romantically rhapsodic about the inscription written there to mark the Gate of the Southern Heaven. Li exclaims that the inscription is beautiful, but the old monk, with tongue in cheek, counters that it's not true, containing both over- and understatements of fact. Li then insists that it is art and thus naturally contains deliberate exaggerations and fabrications, but the old monk remains unconvinced. "You must know," he says, "what is not beautiful is not true and what is not true is not beautiful; if the words do not match reality, how can you talk of art?" (118) At that, the young materialist launches into a long defense of the arts of music, dance, literature and so on, separating them out form science which seeks the truth, sometimes quite ugly truth, as in medicine, and justifying their existence in human life because of their expression of beauty. He concludes, "Therefore, things that are not true not only can be extremely beautiful but are, in fact, regularly the most beautiful of all." (118) The old monk again counters that Li is "completely wrong" because "scientific method" is the standard for evaluating," and Li is forced to argue further the indispensability of the arts and their expression of beauty because, "the search for scientific truth is not really the sum total of humanity's spiritual life." Without the beauty of the arts, "human history would become a dry dull textbook and human life would lose all of its joy!" (118–119)

At this point, having manipulated Li like Socrates's Thrasymachus into arguing his points for him, the old monk suddenly agrees with everything Li said about the value of art in human civilization and proceeds to make exactly the same sort of argument in favor of the value of religion. Li is right that science satisfies that part of human nature that thirsts after Truth; but human beings also crave Beauty, and thus the arts came into being and developed with the development of human civilization. "But," he continues, "you have forgotten something:

Besides Beauty, there is Goodness. Only the pursuit of Truth and Goodness and Beauty constitute the sum total of the spiritual life of mankind. The pursuit of Truth is Science. The pursuit of Beauty is Art. And the pursuit of Goodness is Religion. (119)

The supreme value of religion in human civilization, this old Buddhist monk concludes in a manner characteristic of his faith, is not in the Absolute Truth of its manifold doctrines, but in its ultimate concern with the pursuit of Goodness in human life. As he puts it:

> No matter how many different doctrines proliferate, their fundamental theme is to advise humankind, to make the strong magnanimous and the rich compassionate, to provide a comfort for life's pains and spiritual sustenance for the soul's emptiness. . . . As the ancients said long ago: my heart is my Buddha. So you see, religion is grounded in morality and really has nothing to do with (the realm of) science. (119)

Although Li Huaiping remains skeptical to the end, Li Ping's sympathetic exploration of the value of religion in human civilization and his artful reconciliation of the True, the Good, and the Beautiful as the essence of humanity's spiritual quest is a rare and welcome antiphonal counterpoint to the insistent chorus of anti–religious dogma that has always been a regular part of communist literature. Li Ping's discussion of the relationships between the True, the Good, and the Beautiful is very schematic and does not do justice to what is really a much more complex problem concerning the relationship between facts and values, but it is no more simplistic than the *Red Flag* theoreticians' exposition of Marxism and it is an attempt to transcend the extreme secular humanism of "vulgar Marxism" and open up a dialogue concerning the meaning of religion in society.

The thematic use of natural objects as symbols and metaphors for human thoughts and feelings is most fully developed in Zhang Kangkang's "Aurora Borealis," the first paragraph of which introduces the reader to a world of natural symbols:

> They were once tiny little droplets of water ascending from the broad earth filled with a longing to be purified, but they were sullied once more; and then in the cold temperature of those high altitudes they achieved rebirth in the shape of sparkling crystals — what marvelous news of the contemporary world do they bring back with them as they come floating down out of those boundless fields of clouds? Free, unrestrained, light, and airy, just like angels without a care in the world . . . The entire city reverberates with a soft silent

melody, while they dance enthusiastically to the rhythm that
they themselves have created — gaily self–transcendent . . .
Even the north wind that was lately so cold and cruel seems
to have become warm and gentle as it patiently and evenly
scatters the snowflakes everywhere, giving this bitter cold city
of ice and snow a fresh new mantel of white. (4)

The sight of this winter snowfall in Harbin transports Chen Qinqin
into her own romantic fairytale world peopled by an icy Snow Queen
and a beautiful Princess riding resplendently in an eleven horse sleigh,
until she remembers that she is engaged to be married and that will
surely be the end of her childhood innocence and the graveyard of her
dreams. (5–7) But the snowflakes will stay with her and even help her
in her struggle to be free of that unwanted engagement. They will
help her to see herself as seeking purer spiritual values in a world
poluted with narrowly material desires. (11–12) They will send her
unwanted fiancé off skiing ("imitating cadre children") and leave her
free to meet Fei Yuan and Zeng Chu and to think of a way out of her
predicament. (19) They will delay the coming of spring and the
unwanted marriage, perhaps even because they understand her inner
turmoil. (27–29) Though they may seem like a heavy weight pushing
down the blade of grass that is her heart struggling to be free, they will
help to transform her dropped glove into Zeng Chu's cactus plant and
save her just at the moment when she is about to give in to her family's
pressure to marry someone she does not love. At that point the first
paragraph, up to "marvelous news," will be repeated as she achieves
her own "rebirth" like a "sparkling crystal." (55–57)
    A little deer on her scarf pin that once filled her with longing to run
away (34), will reappear on an aluminum comb in a photographic
studio, flash in the mirror just like the aurora borealis, and give her the
courage to dart out of the studio without sitting for her wedding
pictures. (39–41) Like the cactus and the snow flakes, the deer will
reappear again in her dream as she rides it to freedom (55), the same
deer, no doubt, the sight of which running swiftly through the forest,
brought Zeng Chu back from the brink of despair and suicide in the
1970s. (58–59) In fact, Zeng Chu himself, running back to his ice
hockey (game of life) covered with bruises (wounds of the Cultural
Revolution decade), is "like a happy little deer, darting through the
forest, bounding over the snow, running swiftly without the least
thought of tiring. . . . . . " (45)
    Patterns of "ice flowers" on the schoolroom window recall to her
the beauty and hope of winter mornings in her childhood (the 1950s)

and the sense of innocence, mystery, and excitement surrounding her
first introduction to the aurora borealis, the dominant symbol of the
story. Her heart leaped up then when her uncle first told her of "those
inexhaustibly changing colors appearing in the north polar sky that no
artist's brush could ever create." (12) Her uncle was lost in the snowy
wastes trying to study those lights, but for Qinqin they remain "a
longed for dream world" all her life. (13) She looks for them in the
morning and evening clouds when rusticated to a farm in Suiyuan
Province at eighteen. Most people she asks have never even heard of
them, but she knows they can be seen, however rarely. Her fiancé
thinks that her longing to see the aurora borealis is all a lot of
foolishness. The selfish and nihilistic Fei Yuan looks upon them with
what William Blake called "single vision" and lectures her like a
physics professor. "Polar lights are a kind or arc or belt of brilliantly
flashing lights that is often seen in the clear night sky in the regions of
higher latitude. . . . even if they have appeared before, it is a
phenomenon governed by pure chance." And he warns her that the
northern lights are beautiful but illusory. "The northern lights,
perhaps they are very beautiful and very moving, but which of us has
ever seen them? . . . You must not go on believing that the world can
ever again experience any ideal divine light." (28) Ironcially, this
unbeliever has revealed the true symbolic meaning of the aurora.

The beautiful and moving ideal divine lights that are rerely seen are
a fitting symbol for all of the intangible spiritual values — love,
romance, freedom, idealism, the unending human quest for Truth,
Goodness, and Beauty, and mankind's desire to live a truly civilized life
— that these stories remind us make up the true meaning of human life.
When Qinqin glimpses the mysterious light in the photographer's
mirror for just a fleeting second, she blinks her eyes, sees only herself
in the mirror again, and then the omniscient narrator tells us her
thoughts:

> No, no, she definitely saw it. Only she alone is able to see
> that light of life; only she herself knows where it is. She is
> going to go on looking for it and not stop until she finds it.
> She can do without Fu Yunxiang, can do without the white
> uniform of her instrument assembler's job, can do without a
> comfortable new house; she can do without everything, but
> she cannot live without it! To lose it would be to lose life's
> genuine hope; then what would she do with her body
> bursting with youth? She does not really love Fu Yunxiang,
> not because he's too practical and lacks talent; it isn't for any

of those reasons. Just exactly why is it then? She cannot really say yet. Perhaps it's simply because of those sometimes hidden but sometimes manifest northern lights. Oh, human life: no matter how much the present situation leaves one disatisfied, you still cannot live like Fu Yunxiang and his friends, drifting aimlessly on a great murky yellow sea without any goal or any human quest. . . (39)

When Qinqin finally goes off to join Zeng Chu and his idealistic young friends who believe in Socrates's motto that "the unexamined life is not worth living" (50), she learns that he too has been fascinated by the aurora borealis and he assures her that, "no matter how disappointed we are, science proves that the northern lights have definitely appeared before. . . . No matter whether you've seen them or not or whether you admit it or not, they always exist. In our lifetime, we may or may not see them; but they will certainly appear sometime. . ." (50) The intangible values that have always made human life worth living do exist and can some day be manifested in the individual's everyday life and work. This is the genuine hope of China's post–Mao younger generation, and its literary expression does not seem to be a formalistic response to the Party leadership's call for stories that end on an optimistic note.

Any evaluation of the literary output of China's younger generation, and any evaluation the bulk of post–Mao literature, depends in the final analysis upon whether one applies historical or artistic standards.[27] From a historical point of view, we can only applaud the efforts of this post–Mao "thinking generation" to venture beyond the narrow confines of worker–peasant–soldier literature to express the thoughts and feelings of urban and intellectual youth in a language that begins to reflect both psychological depth and stylistic craftsmanship. The use of metaphor and symbol is at least a first start on the way to a more sophisticated and a more beautiful narrative presentation. Artistically, however, we must ask the deceptively simple question, "is it good art?" and many corollary questions, such as "is there any captivating or enchanting sense of mystery or discovery?" or "is there any sense of the profound irony that seems to lie at the heart of human experience in our century?" Our answers to these questions must, I feel, be negative. The artistic qualities of these more or less romantic works by post–Mao youth have not yet even reached the level of the romantic generation of the May Fourth Era (not to mention world literature), and we must turn back once more to the historical situation for an explanation of this fact.

The youthful literati of the May Fourth Era were in conscious revolt against the traditions of the past, and yet, as the children of the upper classes, they were steeped in the literary traditions of that same Chinese past. They had at their command an enormous number of literary examples to follow, to reject, to parody, and to transform and modernize. Furthermore, although they lived in a time of chaos and disintegration, they had access to any element of the world literary tradition they cared to explore and expropriate ("correctly" or not) for their own purposes. The post-Mao "thinking generation" is also in revolt against politics as a result not only of helplessly watching the suffering of the masses but also of their own bitter experiences at the hands of political commissars. Their renunciation of the Maoist world view is equally as striking as the 1920s revolt against the moribund values of official Confucianism. But where are they to turn for a literary tradition with which to express themselves? The most important literary—historical distinction between them and the May Fourth generation is that they have been doubly robbed of any viable literary traditions. The works of the feudal past were closed to them during their formative years coinciding with the Great Revolution Against Culture (*dage wenhua ming* as the humorist Hou Baoling so aptly termed it) and they were equally cut off from all world literary trends. Experiences they have had and plenty, enough for at least a dozen great works like *War and Peace* and *The Possessed*, or the more recent *Tin Drum* and *One Hundred Years of Solitude*, but it will take time for them to rediscover both their own rich literary heritage, their own language, and the newly accessible and immensely popular literary output of the modern world. And it will require even more time for them to learn how to formulate their own ideas and express their powerful emotional experiences artistically on the basis of the aesthetic lessons learned from "the past, the present, China, and the world." Finally, although classical Chinese and modern Western literatures are once more available, the pressures for ideological conformity are tremendous and these young peoples' inner need for a belief system seems equally pressing. Perhaps the most serious danger facing them as writers (leaving aside the equally troublesome political question of getting published in Party-State controlled journals) is that they will come to believe they have found *the answer* — the ideological solution to human problems which they still seem to be seeking — long before their thinking or their writing has come to grips with the terrible depths of human experience in the past thirty years in China, that is, long before they realize what all great modern writers know — there is no way to understand and to depict the problematic nature of human life in merely ideological terms. I only hope that this does not happen and that writers like Li Ping and Zhang Kangkang can continue their search both for depth of understanding and literary excellence of presentation.

Notes

Notes to Chapter One
Please see first page of Bibliography for abbreviations used in Notes.

1. *Mao Tse-tung on Literature and Art* (Peking: Foreign Languages Press, Second Revised Translation, 1967), pp. 25 and 30. Bonnie S. McDougall, *Mao Zedong's "Talks at the Yan'an Conference on Literature and Art": A Translation of the 1943 Text with Commentary* (Ann Arbor: Center for Chinese Studies, the University of Michigan, 1980), pp. 75 and 78.

2. For a detailed discussion of the effects of Mao's literary theories on Chinese communist literature before the Cultural Revolution, see T.A. Hsia, "Twenty Years After the Yenan Forum," CQ, no. 13 (January–March 1963): 226–53.

3. Merle Goldman has thoroughly analysed these recurrent cycles in two excellent studies, *Literary Dissent in Communist China* (Cambridge: Harvard University Press, 1967) and *China's Intellectuals: Advise and Dissent* (same press, 1981).

4. *Peking Review*, no. 36 (2 September 1977) has a complete text.

5. CQ, no. 72 (December 1977): 873.

6. Ibid., pp. 874–875.

7. Ibid., p. 877.

8. *Documents of the First Session of the Fifth National People's Congress of the PRC* (Peking: Foreign Languages Press, 1978), pp. 125–172 contains a complete English translation.

9. *The Constitution of the People's Republic of China* (Peking: Foreign Languages Press, 1975), article 12.

10. See note 8 above.

11. *Communist China 1955–1959, Policy Documents with Analysis* (Cambridge:Harvard University Press, 1962), p. 291 has a translation of Mao's six criteria of 1957.

12.   Jerome Cohen, "China's Changing Constitution," CQ, no. 76 (December 1978): 835–837. See also Cohen's article, "Due Process?" in Ross Terril, ed. *The China Difference* (N.Y.: Harper Colophon, 1979), pp. 237–259; Chiu Hungdah, "China's New Legal System," *Current History*, vol. 79, no. 458 (September 1980): 29–32 and 44–45; and Leng Shao–chuan, "Criminal Justice in Post–Mao China," CQ, no. 87 (September 1981): 440–469.

13.   *Peking Review*, no. 52 (29 December 1978): 6–16 has the full text of the 22 December "Communique."

14.   CQ, no. 78 (June 1979): 405–408.

15.   Ibid., p. 411; *Peking Review*, no. 9 (2 March 1979): 15–17; *Chinese Law and Government*, vol. X, no. 3 (Fall 1977) is devoted entirely to "The Case of Li I–che."

16.   CQ, no. 79 (September 1979): 663–666, and note 12 above.

Ibid., pp. 650, 670.

18.   Sixteen of the key speeches from this congress are translated in Howard Goldblatt, ed., *Chinese Literature for the 1980s* (Armonk, N.Y.: M.E. Sharpe, Inc., 1982). All my quotations are from this source unless otherwise noted, and page numbers are given in parentheses in the text.

19.   The title of this "Summary" concludes ". . . *with which Comrade Lin Biao Entrusted Comrade Jiang Qing.*" HQ, no. 9 (1967): 11–21, English translation in *Important Documents on the Great Proletarian Cultural Revolution in China* (Peking: Foreign Languages Press, 1970); pp. 201–38.

20.   D.W. Fokkma and Elrud Kunne–Ibsch argue quite persuasively that the literary policies of 1966–76 were a direct extension of Mao's 1942 ideas. See their *Theories of Literature in the Twentieth Century* (New York: St. Martin's Press, 1977), pp. 104–115. See also Fokkma's article, "Chinese Literature Under the Cultural Revolution," *Literature East and West*, vol. 13 (1969), pp. 335–59 for a survey of early Cultural Revolution literature and "the theory that the literary text is never finished," but must be repeatedly revised to keep pace with ever–changing Party policies.

21.   *Shanghen wenxue* and *baolu wenxue* were ˙ terms of opprobrium (the latter from Mao's *Yan'an Talks*) used to attack these works for only depicting the dark side of Chinese social life.

22.   Shao Quanlin's ideas on the depiction of "middle characters" who make up the majority at every level of Chinese life and are unconvinced or uncommitted with regard to socialism–communism was debated at a meeting in Dairen on 2–16 August 1962, excerpted in WYB (August–September 1964), and denounced during the Cultural

Revolution. See Kai-yu Hsü, ed. *Literature of the PRC* (Bloomington: Indiana University Press, 1980), pp. 642–652. The combination of "revolutionary realism" with "revolutionary romanticism" was a slogan put forth for Mao Zedong by Zhou Yang in 1958 to replace the previously venerated (1953–58) Russian concept of Socialist Realism. Zhou Yang, "Xin minge kaituole shige de xin daolu" (New Folk Songs Open a New Road for Poetry), HQ, no. 1 (1958): 33–39. The slogan implied a further move away from the truthful depiction of reality. Such "revolutionary romanticism" became completely dominant during the Cultural Revolution.

23. Reprinted in ChL, no. 1 (1980): 83–91, Mao's "A Talk to Music Workers, 24 August 1956," applied the slogan "socialist in content and national in form" to the "critical inheritance" of the past, both Chinese and Western, a concept derived from earlier Marxist literary theory, discussed by Mao in his *Yan'an Talks*, and repeated most prominently by Zhou Enlai in a June 1961 speech, "Zai wenzi gongzuo zuotanhui he gushipian chuangzuo huiyi shang de jianghua" (Talk at a Forum on Literary and Art Work and a Conference on the Creation of Feature Films), HQ, no. 3 (March 1979): 2–16 and ChL, no. 6 (1979): 83–95.

24. Zhou Yang's entire speech was carried in both RMRB and GMRB of 20 November 1979 as well as WYB, nos. 11–12 (1979). Further excerpts are in ChL, no. 3 (1980): 38–51.

25. Compare D.W. Fokkema, "Strength and Weakness of the Marxist Theory of Literature with Reference to Marxist Criticism in the People's Republic of China," in John J. Deeney, ed. *Chinese-Western Comparative Literature Theory and Strategy* (Hong Kong: The Chinese University Press, 1980), pp. 113–128.

26. Zhou Yang, "The Path of Socialist Literature and Art in China," excerpted in Kai-yu Hsü, ed. *Literature of PRC*, pp. 440–448.

27. Harold Swayze, *Political Control of Literature in the USSR, 1946–1959* (Cambridge: Harvard University Press, 1962), pp. 113–14.

28. Literary critical ideas current for over thirty years, such as the unity of content and form or the ways in which style expresses meaning, are foreign to Chinese Marxist literary criticism to an extent that it hardly qualifies as "literary" criticism.

29. Zhou Yang, note 26 above, p. 443.

30. My account of the events surrounding this controversial play are based on the *China News Analysis*, no. 1205 (24 April 1981) and all of the references given there. The fifth and most important scene of the play is brilliantly translated by Edward M. Gunn in his book

Twentieth Century Chinese Drama (Bloomington: Indiana University Press, 1983), pp. 468–474. See chapter 3, note 62 for complete translation.

31. Hu Yaobang, "Zai juben zuotanhui shang de jianghua" (Talk at the Discussion Meeting on Plays) was first published in WYB, no. 1 (1981), then in pamphlet form, and later in XHWZ, no. 3 (1981): 126–137. My translations are from the latter source with page numbers in the text.

32. Mao Zedong, "On the Correct Handling of Contradictions Among the People," *Selected Works of Mao Tsetung*, vol. V (Peking: Foreign Language Press, 1977), pp. 384–421; in Chinese in *Mao Zedong xuanji*, vol. 5 (Beijing: Renmin chubanshe, 1977), pp. 363–402.

33. Note that these sentiments of Hu Yaobang would seem to be one of the main themes of Bai Hua's film *Bitter Love*; but by the time Hu attacked it in 1981, the dialectic of history had made another turn and Bai Hua had fallen behind.

34. A film version of *What If I Really Were?* was produced in Taiwan, but I have not yet been able to see it.

35. Zhou Yang's speeches, "Jiefang sixiang, zhenshide biaoxian women de shidai" (Emancipate Thinking, Truthfully Reflect Our Age), given on 10 February to this same Drama Forum, WYB, no. 4 (22 February 1981) and BR, no. 15 (13 April 1981): 23–25 and "Jianchi Lu Xun de wenhua fangxiang, fayang Lu Xun de zhandou chuantong" (Persist in Lu Xun's Cultural Direction and Develop Lu Xun's Militant Tradition), given on 25 September 1981 at the Lu Xun Centennial, RMRB, 28 September 1981, ChL, no. 1 (1982): 99–118 both reiterate and elaborate Hu Yaobang's position in the same manner Zhou used to interpret Mao's ideas to the writers.

36. Sha Yexin, "Chedan" (Talking Nonsense), WYB, no. 10 (1980): 7–11.

37. Bai Hua is the subject of Chapter 5 below. Su Shuyang is the author of the anti–Gang of Four play *Danxin Pu* (Loyal Hearts), *Renmin xiju* (May 1978): 16–54 and ChL, no. 10 (1978): 23–105. See *China News Analysis*, no. 1205, (24 April 1981): 6.

38. *Lunyu*, VIII.4 The passage is attributed to Confucius' disciple Zeng Zi. D.C. Lau, *The Analects* (Penguin Books, 1979), pp. 92–93.

39. It is a tribute to the editors of RMRB that Zhao Dan's testament was published on 9 October 1980, two days before his death. My quotations are from the English version published in ChL, no. 1 (1981): 107–111. ChL, no. 4 (1980): 73–92 contains an article by Patricia Wilson on Zhao Dan's "legendary" career in Chinese films.

40. *Dongxiang*, no. 3 (1981): 8–11 and Sha Yexin, "Juben chuangzuo duanxiang lu" (Record of My Thoughts on Playwriting), nos. 1–3, in *Shanghai xiju*, nos. 3, 5, and 6 (1980): 59–60; 22–23; and 2–5 respectively. Number 2 is subtitled "The Arts and Politics," and number 6 is "Concerning *What If I Really Were?*"

41. JFJB 10, 17, and 20 April 1981. Bi Hua and Yang Ling, eds., *Bai Hua jinzuo xuan* (Hong Kong, 1981) reprints the article entitled "Sixiang yuanze burong weifan -- ping dianying wenxue juben *Kulian*" (The Four Fundamental Principles Cannot Permit Betrayal -- A Critique of the Filmscript *Kulian*), pp. 223–230.

42. *Kulian* was first published in the literary quarterly *Shiyue* (October) in September 1979. It was written by Bai Hua and Peng Ning in April and May of that year and had already been made into a movie directed by Peng in 1980 and 1981. The text was reprinted in *Shidai de baogao* (Report of the Age), special edition for 23 April 1981, pp. 5–8 as part of their attack in support of the *PLA Daily*'s position. Peng Ning was not attacked by name, and so I have considered Bai Hua only in this chapter.

43. Liao Gailong, "Zhonggong 'gengshen gaige' fangan" (Draft of Chinese Communists' *gengshen* Reforms) QSND (March 1981): 38–47. *Gengshen* is 1980; this "draft document" was circulated throughout the year within the CCP.

44. See BR, no. 27 (6 July 1981) for a full report on this meeting.

45. BR, no. 36 (7 September 1981): 13. Deng Xiaoping, who was himself very much opposed to Jiang Qing's cultural policies, has all along been the main force behind Hu Yaobang and Zhou Yang's efforts to reestablish Party control over all aspects of cultural life. See, for example, his unpublished speech of 16 January 1980 (one month before Hu's Drama Forum speech) in which he called for such control and also announced that the "four big freedoms," including the freedom to put up big character posters, would be removed from the 1978 Constitution. The speech was printed in ZM (Hong Kong), no. 29 (March 1980): 11–23.

46. BR, no. 27 (6 July 1981), p. 14.

47. BR, no. 38 (21 September 1981): 15.

48. That is, as an "objective law," i.e., an inevitable consequence of a CCP–style socialist society.

49. Wang Xizhe, principle author of the famous 1974 *Li Yizhe dazibao*, was arrested in May 1981 and was given a 14–year sentence for "inflamatory counter–revolutionary propaganda" in May 1982 by the Canton People's Court. See QSND (August 1982): 42–43 and many previous reports of the Hong Kong Students' Associations's

1981–82 attempts to ascertain the truth about Wang's case as reported in this same journal.

50. BR, no. 38 (21 September 1981): 13.

51. See Merle Goldman, "The Political Use of Lu Xun," CQ, no. 91 (September 1982): 446–461 for a historical survey; T.A. Hsia, "Lu Hsün and the Dissolution of the League of Leftist Writers," in Hsia's *The Gate of Darkness* (Seattle: Univ. of Washington Press, 1968), pp. 101–145 for Lu Xun's actual relations with CCP leaders during his lifetime; and John Chinnery, "Lu Xun and Contemporary Chinese Literature," and W.J.F. Jenner, "Lu Xun's Last Days and After," in the same CQ above, pp. 411–421 and 424–445 for Lu Xun's continuing inspiration to PRC writers who try to use irony to satarize moral and political corruption. BR, no. 40 (5 October 1981): 11–16 has an English translation of Hu's September 25 speech at the Lu Xun Centennial.

52. HQ, no. 19 (7 October 1981): 9–16.

53. Written on 25 November, the letter was published in the JFJB of 23 December, the RMRB of 24 December, WYB, no. 1 (1982), and XHWZ, no. 2 (1982): 158–159. For an analysis, see Mu Fu, "Yichang daijia gaoang de biaoyan: Bai Hua shijian huigu" (A Costly Performance: A Retrospectus on the Bai Hua Incident) QSND (February 1982): 12–14.

54. Although *Kulian* was never shown, Bai Hua did continue to write and be published, scoring a popular triumph in the spring of 1983 with his historical play "Wu Wang jinge Yue Wang jian" (The Wu King's Golden Spear and the Yue King's Sword), SY, no. 2 (1983): 65–95, a study of the moral corruption brought about by an excessive will to power on the part of the legendary Yue King Gou Jian that seems to be a transparent critique of Mao Zedong's later years in substantial agreement with the present official assessment, but that (unlike *Kulian*) avoids a general condemnation of the communist era by treating the familiar "power corrupts" theme more in terms of universal human psychology than of Marxist historical inevitabilities of any sort. A RMRB article of 10 May 1983 warned audiences away from taking the "historical lesson" of the play as a direct reflection of present day realities in what appeared to be a laudable attempt to protect Bai Hua by forstalling a Maoist attack on his work. See Huai Bing, "Ping Bai Hua xinzuo 'Wu Wang jinge Yue Wang jian'" (A Critique of Bai Hua's New Work . . .), ZM (October 1983): 54–55.

55. "Nuli jianshe gaodu shehui zhuyi jingshen wenming" (Work Hard to Establish a High Level Socialist Spiritual Civilization), HQ, no. 19 (1982): 2–9; English text in BR, no. 45 (8 November 1982): 13–17.

56. Complete English text in BR, no. 52 (27 December 1982): 10–29. See also, Peng Zhen, "Report on the Draft of the Revised Constitution. . .," a speech made on 26 November 1982 to the National People's Congress, in BR, no. 50 (13 December 1982): 9–24.

57. About the same time that the new 1982 Constitution was being debated and the HQ article was being prepared, Hu Yaobang repeated most of the same points in his speech to the 12th National Congress of the CCP, 1 September 1982, "Create a New Situation in All Fields of Socialist Modernization," BR, no. 37 (13 September 1982): 11–39. See especially Part III, "Strive to Build a High Level of Socialist Spiritual Civilization," in which he stressed the necessary communist ideological content of all education, science, art, and literature. Premier Zhao Ziyang's, "Report on the Work of the Government," delivered on 6 June 1983 to the National People's Congress, continued the attack on "the tendency towards bourgeois liberalism . . . and disregard for social consequences" of art and literature that had begun in 1980. BR, no. 27 (4 July 1983): I–XXIV, especially pp. XVIII–XIX.

58. Among the plethora of articles on the "alienation," "modernism," and "spiritual pollution" campaigns, the following are most useful: Mu Fu. "Yihua lilun yu jingshen wuran" (The Theory of Alienation and Spiritual Pollution). QSND (December 1983): 56–60. Su Liwen. "'Xiandai pai' zuojia mianlin chongji" ("Modernist" Writers Face Attack). QSND (December 1983): 62–64. Lo Bing. "'Fan wuran' tuichao toushi" (Perspective on the Decline of the Spiritual Pollution Campaign). ZM (January): 9–12. Lee Oufan. "'Xiandai zhuyi' wenxue suo mianlin de 'wuran'" (The "Pollution" that "Modernism" Faces). QSND (January 1984): 78–79. The first issue of the *Journal of Modern Chinese Literature* (September 1984) is devoted to an analysis of "modernism" in Chinese literature.

Notes to Chapter Two

1. *The following articles on the realism dabate are particularly useful*: Chen Shen, "Chong du 'Xianshi zhuyi guangkuo de daolu.'" (Re–reading 'Realism, the Broad Road'), *Yanhe*, no. 5 (1979): 63–71. (On Qin Zhaoyang's controversial concept of realism.) Huang Xiuji, "Lu Xun de 'bingcun' lun zui zhengque." (Lu Xun's Theory of Coexistence is Most Correct), WPL, no.5 (1978): 27–36. Li Jie, "Jiaru wo shi yige zuojia." (If I Were a Writer), *Yuhua*, no. 7 (1979). Li Xiaoba, "Cong 56–nian He Zhi de wenzhang tanqi." (Remarks Prompted by He Zhi's 1956 Article), *Yanhe*, no. 4 (1979): 32–38. (Also on Qin Zhaoyang's concept of realism.) Liu Binyan, "Guanyu 'xie yin'an mian' he 'ganyu shenghuo.'" (On 'Writing about the Dark

Side' and 'Interfering in Real Life'), SHWX, no. 3 (1979): 49–57. Qin Mu, "Fayang guangda geming wenxue de xianshi zhuyi chuantong." (Carry Forward the Great Tradition of Revolutionary Realism), *Nanfang ribao*, 2 April 1980. Su Shuyang, "Cong shiji shenghuo cufa suozao renwu." (Create Characters from Real Life), *Renmin xiju*, no. 5 (1978): Wang Chunyuan, "Guanyu xie yingxiong renwu lilun wenti de tantao." (Exploration of the Theoretical Question of Writing About Heroic Characters), WXPL, no. 5 (1979). Wang Meng, "Zhengkai yanjing, mianxiang shenghuo." (Open Your Eyes and Look at Life), GMRB 5 September 1979. Xu Congzhe, "Zhonggong de wenyi luxian." (The Chinese Communits Literary Line), QSND (December 1979): 15–19. (Contains a summary of the 1979 literary debates.) Zhou Yang, "Zhou Yang on Reality in Literature and Other Questions," ChL, no. 1 (1980): 92–96. (An October 1979 interview with the editors.) "Zuojia you quanli tichu shenghuo zhong de wenti." (Writers Have the Right to Raise Questions About Life), WYB no. 9 (1980).

2. Liu Xinwu, "Shenghuo de chuangzaozhe shuo:zou zhei tiao lu!," (The Creator of Life Says: Take This Road!), WXPL, no. 5 (1978): 53–64. Lu Xinhua, "Tantan wo de xizuo *Shanghen*," (Talking About My Exercise *Shanghen*), WHB 14 October 1978. Xiang Tong, "Wenyi yaobuyao fanying shehui zhuyi shiqi de beiju — cong 'Shanghen' tanqi." (Should Literature and Art Reflect Tragedies in the Socialist Era — Beginning with *Shanghen*), GMRB 3 November 1978.

3. *On the 'praise and blame" debate, see*: Heng Guo, "Cong 'Gede pai' xiangqi." (Thoughts on the "Praise Faction"), CJWY, no. 7 (1979): 76–77. Hu Yu, "Rang 'baihua zhengming' de fangzhen zai wenyijie kaihua jieguo." (Let the 'Hundred Schools Contending' Line Blossom and Bear Fruit in Literature and Art), WYB, no. 7 (1979): 61–64. Li Jian, "Gede yu quede." (Praising Virtue and Lacking Virtue), *Hebei wenyi*, no. 6 (1979). Reprinted in RMRB 31 July 1979. Wang Ruowang, "Chuntianli de yige lengfeng." (A Cold Wind in Spring), GMRB 20 July 1979; and, "Tan wenyi de 'wuwei er zhi.'" (Discussing 'Ruling by Nonaction' in Literature and Art), HQ, no 9 (1979). Yan Xiu, "Lun 'Gede pai.'" (On the 'Praise Faction'), *Dushu*, no. 7 (1979). Reprinted in XHYB(WZB), no. 12 (1979):168–175.

4. *On literature and democracy, see*: Fang Yumin, "Tushuguan bixu simen dakai." (The Libraries Should Open Wide Their Doors), *Dushu*, no. 2 (May 1979): 11–16. "Minzhu yu yishu." (Democracy and Art), *Shanghai wenyi*, no. 11 (1978): 4–10. Xia Zhennong, "Meiyou minzhu jiu meiyou shehui zhuyi." (Without Democracy There Is No Socialism), *Fudan xuebao (shehui kexue ban)*, no. 1 (1978).

5. *On humanism in literature, see*: Lu Yifan, "Ping jianguo yilai dui 'rendao zhuyi' de pipan." (A Critique of Criticisms of 'Humanism' Since the Founding of the PRC), *Xin wenxue luncong*, no. 3 (1980). Yu Jianzhang, "Lun dangdai wenxue chuangzuo zhong de rendao zhuyi chaoliu." (On the Humanist Tide in Contemporary Literary Creation), WXPL, no. 1 (January 1981).

6. W.J.F. Jenner, "1979: A New Start for Literature in China?" CQ, no. 86 (June 1981): 274–303, for analysis and further bibliography. Howard Goldblatt, ed. *Chinese Literature for the 1980s* contains the outspoken speeches of Bai Hua, Ke Yan, Chen Dengke, and Liu Binyan at the Fourth National Congress of Writers and Artists.

7. "'Wenyi de shehui gongneng' — wuren tan." (A Five Person Discussion of 'the Social Function of Literature and Art'), WYB, no.1 (January 1980): 29–36.

8. Kaiyu Hsü, ed. *Literature of the PRC*, (Bloomington: Indiana University Press, 1980), pp. 90–102 is a translation of Li Zhun's model story, "Can't Take That Road" (Buneng zou neitiao lu), originally published in the *Henan ribao*, 20 November 1953.

9. See Chapter Four, note 20.

10. See Li Zhun's short story "Mango" (Manguo), RMWX, no 10 (1981): 35–42.

11. "Bujian baodao de yici wenyi zuotanhui — ji Huangshan bihui." (An Unreported Literature and Art Discussion Meeting — Report on the Huangshan Writers' Conference), QSND (January 1981): 98–105.

12. Paul and Rita seem to be characters in some revolutionary novel that I have been unable to identify.

13. Zhang Jie, "Ai, shi buneng wangji de," BJWY, no. 11 (1979); translated in Siu and Stern, *Mao's Harvest*, pp. 92–106.

14. In light of what is currently known about Karl Marx's private life, these remarks may seem as humorous to us as they are serious in the PRC.

15. *The Imposter* is another name for the play *What If I Really Were?* Liu Ke, "Fei Tian," SY, no. 3 (September 1979), is the story of a young woman who is raped by a high ranking PLA officer.

16. For a sadly ironic fictional depiction of the inability to say "no" to the Party, see Dai Qing's 1981 story "No" (Bu) in Dai Qing, *Bu*, (Guangzhou: Huacheng chubanshe, 1982) pp. 73–90.

17. See Chapter Four, pp. 110–117 and p. 229, note 2.

18. Bai Hua, "Jinye xingguang canlan," SH, no. 2 (March 1979).

19. Xu Mingxu, "Diao dong," *Qingming*, no. 2 (October 1979).

20. John K. Fairbank, "Self-Expression in China," in Ross Terril, ed. *The China Difference* (New York: Harper Colophon, 1979), p. 83.

Notes to Chapter Three

1. René Wellek, *Concepts of Criticism* (New Haven: Yale University Press, 1963), pp. 252–253.

2. The best selection of neo–realist fiction (also including some plays, film scripts and poems) in Chinese is in four volumes edited by the editors of *Qishi niandai* magazine in Hong Kong: *Zhongguo xin xieshi zhuyi wenyi zuopin xuan*, vol. 1 (Lee Yee, ed., 1980); vol. 2 (Lee Yee and Bi Hua, eds., 1980); vol. 3 (Bi Hua and Yang Ling, eds., 1982); vol. 4 (Bi Hua and Yang Ling, eds., 1984). See also Bi Hua. *Zhongguo xin xieshi zhuyi wenyi lungao* (Essays on China's New Realist Literature, Hong Kong: Dangdai, 1984). A number of anthologies of English translations are also available, including the following: Perry Link, ed. *Stubborn Weeds: Popular and Controversial Literature After the Cultural Revolution* (Bloomington: Indiana University Press, 1983), *People or Monsters?* (stories and reportage by Liu Binyan; same press, 1983), and *Roses and Thorns: The Second Blooming of the Hundred Flowers in Chinese Fiction* (Berkeley: University of California Press, 1984); Helen Siu and Zelda Stern, eds. *Mao's Harvest: Voices from China's New Generation* (N.Y.: Oxford University Press, 1983); Mason Wang, ed. *Perspectives in Contemporary Chinese Literature* (University Center, Michigan: Green River Review Press, 1983); Michael S. Duke, ed. *Contemporary Chinese Literature: An Anthology* (Armok, N.Y.: M.E. Sharpe, Inc./East Gate Books, 1985), first published in part in the *Bulletin of Concerned Asian Scholars* (July–September 1984). A major international literary conference was held in May 1982 at St. John's University in New York on the theme of post–Mao neo–realism and Jeffrey C. Kinkley has edited a volume entitled *After Mao: Chinese Literature and Society, 1978-1981* (Cambridge: Harvard University East Asian Monograph, 1984) containing seven of the forty plus conference papers.

3. My list of taboos is slightly modified from D.E. Pollard, "The Short Story in the Cultural Revolution," CQ, no. 73 (March 1978): 99–121.

4. Wellek, *Concepts of Criticism*, p. 242.

5. *Nineteen Eighty-Four*, any edition. David S.G. Goodman, *Beijing Street Voices* (London: Marion Boyars, 1981) is an anthology of poetry and politics from the Peking Spring.

6. Gong Qianshan, "Zhonggong gaige pai gongkai fenlie" (Chinese Communsit Reform Faction Openly Splits), *Zhongguo zhi chun* (New

York), no. 8 (December 1983): 11–18, relates the recollection of the first editors of *Beijing zhi chun* (Peking Spring) that, "we went to their [the reform leaders] homes regularly to talk for hours" and "they urged on us the necessity for democracy, taught us how to attack the conservatives, and so on." (p. 12)

7. *Tansuo* (25 March 1979), reprinted in MB (January 1980): 29–30 and translated in Gregor Benton, ed. *Wild Lillies and Poisonous Weeds* (London: Pluto Press, 1982), pp. 45–50.

8. Liu Qing (Liu Jianwei), *Prison Memoirs*, edited and introduced by Stanley Rosen and James Seymour in *Chinese Sociology and Anthropology*, Vol. XV, no. 1–2 (Fall–Winter 1982/83).

9. Chen, Ruoxi. *Democracy Wall and the Unofficial Journals* (Berkeley: Institute of East Asian Studies, 1982) and articles in *Zhongguo shibao* (Taipei), *fukan*, 26 and 27 April 1981.

10. Wei Jingsheng's *Tansuo* article, "Di wuge xiandaihua — minzhu ji qita" is reprinted in Chinese in the invaluable collection of *Documents on the Chinese Democratic Movement 1978–80*, edited, introduced in French and English by Claude Widor, and published by the Centre de Récherches et de Documentation sur la Chine Contemporaine de l'Ecole des Hautes Etudes en Science Sociales, Paris (Hong Kong: Observer Publishers, vol. 1, 1981): 50–58 and 60–69.

11. Wang Xizhe, "Mao Zedong yu wenhua da geming," QSND (February 1981): 26–49. For an analysis of Wang's critique and its intellectual sophistication, see Josephine Chiu–Duke, "Wang Xizhe's Critique of Mao Zedong and the Cultural Revolution," unpublished M.A. Thesis in Chinese History, University of Wisconsin, Madison, 1983.

12. This brief survey is based on an unpublished St. John's conference paper by Pan Yuan and Pan Jie that will appear in Kinkley, *After Mao*, as "The Non–official Magazine *Today* and the Younger Generation's Ideals for a New Literature." My quotations are from the earlier version.

13. Ibid., p. 6.

14. A scene related by the poetess Ke Yan in "A Few Words in Defense of New Poetry and the Literary Contingent," at the Fourth Congress of Writers and Artists, translated by Betty Ting in Howard Goldblatt, ed. *Chinese Literature for the 1980s*, pp. 79–80.

15. Marian Galik, "Some Remarks on 'Literature of the Scars' in the People's Republic of China (1977–1979)," *Asian and African Studies*, vol. XVIII (1982): 53–74.

16. See Chapter One for Deng Xiaoping and Zhou Yang's positive evaluation and defense of this 1977–78 literature, specifically

mentioning its political usefulness as an attack on the Gang of Four. The "whatever faction" (*fanshi pai*) were the Maoists led at the time by Hua Guofeng who were said by the reformers to believe that "whatever" Chairman Mao said was always right.

17. Galik, "Some Remarks. . .," p. 73.

18. Howard Goldblatt's statement that in these stories "one finds no sophistication, no imagination, no style — in a word, no art" may appear to be extreme, but it's not far off the mark. See his review of *The Wounded and Stories of Contemporary China* in CLEAR, vol. 2, no. 2 (July 1980): 293–294.

19. Liu Xinwu, "Shenghuo de chuangzaozhe shuo: zou zhei tiao lu!" (The Creator of Life Says: Take This Road!), WXPL, no. 5 (1978): 53–64, and RMWX, no. 2 (1978): 101–107.

20. *The Wounded*, p. 11.

21. Joseph S.M. Lau also pointed out this feature in a paper entitled "The Wounded and the Fatigued: Reflections on Post–1976 Chinese Fiction." *Journal of Oriental Studies*, vol. 20 (1979).

22. "Zhufu" (1924) is in *Lu Xun quanji* (Beijing: Renmin wenxue chubanshe, 1981), vol. 2, pp. 5–23. Liu Shaoming (Joseph S.M. Lau), "Chaoliu yu diandi—xieshi xiaoshuo de liangzhong leixing" (Main Currents and Tributaries—Two Types of Modern Chinese Realist Narrative), MB (September 1982):97–101, discusses Lu Xun's suspension of judgement in a survey of pre–1949 realism in Chinese fiction. Lu Xinhua discusses his inspiration and intensions in "Tantan wo de xizuo 'Shanghen'" (Talking About My Exercise "The Wounded"), WHB 14 October 1978.

23. Ba Jin's Love Trilogy is quoted from the discussion in C.T. Hsia, *A History of Modern Chinese Fiction* (New Haven: Yale University Press, rev. ed., 1971), p. 248. Liu Xinwu's story, originally in RMWX in 1978, appeared in ChL, no. 1 (1979): 36–57; quote is from p. 52.

24. SH, no. 3 (May 1979), reprinted in Lee Yee, vol. 1, pp. 10–22 and translated in ChL, no. 3 (1980): 68–91.

25. SHWX, no. 4 (1979); my translation is in Perry Link, ed. *Roses and Thorns*, pp. 221–243.

26. The best available collection of these stories is Lin Yemu, ed. *Zai feixu shang* (On the Ruins; Taibei: Shibao wenhua chuban shiye, 1982); some of the stories in this collection have been changed slightly from their original wording in the unnofficial publications. See also Wu Mang, "Feixu shang de huhuan," (Calling from the Ruins), ZB (June 1980): 92–96.

27. I do not accept Wu Mang's interpretation that Wang Qi has realized that the intellectuals are largely responsible for all of the disasters of Chinese history since 1860, although he may be regarded as having just realized, like Party Secretary Zhu Chunxin, that the common people are suffering even more than the urban intellectuals.

28. ZB (June 1980): 108–109, has a translation of a discussion by Heinrich Böll of the post–war "literature of the ruins" in Germany. For my translation of "Open Terrain" I am indebted to Jeffrey Kinkley of St. John's University for sending me a copy of the original *Today* magazine. A complete translation by Bonnie S. McDougall entitled "Open Ground" is in Michael S. Duke, ed. *An Anthology.*

29. My choices in this section and the rest of this chapter, although based on over three years of reading, are still highly selective. I have tried to discuss at length only those stories that I feel have artistic rather than merely sociological interest. I have tried to discuss works in which the style is both interesting and an integral part of the theme or meaning. I have not included Wang Meng's well known story "The Bolshevik Salute" (*Buli*, DD, no. 3, September 1979) nor the very controversial novella "A Tale of Tianyun Mountain" (*Tianyunshan chuanqi*) by Lu Yanzhou (*Qingming*, July 1979); the former because I find it trivializes rather than dramatizes the events presented and reads like an application to rejoin the Party organization (in short, it is a belated "wounded" story), and the latter because it is of more political than artistic interest, combining realism about the past with faith in the present Party leadership. The controversy surrounding it is a page in a chapter of post–Mao inner Party factionalism which I have simply chosen not to chronicle. Interested readers can refer to Shiao–ling Yu, "The Cultural Revolution in Post–Mao Literature," unpublished Ph.D. dissertation, University of Wisconsin, Madison, 1983, pp. 73–80 and 62–73 for a synopsis and discussion of these two works respectively.

30. RMWX, no. 2 (1979): 65–76.

31. My complete translation of this story will be in Michael S. Duke, ed. *An Anthology*, but I do not know the origin of the story, a xerox copy of which was sent to me from China by a friend. It may be from the Peking journal *Chou xiaoya* (Ugly Duckling).

32. This refers to the cave dwelling she guarded for her master.

33. SHWX, no. 5 (1979); my translations are from Lee Yee, vol. 1, pp. 23–30 with page numbers given in the text. A complete translation by Wendy Larson will also appear in *An Anthology.*

34. Li's words ironically recall Confucius' saying that bad government is worse than a fierce tiger.

35. CQ, no. 78 (June 1979): 413.

36. Originally published in WHB 11 February 1979; my translations are from *Qiao changzhang shangren ji* (Manager Qiao Takes Office; Jiangsu renmin chubanshe, 1979), pp. 415–431 with page numbers in text. A complete translation is in Perry Link, ed. *Stubborn Weeds*, pp. 57–73. I differ with Link's characterization of the story as "crudely written and psychologically shallow" because it seems to me that the scenic background and battle scenes are quite well done in relation to the theme and that the psychological shallowness of twenty year old fanatics ("romantic revolutionaries") is realistic characterization.

37. Joseph S.M. Lau, C.T. Hsia, and Leo Ou-fan Lee, eds. *Modern Chinese Stories and Novellas 1919–1949* (N.Y.: Columbia University Press, 1981), p. xx.

38. Published in *Zhongshan*, no. 1 (1980) and *Xiaoshuo jikan* (December 1980), "The Web" is translated by Richard King in *Renditions* (Autumn 1981): 112–153. Lu Xun's classic story from *Panghuang* (Hesitations, 1926) is in Lau, Hsia, and Lee, *Stories and Novellas*, pp. 17–26.

39. Lu Xun, Ibid., p. 24 and *Renditions*, (Autumn 1981): 113.

40. *Renditions*, p. 121; I have changed King's last line slightly to conform more closely to the original. The next paragraph makes the symbolism explicit when Toughie feels that she too is "caught in a great web" being sucked dry by a spider. Then she dies. According to King, who is aquainted with the author, the editors of *Xiaoshuo jikan* added a false ending in which the Deng Xiaoping "wind" blows the web away and she wakes up as if from a nightmare.

41. "Big rat, big rat,/Do not gobble our millet!" begins *Mao shi* number 113 in Arthur Waley, *The Book of Songs*, N.Y.: Grove Press, 1960, p. 309), traditionally regarded as a peasant's lament against the extortions of oppressive officials. *Zhuang zi* chapter 29 is a fictionalized diatribe against all the Confucian moralists who "eat without ever plowing, clothe (themselves) without ever weaving" and live off the peasants' labor while forever lecturing about "right and wrong." Burton Watson, *The Complete Works of Chuang Tzu* (N.Y.: Columbia University Press, 1968), pp. 323–338.

42. *Renditions*, p. 119.

43. SH, no. 1 (1980). My translations are from *Shen Rong xiaoshuo xuan* (Beijing chubanshe, 1981), pp. 181–286. There is an abridged translation in ChL, no. 10 (1980): 3–63 and a complete translation in Perry Link, ed. *Roses and Thorns*. For another discussion of this story, see Joseph S.M. Lau, "The Wounded and the Fatigued."

44. "Zai yiyuan zhong," *Ding Ling duanpian xiaoshuo xuan* (Beijing: Renmin wenxue chubanshe, 1981), vol. 2, pp. 569–589, is translated in Lau, Hsia, and Lee, *Stories and Novellas*, pp. 279–291.

45. The complete list of 1977–1980 prize winners is in RMWX, no. 6 (1981): 9–12.

46. This most important section 9, in which another doctor, Liu Xueyao, decides to leave China due to his ill–treatment during the Cultural Revolution, and the title is explained to mean "when one reaches middle age he is busy with a million things to do," is unfortunately deleted from the ChL translation.

47. "Huainian Xiao Shan" was originally published in ZP, no 4 (1979) and reprinted in *Suixiang lu* (A Record of Random Thoughts; Hong Kong: Sanlian, 1980), pp. 14–32; my complete translation is in Mason Wang, ed. *Perspectives*, pp. 113–133. Yang Jiang's work was first published by non–PRC presses in Hong Kong before being put out by Sanlian in July 1981. The "authorized" translation by Geremie Barmé and Bennett Lee, entitled *A Cadre School Life: Six Chapters* (Hong Kong: Joint Publishing Co., 1982), is, like their "wounded" book, a terrible translation full of flat phraseology that is a disservice to Yang Jiang's craftsmanship. Fortunately we have Howard Goldblatt's masterful version, entitled *Six Chapters from My Life 'Downunder,'* *Renditions* (Autumn 1981): 6–43, which manages to capture the stylistic flavor of the original. My quotations are all from Goldblatt's version.

A comparison of Barmé and Lee's version of the "tempering people" (*lianren*) passage which they mysteriously render as "tempering hardened intellectuals" before completely mistranslating the next line, gives a good idea of what I mean; but I cannot resist one other example that demonstrates how misleading and banal a bad translation can be. In Chapter Three, Yang employs a masterful double entendre to suggest the terrible waste that the cadre schools involve when she points out that the intellectual's night soil was "pilfered, for local wisdom had it that the waste produced in the cadre school was the best around." Thus Goldblatt, capturing exactly Yang's style *and* meanings. Barmé and Lee murder this with "because the peasants believed that the faeces from the cadre school were especially effective as a fertilizer." Instances could be multiplied, but these should suffice.

48. Zhao Shuli used a number of traditional storyteller's techniques such as the persona of the implied oral narrator, peasant proverbs, puns, direct address to the reader, instructive digressions, and reference to popular mythology in the construction of his mainly pro–land

reform stories and novels. For a detailed analysis, see Cyril Birch, "The Persistence of Traditional Forms," in Birch, ed. *Chinese Communist Literature* (N.Y.: Praeger, 1963), pp. 74–91. Birch also analyzed many of Hao Ran's traditional stylistic devices in his "Change and Continuity in Chinese Fiction," in Merle Goldman, ed. *Modern Chinese Literature in the May Fourth Era* (Cambridge: Harvard University Press, 1977), pp. 385–404.

49. Originally published in *Yuhua* (Rain Flowers), no. 7 (1979) and reprinted in Lee Yee, vol. 1, pp. 41–48. An accurate, though sometimes stylistically lacking, translation is in Mason Wang, ed. *Perspectives*, pp. 193–227.

50. Leo Ou–fan Lee, "Technique As Dissidence: A Perspective of Contemporary Fiction," a St. John's conference paper, will appear in Jeffrey C. Kinkley, ed. *After Mao*; the quotation given here is from M.H. Abrams, *A Glossary of Literary Terms*, 3rd. ed. (N.Y.: Holt, Rinehart and Winston, 1971), p. 81. It is worth noting that Gao Xiaosheng told Lee that he was mistaken to find such ironies in his story. He claimed that he was only describing the reality of rural China as honestly as possible (personal communication from Lee). In Vancouver Shen Rong, too, was quite evasive about any interpretations of her stories, saying that she likes to leave that to the "literary experts." Since interpretations tend to be more straightforward and easily understood, it is not surprising that PRC writers are concerned about what might be classified as the bad "social effects" of their works.

51. Page numbers for my translation refer to Lee Yee, volume 1.

52. Chen Huansheng goes from a bemused visitor to town to a bumbling but successful factory purchasing agent in a series of gently satirical stories that poke good natured fun at many of the foibles of contemporary PRC society. References are in the bibliography. For an assessment of the results of the post–Mao economic reforms, both rural and urban, see W. Klatt, "The Staff of Life: Living Standards in China, 1977–81," CQ, no 93 (March 1983): 17–50.

53. For a review of factory fiction, see Michael Gotz, "Images of the Worker in Contemporary Chinese Fiction (1949–1964), unpublished Ph.D. dissertation, University of California, Berkeley, 1977 and parts of Joe C. Huang, *Heroes and Villains in Communist China* (N.Y.: Pica Press, 1973).

54. Helen Siu and Zelda Stern, eds. *Mao's Harvest*, pp. 128–146 and Perry Link, ed. *Stubborn Weeds*, pp. 142–161.

55. RMWX, no. 7 (1979) and no 2 (1980), translated in part in ChL, no. 2 (1980): 25–62 and no. 9 (1980): 3–39; my translations and

page numbers are from Lee Yee, vol. 1, pp. 49–72 and 269–287.

56. Originally published in *Xingang* (New Harbor), no. 5 (1980), partially translated in ChL, no. 12 (1980): 32–53, and reprinted in *Kaituozhe* (Pioneers; Beijing: Zhongguo qingnian chubanshe, 1981), pp. 212–239; page numbers in the text are from the translation/the book reprint.

57. The last line reads literally: "If we don't have a thorough grasp of sociology and personal relations (*chitou shehuixue, guanxixue*), we can't move an inch." Jiang is using Party jargon [for *chitou*, the *Pinyin Dictionary* example is *chitou wenjian jingshen*, "grasp the spirit of a document"] in a serious, but ironic fashion.

58. I've changed the translation by deleting four words and replacing the ironically rhetorical question.

59. See Chapter One, note 30. Another complete translation is in Perry Link, ed. *Stubborn Weeds*, pp. 198–250..

60. My discussion of this play owes much to Gunn's unpublished St. John's conference paper, "At Play in the Fields of the Word."

61. Ibid., p. 2.

62. The original Chinese text is in QSND (January 1980): 83; translation from Link, *Stubborn Weeds*, pp. 216–217.

63. Original p. 93; Link, p. 244.

64. Original p. 95; Link, p. 248. It is interesting to note that Li's admission of being "wrong" (*cuo*) rather than guilty of a "crime" (*zui*) exactly parallels the Party's post–Mao assessment of its own "mistakes" (*cuowu*).

65. Original p. 96; Link, p. 250. On the justification for the latest rectification campaign, see Lowell Dittmer, "The 12th. Congress of the Communist Party of China," CQ, no. 93 (March 1983): 108–124. On page 119 Dittmer quotes from a 10 September 1982 RMRB article concerning the decline in "party spirit" since the CCP became, in Hu Yaobang's phrase, "a Party in power":

> Since the founding of the People's Republic our Party has been a Party in power and many Party members have become leading cadres of varying ranks. This change in their positions is a severe test for Party members. Some comrades whose Party spirit has not been adequately tempered often gradually become muddled in their understanding and forget that the Party's basic aim is to serve the people wholeheartedly. Those comrades no longer serve the people wholeheartedly. On the contrary, they serve the

people with only half their heart, with the other half being used to plan for their own interests.

66. WYB, no. 1 (January 1980): 15.

67. George Becker, *Documents of Modern Literary Realism* (Princeton, N.J.: Princeton University Press, 1963), pp. 597–598.

Notes to Chapter Four

1. Carlos Fuentes, "Writing in Time," *democracy* (January 1981): 65.

2. Translated in full by James V. Feinerman and Perry Link as "People or Monsters?" in Link, ed. *People or Monsters?* (Bloomington: Indiana University Press, 1983), pp. 11–68, "Ren yao zhijian" first appeared in RMWX, no. 9 (1979) and was later reprinted in *Liu Binyan baogao wenxue xuan* (Selected Reportage Fiction of LBY; Beijing chubanshe, 1981). Page numbers in the text of this chapter are from this book unless otherwise noted. "Guanyu 'Ren yao zhijian': da duzhe wen" (Answering Readers' Questions Concerning "Between Men and Monsters"), RMWX, no. 1 (1980): 100.

3. Northrop Frye, *Anatomy of Criticism* (Princeton: Princeton University Press, 1957), pp. 40–41.

4. Liu's conception of literary realism is an article of faith that he, ironically, reconciles with or even derives from his deeper faith in the superiority of socialist over capitalist society. See: "Ren shi mudi, ren shi zhongxin" (Human Beings are the Aim, Human Beings are the Center), WXPL, no. 6 (1979): 10–15, translated in Howard Goldblatt, ed. *Chinese Literature for the 1980s*, pp. 121–131. Liu reiterated this view of realism and discussed the influence of 19th century European literature on the formation of his social consciousness and revolutionary political ideals in a revealing and important interview in October 1982 at the University of Iowa with Lee Yee, editor of the Hong Kong monthly *The Seventies*; see, QSND (December 1982): 64–76, hereafter referred to as "Interview."

5. Frye, *Anatomy of Criticism*, pp. 34–35, emphasis added throughout.

6. Ibid., p. 41.

7. Ibid., p. 221.

8. Ibid., p. 41.

9. Ibid., pp. 39–40.

10. Ibid., p. 40.

11. The "literature of the wounded" (Chapter Three) concerns the effects of the Cultural Revolution on the spirit of the Chinese people,

but the best eye–witness account of the human cost of the period from 1958 to 1980 is Liang Heng and Judith Shapiro's *Son of the Revolution* (New York: Alfred A. Knopf, 1983; Chinese translation: *Geming zhi zi*, Taibei: Shibao wenhua chubanshe, 1983). Penetrating accounts of the gangland style political and moral corruption of the Maoist hierarchy are to be found in Hsia Chih–yen's novel *The Coldest Winter in Peking* (New York: Doubleday, 1978) and Yao Mingle's *The Conspiracy and Death of Lin Biao* (New York: Knopf, 1983) which is perhaps highly fictionalized but quite accurate as to the motives and modes of operation among the Maoist elite.

12. See the BR, no. 52 (28 December 1981): 3, where this view is stated quite frankly and with no intended irony, and Jerome Cohen, "China's Changing Constitution," CQ, no. 76 (December 1978): 835–837.

13. The persistence of Mao's legacy was in very great evidence during the celebrations surrounding the 90th anniversary of his birth on 26 December 1983. See especially Hu Yaobang's speech, "The Best Way to Remember Mao Zedong," BR, no. 1 (2 January 1984): 16–18, Li Weihan, "Mao Zedong's Unique Contribution," same issue, pp. 19–22, and the many articles in the Chinese press immediately before and after the celebrations which included the publication of many of Mao's letters in both Chinese and English. To some extent the "early Mao" is being quoted by the Deng–Hu–Zhao leadership in order to overcome the bad effects of the "late Mao," but the one party one ideology style of propaganda control has not changed.

14. Ibid., p. 75. Liu Binyan actually wrote such a letter to Chairman Mao at the time, but he never mailed it. It is just one more irony of his life that during the Anti–Rightist Campaign, he had to hand it over to the Party and it formed part of the case against him. "Interview," p. 70.

15. Merle Goldman, *Literary Dissent in Communist China* (Cambridge: Harvard University Press, 1967), p. 237 and note 80, p. 302; Maurice Meisner, Mao's China (New York: The Free Press, 1977), pp. 192–193.

16. "Interview," pp. 68–70.

17. Ibid., pp. 71–72.

18. Liu Binyan, "Shidai de zhaohuan" (The Call of the Times), *Wenxue xuan*, pp. 1–24; translated in Howard Goldblatt, ed. *Chinese Literature for the 1980s*, pp. 103–120.

19. For the "Sixteen Points," see K.H. Fan, ed. *The Chinese Cultural Revolution: Selected Documents* (New York: Grove Press, 1968), pp. 161–173.

20. Jacques Guillermaz, *The Chinese Communist Party in Power, 1949-1976* (Boulder, Colorado: Westview Press, 1976), pp. 452-469. Zhang Zhixin was executed after undergoing sadistic torture including having her throat cut to prevent her from speaking out against the new order; see Jonathan Chaves, "A Devout Prayer of the Passion of Chang Chi-hsin," in *Modern Chinese Literature Newsletter* (Spring 1980):8-24.

21. "Guanyu 'Ren yao zhijian': da duzhe wen," pp. 99-101.

22. "Cong 'Ren yao zhijian' yinqi de" (Events Touched Off By "Between Men and Monsters"), RMWX, no. 12 (1980):86-90.

23. The ZP, no. 1 (1980) story is translated in Perry Link, ed. *People or Monsters?*, pp. 69-78. For the letter, see "Liu Binyan tongzhi de yifeng xin" (A Letter from Comrade Liu Binyan), *Wenyi qingkuang* (23 June 1980): 14.

24. *Wenxue xuan*, p. 210. On the dossier kept on every Chinese employee by his "work unit," see Fox Butterfield, *China: Alive in the Bitter* (New York: NY Times Books, 1982), p. 323; Butterfiled's entire chapter on "the control apparatus" is extremely thought provoking in relation to our consideration of the chances for the realization of Liu Binyan's ideal of a "democratic" or "humanistic" Chinese Communist Party.

25. Benjamin I. Schwartz, "The Reign of Virtue: Some Broad Perspectives on Leader and Party in the Cultural Revolution," in John Wilson Lewis, ed. *Party Leadership and Revolutionary Power in China* (Cambridge: Cambridge University Press, 1970), pp. 149-169.

26. "Feng yu zhaozhao," RMWX, no. 6 (1981): 52.

27. Lee Ou-fan, "Liu Binyan yu 'Ren yao zhijian,'" QSND (October 1980): 79-82. 28. Liu Binyan, "Luzi hai keyi geng kuan xie" (Our Approach Could Still be Somewhat More Flexible), WYYJ, no. 4 (1980): 76-77. During the St. John's Conference, Rudolf Wagner of the Free University of Berlin pointed out to me that Liu Binyan's "reportage literature" is ultimately derived from the 19th century *esquisse physiologique* which was popularized as the *očerk* in Russia and taken up again by the Soviet writer Ovechkin during "the thaw" after Khrushchev's Twentieth Congress speech. Liu visited with Ovechkin in 1956 and was inspired by his use of what Liu and his editor, Qin Zhaoyang, then called *zhencha wenxue* or "investigative literature." Liu also discusses this period of his life in "Interview," p. 68.

29. Liu Binyan, "Luzi hai keyi geng kuan xie," p. 77.

30. John Hollowell, *Fact and Fiction: the New Journalism and the Nonfiction Novel* (Chapel Hill: University of North Carolina Press,

1977).

31. In "Interview" pp. 73–75, Liu expresses guarded optimism concerning the present Party line which seems to him to be close to the correct Marxist–Leninist position and program.

32. "Cong 'Ren yao zhijian' yinqi de," p. 86.

33. The day after I delivered this speech at St. John's University, the writer Wang Meng, a close friend of Liu Binyan and currently (January 1984) Chief Editor of *People's Literature*, commented that I had greatly misunderstood Liu Binyan and his writings. He said that Liu Binyan is now and always has been a devoted follower of Lenin. I do not believe that I said he was not and I fully understand Wang Meng's concern lest he or Liu Binyan be regarded as "bourgeois liberals" or anti–Party "dissenters." I believe I have made it clear that I think that one of the ironies of Liu Binyan's life is precisely the fact that he has never given up his Leninist faith despite all of the harm such an ideology has done to China. Liu Binyan is much more pragmatic and much less ideological than many other PRC writers and is honestly concerned with the material and spiritual wellbeing of the Chinese people, but he is in no way a dissident from the Marxist–Leninist–socialist policies of the PRC government and the Communist Party. It is probably inevitable that my interpretation of his life and work differs from his own or that of his close friends.

Notes to Chapter Five

1. My translations are from the *Shidai de baogao* (23 April 1981) text.

2. Bai Hua, "Meiyou tupo, jiu meiyou wenxue" (No Breakthrough, No Literature), RMRB 13 November 1979; translated in Howard Goldblatt, ed. *Chinese Literature for the 1980s*, pp. 56–67.

3. Goldblatt, p. 57.

4. Ibid., p. 58.

5. Bai Hua, "A Question That Must Be Answered," translated from *Wenhui zengkan*, no. 1 (1980) : 7–8 by Madelyn Ross in Mason Y.H. Wang, ed. *Perspectives in Contemporary Chinese Literature* , pp. 105–106.

6. Ibid., p. 110, with one minor change.

7. Ibid., p. 111.

8. Erwin Panofsky, *Meaning in the Visual Arts* (N. Y., 1955), pp. 1–2. Two general surveys are Werner Jaeger, *Paideia: The Ideals of Greek Culture*, 3 vols., translated by Gilbert Highet (N.Y., 1939–44) and Gilbert Highet, *The Classical Tradition: Greek and Roman Influences on Western Literature* (N.Y., 1949).

9. Lin Yü-sheng, "The Evolution of the Pre-Confucian Meaning of *Jen* and the Confucian Concept of Moral Autonomy," *Monumenta Serica*, vol. 31 (1974-75): 184, italics added.

10. Ibid., p. 185.

11. Ibid., p. 190.

12. Ibid.

13. D.C. Lau, *Mencius* (Penguin Books, 1970), pp. 12-13.

14. Lin Yü-sheng, p. 194; and Tu Wei-ming, "Creative Tension Between *Jen* and *Li*, " *Philosophy East and West*, XVIII, Nos. 1-2 (January-April, 1968): 29-39.

15. Lin Yü-sheng, p. 198.

16. For Ai Qing, see Zhang Cuo, "Ai Qing de dubai yu gongming" (Ai Qing's Monologue and Response), QSND (November 1980): 106-108. For Ba Jin and his wife Xiao Shan, who died of cancer during this period due to lack of proper treatment, see "Huainian Xiao Shan" (Remembering Xiao Shan), in Ba Jin, *Suixiang lu* (Random Thoughts, Hong Kong, 1980): 14-32, translated by Michael S. Duke in Mason Y.H. Wang, ed. *Perspectives in Contemporary Chinese Literature*, pp. 113-133.

17. *Shishuo xinyu*, Sibu beiyao, p. 22b.

18. "Chunchao zaiwang," in *Bai Hua jinzuoxuan*, (Hong Kong: Tiandi tushu, 1981), pp. 14-21. This line is on page 15.

19. *Li sao*, line 97, following (with changes) David Hawkes, *Ch'u Tz'u* (Boston: Beacon, 1962), p. 28. For the Qu Yuan legend in Chinese history and literature, see Laurence A. Schneider, *A Madman of Ch'u* (Berkeley: University of California Press, 1980).

20. *Li sao*, line 43. Hawkes, p. 24. Bai Hua's intentionally courageous stance is also reflected in his poem "Chuan" (The Ship), *Shikan* (Poetry), no. 1 (1981), reprinted in QSND (June 1981), p. 41, in which he predicts (quite correctly) that a ship sailing heavy seas might will see the wreckage floating on the sea and know that a great ship (himself) had passed that way.

21. Hawkes, p. 56.

22. Bai Hua is not really a dissident, despite his "comradely critics" attempts to make him out to be one. He is a loyal CCP member whose "Party spirit" is very high. He is a Chinese Marxist who believes that a good deal of literary freedom is quite compatible with his ideology. When he wrote *Kulian* he supported the Deng Xiaoping reform program and the Zhou Enlai position on literature and art. For truly dissident writings, see Leo Ou-fan Lee, "Dissent Literature from the Cultural Revolution," *Chinese Literature: Essays, Articles, Reviews*, vol. 1 (1979): 59-79 and Bonnie McDougall, "Dissent Literature:

Official and Non–official Literature In and About China in the Seventies," *Contemporary China*, vol. 3 (Winter 1979): 49–79.

23.   Ding Wang, "Fenxi Bai Hua de daibiaozuo '*Kulian*,'" (Analyzing Bai Hua's Representative Work '*Bitter Love*'), *Lianhebao* (United Daily, overseas edition), 10–13 June 1981 (four articles), also pointed out this fact in another excellent discussion of Bai Hua's humanism from a slightly different point of view.

24.   Blaise Pascal, *Thoughts*, translated by Howard E. Hugo, in Maynard Mack et al., eds.   *The Continental Edition of World Masterpieces* (N.Y., 1966), vol. 2, p. 5.

25.   See D.C. Lau, *Mencius*, pp. 131, 182, and 168 for translations of *Meng zi* chapters 4.B.19, 7.A.1, and 6.A.15.

26.   The re–evaluation of Mao Zedong culminated in the *Resolution on Certain Questions in the History of Our Party Since the Founding of the People's Republic of China*, a document debated throughout 1980 and adopted at the Sixth Plenum of the Eleventh Central Committee on 27 June 1981.   In this "historic resolution" Mao Zedong is personally blamed for the Cultural Revolution, but the Party is extoled for its ability to admit and correct its "mistakes;" Mao's merits are declared to have been "primary" and his errors only "secondary" in importance; and Mao Zedong Thought is given the status of an infallible scientific dogma that, curiously enough, does not include any of the erroneous ideas of the man buried in Mao's tomb and that is a "valuable spiritual asset" and "will be our guide to action for a long time to come."   For a complete English text, see BR, no. 27 (6 July 1981).   See Chapter 4, note 13.

27.   *Miaotang* is a term specifically applicable to the imperial court temple, and Bai Hua has chosen to employ it in place of the more usual *miaoyu* in order to directly associate the cult of Mao with the "feudalistic superstition" of the Chinese empire.   This usage was particularly galling to the critics of *Shidai de baogao*, who regarded it as a caricature of Chairman Mao and an attack on the CCP and communism as a form of religious superstition.

28.   *Ephesians*, 6:12, "For our contention is not with the flesh and blood, but with dominion and authority, with the world–ruling powers of this dark age, with the spirit of evil in things heavenly."

29.   We might do well to ponder deeply the unexplored depths of *Bitter Love*'s implications concerning the ironic rather than dialectic relationship that seems to exist (even becoming apparent to Chinese Marxists like Bai Hua and Liu Binyan) between altogether laudable socialist goals and their unfortunate results.   I can think of no better aid to such rumination than Friedrich A.   Hayek's three volume

reinterpretation of classical liberalism, *Law, Legislation, and Liberty* (Chicago: University of Chicago Press, 1973– 1979).

In a later story, "Yi shu xinzha" (A Bundle of Letters), RMWX, no. 1 (1980): 24–40, Bai Hua does probe deeper into the corruption and special privileges of the CCP bureaucratic elite. The cynical credo of that class is stated quite openly by the wife of a PLA general: "As soon as you have power, no matter what liberties you take, you're still a good cadre; but once you lose power, no matter how careful you are, you're still a 'capitalist roader' and you'll still be a target for attack." (p. 26) Complete translation in Perry Link, ed. *Stubborn Weeds*, pp. 114–142.

30. According to Bi Hua, "Yong bu ximie de aiguo qingyan" (The Never Extinguished Flames of Patriotic Feeling), QSND (June 1981): 38–40, this episode and much else in *Bitter Love* is based on the real life experiences of the painter Huang Yongyu, whose works were very popular with Zhou Enlai.

31. *Faust, Part One.* Translations by Theodore Roszak, in *Where the Wasteland Ends* (N.Y.: Anchor, 1973), p. 317 and Louis Macniece, in Maynard Mack, *World Masterpieces*, p. 315.

32. See Qi Xin, QSND, (June 1981): 11–12 for a jingle popular in the PRC at that time: "In the fifties it was 'people help people' (*ren bang ren*); in the sixties it was 'people attack people' (*ren dou ren*); in the seventies it was 'people fear people' (*ren pa ren*); and in the eighties it is 'every man for himself' (*geren gu geren*)."

33. See Chen Jisun, "Cixu bixu diandao guolai" (The Order Should Be Reversed), QSND (June 1981): 37.

34. For a very perceptive appraisal of the morally debilitating effects of the CCP's alternating policies of repression and relaxation on the intellectuals, see Lee Yee's discussion with Xu Fuguan, "Xu Fuguan tan zhonggong zhengju". (Xu Fuguan Discusses the Chinese Communist Political Situation), QSND (May 1981): 8–16.

35. On the CCP patriotism campaign of 1980–81, see Lee Yee, "Aiguo zhuyi de huhuan" (The Call to Patriotism), QSND (June 1981): 42–46, and Yuan Fang, "*Kulian* yu zhishi fenzi de aiguo xin" (*Bitter Love* and the Patriot ism of the Intellectuals), HQ, no. 9 (1 May 1981): 27–33.

36. As in Stalin's Russia, so in the last ten years of Mao's China, demonology is an important point of departure for understanding. See George Urban, "A Conversation with Leszek Kolakowski: The Devil in History," *Encounter* (January 1981): 9–26. Parallels with China in this distinguished Polish historian's discussion of communist theodicy are striking.

37. Note the hesitation here: how difficult for a PLA officer to speak these words.

38. Ignazio Silone, *Bread and Wine*, 1955 version (N.Y.: Signet, 1962), p. 183.

39. Bai Hua, as we have seen above, went on to write again, his first published work after the "*Kulian* Incident" was the novella, "Dongri meng zhong de da leiyr," (A Great Thunderstorm in a Winter Dream), SY, no. 3 (1981): 39–68, 103.

Notes to Chapter Six

1. I have not read all of the novels published since 1978, but I have followed the criticisms and reviews of them in *Wenyibao, Wenxue pinglun* and other journals. I had originally thought to include Zhang Jie's *Chenzhong de chibang* (Leaden Wings. Peking: Renmin wenxue chubanshe, 1981) in this chapter on confession and affirmation, but I found it extremely dull, pedantic, didactic, and, in terms of characterization, rather unbelievable; not really a novel, but rather a series of lectures on political economy, sociology, management theory, and behaviorism interspersed with brief sketches of people from all walks of life. It has, however, received fairly good press and belongs in the category of factory fiction where it is outshined by Jiang Zilong's short stories. Other works worthy of mention and perhaps study are Yao Xueyin's multi–volume historical novel *Li Zicheng* (Peking: Zhongguo qingnian chubanshe, 1963–1979) and Zhu Lin's *Shenghuo de lu* (The Road of Life. Peking: Renmin, 1979). Gladys Yang is now working on an abridged translation of *Leaden Wings*, and Richard King is doing a doctoral thesis (UBC) which includes an analysis of *The Road of Life* and intellectual youth in Chinese fiction before and after the Cultural Revolution.

2. Dai Houying, *Ren a, ren!*, Guangdong renmin chubanshe, 1980 and Huacheng chubanshe, 1982 (forth printing). Page numbers to all quotations will be given in the text. Dai Houying's first novel, *Shiren zhi si* (The Death of a Poet) was published after the success of *Ren a, ren!* (Fuzhou: Fujian renmin chubanshe, 1982) and is a much less successful investigation of the Gang of Four's mistreatment of artists and intellectuals during the Cultural Revolution, although its humanistic tone is still quite laudable. The *Zhongguo shibao* (*China Times*, North American edition) of 25 October 1983 reported that *Ren a, ren!* was banned by a directive from the Propaganda Bureau. I learned in 1982 from a friend and would–be translator that the Writers Union refused permission for an authorized English translation of *Ren a, ren!* Jeannette Faurot's translation of Chapter 20 will appear in

Michael S. Duke, ed. *An Anthology.*

3. *China News Analysis*, no. 1231 (23 April 1982) offers an English summary and discussion of the following Chinese articles: from the *Nanfang ribao* — Lin Xianzhi, "Shilun *'Ren a, ren!'* de xinren xingxiang," (January 8, 1982, very favorable), Qi Junmin, "Cuowu de denghao — guanyu *'Ren a, ren!'* zhong de rendao zhuyi wenti," (22 January 1982, mostly unfavorable; Marxism is not equal to humanism); from WHB — Yao Zhengming and Wu Ming-ying, "Sisuo shemme yang de 'shenghuo zheli' — ping changpian xiaoshuo *'Ren a, ren!'* (17 October 1981), p. 3; Ai Ye, "Shemme shi 'makesi zhuyi de rendao zhuyi?' — ping "*Ren a, ren!*' de zhuti," Ouyang Pinghua, "Shengdong de renwu xingxiang;" Jin Qing, "Tichang ziyou taolun;" and Yin Ming, "Yige tujie de renwu xingxiang — Xi Liu," (all on 3 November 1981), p. 3; Xi Bian, Fang Keqiang, and Gu Changhao, "Bingfei kongshan bujian ren — du *'Ren a, ren!'* de yishu chuangxin jian yu He Manzi tongzhi shangquan," and two letters from readers (December 18, 1981), p. 3; Cheng Gu, "Zuopin yao xianchu sixiang de 'liangse' — wo du *'Ren a, ren!'* (24 December 1981, this reviewer found the work most depressing and lacking in any "brightness"), p. 3.

4. Edward J. Brown, *Russian Literature* Since the Revolution, (Cambridge: Harvard University Press, 1982), pp. 190–221. Parallels between 1953–56 in the USSR and 1978–81 in the PRC are striking, except that there is no Chinese Pasternak or Solzhenitsyn.

5. Mark Schorer, "Technique as Discovery," in Philip Stevick, ed. *The Theory of the Novel* (N.Y.: Free Press, 1967), p. 67.

6. Czeslaw Milosz, *The Captive Mind* (N.Y.: Vintage Books, 1981, originally published in 1953), pp. 200–201 discusses the manner in which dialectical materialism gives intellectuals "the illusion of full knowledge" and confuses the humanities with the natural sciences. Boris Pasternak is quoted in Brown, *Russian Literature*, p. 217: "We cease to recognize reality. It appears to us in some new category. And this category seems a condition belonging to it rather than to us. Apart from this condition everything else in the world has been named. New and unnamed is it alone. We try to name it. The result is art . . ."

7. Milosz, *Mind*, p. 73: In East European countries (and in the PRC), "one of the most ominous reproaches leveled against writers is the suspicion that their verses, plays, or novels contain a 'metaphysical residue.' Since a writer is a civilizer who dares not be a shaman or a sorcerer, the slightest signs of a metaphysical tendency in him are unforgivable." Witness Jiang Qing's prolonged campaign against ghosts in Chinese drama and more recent criticism of post-Mao writers who use words like *linghun* ("soul") in their discussion of *renxing*

("human nature," itself regarded as a "metaphysical" — non-dialectical materialist — concept in Mao Zedong's *Yan'an Talks.*

8. C.T. Hsia, *The Classic Chinese Novel* (N.Y.: Columbia University Press, 1968) pp. 271–276.

9. Postface to *Ren a, ren!* p. 358.

10. Brown, *Russian Literature*, 202.

11. Milosz, *Mind*, p. 209: "When people are divided into 'loyalists' and 'criminals' a premium is placed on every type of conformist, coward, and hireling; whereas among the 'criminals' one finds a singularly high percentage of people who are direct, sincere, and true to themselves." In China since 1957, the "Rightists" have always been considered "criminals," and one of the main themes of post-Mao literature from 1978 through 1981 has been the honesty, sincerity, and goodness of these people in contrast to the venality of CCP "loyalists."

12. Milosz, *Mind*, p. 48: "At every step, be it in the realm of aesthetics or ethics, one encounters the opposition that the strangeness of man raises against the wisest of theories. It is reasonable that a responsibly raised child should inform on his father . . . (as was done in China during the Cultural Revolution) And yet the disgust such behavior awakens in many people is just as inexplicable as their preference for Manet over Russian nineteenth century realists." In China, the contrast would be between traditional Chinese vernacular fiction, especially the *Dream of the Red Chamber* that He Jingfu carries with him everywhere, and the works of "socialist realism" or "revolutionary romanticism" of the years 1949–1977, works that caused cultural bureaucrats like Zhou Yang to complain on numerous occasions that Chinese readers did not like them. Note that Xi Liu's exclamation, including the title of the book, "People, oh people!," contains a tacit admission that communist indoctrination has to constantly "struggle" against universal human nature.

13. I suppose the publication guarantee cited here refers to the constitutional guarantees mentioned in Chapter One; and this novel offers a good example of how they might be treated in sensitive cases.

14. *China News Analysis*, no. 1243 (8 October 1982): 4. The complete text of Hu Yaobang's report, "Create a New Situation in All Fields of Socialist Modernization," is in BR, no. 37 (13 September 1982): 11–40.

15. "Su Qin liezhuan" is in the *Shiji* (Records of the Grand Historian), chapter 69, volume 7, pp. 2241– 2277 of Zhonghua shuju's 1959 edition.

16. Li Zehou, "Letter to L.J.," WYB, no. 2 (1981): 44; partially translated in Li Zehou and Vera Schwarcz, "Six Generations of

Modern Chinese Intellectuals," unpublished paper presented at the AAS meeting in Chicago, 4 April 1982. My thanks to Li Zehou for giving me a copy.

17. BR, no. 47 (22 November 1982), p. 5 and no. 52 (27 December 1982): 4.

18. Milosz, *Mind*, pp. 197–198.

19. C.T.Hsia, "Residual Femininity: Women in Chinese Communist Fiction," in Cyril Birch, ed. *Chinese Communist Literature* (N.Y.: Praeger, 1963), pp. 158–179. Milosz, *Mind*, p. 6: "For the intellectual, the New Faith is a candle that he circles like a moth. In the end, he throws himself into the flame for the glory of mankind. We must not treat this desire for self–immolation lightly ... We are concerned here with questions more significant than mere force."

20. Northrop Frye, "Introduction" to *The Tempest*, in *The Complete Pelican Shakespeare: The Comedies and Romances*, Penguin, 1969, p. 506.

21. Theodore Spencer, "Shakespeare and the Nature of Man: *The Tempest*," in Leonard F.Dean, ed. *Shakespeare: Modern Essays in Criticism* (N.Y.: Oxford University Press, 1961), pp. 411–416. Frank Kermode, excerpt from "A Salvage and Deformed Slave;" Theodore Spencer, "Shakespeare's Last Plays;" and Hallett Smith, "Introduction: *The Tempest* as a Kaleidoscope;" in Hallett Smith, ed. *Twentieth Century Interpretations of "The Tempest"* (Englewood Cliffs, N.J.: Prentice Hall, 1969), pp. 91–96, 43–46, and 1–11.

22. Just what Hu Yaobang told Sha Yexin et al. in February 1980.

23. Milosz, *Mind*, p. 55.

24. In the post–Mao era, there has been a great deal of discussion of the "feudalistic" Chinese "national character" and how to change it; among the better presentations, one that basically agrees with He Jingfu is Liu Binyan's "Man is the Aim, Man is the Center," WXPL, no. 6 (1979). in Howard Goldblatt, ed. *Chinese Literature for the 1980s*, pp. 121–131. (None of the discussions I have seen has actually transcended the CCP's own Rousseauist view that the ruling party, of which there can only be one, by definition has the same interests as "the people" and represents the "general will.") See also Kwang–ching Liu, "World View and Peasant Rebellion: Reflections on Post–Mao Historiography," *Journal of Asian Studies*, vol. XL, no. 2 (February 1981): 295–326, in which many PRC historians downplay the importance of mass movements in the making of history, thus lending support to He Jingfu's assertion of the historical importance of individuals of genius. All of this return to a more reasonable view of

history is supportive of the importance of intellectuals in the current Four Modernizations drive and can only be considered a welcome relief from the Maoist idea that "class struggle" is the only important causitive factor in history.

25. Karl Marx and Frederick Engels, *The German Ideology*, Part One (N.Y.: International Publishers, 1970), p. 53. Maurice Meisner, *Mao's China* (N.Y.: Free Press, 1977), p. 234.

26. He Jingfu's idea of "bourgeois humanism" and the "bourgeois state," like that of Hu Yaobang noted above seems to fit a vision of the capitalist world of the 1840s such as might be reflected in the works of Charles Dickens.

27. T.A.Hsia, "Twenty Years After the Yenan Forum," and Howard L. Boorman, "The Literary World of Mao Tse–tung," in Birch, *Chinese Communist Literature*, pp. 226–253 and 15–38, both discuss the profoundly antihumanistic thrust of Mao's *Yan'an Talks*. On the literary and class struggle line for 1981–82, see: "Socialist Spiritual Civilization," HQ, no. 19, 1982 in BR, no. 45 (8 November 1982): and "Scientifically Understand and Handle Class Struggle in China," JFJB 9 October 1982 and BR, no. 49 (6 December 1982).

28. Jean Boudout, "Introduction," Victor Hugo's *Quatrevingt–Treize*, (Paris: Editions Garnier Freres, 1963), p. i.

29. *China News Analysis*, no. 1231, suggests the comparison with Myshkin, but does not make it.

30. Fyodor Dostoyevsky, *The Idiot*, (N.Y.: New American Library, 1969), p. 632. See also Harold Rosenberg's "Introduction" to this edition.

31. This is not the place to go into a detailed discussion of Karl Marx's humanism and or Dai Houying and other PRC writers' faithfulness to it. Suffice it to say that many of them consider their humanism to be of a piece with Marx's. As has been the case in Italy and Eastern Europe for some time, Chinese writers and intellectuals's attempts to emphasize the "humanistic Marxism" of the "early Marx" will continue to play an important role in the overall democratization of Chinese political and cultural life for some time to come.

Notes to Chapter Seven

1. The intellectual historian George L. Mosse makes Romanticism, for better and for worse, the main theme of his original textbook–essay, *The Culture of Western Europe, 19th and 20th Centuries* (Chicago: Rand McNally, second revised edition, 1974). Good surveys of recent critical discussions are *Romanticism: Points of View*, edited by Robert F. Gleckner and Gerald E. Enscoe

(Englewood Cliffs, N.J.: Prentice–Hall, Inc., second edition, 1970) and *Romanticism Reconsidered: Selected Papers from the English Institute*, edited by Northrop Frye (N.Y.: Columbia University Press, 1963).

2. René Wellek, "The Concept of Romanticism in Literary History" (1949) and "Romanticism Re–examined," in *Concepts of Criticism* (New Haven: Yale University Press, 1963), pp. 220, 160–161.

3. Ibid., p. 161. 4. For a more exhaustive list of romantic criteria, see Henry H.H. Remak, "West European Romanticism: Definitions and Scope," in Newton P. Stallknecht and Horst Frenz, eds. *Comparative Literature: Method and Perspective* (Carbon dale, Ill: Southern Illinois University Press, revised edition, 1971), pp. 275–311.

5. C.T. Hsia, "Hsü Chen–ya's *Yü–li hun*: An Essay in Literary History and Criticism," Taipei: Academica Sinica International Sinological Conference reprint (October 1981), p. 259.

6. Cambridge: Harvard University Press, 1973. For a succinct summary of Lee's major conclusions, see his "The Romantic Temper of May Fourth Writers," in Benjamin I. Schwartz, ed. *Reflections on the May Fourth Movement: A Symposium* (Cambridge: Harvard University East Asian Research Center, 1972), pp. 69–84.

7. Bonnie S. McDougall, *The Introduction of Western Literary Theories Into Modern China, 1919–1925* (Tokyo: Centre for East Asian Cultural Studies, 1971). Chapter 3, "Romanticism and Neo–Romanticism," especially pages 88–108, discuss Tian Han's association of China's "poetry expresses intention (inclination, determination, or will)" with various European romantic theories of literature. For a further exposition of the *shi yan zhi* theory in Chinese tradition, see chapters 3 and 7 of James J.Y. Liu, *Chinese Theories of Literature* (Chicago: University of Chicago Press, 1975).

8. T.A.Hsia, *The Gate of Darkness: Studies on the Leftist Literary Move ment in China* (Seattle: University of Washington Press, 1968), p. 71 passim.

9. Edward M. Gunn, *Unwelcome Muse: Chinese Literature in Shanghai and Peking, 1937–1945* (N.Y.: Columbia University Press, 1980). Leo Ou–fan Lee, *Romantic Generation*, Part Three, "The Romantic Left" and Merle Goldman, *Literary Dissent in Communist China* (Cambridge: Harvard University Press, 1967.)

10. Kai–yu Hsü and Ting Wang, eds. *Literature of the People's Republic of China* (Bloomington: Indiana University Press, 1980). Nieh Hualing, ed. *Literature of the Hundred Flowers* (N.Y.: Columbia University Press, 1981, 2 vols).

11. See Robert Scholes and Robert Kellog's remarks on "pure romance" in *The Nature of Narrative* (N.Y.: Oxford University Press, 1966), p. 99, which reads like an ironic comment on the "non-representational" nature of PRC "realism," whether "socialist," "revolutionary," or combined with "revolutionary romanticism."

12. Cyril Birch, "The Particle of Art," in Birch, ed. *Chinese Communist Literature* (N.Y.: Praeger, 1963), pp. 3–14.

13. Li Zehou, "Letter to L.J.," WYB, no. 2 (1981): 44; translated by Vera Schwarcz in an unpublished AAS Conference paper co-authored with Li entitled "Six Generations of Modern Chinese Intellectuals." (Chicago, 4 April 1982).

14. The concluding section, "Autumn," of Li Ping's long novella has now been translated by Daniel Bryant and will appear in Michael S. Duke, ed. *An Anthology.* "Winter Fairytale" is autobiography plain and simple. "Spring Fairytale" has a first person narrator, Xiao Shan, and all of the characters' names are changed; but it is obviously autobiographical and everyone has, with the author's encouragement, read it that way. "Sunset Clouds" is a first person narrative with a short preface by the author describing it as a record of his experiences written to help others of his age deal with similar circumstances that are bound to arise in their lives. "Open Love Letters," written by a husband and wife team, two scientists, and telling the story of how the female protagonist was won over by the male protagonist to a life of love and scientific study, is certainly autobiographical despite its later revision for publication. "Aurora Borealis," the only one of the five written from the third person omniscient point of view with only one direct authorial comment, is perhaps not wholly autobiographical in the sense that the other stories are, despite the fact that one young woman is the sole center of consciousness.

15. All page numbers in the text in parentheses refer to the journals mentioned above for each piece. Elipses of this sort (. . .) are mine, while those of this sort (. . . . . .) are in the originals.

16. "Sinking" is translated in Joseph S.M. Lau, C.T. Hsia, and Leo Ou-fan Lee, eds. *Modern Chinese Stories and Novellas, 1919–1949* (N.Y.: Columbia University Press, 1981), pp. 123–141 and "The Diary of Miss Sophia" is translated in Harold R. Isaacs, ed. *Straw Sandals* (Cambridge: The MIT Press, 1974), pp. 129–169.

17. QSND carried two articles on popular reactions to Yu Lojin and her stories in the PRC: Mu Fu, "Yu Lojin: xin shiqi de panni nuxing" (A New Feminist Rebel), (July 1982): 79–81 and Cheng Mumu, "Jida xuesheng zuotan 'Chuntian de tonghua,'" (Jinan University Students Discuss "Spring Fairytale"), (November 1982):

92–93. Despite the adverse publicity, Yu Lojin's story has a happy ending. She was recently remarried, for the first time married for love to the man of her choice. For a sociological analysis of the Yu Lojin case and the questions it raises concerning the possition of women in PRC society today, see Emily Honig, "Private Issues, Public Discourse: The Life and Times of Yu Lojin," in *Pacific Affairs* (Summer 1984): 252–265.

18. Jin Fan's conception of mankind's search for truth is strikingly similar to the exposition of "Intellectual Passions" and "Commitment" in chapters 6 and 10 of Michael Polanyi's *Personal Knowledge: Towards a Post–Critical Philosophy* (Chicago: University of Chicago Press, 1958, 1962.)

19. Su Liwen, "'Aiqing re' manbu Zhongguo wentan," ('Hot Love' Flourishes in Chinese Literature"), QSND (February 1982): 76–79.

20. I cannot be certain, but this epigraphic quotation might be from some Chinese translation of Sophocles' *Oedipus at Colonus*, lines 1514–15; in the volume *Sophocles I*, volume 3 of David Grene and Richmond Lattimore, eds. *The Complete Greek Tragedies* (N.Y.: Washington Square Press, 1967), p. 149, Theseus ask Oedipus, "What proof have you that your hour has come?" and Oedipus answers, "The great, incessant thunder and continuous / Flashes of lightning from the hand of God." Translated by Robert Fitzgerald.

21. Yu Lojin's father actually took out an advertisement in order to marry his daughter off to a "relatively well–to–do farming village." (84)

22. In two other places, pages 106 and 107, Yu Lojin also describes visions of Yu Loke's spirit as a Titan among the dawn and evening clouds.

23. "Hymn to Intellectual Beauty," lines 75–77, in *The Norton Anthology of English Literature*, volume 2A, 1968, p. 411.

24. Wordsworth, "Ode: Intimations of Immortality," stanza 10, in Ibid., p. 153.

25. M.H. Abrams, "English Romanticism: The Spirit of the Age," in *Romanticism: Points of View*, pp. 314–330. The quotation is from Shelley's "Prometheus Unbound," Act IV, lines 570–574, p. 329 of Abrams' article.

26. Although primarily influenced by Chinese Marxism, Li Huaiping's views are typical of 19th century Positivism while the old monk's arguments resemble, in a much less sophisticated manner, those of Michael Polanyi's *Meaning* (Chicago: University of Chicago Press, 1975) in which he considers the implications of his post–critical epistemology for art, literature, myth, and religion.

27. I am indebted to Leo Ou–fan Lee's comments on an earlier draft of this chapter (at the Fourth International Comparative Literature Conference, August 1983, at Tamkang University, Taipei, Taiwan) for urging my thoughts in the direction of these concluding remarks.

Bibliography

It goes without saying that the following four part bibliography is not intended as a complete bibliography of Chinese literature from late 1977 to date. I have listed here only those works either (1) mentioned in the text, (2) by writers discussed in the text, or (3) read and found useful as background to this period of Chinese literature.

Abbreviations

AHWX . . . . Anhui wenxue (A. Literature)
AJCA . . . . Australian Journal of Chinese Affairs
BFWX . . . . Beifang wenxue (Northern L.)
BJWX . . . . Beijing wenxue (Peking L.)
BJWY . . . . Beijing wenyi (Peking Literature and Art)
BR . . . . Beijing Review
ChL . . . . Chinese Literature
CJ . . . . Changjiang (Yangzi River)
CJWY . . . . Changjiang wenyi (Y.R. Lit/Art.)
CQ . . . . China Quarterly
DD . . . . Dangdai (This Generation)
DS . . . . Dushu (Reading)
GMRB . . . . Guangming ribao (Intellectual Daily)
HC . . . . Huacheng (Flower City)
HQ . . . . Hongqi (Red Flag)
JFJB . . . . Jiefangjun bao (PLA Daily)
MB . . . . Mingbao yuekan (MB Monthly)
QSND . . . . Qishi niandai (The Seventies)
RMRB . . . . Renmin ribao (People's Daily)
RMWX . . . . Renmin wenxue (People's Lit.)
SH . . . . Shouhuo (Harvest)
SHWX . . . . Shanghai wenxue (Shanghai Lit.)
SY . . . . Shiyue (October)

WHB .... Wenhuibao (Literary Daily)
WXPL .... Wenxue pinglun (Literary Critique)
WYB .... Wenyibao (Literary Gazette)
WYYJ .... Wenyi yanjiu (Lit/Art Research)
XHWZ .... Xinhua wenzhai (New China Literary Digest)
XHYB(WZB) .... Xinhua yuebao (wenzhaiban) (New China
    Monthly, Literary Supplement)
YLJ .... Yalüjiang (Y. River)
ZM .... Zhengming (Contension)
ZB .... Zhongbao yuekan (China Monthly)
ZP .... Zuopin (Works)

Unless otherwise noted all place names that appear in the position reserved for publishers are understood to be followed by *renmin chubanshe* (People's Publishing Company). The only exception is that the notation *Renmin* itself stands for the *Renmin wenxue chubanshe* (People's Literature Publishing Company). For example, the entry: Jiang, Zilong, et al. *Ai de quanli* (The Right to Love). Chengdu: Sichuan, 1980, means that the work was published by the People's Publishing Company of Sichuan. The entry: Wang Meng, *Dongyu* (Winter Rain). Peking: Renmin, 1980, means the work was published by the People's Literature Publishing Company.

I. ANTHOLOGIES

Aiqing xiaoshuoji (Anthology of Love Stories). Shanghai: Wenyi chubanshe, 1979.

Barmé, Geremie and Bennet Lee, eds. *The Wounded.* Hong Kong: Joint Publishing Company, 1979.

Bei dou (Dipper), ed. *Fanxiulou: hongweibing de haojie wenxue* (The Anti-revisionist Tower: Red Guard Literature of the Great Catastrophe). Hong Kong: Bei dou, 1979.

Benton, Gregory, ed. *Wild Lilies, Poisonous Weeds: Dissident Voices from People's China.* London: Pluto Press, 1982.

Bi, Hua and Yang Ling , eds. *Zhongguo xin xieshi zhuyi zuopin xuan* (Selected Works of China's New Realism). Vol. 3. Hong Kong: QSND, 1982.

---------- , eds. same title. Vol. 4. same publisher, 1984.

---------- , eds. *Jueqi de shiqun — Zhongguo dangdai menglong shi yu shilun xuanji* (Newly Emerging Poetry — An Anthology of Contemporary Chinese "Obscure Poetry" and Poetry Criticism). Hong Kong: Dangdai wenxue yanjiushe, 1984.

Cen, Ying , ed. *Zhongguo dalu zui'an xiaoshuo xuan* (An Anthology of China Mainland Crime Stories). Hong Kong: Tongjin, n.d. (1981?).

—————— , ed. *Zhongguo dalu zhentan xiaoshuo xuan* (An Anthology of China Mainland Dectective Stories). Hong Kong: Tongjin, n.d. (1981?).

Chongfang de xianhua (Second Blooming Fragrant Flowers). Shanghai: Baihua wenyi, 1979.

Chun lei (Spring Thunder, stories from SY). Peking: Beijing chubanshe, 1981.

Ding, Ling, ed. *Dangdai nü zuojia zuopin xuan* (An Anthology of Works by Contemporary Women Writers). Guangzhou: Guangdong, 1980.

Duke, Michael S., ed. "Chinese Literature in the Post–Mao Era," a special issue of *The Bulletin of Concerned Asian Scholars* (July–September 1984).

——————, ed. *Contemporary Chinese Literature: An Anthology.* Armonk, N.Y.: M.E.Sharpe/East Gate Books, 1985. (Contains all of the BCAS special issue plus several additional works.)

Gao Shangqin , ed. *Zhongguo dalu kangyi wenxue* (Mainland China Protest Literature). Taibei: Shibao wenhua chuban shiye, 1979.

Goldblatt, Howard, ed. *Chinese Literature for the 1980s: The Fourth Congress of Writers and Artists.* Armonk, N.Y.: M.E.Sharpe, 1982.

Goodman, David S.G., ed. *Beijing Street Voices.* London: Marion Boyars, 1981.

Gunn, Edward M., ed. *Twentieth Century Chinese Drama: An Anthology.* Bloomington: Indiana University Press, 1983.

Hsü, Kai–yu, ed. *Literature of the People's Republic of China.* Bloomington: Indiana University Press, 1980.

Isaacs, Harold R., ed. *Straw Sandals.* Cambridge: MIT Press, 1974.

Jiang, Zilong , et al., eds. *Ai de quanli* (The Right to Love). Chengdu: Sichuan, 1980.

——————, et al., eds. *Qiao changzhang shangren ji* (Manager Qiao Takes Office and Other Stories). Jiangsu: Jiangsu, 1979.

Lau, Joseph S.M., C.T.Hsia, and Leo Ou–fan Lee, eds. *Modern Chinese Stories and Novellas, 1919–1949.* N.Y.: Columbia University Press, 1981.

Lee, Yee, ed. *Zhongguo xin xieshi zhuyi wenyi zuopin xuan* (Selected

Works of China's New Realism). Vol. 1. Hong Kong: QSND, 1980.

----------and Bi Hua , eds. same title. Vol. 2. Hong Kong: QSND, 1980.

Lee, Yee, ed. *The New Realism: Writings from China After the Cultural Revolution.* N.Y.: HIP, 1983.

Lin, Yemu , ed. *Zai feixu shang* (On the Ruins). Taibei: Shibao wenhua chuban gongsi, 1982.

Link, Perry, ed. *People or Monsters? Stories and Reportage by Liu Binyan.* Bloomington: Indiana University Press, 1983.

----------, ed. *Stubborn Weeds: Popular and Controversial Literature After the Cultural Revolution.* Bloomington: Indiana University Press, 1983.

----------, ed. *Roses and Thorns: The Second Blooming of the Hundred Flowers in Chinese Fiction.* Berkeley: University of California Press, 1984.

Lu Xinhua , et al., eds. *Shanghen* (The Scar). Hong Kong: Sanlian shudian, 1978.

Nieh, Hualing, ed. *Literature of the Hundred Flowers.* 2 Vols. N.Y.: Columbia University Press, 1981.

Quanguo youxiu duanpian xiaoshuo ji (Best Short Stories of 1978-1979). Jiangsu: Jiangsu, 1979.

Rao, Zhonghua , ed. *Kexue shenhua: 1979-1980 kexue huanxiang zuopin ji :1979-1980* (Anthology of Science Fiction of 1979-1980). Peking: Haiyang, 1980.

RMWX, ed. *Duanpian xiaoshuo xuan* (Selected Short Stories). Vol. 7. Peking: Renmin, 1981.

----------, ed. *Yijiu baling nian duanpian xiaoshuo xuan* (Selected Short Stories of 1980). Peking: Renmin, 1981.

----------, ed. *Yijiu baling nian quanguo youxiu duanpian xiaoshuo pinxuan huojiang zuopin ji* (Prize Winning Short Stories of 1980). Shanghai: Shanghai wenyi chubanshe, 1981.

----------, ed. *Yijiu bayi nian duanpian xiaoshuo xuan* (Selected Short Stories of 1981). Peking: Renmin, 1982.

----------, ed. *Yijiu bayi zhongpian xiaoshuo xuan* (Selected Novellas of 1981). Peking: Renmin, 1982.

----------, ed. *Yijiu qiba nian quanguo youxiu duanpian xiaoshuo pingxuan zuopin ji* (Prize Winning Short Stories of 1978). Peking: Renmin, 1980.

----------, ed. *Yijiu qijiu nian quanguo youxiu duanpian xiaoshuo pingxuan huojiang zuopin ji* (Anthology of Prize Winning Short Stories of 1979). Shanghai: Shanghai wenyi chubanshe, 1980.

----------, ed. *Yijiu qijiu–yijiu baling zhongduanpian xiaoshuo xuan* (Selected Short Stories and Novellas of 1979–1980). Vol. 2. Peking: Renmin, 1981.

----------, ed. *Zhongpian xiaoshuo xuan* (Selected Novellas, 1979–1980). 4 Vols. Peking: Renmin, 1981.

Tung, Robert, ed. *Proscribed Chinese Writings*. London: Curzon Press, 1976.

Siu, Helen and Zelda Stern, eds. *Mao's Harvest: Voices from China's New Generation*. N.Y.: Oxford University Press, 1983.

Tiananmen Revolutionary Poems. Hong Kong: Wenhua ziliao gongying chubanshe, 1979.

Wang, Mason, ed. *Perspectives in Contemporary Chinese Literature*. University Center, MI: Green River Review Press, 1983.

Widor, Claude, ed. *Documents on the Chinese Democratic Movement 1978–80*. Vol. 1. Hong Kong: Observer Publishers, 1981.

Wu, Mang, ed. *Gan you geyin dong di ai — wenhua da geming hou Zhongguo qingnian shiwen xuan* (Songs That Grieve the Earth — Selected Poems and Prose of Chinese Youth after the Cultural Revolution). Hong Kong: Qiling niandai shuang zhoukan, 1974.

Xiaoshuo yuekan, ed. *Qingnian jiazuo* (Excellent Youth Works). Peking: Zhongguo qingnian chubanshe, 1981.

Yang, Winston L.Y. and Nathan K.Mao, eds. *Stories of Contemporary China*. N.Y.: Paragon, 1979.

II. INDIVIDUAL CREATIVE WORKS

Ba, Jin. *Suixiang lu* (Record of Random Thoughts). Vol. 1. Hong Kong: Sanlian, 1979.

Bai Hua jinzuo xuan (An Anthology of Bai Hua's Recent Works). Edited by Bi Hua and Yang Ling . Hong Kong: Tiandi tushu, 1981.

Bai Hua juan (Bai Hua Volume). Edited by the Hong Kong Movement to Support Chinese Writers. Hong Kong: publisher unlisted, 1981.

Bai, Hua. "Jinye xingguang canlan" (The Stars Are Bright Tonight). SH, no. 2 (March 1979).

----------. "Kulian" (*Bitter Love*). SY, no. 3 (September 1979) and *Shidai de baogao* (Report of the Age) 23 April 1981: 5–8.

----------. "Assiduous Love," a translation of *Kulian* appended to Wang Chang–ling. *Bai Hua de lu*, listed below.

----------. "'Xiangqian kan' de gushi" (A Story About 'Looking to the Future'). RMWX, no. 9 (1979).

----------. "Yishu xinzha" (A Bundle of Letters). RMWX, no. 1 (1980).

----------. "Dongri mengzhong de da lei" (Dreaming of a Winter Thunderstorm). SY, no. 3 (1981).

----------. "Wu Wang jin'ge Yue Wang jian" (The Wu King's Golden Lance and the Yue King's Sword). SY, no. 2 (1983).

Bei Dao (Zhao Zhenkai), poems and stories, see Bonnie S. McDougall.

Cao, Yumo . "Ai....!" (Ai!). SHWX, no. 1 (1980).

Chen, Cun . "Liang dai ren" (Two Generations). SHWX, no. 9 (1979).

Chen, Guokai . "Wo yinggai zemme ban?" (What Should I Do?). ZP, no. 2 (1979).

Chen, Haiying . "Hei haichao" (Black Tide). *Hongdou* (Red Bean), no. 2 (1979) and *Zheyidai*, no. 1. (This Generation, November 1979).

Chen, Jo–hsi (Ruoxi). *The Execution of Mayor Yin and Other Stories of the Great Proletarian Cultural Revolution.* Bloomington: Indiana University Press, 1978.

Chen, Shixu . "Xiaozhen shang de jiangjun" (The General and the Small Town). SY, no. 3 (1979) and ChL, no. 6 (1980).

Cong, Weixi . "Daqiang xia de hong yulan" (The Blood–Stained Magnolia). SH, no. 2 (1979) and ChL, no. 4 (1980).

----------. "Dishige dankong" (The Tenth Bullet Hole), SY, no. 1 (1979).

Dai, Houying . *Ren a, ren*! (People, Oh People!). Guangdong: HC chubanshe, 1980.

----------. "Diaoxiang" (Sculpturing). ZP, no. 5 (1982).

----------. *Shiren zhi si* (The Death of a Poet). Fuzhou: Fujian, 1982.

Dai, Qing . *Bu* (No, a collection of short stories). Guangdong: HC chubanshe, 1982.

Feng, Jicai . "Puhua de qilu" (The Wayward Path Strewn With Flowers). SH, no. 2 (1979).

Gao, Xiaosheng . *Gao Xiaosheng yijiu baling nian xiaoshuo ji* (Gao Xiaosheng's Selected Stories of 1980). Peking: Renmin, 1981.

----------. *Qijiu xiaoshuo ji* (1979 Short Stories). Nanjing: Jiangsu, 1980.

----------. "Li Shunda zao wu" (Li Shunda Builds a House). *Yuhua* (Rain Flowers), no. 7 (1979).

----------. "Manchang de yitian" (A Very Long Day). RMWX, no. 8 (1979).

----------. "All the Livelong Day." ChL, no. 3 (1980).

----------. "Chen Huansheng shang chen" (Chen Huansheng's Adventure in Town). RMWX, no. 2 (1980) and ChL, no. 12 (1980).

----------. "Qianbao" (The Briefcase). *Yanhe*, no. 5 (1980) and ChL, no. 12 (1980).

----------. "Jiqi jiandan de gushi" (An Extremely Simple Story). SH, no. 2 (1981).

----------. "Shui dong liu" (The River Flows East). RMRB, 21 February 1981 and ChL, no. 10 (1981).

----------. "Chen Huansheng baochan" (Chen Huansheng Takes the Responsibility System). RMWX, no. 3 (1982).

----------. "Chen Huansheng zhuanye" (Chen Huansheng Transferred). XSYB (April 1982) and ChL, no. 4 (1982).

Gu, Cheng . "Guanyu 'Xiaoshi liushou' de yifeng xin" (A Letter On *Six Little Poems*). QSND, (December 1982): 84–85.

Gu, Hua . "Paman qingteng de muwu" (The Ivy-covered Cottage). *Xiaoshuo xuankan* (Short Story Selections), no. 5 (1981).

Han, Jianghong (Li Hong). *Wenge fengyu hua shanxiang* (A Mountain Village in the Cultural Revolution Storms). Hong Kong: Zhongbao, 1969.

----------. *Sha xiao-er de qing-ai* (The Loves of Foolish Xiaoer). n. p. (Hong Kong?): Chuangzao chubanshe, 1978.

He, Shiguang . "Xiangchang shang" (In the Village Street) and ChL, no. 1 (1982).

Hsia, Chih-yen. *The Coldest Winter in Peking.* N.Y.: Doubleday, 1978.

Hu, Zonghua . *Yige kexuejia de gushi.* Guanchajia (Observer) nos. 14–22 (December 1978–August 1979). Serialization of a different version of Zhang Yang's novel *The Second Handshake.*

Jiang, He . "Meiyou xiewan de shi" (Unfinished Poems). *Jiushi niandai* (The Nineties, Hong Kong, June 1984).

Jiang, Zilong . *Jiang Zilong duanpian xiaoshuo ji* (Selected Short Stories of JZL). Peking: Zhongguo qingnian chubanshe, 1980.

----------. Kaituozhe (Pioneers). Peking: Zhongguo qingnian chubanshe, 1981.

----------. "Qiao changzhang shangren ji" (Manager Qiao Assumes Office). RMWX, no. 7 (1979) and ChL, no. 2, 1980.

----------. "Jichu" (The Foundation). SHWX, no. 12 (1979).

----------. "Qiao changzhang houzhuan" (More About Manager Qiao). RMWX,no.2 (1980) and ChL, no. 9 (1980).

----------. "Jinnian de qihao taifeng" (No. 7 Typhoon). *Wenhui zengkan* , no. 4 (1980) and ChL, no. 3 (1981).

——————. "Yige gongchang mishu de riji" (Pages from a Factory Secretary's Diary). *Xingang* (New Harbor), no. 5 (1980) and ChL, no. 12 (1980).

——————. "Yige nü gongchengshi de zishu" (A Female Engineer's Personal Report). *Wenhui yuekan*, no. 5 (1981).

Jin, He . "Chongfeng" (Re-encounter), SHWX, no. 4 (1979).

——————. "Wo weishemme xie 'chongfeng'" (Why I Wrote 'Re-encounter'). SHWX, no. 8 (1979).

——————. "Modiao mingzi de ren" (The Man Whose Name Had Been Erased). SH, no. 1 (1980).

——————. "Dai xiesi de yanjing" (Bloodshot Eyes). YLJ, no. 10 (1980).

Jin, Shui (Shi Tiesheng). "Jiushi zhege jiaoluo" (Our Corner). *Xiaoshuo jikan* (Short Story Quarterly), no. 3 (1980) and ChL, no. 5 (1981).

Jin, Yun and Wang Yi . "Benren Wang Laoda" (Stupid Wang). BJWY, no. 7 (1980).

Ke, Yunlun . "Sanqianwan" (Thirty Million Yuan). RMWX, no. 11 (1980) and ChL, no. 8 (1981).

Kong, Jiesheng . "Zai xiaohe neibian" (On the Other Side of the Stream). ZP, no. 3 (1979).

——————. "Yinyuan" (Marriage) and ChL, no. 5 (1979).

——————. "Yinwei youle ta" (Because of Her). RMWX, no. 10 (1979).

Li, Chao . "Chun han" (Spring Chill). *Zhongshan* , no. 3 (1979).

Li, Honglin . "Dahai zuozheng" (The Sea Is My Witness). YLJ, no. 10 (1979).

Li, Jian . "Nü'erqiao" (Daughters' Bridge). *Fang cao* , no. 2 (1981).

——————. "Jing zheyao" (Bowing and Scraping). *Hebei wenyi*, no. 2 (1981).

Li, Kewei . "Nü Zei" (Girl Thief). *Dianying chuangzuo* (Film Creation), no. 11 (1979).

Li, Ping . "Wanxia xiaoshi de shihou" (When Evening Clouds Disappear). SY, no. 1 (1981).

Li, Zhun . "Manguo" (Mango). RMWX, no. 10 (1980).

Ling, Geng . *Tian chou* (The Revenge of Heaven). Hong Kong: Xinqing chuanpo gongsi, 1972. Translation published in New York by G.P. Putnam's Sons, 1972.

Liu, Binyan . *Liu Binyan baogao wenxue xuan* (Selected Reportage Fiction of LBY). Peking: Beijing chubanshu, 1981.

——————. "Ren yao zhijian" (Between Men and Monsters). RMWX, no. 9 (1979) and QSND (December 1979).

----------. "Lu manman qi xiu yuan xi..." (The Road is Long and Slow). RMWX, no. 1 (1981).

----------. "Fengyu zhaozhao" (In the Wind and Rain). RMWX, no. 6 (1981).

---------- and Yu Yitai . "Qianqiu gongzui" (Lasting Merit and Faults). SY, no. 3 (1982).

Liu, Ke . "Fei Tian" (Fei Tian). SY, no. 3 (1979).

Liu, Xinwu . "Ban zhuren" (The Class Teacher), RMWX, no. 11 (1977) and ChL, no. 1 (1979).

----------. "Aiqing de weizhi" (A Place for Love), SY, no. 1 (1978).

----------. "Liti jiaotaqiao" (The Overpass). SY,no. 2 (1981).

Liu, Zhen . "Ta haoxiang mingbaile yidiandian" (The Girl Who Seemed to Understand). *Qingming* (April Fifth), no. 2 (1979).

----------. "Hei qi" (Black Flag). SHWX, no. 3 (1979) and ChL, no. 5 (1980).

Lu, Wenfu . "Xianshen" (Dedication). RMWX, no. 4 (1978).

Lu, Xinhua . "Shanghen" (The Scar). WHB 11 August 1978 and ChL, no. 3 (1979).

Lu, Yanzhou . "Tianyunshan chuanqi" (A Tale of Tianyunshan). *Qingming* (April Fifth), no. 1 (1979).

McDougall, Bonnie S., ed. and trans. *Notes From the City of the Sun: Poems by Bei Dao.* Ithaca, N.Y.: Cornell University Press, 1983.

Qiao, Shi . "Guan fan" (Providing a Meal). SHWX, no. 5 (1979).

Qin, Fan . "Gongkai de qingshu" (Open Love Letters). SY, no. 1 (1980).

Ru, Zhijuan . "Jianji cuole de gushi" (A Misedited Story). RMWX, no. 2 (1979).

----------. "Caoyuan shang de xiaolu" (The Path Through the Grassland). SH, no. 3 (1979) and ChL, no. 3 (1980).

----------. "Ernü qing" (Children's Feelings). SHWX, no. 1 (1980).

Sha, Yexin , Li Shoucheng , and Yao Mingde . "Jiaru wo shi zhende" (What If I Really Were?). QSND (January 1980).

Shen, Rong . *Shen Rong xiaoshuo xuan* (Selected Short Stories of SR). Peking: Beijing chubanshe, 1981.

----------. *Guangming de heian* (Bright Darkness).Peking: Renmin, 1978.

----------. "Ren dao zhongnian" (Reaching Middle Age). SH, no. 1 (1980). Abridged in ChL, no. 10 (1980).

----------. "Bing zhong" (In Sickness). *Wenhui zengkan* , no. 5 (July 1980).

----------. "Zhoumo" (Weekend). RMWX, no. 8 (1980).

----------. "Bai xue" (Snow). SY, no. 4 (1980).

----------. "Tongku zhong de jueze" (A Painful Decision). WHB 7 January 1981.

----------. "Zan ge" (Hymn). SH, no. 1 (1981).

Shi, Mo (Zhao Zhenkai). "Zai feixu shang" (On the Ruins). *Jintian* (Today), no. 1 (1979) and ZB, no. 6 (1980).

----------. "Guilaide moshengren" (The Homecoming Stranger). *Jintian* (Today), no. 1 (1979).

Shi, Tiesheng . "Meiyou taiyang de jiaoluo" (A Sunless Corner). *Weiminghu* (a Peking University student publication), no. 1 (1980). Republished with a happy ending in *Xiaoshuo yuekan* (Short Story Monthly), no. 3 (1980). Translated as "Our Corner" by Jin Shui in ChL, no. 5 (1981).

----------. "You nemme yizhi ge" (There Was Such a Song). Xerox copy from a friend of the author in Peking. Written 31 May 1982.

----------. "Heihei" (Blacky). Probably from *Chou xiaoya* (Ugly Duckling, a Peking University student publication); written in 1981 or 1982.

----------. "Zai yige dongtian de wanshang" (One Winter's Evening). *Chou xiaoya* (October 1982).

----------. "Wucan ban xiaoshi" (Half an Hour Lunch Break). *Xiaoshuo xuankan* (Short Story Selections), no. 1 (1981). Reprinted and commented on positively and negatively in XHWZ, no. 3 (1981).

Shu, Ting . "Jiaotangli de qinsheng" (Sound of the Organ in the Church). *Jintian* (Today), no. 5 (1979) and ZB, no. 6 (1980).

----------. *Xinge ji* (Songs of the Heart). Fujian wenyi, 1980.

Su, Shuyang . "Danxin pu" (Loyal Hearts). *Renmin xiju* (People's Theatre, May 1978) and ChL, no. 10 (1978).

----------. "Jinshuiqiao ban" (At the Gold Water Bridge). *Juben* (Plays, July 1979).

Sun, Yuchun . "Jiu hou tu zhen yan" (In Vino Veritas). *Anhui wenyi* (Anhui Literature), no. 4 (1979) and ChL, no. 12 (1979).

"Tiananmen Poems," ChL, no. 1 (1979).

Wan, Zhi (Chen Maiping). "Kaikuo di" (Open Terrain). *Jintian* (Today), no. 5 (1979) and ZB, no. 6 (1980).

Wang, Jiancheng and Wen Xiaojue . "Biele zhili" (Goodbye Caltrop). SH, no. 1 (1982).

Wang, Jing . "Zai shehui de dangan li" (In the Files of Society). *Wotu* (Fertile Soil), no. 2 (1979) and *Dianying chuangzuo* (Film

Creation), no. 10 (1979).

Wang, Meng . *Qingchun wansui* (Long Live Youth). Peking: Renmin, 1979.

----------. *Dongyu* (Winter Rain). Peking: Renmin, 1980.

----------. *Wang Meng xiaoshuo baogao wenxue xuan* (Selected Short Stories and Reportage of WM). Peking: Beijing chubanshe, 1981.

----------. *Wang Meng jinzuo xuan* (Selected Recent Works of WM). Hong Kong: Hai tao chubanshe, n.d. Contains many essays as well as stories.

----------. "Zuzhibu xin laide nianqingren" (A Young Man Newly Arrived in the Organization Department). RMWX, no. 9 (1956).

----------. "Zui baoguide" (Something Most Precious). ZP, no. 7 (1978).

----------. "Bu li" (The Bolshevik Salute). DD, no. 3 (1979).

----------. "Ye de yan" (The Eyes of the Night). GMRB 21 October 1979. Translated in ChL, no. 7 (1980) as "A Night in the City."

----------. "Shuoke yingmen" (A Spate of Visitors). RMRB 12 January 1980 and ChL, no. 7 (1980).

----------. "Youyou cuncao xin" (A Worried Mind). SHWX, no. 9 (1979) and ChL, no. 7 (1980) as "The Barber's Tale."

----------. "Hu die" (The Butterfly). SY, no. 4 (1980) and ChL, no. 1 (1981).

----------. "Chun zhi sheng" (Voices of Spring). RMWX, no. 5 (1980) and ChL, no. 1 (1982).

----------. "Fengzheng piaodai" (Kite Streamers). ChL, no. 3 (1983). Original in *xiaoshuo baogao wenxue xuan* above.

Wang, Peng . "Pipanhui shang (At the Denunciation Meeting). RMWX, no. 11 (1979).

Wang, Ruowang . "Ji'e sanbu qu" (Hunger Trilogy). SH, no. 1 (1980).

----------. "Shangxingou, dai xu" (Preface to 'The Sad Canal'). SHWX, no. 6 (1980).

Wen, Po . "Qiushui" (Autumn Waters). YLJ, no. 1 (1982).

Wu, Huan . "Dahei" (Big Blacky). DD, no. 1 (1982).

Xing, Yixun . "Quan yu fa" (Power Versus Law). *Juben* (Plays), no. 10 (1979) and ChL, no. 6 (1980).

Xu, Mingxu . "Diaodong" (The Transfer). *Qingming* (April Fifth), no. 2 (1979).

Yang, Jiang . *Ganxiao liuji* (Cadre School Six Memoirs). Hong Kong: Sanlian shudian, 1981. Translated by Howard Goldblatt as *Six*

Chapters From My Life 'Downunder', in *Renditions*, no. 16 (Autumn 1981) and by Geremie Barmé and Bennet Lee as *A Cadre School Life: Six Chapters*, Hong Kong: Joint Publishing Co., 1982.

Yao, Xueyin . *Li Zicheng* (Li Zicheng) 3 vols.. Peking: Zhongguo qingnian chubanshe, 1963, 1979.

Yu, Lojin . "Yige dongtian de tonghua" (A Winter Fairytale). DD, no. 3 (1980).

----------. "Chuntian de tonghua" (A Spring Fairytale). HC, no. 1 (1982).

Yu, Long . "Ta shuyu nayilei ren?" (What Kind of Person is He?). ZP, no. 4 (1979).

Yu, Mei . "A, ren...." (Oh, Mankind....). *Hua xi* (Flower Stream), no. 10 (1980).

Zhang, Jie . *Ai, shi buneng wangji* (Love Cannot Be Forgotten, collected stories). Guangdong: Guangdong, 1980.

----------. *Zhang Jie xiaoshuo juben xuan* (Selected Stories and Plays of ZJ). Peking: Beijing chubanshe, 1980.

----------. *Chenzhong de chibang* (Leaden Wings). Peking: Renmin, 1981.

----------. "Ai, shi buneng wangji de" (Love Cannot Be Forgotten). BJWY, no. 11 (1979).

----------. "Chanhui" (Remorse). BJWY, no. 11 (1979).

----------. "Fang zhou" (The Ark). SH, no. 2 (1982).

Zhang, Kangkang . "Ai de quanli" (The Right to Love). SH, no. 2 (1979).

----------. "Youyuan zhong sheng" (The Tolling of a Distant Bell). SY, no. 3 (1980).

----------. "Dandan de chenwu" (Light Morning Mist). SH, no. 3 (1980).

----------. "Huo de jingling" (The Fire Spirit). DD, no. 3 (1981).

----------. "Beijiguang" (Aurora Borealis). SH, no. 3 (1981).

----------. "Kongbai" (The Wasted Years). *Xiaoshuo jikan* (Short Story Quarterly), no. 2 (1981) and ChL, no. 3 (1981).

Zhang, Xian . "Jiyi" (Memories). RMWX, no. 3 (1979).

----------. "Bei aiqing yiwang de jiaoluo" (A Corner Forsaken by Love). SHWX, no. 1 (1980).

----------. "Weiwangren" (The Widow). *Wenhui yuekan* (Literary Monthly), no. 1 (1981).

Zhang, Xinxin . "Wo zai nar cuoguole ni?" (Where Did I Miss You?). SH, no. 5 (1980).

——————. "Zai tong yige dipingxian shang" (On the Same Horizon). SH, no. 6 (1981).

Zhang, Yang . *Di'erci woshou* (The Second Handshake). Peking: Zhongguo qingnian chubanshe, 1979.

Zhang, Yigong . "Fanren Li Tongzhong de gushi (The Criminal Li Tongzhong). SH, no. 1 (1980).

——————. "Zhao Juetou de yizhu" (Zhao Juetou's Will). SH, no. 2 (1981).

——————. "Heiwa zhaoxiang" (Little Blacky Takes a Picture). SHWX, no. 7 (1981).

Zhao, Guoqing . "Jiujiu ta" (Save Her). XHYB(WZB), no. 2 (1980) and *Gongren ribao* (Workers' Daily) 21–26 December 1979.

Zhao, Zhenkai . *Waves and Other Stories.* Edited by Bonnie S.McDougall. Hong Kong: Chinese University Press (Chinese edition, *Bodong,* to be published at same time), forthcoming.

——————. "Po dong" (Waves). CJ, no. 1 (1981). First written in 1974 and published in *Jintian* (Today) in 1979.

——————. "Gaozhi shang de yueliang" (Moonlight on Writing Paper). SH, no. 5 (1981).

Zhao, Zhizhen . "Diaodong zhihou" (After the Decision of My Transfer). *Qingchun* (Youth), no. 7 (1981) and ChL, no. 4 (1982).

Zheng, Yi . "Feng" (Maple). WHB 11 February 1979.

Zhu, Lin . *Shenghuo de lu* (The Road of Life). Peking: Renmin, 1979.

——————. "Wang" (The Web). *Zhongshan* , no. 1 (1980).

Zong, Fuxian . "Yu wusheng chu" (In A Land of Silence). *Renmin xiju* (People's Theatre), no. 12 (1978).

Zong, Pu . "Hong dou" (Love Berries). RMWX, no. 7 (1957).

——————. "Xuanshang de meng" (Melody in Dreams). RMWX, no. 12 (1978) and ChL, no. 8 (1979).

III. CRITICAL STUDIES, ESSAYS, AND SPEECHES

Ai, Ye . "Shemme shi 'makesi zhuyi de rendao zhuyi?' —ping '*Ren a, ren!*' de zhuti — (What is Marxist Humanism? — A Critique of the Theme of *Ren a, ren*!). WHB 3 November 1981.

Anhui wenxue , no. 3 (1980) has several articles on Zhu Lin and her *Shenghuo de lu.*

Bai, Hua . "Wenxue yishu yu minzhu" (Literature, Art, and Democracy). *Meishu yanjiu* (Art Research, January 1979).

——————. "Meiyou tupo jiu meiyou wenxue" (No Breakthrough,

No Literature). RMRB 13 November 1979.

----------. "Yige bixu huida de wenti" (A Question That Must Be Answered). *Wenhui zengkan* (Literary Supplement, January 1980): 7-8.

----------. "Shidai zai huhuan zuojia" (The Age is Calling to Writers). WHB 21 November 1980.

----------. "Bai Hua Criticizes Himself," BR, no. 2 (11 January 1982): 29-30. A newsbrief with translated excerpts from Bai Hua's letter of self-criticism which was printed in JFJB of 23 December 1981 and RMRB of the following day and reprinted in WYB, no. 1 (1982) and XHWZ, no. 2 (1982): 158-159.

Bai, Xia . "Zhao Dan huanju qu liao" (Zhao Dan Died Happy). RMRB 18 October 1980.

Barmé, Geremie. "Flowers or More Weeds?" AJCA, no. 1 (January 1979): 125-131.

----------. "Chaotou Wenxue – China's New Literature." AJCA, no. 2 (July 1979): 137-148.

Bernard, Suzanne. "An Interview with Ru Zhijuan." ChL, no. 3 (1980): 92-98.

Bi, Hua . *Zhongguo xin xieshi zhuyi wenyi lungao* (Collected Essays on China's Neo-Realist Literature). Hong Kong: Dangdai wenxue yanjiu she, 1984.

----------. "Yong bu ximie de aiguo qingyan" (The Never Extinguished Flames of Patriotic Feeling). QSND (June 1981): 38-40.

----------. "Yong heise de yanjing xunzhao guangming – ping Gu Cheng de shi" (Using Black Eyes to Search for Light – a Critique of Gu Cheng's Poetry). QSND (December 1982): 81-83.

----------. "Zhongguo wenyi zuopin zhong de gaigezhe qunxiang" (A Group Portrait of the Reformers in Chinese Literature and Art). QSND (May 1983): 86-88.

----------. "'Lijing pandao' de xiandai shilun" (Iconoclastic Modern Poetry Discussion). QSND (June 1983: 103-105.

----------. "Beida xuesheng zui xi'ai de yipian xiaoshuo – Li Ping 'Wanxia xiaoshi de shihou'" (Peking University Students' Best Loved Short Story – Li Ping's 'When Evening Clouds Disappear). QSND (July 1983): 89-91.

"Bujian baodao de yici wenyi zuotanhui – ji Huangshan bihui (An Unreported Literature and Art Discussion Meeting – Report on the Huangshan Writers' Conference). QSND (January 1981): 98-105.

Chan, Peter. "Popular Publications in China: A Look at the Spring of

Peking." *Contemporary China* (Winter 1979): 103–111.

Chan, Sylvia. "The Blooming of the 'Hundred Flowers' and the Literature of the 'Wounded Generation.'" in Bill Brugger, ed. *China Since the "Gang of Four."* N.Y.: St. Martin's Press, 1980: 174–201.

–––––––––––. "Realism or Socialist Realism?: The 'Proletarian' Episode in Modern Chinese Literature 1927–1932." AJCA, no. 9 (January 1983): 55–74.

Chang, Ts'o (Dominic Cheung). "Ai Qing de dubai yu gongming" (Ai Qing's Monologue and Response). QSND (November 1980): 106–108.

Chao, Pien. "Liu Hsin-wu's Short Stories." ChL, no. 1 (1979):89–93.

Chaves, Jonathan. "A Devout Prayer of the Passion of Chang Chi-hsin [Zhang Zhixin]." *Modern Chinese Literature Newsletter* (Spring 1980): 8–24.

Chen, Jisun . "Cixu bixu diandao guolai" (The Order Should Be Reversed). QSND (June 1981): 37.

Chen, Ruoxi. *Democracy Wall and the Unofficial Journals.* Berkeley: University of California, Center for Chinese Studies/Institute of East Asian Studies, 1982.

Chen, Shen . "Chongdu 'Xianshi zhuyi — guangkuode daolu'" (Rereading 'Realism, the Broad Road'). *Yanhe* (Yan River), no. 5 (1979): 63–71.

Chen, Yu-shih . "Tantan jipian guonei xiaoshuo zhong renwu zaoxing de qingxiang" (Discussing Characterization in Several Stories from China). QSND (December 1980): 87–89.

Chen, Yun . "Guanyu dang de wenyi gongzuozhe de liangge qingxiang wenti" (On the Problem of the Two Tendencies Among the Party's Literary Workers). RMRB 23 May 1982.

Cheng, Gu . "Zuopin yao xianchu sixiang de 'liangse' — wo du *Ren a, ren!*" (Literary Works Should Show Bright Thoughts — My Reading of *Ren a, ren!*). WHB 24 December 1981.

Cheng, Mumu . "Jida xuesheng zuotan 'Chuntian de tonghua'" (Jinan University Students Discuss 'Spring Fairytale'). QSND (November 1982): 92–93.

Chih, Pien. "'The Wound' Debate." ChL, no. 3 (1979): 103–105.

China News Analysis (Hong Kong). The following numbers:
    1199: The trial of the Gang of Four.
    1205: On the play *What If I Really Were?*
    1214: On Marxism in China after Mao's death.
    1215: On the campaign to suppress criminality.

1220: On the struggle between the reformers and the Maoists.

1231: On the novel *Ren a, ren*!.

1234: On history and historians in the Post–Mao Era.

1242: More on post–Mao Marxism.

1243: On the Twelfth Party Congress.

1245: On the *PLA Daily*'s attack on the reformers and Deng Xiaoping's response.

Chinnery, John. "Lu Xun and Contemporary Chinese Literature." CQ, no. 91 (September 1982): 411–421

Chiu–Duke, Josephine. "Wang Xizhe's Critique of Mao Zedong and the Cultural Revolution." Unpublished M.A. thesis, University of Wisconsin, Madison, 1983.

Chou, Yushan. "Liberation of the Writers of the 1930s." *Issues and Studies*, no. 2 (1978): 37–52.

Da, Wen . "Dalu wenxue de sichao he luxiang" (The Thought Currents and Direction of Mainland Literature). *Dangdai wenyi* (Hong Kong, March 1983):40–49.

––––––––––. "Dalu de 'qingchun wenxue'" (Mainland 'Youth Literature'). *Dangdai wenyi* (June 1983): 42–48.

Deng, Xiaoping . "Zai Zhongguo wenxue yishu gongzuozhe disici daibiao dahui shang de zhici" (Speech at the Fourth Congress of Literary and Art Workers). WYB, no. 11–12 (November–December 1979): 2–5.

––––––––––. "DXP guanyu muqian xingshi he renwu de baogao" (DXP's Report on the Present Situation and Tasks). A speech given on 16 January 1980 but never openly published in the PRC. In ZM, no. 29 (March 1980): 11–23.

Ding, Ling. "A Few Words From My Heart." ChL, no. 4 (1980): 106–109. Her remarks at the Fourth Congress of Writers and Artist.

Ding, Zhenhai and Zhu Bing . "Tuidong sihua jianshe de hao zuopin – ye ping 'Qiao changzhang shangren ji' bing yu Shao Ke tongzhi shangque" (A Good Work for Promoting the Four Modernizations – Critique of 'Manager Qiao Takes Office" and Debate with Comrade Shao Ke). RMRB 18 October 1979.

Documents of the First Session of the Fifth National People's Congress of the People's Republic of China. Peking: Foreign Languages Press, 1978.

Dolezalova, Anna. "Two Waves of Criticism of the Film Script *Bitter Love* and of the Writer Bai Hua in 1981." *Asian and Africal Studies*, vol. XIX (1983): 27–54.

Dong, Jian . "Dui shenghuo he yishu de tanqiu jingshen – du Gao

Xiaosheng de duanpian xiaoshuo" (Questing Spirit in Life and Art — Reading GXS's Short Stories). RMRB 28 May 1980.

Du, He. "The Short Stories of 1978." ChL, no. 6 (1979): 113–117.

Duan, Gengxin . "Beiju mingyun, yingxiong xingge" (Tragic Fate and Heroic Character). CJWY (April 1981): 63–68.

Duke, Michael S. "The Second Hundred Flowers: Chinese Literature in the Post–Mao Era." In Mason Wang, ed. *Perspectives in Contemporary Chinese Literature*. University Center, MI: Green River Review Press, 1983: 1–48.

––––––––––. "Chinese Literature in the Post–Mao Era: The Return of 'Critical Realism,' the introduction to BCAS and M.E. Sharpe anthologies listed above.

––––––––––. "Wang Meng's Conception of the 'Stream–of–Consciousness' Technique." *Journal of Modern Chinese Literature*, no. 1 (September 1984).

"Duzhe dui 'zai shehui de dang'an li' de fanying" (Readers" Responses to 'In the Files of Society'). *Dianying chuangzuo* (Film Creation), no. 1 (1980): 93–96.

Feng, Xiaoxiong. "Ding Ling's Reappearance on the Literary Stage." ChL, no. 1 (1980): 3–16.

Fokkema, D.W. *Literary Doctrine in China and Soviet Influence, 1956–1960*. The Hague: Mouton and Co., 1965.

––––––––––– and Elrud Kunne–Ibsch. *Theories of Literature in the Twentieth Century*. N.Y.: St. Martin's Press, 1977.

––––––––––. "Chinese Criticism of Humanism: Campaigns Against the Intellectuals 1964–1965." CQ, no. 28 (1966): 68–81.

––––––––––. "Chinese Literature Under the Cultural Revolution." *Literature East and West*, vol. 13 (1969): 335–359.

––––––––––. "Strength and Weakness of the Marxist Theory of Literature with Reference to Marxist Criticism in the PRC." In John J. Deeney, ed. *Chinese–Western Comparative Literature Theory and Strategy*. Hong Kong: The Chinese University Press, 1980: 113–128.

Fu, Hu. "Let Thorny Flowers Blossom." ChL, no. 11 (1979): 101–109.

––––––––––."Controversial Plays." ChL, no. 8 (1980): 116–119.

Galik, Marian. "Some Remarks on 'Literature of the Scars' in the People's Republic of China (1977–1979)." *Asian and African Studies*, vol. XVIII (1982): 53–74.

Gao, Xiaosheng . "Zhagen yu shenghuo de turang" (Strike Roots Deep in the Soil of Life). RMRB 28 January 1981.

Gao Xiaosheng yanjiu ziliao (Research Materials on GXS). Edited by Lianyungang shi jiaoshi jinxiu xueyuan. No Publisher: July 1981.

Goldblatt, Howard. "Contemporary Chinese Literature and the New *Wenyi Bao.*" *World Literature Today,* no. 4 (Autumn 1979): 617–618.

——————. Review of *The Wounded* and *Stories of Contemporary China, Chinese Literature: Essays Articles Reviews,* no. 2 (July 1980): 293–294.

——————. trans. *Six Chapters From My Life 'Downunder.'* (Yang Jiang's Cultural Revolution memoir.) *Renditions,* no. 16 (Autumn 1981): 6–41.

——————. "Fresh Flowers Abloom Again: Chinese Literature on the Rebound." *World Literature Today,* no. 1 (Winter 1981): 7–10.

Goldman, Merle. "The Fall of Chou Yang." CQ, no. 27 (July–September 1966): 132–148.

——————. "The Political Use of Lu Xun." CQ, no. 91 (September 1982): 446–461.

Gong, Qianshan . "Zhonggong gaige pai gongkai fenlie" (Chinese Communist Reform Faction Openly Splits). *Zhongguo zhi chun* (China Spring, N.Y.), no. 8 (December 1983): 11–18.

Gu, Xiang . "Lu Wenting de xingxiang shi shidai de chanwu" (Lu Wenting's Image is a Product of the Age). WYB, no 9 (1980): 11–13.

——————. "Aiqing yu wenyi duanxiang" (Thoughts on Love and Literature). GMRB 10 December 1981.

Gu, Zhicheng, "'The Second Handshake,' a New Bestseller." ChL, no. 1 (1980): 101–104.

"Guanyu xiaoshuo 'Ai shi buneng wangji de' de taolun" (Discussion Concerning the Short Story 'Love Cannot be Forgotten'). XHYB(WZB), no. 22 (October 1980): 161–168.

"Guanyu 'Zai shehui de dang'an li' deng zuopin de taolun" (Discussion Concerning 'In the Files of Society' and Other Works). XHYB(WZB), no. 23 (November 1980): 141–152.

GMRB Commentator. "Yong kexue de taidu jianshe jingshen wenming" (Use a Scientific Attitude to Build a Spiritual Civilization). GMRB 6 March 1981 and XHWZ, no. 4 (1981): 1–3.

GMRB Special Commentator. "Renmin minzhu zhuanzheng shishishang shi wuchan jieje zhuanzheng" (The People's Democratic Dictatorship Is in Essence the Dictatorship of the Proletariat). GMRB 21 April 1981. Abridged translation in BR, no. 19 (11 May 1981): 15–20.

Gunn, Edward M. "At Play in the Fields of the Word." Unpublished

St. John's conference paper, 1982.

Guo, Linxiang. "Zhang Jie, a New Woman Writer." ChL, no. 9 (1979): 103–104.

He, Jingzhi . "Zongjie jingyan, suzao xinren" (Sum Up Experiences, Portray New People). RMRB 15 April 1981.

Hongqi Commentator, "Socialist Spiritual Civilization." BR, no. 45 (8 November 1982): 13–17.

Honig, Emily. "Private Issues, Public Discourse: The Life and Times of Yu Lojin," *Pacific Affairs* (Summer 1984): 252–265.

Hou, Mingze "'Ganxiao liuji' du hou" (After Reading *Ganxiao liuji*). *Dushu* (Reading, September 1981): 9–13.

Hsia, T.A. "Heroes and Hero–worship in Chinese Communist Fiction." In Cyril Birch, ed. *Chinese Communist Literature.* N.Y.: Praeger, 1963.

Hu, Qiaomu. "Questions on the Ideological Front." BR, no. 5 (25 January 1982): 15–18. Highlights of 8 August 1981 speech to CCP Propaganda Department.

"Hu Qiaomu on Bourgeois Liberalization and Other Problems." BR, no. 23 (7 June 1982): 20–21.

Hu, Yaobang . "Zai juben chuangzuo zuotanhui shang de jianghua" (Talk at the Drama Forum). WYB, no. 1 (1981), HQ, no. 20 (1981), and XHWZ, no. 3 (1981): 126–137. Hu's February 1980 speech was only publicly released in January 1981. Translated in full as "Hu Yao–pang's Speech to the 'Forum on Script Writing.'" *Issues and Studies* (February 1982): 67–106.

——————. "Zai Lu Xun dansheng yibai zhounian dahui shang de jianghua" (Speech at the Commemorative Convention of the Hundredth Anniversary of the Birth of Lu Xun). RMRB and GMRB 26 September 1981. Translated in BR, no. 40 (5 October 1981): 11–16.

——————. "Create a New Situation in All Fields of Socialist Modernization." 1 September 1982 report to the Twelfth Congress. In *The Twelfth National Congress of the Communist Party of China* (September 1982). Peking: Foreign Languages Press, 1982.

——————. "Nuli jianshe gaodu shehui zhuyi jingshen wenming" (Work Hard to Establish a High Level Socialist Spiritual Civilization). HQ, no. 19 (1982): 2–9 and BR, no. 45 (8 November 1982): 13–17.

——————. "The Best Way to Remember Mao Zedong." BR, no. 1 (2 January 1984): 16–18.

Hu, Yu . "Rang 'Baihua zhengming' de fangzhen zai wenyijie kaihua jieguo" (Let the Line of 'A Hundred Schools Contending'

Blossom and Bear Fruit in Literature and Art). WYB, no. 7
(1979): 61–64. Response to Li Jian and the "Praise Faction."

Huai, Bing (Bi Hua). "Toujin zhonggong shitan de yimei zhadan –
Xu Jingya de 'Jueqi de shiqun' shuping" (A Bombshell Thrown
onto the Chinese Communist Literary Stage – On Xu Jingya's
'Newly Emerging Poetry'). ZM, no. 5 (1983): 56–58.

––––––––––. "Ping Bai Hua xinzuo 'Wu Wang jin'ge Yue Wang
jian'" (A Critique of Bai Hua's New Work 'The Wu King's
Golden Lance and the Yue King's Sword). ZM, no. 10 (October
1983): 54–55.

Huang, Ansi . "Xiang qian kan a! wenyi" (Look Forward, Literature
and Art). Guangzhou ribao (Canton Daily) 15 April 1979.

Huang, Gang . "Zheshi yibu shemme yang de 'dianying shi'?" (What
Kind of a 'Film Poem' is This?). Shidai de baogao (Report of the
Age) 23 April 1981.

Huang, Joe. Heroes and Villains in Communist China. N.Y.: Pica
Press, 1973.

Huang, Mei . "Guanyu dianying juben 'Zai shehui de dang'an li'" (On
the Film Script 'In the Files of Society'). XHYB(WZB), no. 6
(1981): 176–184. Originally in Dianying yishu (Film Art), no. 4
(1980).

––––––––––. "A Dan busi" (Zhao Dan Didn't Die). RMRB 18
October 1980: 5.

Huang, Qiuyun . "Guanyu Zhang Jie zuopin de duanxiang" (Thoughts
on Zhang Jie's Works). WYB, no. (1980): 26–29.

Huang, Xiuji "Lu Xun de 'bingcun' lun zui zhengque" (Lu Xun's
Coexistence Theory is Most Correct). WXPL, no. 5 (1978):
27–36.

Jenner, W.J.F. "The Hundred Flowers." Index on Censorship
(February 1980): 7–12.

––––––––––. "A New Start for Literature in China?" CQ, no. 86
(June 1981): 274–303.

Ji, Lu. "Symposium on Lu Xun." ChL, no. 1 (1982): 119–123.

Jiang, Zilong . "'Qiao changzhang shangren ji' de shenghuo zhang"
(The Life Behind 'Manager Qiao Takes Office'). SY, no. 4 (1979)
and XHYB(WZB), no. 3 (1980): 151–154.

Jiefangjun bao Commentator, "Yi sixiang yuanze wei wuqi kefu cuowu
sixiang yingxiang (Use the Four Fundamental Principles as a
Weapon to Overcome Incorrect Thinking). RMRB 27 April 1981.

––––––––––. "Scientifically Understand and Handle Class Struggle
in China." BR, no. 49 (6 December 1982): 16–21.

Jin, Qing . "Tichang ziyou taolun" (Advocating Freedom of

Discussion). WHB 3 November 1981: 3.

Jin, Shan . "Mingxing yunluo" (A Star Falls). RMRB 15 October 1980: 3. (On Zhao Dan)

"Juben chuangzuo zuotanhui qingkuang jianshu (Brief Report on the Drama Forum). XHYB(WZB), no. 6 (1980): 171–176.

Kane, Anthony J. "Literary Politics in Post–Mao China." *Asian Survey*, no. 7 (July 1981): 775–794.

King, Richard. "'Wounds' and 'Exposure': Chinese Literature after the Gang of Four." *Pacific Affairs* (Spring 1981): 82–100.

——————. "Chinese Film Controversy." *Index on Censorship* (May 1981): 36–37.

Kinkley, Jeffrey C., ed. *After Mao: Chinese Literature and Society, 1978–1981.* Cambridge: Harvard University East Asian Monograph, 1984. Seven papers from May 1982 St. John's University conference on Realism in Contemporary Chinese literature.

Lau, Joseph S.M. (Liu Shao–ming). "Pibei de linghun: tan 'shanghen wenxue'" : (Tired Souls: On 'Scar Literature'). MB, no. 8 (1981): 72–76.

——————. "The Wounded and the Fatigued: Reflections on Post–1976 Chinese Fiction." *Journal of Oriental Studies*, vol. 20 (1979).

——————, "Chaoliu yu diandi–xieshi xiaoshuo de liangzhong leixing" (Main Currents and Tributaries–Two Types of Modern Chinese Realist Narrative). MB (September 1982): 97–101.

——————. "Between Two Worlds: the Marginality of *T'e–chü wen–hsüeh* (Literature of the Special Areas)." Unpublished conference paper, March 1983.

——————. "Menglong xiuzou" (Don't Go Away Obscurity). *Jiushi niandai* (June 1984): 99–100.

Lee, Leo Ou–fan (Lee Ou–fan). "Dissent Literature from the Cultural Revolution." *Chinese Literature: Essays Articles Reviews*, no. 1 (January 1979): 59–79.

——————. "Recent Chinese Literature: A Second Hundred Flowers." In Robert Oxnam, ed. *China Briefing.* Boulder, CO: Westview Press, 1980: 65–73.

——————. "Gao Xiaosheng de 'Li Shunda zao wu' yu fanfeng yiyi (GXS's 'Li Shunda Builds a House' and Its Ironic Meaning). *Dangdai* (Contemporary, Hong Kong), no. 4 (1980): 4–8.

——————. "Technique as Dissidence: A Perspective on Contemporary Chinese Fiction." In Jeffrey Kinkley, ed. *Respite From Politics.*

----------. "'Xiandai zhuyi' wenyi suo mianlin de 'wuran'" (The "Pollution that "Modernism" Faces). QSND (January 1984): 78-79.

Lee, Yee . "Xu Fuguan tan zhonggong zhengju" (Xu Fuguan Discusses the Chinese Communist Political Situation). QSND (May 1981): 8-16.

----------. "Aiguo zhuyi de huhuan" (The Call to Patriotism). QSND (June 1981): 42-46.

----------. "Zhongguo weishemme dui wenyi ruci mingan?" (Why is China so Sensitive About Literature and Art?). QSND (July 1982): 90-93.

----------. "Liu Binyan he ta de shidai" (Liu Binyan and His Age). QSND (December 1982): 64-76. October 1982 interview at the University of Iowa.

Lei, Da and Liu Xicheng . "San nian lai xiaoshuo chuangzuo fazhan de lunkuo" (An Outline of Short Story Development in the Last Three Years). WYB (October 1979): 6-12.

Li, Jian . "Gede yu quede" (Praising Virtue and Lacking Virtue). *Hebei wenyi* (Hebei Literature, June 1979), RMRB 31 July 1979, and XHYB(WZB), no. 8 (1979): 173-174.

Li, Jie . "Jiaru wo shi yige zuojia" (If I Were a Writer). *Yuhua* (Rain Flowers), no. 7 (1979).

Li, Weihan. "Mao Zedong's Unique Contribution," BR, no. 1 (2 January 1984): 19-22.

Li, Weishi . "Sikao, dan bie wangle wenxue" (Think, but Don't Forget Literature). GMRB 6 March 1979.

Li, Xiaoba . "Cong wuliu nian He Zhi de wenzhang tanqi" (Remarks Prompted by He Zhi's 1956 Article). *Yanhe* (Yan River), no. 4 (1979): 32-38.

Li, Xifan . "Tangruo you suowei tianguo ..." (If There is a So-called Heavenly Country...). WYB, no. 5 (1980): 47-51.

Li, Zehou . "Hualang tan mei — gei L.J. de xin" (Speaking of Beauty at a Painting Exhibition — a Letter to L.J.). WYB, no. 2 (1981): 41-44.

---------- and Vera Schwarcz. "Six Generations of Modern Chinese Intellectuals." Unpublished AAS conference paper, April 1982.

Liang, Heng and Judith Shapiro. *Son of the Revolution.* N.Y.: Knopf, 1983. In Chinese as *Geming zhi zi* . Taipei: Shibao wenhua chubanshe, 1983.

----------. "Zhongguo dalu minjian wenxue jianjie" (A Brief Introduction to Popular Literature on the China Mainland).

Unpublished St. John's conference paper, 1982.

Liao, Gailong . "Zhonggong 'gengshen gaige' fang'an" (Draft of the Chinese Communists' 1981 Reforms). QSND (March 1981): 38–47.

Lin, Boye and Shen Che . "Ping suowei fandui guanliao zhuyizhe jieji" (A Critique of the So-called Opposition to a Bureaucratic Class). HQ, no. 6 (1981): 12–18.

Lin, Hua . "Cong pingjia 'Kulian' kan dangqian zhonggong de zhengju" (Chinese Communists' Present Political Situation as Seen from the Criticism of Bitter Love). ZB (June 1981):38–41.

Lin, Xianzhi . "Shilun Ren a, ren! de xinren xingxiang" (Tentative Discussion of the Images of New People in Ren a, ren!). Nanfang ribao (Southern Daily) 8 January 1982.

Link, Perry. "Fiction and the Reading Public in Guangzhou and Other Chinese Cities, 1979–80." unpublished conference paper, 1982.

Liu, Binyan . "Guanyu 'xie yin'an mian' he 'ganyu shenghuo'" (On Writing About the Dark Side and Interfering in Real Life). SHWX, no. 3 (1979): 49–57.

——————. "Liu Binyan zishu – zai Heilongjiang qingnian wenxue chuangzuo huiyi shang de jianghua" (Liu Binyan Speaks at the Conference on Youth Literature in Heilongjiang). May 1979: 1–38. Source unknown, I received a xerox copy from a friend in Hong Kong. Another complete text of this brutally frank speech was printed in Guangjiaojing (Wide Angle, March 1980): 10–23.

——————. "Shidai de zhaohun" (The Call of the Age). WYB (November–December 1979): 36–46.

——————. "Ai shi buke queshao de" (Love is Indispensable). Wenhui zengkan (Literary Supplement, January 1980): 9–12.

——————. "Guanyu 'Ren yao zhijian': da duzhe wen' (Answering Readers' Questions Concerning 'Between Men and Monsters'). RMWX, no. 1 (1980).

——————. "Luzi hai keyi geng kuan xie" (Our Approach Could Still Be Somewhat More Flexible). WYYJ, no. 4 (1980): 76–77.

"Liu Binyin tongzhi de yifeng xin" (A Letter from Comrade LBY). Wenyi qingkuang (Literary Situation) 23 June 1980: 14.

——————. "Cong 'Ren yao zhijian yinqi de" (Events Touched Off by "Between Men and Monsters") RMWX, no. 12 (1980): 86–90.

——————. "Ying shi longteng huyue shi" (It Should be a Time of Great Development). DD, no. 5 (1982).

Liu, Jin . "Yiduan chahua" (An Interjection). WYB, no. 2 (1981):

38–39. Refusal to rewrite *What If I Really Were?*

Liu, Mengxi . "Wenxue de mingyun he zuojia de ziren" (The Fate of Literature and the Responsibility of Writers). RMRB 23 January 1980: 5.

----------. "Lüelun yijiubaling nian wenxue fazhan de zhuchao' (A Brief Discussion of the Main Trends of Literary Development in 1980). HQ, no. 3 (1981): 30–34.

Liu, Shaotang. "A Profile of Cong Weixi." ChL, no. 4 (1980): 57–60.

Liu, Xinwu . "Shenghuo de chuangzaozhe shuo: zou zhei tiao lu!" : (The Creator of Life Says: Take This Road!). WXPL, no. 5 (1978): 53–64.

Lo, Bing. "'Fan wuran' tuichao toushi" (Perspective on the Decline of the Anti–Spiritual Pollution Campaign). ZM (January 1984): 9–12.

Louie, Kam. "Discussions on Exposure Literature since the Fall of the Gang of Four." *Contemporary China*, no. 4 (Winter 1979): 91–102.

----------. "New Forms of Realism in Chinese Literature: the St. John's University Conference." AJCA, no. 9 (January 1983): 99–113.

Lu, Da . "Zhonggong wenyi zhengci zai shou menglie pengji" (Chinese Communist Literary Policy Under Heavy Criticism Again). *Nanbeiji* (North–south Pole, Hong Kong), no. 126 (16 November 1980): 46–49. On Zhao Dan's testament.

Lu, Xinhua . "Tantan wo de xizuo 'Shanghen'" (Talking About my Exercise *Shanghen*). WHB, no. 14 (1978) and XHYB(WZB), no. 1 (1979): 206–209.

Lu, Yifan . "Ping jianguo yilai dui 'rendao zhuyi' de pipan" (Critique of the Criticisms of 'Humanism' Since the Founding of the PRC). XHWZ, no. 6 (1981): 176–184.

Mackerris, Colin. "The Taming of the Shrew: Chinese Theatre and Social Change Since Mao." AJCA, no. 1 (1979): 1–18.

----------. "Chinese Language Periodicals on Literature and the Arts." Ibid., no. 6 (1981): 220–226.

McDougall, Bonnie S. "Dissent Literature: Official and Nonofficial Literature in and about China in the Seventies." *Contemporary China*, no. 4 (Winter 1979): 49–79.

----------. "Underground Literature: Two Reports from Hong Kong." Ibid.: 80–90.

----------. *Mao Zedong's 'Talks at the Yan'an Conference on Literature and Art.'* Ann Arbor: University of Michigan Center for Chinese Studies, 1980.

——————. "Zhao Zhenkai's Fiction: A Study in Cultural Alienation." *Journal of Modern Chinese Literature*, no. 1 (September 1984).

Mao, Zedong. *Mao Tse-tung on Literature and Art*. Peking: Foreign Languages Press, 1967.

——————. "A Talk to Music Workers, August 24, 1956." ChL, no. 1 (1980): 83–91.

——————. "Mao Zedong's Letters on Literature." BR, no. 22 (31 May 1982): 5–6, 23–29. Original published in RMRB 23 May 1982.

Meng, Weizai. "Youyi de qishi — tan Liu Binyan de baogao 'Ren yao zhijian'" (A Helpful Revelation — Discussing LBY's 'Between Men and Monsters'). WYB, no. 11–12 (1979): 82–85.

Min, Ze. "'Ren dao zhongnian' de daode liliang" (The Moral Force of 'Reaching Middle Age'). *Wenhui zengkan* (Literary Supplement), no. 4 (May 1980): 60–61.

"Minzhu yu yishu" (Democracy and Art). *Shanghai wenyi* (Now SHWX), no. 11 (1978): 4–10.

Mo, Yan. "Chifa de gaojian — ping 'Zai shehui de dang'an li'" (A Late Draft — Critique of 'In the Files of Society'). WYB, no. 9 (1980) and XHYB(WZB), no. 11 (1980):141–143.

Mu, Fu. "Yichang daijia gao'ang de biaoyan: Bai Hua shijian huigu" (A Costly Performance: Recalling the Bai Hua Incident). QSND (February 1982): 12–14.

——————. "Yu Lojin: xin shiqi de panni nüxing" (YLJ: A Feminist Rebel in the New Age). QSND (July 1982): 79–81.

——————. "Cong 'Muma ren' kan zhonggong wenyi xin moshi" (Chinese Communists' New Literary Model as Seen in *The Herdsman*). QSND (November 1982): 89–91.

——————. "Yihua lilun yu jingshen wuran" (The Theory of Alienation and Spiritual Pollution). QSND (December 1983): 56–60.

Ouyang, Pinghua. "Shengdong de renwu xingxiang" (Moving Characterizations, in *Ren a, ren*!). WHB 3 November 1981.

Pai, Hsien-yung. "Yibu beizhuang chentong de liuwangqu: du 'Fanxiulou' tan 'Beidouren'" (A Tragically Moving Wanderer's Song: Reading *The Anti-revisionist Tower* and Discussing the Dipper Writers). ZB, no. 3 (1980): 13–15.

Pan, Xiao. "Rensheng de yiyi jiujing shi shemme?" (What is the Meaning of Life After All?). *Zhongguo qingnian* (Chinese Youth, April 1980) and QSND (January 1981): 82–90.

Peng, Yunqiang and Yang Zhijie. "Fandui guanliao zhuyi shi shehui zhuyi wenxue de zhongyao shiming" (Opposing Bureaucratism is an Important Mission of Socialist Literature). SHWX, no. 9 (1979) and XHYB(WZB), no. 1 (1980): 160–162.

Pollard, D.E. "The Short Story in the Cultural Revolution." CQ, no. 73 (March 1978):99–121.

Qi, Fang . "Zhongguo wenxue he zhongguo xianshi." (Chinese Literature and Chinese Realities). WYYJ, no. 1 (1981): 126–132. Critical of Lee Yee's "new realism" selections.

Qi, Junmin . "Cuowu de denghao — guanyu *Ren a, ren*! zhong de rendao zhuyi wenti" (A Mistaken Equivalence — On the Problem of Humanism in *Ren a, ren*!). *Nanfang ribao* (Southern Daily) 22 January 1982.

Qi, Xin . "Zhonggong wanchengle jizhuanwan: san zhong quanhui de taiqian–muhou" (The CCP Completes a U–turn: Inside Story of the Third Plenum). QSND (February 1979): 7–17.

—————. "Cong Deng Xiaoping guanyu tequan wenti de jianghua tanqi — jiantan huaju 'Jiaru wo shi zhende' de shehui beijing" (Beginning with DXP's Speech on Bureaucratism — also Discussing the Social Background of the Play *What If I Really Were?*). QSND (January 1980): 74–75.

Qian, Hai and Li Yan . "Wenxue de fanrong he zuojia de zeren" (Literature's Flourishing and the Writers' Responsibilities). RMRB 25 May 1981: 2.

—————. "Zhengque kaizhan wenyi piping, zengqiang zuojia de shehui zerengan" (Corrrectly Develop Literary Criticism, Strengthen Writers' Sense of Social Responsibility). WYYJ, no. 2 (1981) and XHWZ, no. 7 (1981): 163–164.

Qin, Mu . "Fayang guangda geming wenxue de xianshi zhuyi chuantong" (Carry On the Great Tradition of Realism in Revolutionary Literature). *Nanfang ribao* (Southern Daily) 2 April 1980.

Qin, Zhaoyang. "The Writer Wang Meng." ChL, no. 7 (1980): 3–8.

Qu, Liuyi . "Yishu shi zhen shan mei de jiejing — dui 'Jiaru wo shi zhende,' 'Zai shehui dang'an li,' deng zuopin de ganxiang" (Art is the Crystalization of Truth Goodness and Beauty — Reflections on *What If I Really Were?*, 'In the Files of Society,' and Other Works). WYB, no. 4 (1980): 49–53.

RMRB Reporter. "Zhengque fanying xin shidai, suzao shehui zhuyi xinren" (Correctly Reflect the New Era, Portray Socialist New People). RMRB 25 April 1981:4. A report on He Jingzhi's discussions with the editors of *Zuopin yu zhengming* (Works and Contention).

RMRB Special Commentator. "Zhixing sanzhong quanhui luxian, jianchi sixiang jiben yuanze" (Implement the Third Plenum Line, Uphold the Four Fundamental Principles). RMRB 24 April 1981: 1. Summarized in the English language *Ta Kung Pao* of 30 April 1981: 3.

RMRB Commentator. "Zhengque jinxing fanqingxiang de douzheng" (Correctly Carry Out the Anti-tendencies Struggle). RMRB 26 April 1981.

———————. "Wenyi shi yindao renmin qianjin de 'denghuo'" (Literature and Art are the Lamplights Which Lead the People Forward). RMRB 6 February 1980: 5.

———————. "Zhangwo hao wenyi piping de wuqi" (Master Well the Weapon of Literary Criticism). RMRB 18 August 1981 and XHWZ, no. 10 (1981): 154.

RMRB Special Commentator. "Ping 'zuo bi you hao'" (Critique of 'Left is Better than Right'). RMRB 27 May 1981 and XHWZ, no. 7 (1981): 8–9.

———————. "Huifu piping yu ziwo piping de dangfeng" (Revise the Party Practice of Criticism and Self-criticism). RMRB 11 May 1981 and XHWZ no. 7 (1981): 9–11.

———————. "Tigao shehui zeren, zhengque miaoxie aiqing" (Raise Our Sense of Social Responsibility, Write Correctly About Love). RMRB 11 November 1981: 5.

Rubin, Kyna. "An Interview with Mr. Wang Ruowang." CQ, no. 87 (September 1981): 501–517.

Sha, Yexin . "Chedan" (Talking Nonsense). WYB, no. 10 (1980): 7–11.

———————. "Juben chuangzuo duanxiang lu" (Record of My Thoughts on Playwriting). *Shanghai xiju* (Shanghai Theatre), nos. 3, 5, and 6 (1980): 59–60, 22–23, and 2–5. The last piece specifically refers to *What If I Really Were?*

Shao, Ke . "Ping xiaoshuo 'Qiao changzhang shangren ji'" (Critique of the Story 'Manager Qiao Takes Office'). *Tianjin ribao* (Tianjin Daily) 12 September 1979 and XHYB(WZB), no. 12 (1979): 180–183.

Shi, Jian . "Jiefang sixiang de yige zhongyao wenti" (An Important Problem with Emancipation of the Mind). HQ, no. 3 (1982) and BR, no. 16 (19 April 1982): 24–25.

Su, Liwen . "'Aiqing re' manbu zhongguo wentan" ('Hot Love' Flourishes in Chinese Literature). QSND (February 1982): 76–79.

———————. "Dalu shitan de yichang da hunzhan" (A Great Battle in Mainland Chinese Poetic Circles). QSND (November 1981):

38–44.

——————. "'Xiandai pai' zuojia mianlin chongji" ("Modernist"
Writers Face Attacks). QSND (December 1983): 62–64.

Su, Shuyang . "Cong shiji shenghuo chufa suzao renwu" (Create
Characters from Real Life). *Renmin xiju* (People's Theatre, May
1978).

——————. "How I Came to Write 'Loyal Hearts'." ChL, no. 10
(1978): 106–107.

Sun, Wuchen. "Tandao ruhe fanying xin de shiqi de shehui maodun
wenti" (Discussion of How to Reflect Current Social
Contradictions). *Xiangjiang wenyi* (Xiang River Literature,
January 1981): 71–74.

Tan, Tianming . "Yao yindao renmin zhengque renshi shenghuo" (We
Must Lead the People to Correctly Understand Life). WHB 24
February 1981: 3.

Tang, Yin and Tang Dacheng . "Lun *'Kulian'* de cuowu qingxiang"
(On the Mistaken Tendency in *Bitter Love*). HQ, no. 19 (1981):
9–16.

Tang, Yuan . "Guanyu yijiu sanliu nian 'liangge kouhou' lunzhan de
xingzhi wenti" (On the Question of the Nature of the 1936 Battle
of the Two Slogans). WXPL, no. 3 (1978): 10–19.

Tay, William. "How Obscure Is 'Obscure Poetry'?" In Jeffrey C.
Kinkley, ed. *Respite From Politics.*

Ting, Wang . "Fenxi Bai Hua de daibiaozuo *'Kulian'*" (Analyzing Bai
Hua's Representative Work *Bitter Love*). *Lianhebao* (United
Daily, overseas edition) 10–13 June 1981.

——————. "Chuye quan yu beiju wenxue" (The Right of the
First Night and Tragic Literature). MB, no. 7 (1982): 22–25 and
no. 9 (1982): 58–62.

——————. "Beiju wenxue yu liangxing guanxi" (Tragic
Literature and the Relations Between the Sexes). *Lianhebao
fukan* (United Dailey, overseas edition) 31 May 1982.

Wagner, Rudolf G. "The Real Future in the Passing Present: Science
Fiction in the PRC." In Jeffrey C. Kinkley, ed. *Respite From
Politics.*

Wang, Chang–ling . *Bai Hua de le* (Pai Hua's Road). Taibei: Liming
wenhua shiye gongsi, 1982.

Wang, Chunyuan . "Guanyu xie yingxiong renwu lilun wenti de
tantao" (Preliminary Discussion of the Theoretical Problems
Concerning Creating Heroic Characters). WXPL, no. 5 (1979).

——————. "Lu Wenting de beiju yu shenghuo de yinying" (Lu
Wenting's Tragedy and Life's Dark Shadows). WYB, no. 9

(1980): 10–11.

Wang, Fu. "A Difficult Path — Introducing the Amateur Writer Jiang Zilong." ChL, no. 2 (1980): 63–66.

Wang, Meng . *Dang ni naqi bi* (When You Take Up Your Pen). Peking: Beijing chubanshe, 1981.

──────────. "Zhengkai yanjing, mianxiang shenghuo" (Open Your Eyes and Look at Life). GMRB 5 September 1979.

──────────. "Guanyu 'yishiliu' de tongxin" (Open Letter on Stream-of-Consciousness). YLJ, no. 2 (1980): 70–72.

──────────. "Buduan tansuo xin de biaoxian shoufa" (Constantly Searching for New Methods of Expression). *Beijing wanbao* (Peking Evening News) 2 July 1980.

──────────. "Gei Yan Wenjing tongzhi de huixin" (A Letter of Reply to Comrade Yan Wenjing). Ibid. 5 July 1980.

──────────. "Zai tansuo de daolu shang" (On the Road of Exploration). XHWZ, no. 1 (1981): 148–151.

──────────. "For a Better Life." ChL, no. 2 (1981): 130–134.

──────────. "My Exploration." ChL, no. 3 (1981): 56–63.

──────────. "Weile gengjia chengshou de wenxue" (For a More Mature Literature). WYB, no. 6 (1981): 12–15.

──────────. "Shenghuo, qingxiang, bianzhengfa, he wenxue" (Life, Tendencies, Dialectics, and Literature). WYB, no. 6 (1981): 175–181.

──────────. "Zhongguo wenxue de mingyun yu zuojia de shiming" (The Fate of Chinese Literature and the Writers' Mission). Unpublished St. John's conference paper, 1982.

──────────. "Qingtingzhe shenghuo de shengxi" (Listening Carefully to the Sounds of Life). In Wang's *Manhua xiaoshuo chuangzuo* (Talks on Literary Creation). Shanghai: Shanghai wenyi chubanshe, 1983: 3–19.

Wang, Ruoshui . "Zhenli biaojun yu lilun yanjiu" (The Standard of Truth and Theoretical Research). *Dushu* (Reading) no. 1 (1980) and XHYB(WZB), no. 3 (1980): 11–15.

Wang, Ruowang . "Lun 'gede pai'" (On the 'Praise Faction'). *Dushu*, no. 7 (1979) and XHYB(WZB), no. 12 (1979): 168–175.

──────────. "Chuntianli de yige lengfeng" (A Cold Wind in Spring). GMRB 20 July 1979: 3.

──────────. "Tan wenyi de 'wuwei er zhi'" (Discussing Non-action in Literature and Art). XHYB(WZB), no. 10 (1979): 190–91.

──────────. "Wenyi yu zhengzhi bushi congshu guanxi" (The Arts are not in a Subordinate Relationship with Politics). WYYJ, no. 1

(1980): 61–65.

Wang, Xiyan . "Cong niupeng dao laodongying — wenge haojie zhong de Ba Jin" (From Cow Shed to Labor Camp — Ba Jin During the Cultural Revolution Calamity). *Lianhebao* (United Daily, overseas edition) 12 and 13 April 1984: 4.

Wang, Xizhe . "Mao Zedong yu wenhua da geming" (MZD and the Cultural Revolution). QSND (February 1981): 26–49.

Wei, Jianlin . "Zuojia de shehui zeren he zuopin de shehui xiaoguo" (Writers' Social Responsibility and the Social Effects of Works). HQ, no 6 (1981): 30–35.

WHB editors. "Tongxin xieli jianshe shehui zhuyi jingshen wenming" (Cooperate and Work Hard to Build Socialist Spiritual Civilization). WHB 1 March 1981. Excerpts from various PRC periodicals.

WYB editors. "'Wenyi de shehui gongneng' wuren tan" (A Five Person Discussion of the Social Function of Literature and Art). WYB, no. 1 (1980): 29–36.

——————. "Lianghao de kaiduan" (A Good Beginning). WYB, no. 3 (1980): 6. On the Drama Forum of January–February 1980.

Wilson, Patricia. "'. . . I Sought the Jewel of Art': Introducing Zhao Dan." ChL, no. 4 (1980): 73–92.

Wong, Wei-leung . "Mainland China from the Perspective of Its Emigré Writers in Hong Kong." Unpublished St. John's conference paper, 1982.

Wood, Francis. "Official Publishing." *Index on Censorship* (February 1980): 42–46.

Wu, Mang . "Feixu shang de huhuan: lun dalu 'feixu wenxue'" (A Cry from the Ruins: On Mainland 'Literature of the Ruins'). ZB, no. 6 (1980): 92–95.

Xi, Bian , Fang Keqiang , and Gu Changhao . "Bingfei kongshan bujian ren — tan *Ren a, ren!* de yishu chuangxin jian yu He Manzi tongzhi shangquan" (Certainly Not a Case of Empty Talk — Discussing the Artistry of *Ren a, ren!* and Debating Comrade He Manzi). WHB 18 December 1981.

Xia, Zhengnong . "Meiyou minzhu jiu meiyou shehui zhuyi" (Without Democracy there's no Socialism). XHYB(WZB), no. 1 (1979): 1–6.

Xiang, Tong . "Wenyi yaobuyao fanying shehui zhuyi shiqi de beiju — cong '*Shanghen*' tanqi" (Should Literature Reflect Tragedies of the Socialist Era — Beginning with '*Shanghen*'). GMRB 3 November 1978.

Xie, Yongwang . "Du shu yi zhi — ping Gao Xiaosheng de xiaoshuo"

(Raising a Solitary Banner — Critique of GXS's Short Stories). WYB, no. 2 (1980): 5–10.

XHYB Reporters. "Xin zi, duanpian xiaoshuo 'chongfeng' ji qi taolun" (New Data on the Short Story 'Re–encounter' and the Debate Surrounding It). XHYB(WZB), no. 8 (1979): 201.

Xu, Congzhe . "Zhonggong de wenyi luxian" (The Chinese Communist Literary Line). QSND (December 1979): 15–19. Summary of 1979 debates.

Xu, Dayuan . "Ye tan shehui zhuyi shidai de beiju wenti" (Also Discussing the Question of Tragedies in the Socialist Era). *Guangzhou wenyi* (Canton Literature), no. 6 (1979): 39–40.

Yan, Xiu . "Lun 'gede pai'" (On the 'Praise Faction'). XHYB(WZB), no. 12 (December 1979): 168–172.

Yang, Gladys. "'Power Versus Law' — a Courageous, Topical Play." ChL, no. 6 (1980): 92–97.

––––––––––. "A New Woman Writer Shen Rong and Her Story 'At Middle Age.'" ChL, no. 10 (1980): 65–70.

Yang, Xueying. "'Save Her' — A Play About Juvenile Delinquency." ChL, no. 8 (1980): 111–115.

Yang, Yi. "A Man Who Conquered Fate." ChL, no. 8 (1979): 3–15. An Interview with Ba Jin.

Yang, Zhansheng . "Ping 'liangge kouhao' de lunzheng" (Critique of the Battle of the Two Slogans). WXPL, no. 3 (1978): 20–26.

Yao, Zhengming and Wu Mingying . "Sisuo shemme yang de 'shenghuo zheli' — ping changpian xiaoshuo *Ren a, ren*!" (What Kind of 'Life Philosophy' are You Thinking About — Critique of the Novel *Ren a, ren*!). WHB 17 October 1981.

Ye, Yun . "Zhonggong wentan you qi zhenglun" (Chinese Communist Literary Debates). QSND (September 1979): 31–33.

Ye, Zhicheng. "The String That Will Never Break — Introducing the Writer Gao Xiaosheng." ChL, no. 12 (1980): 26–31.

Yeh, Wei–lian (William Yip). "Weiji wenxue de lilu — dalu menglongshi de shengbian" (The Logic of Crisis Literature — The Rise and Development of Mainland Obscure Poetry). *Jiushi niandai* (The Nineties, June 1984): 90–95.

Yi, Jun . "'Zai shehui de dang'an li' si ti" (Four Questions about 'In the Files of Society'). WYB, no. 5 (1980): 60–64.

Yi, Yan . "Wei zhongnian ganbei" (A Toast to Middle Age). WYB, no. 3 (1980): 16–18. On Shen Rong's story.

Yi, Zhun . "Ping 'chuntian de tonghua' de cuowu qingxiang" (Critique of the Mistaken Tendency in 'Spring Fairytale'). ZP, no. 6 (1982):52–56.

Yin, Ming . "Yige tujie de renwu xingxiang — Xi Liu" (A Graphic Characterization — Xi Liu). WHB 3 November 1981: 3.

Yu, Congzhe . "Sheng Ruowang wenxue taolunhui shang de zhenglun" (Polemics at the St. John's Literature Conference). QSND (July 1982): 31–32.

Yu, Jianzhang . "Lun dangdai wenxue chuangzuo zhong de rendao zhuyi chaoliu" (On the Tide of Humanism in Contemporary Literary Creation). WXPL, no. 1 (1981): 22–33.

Yuan, Fang . "'*Kulian*' yu zhishi fenzi de aiguo xin" (*Bitter Love* and the Patriotism of the Intellectuals). HQ, no. 9 (1981): 27–33.

Zhang, Guangnian . "Zhengqu wenxue shiye riyi fanrong" (Strive for a Situation of Day–by–Day Literary Flourishing). RMRB 21 April 1981: 2. Speech at the presentation of the 1980 short story prizes.

–––––––––. "Fazhan baihua qifang de xin jumian" (Develop the New Situation of A Hundred Flowers Blooming). RMRB 10 June 1981 and RMWX, no. 6 (1981): 3–6.

Zhao, Cong . "Bai Hua shijian yu wenyi zhengce" (The Bai Hua Incident and Literary Policy). MB (June 1981): 15–18.

Zhao, Dan ."Guan de tai juti, wenyi mei xiwang" (Watched Too Closely, Literature and Art Have No Hope). RMRB 8 October 1980: 5. Translated as "Rigid Control Ruins Art and Literature" in ChL, no. 1 (1981): 107–111. See *Dongxiang* (Tendency), no. 3 (1981): 8–11 for a discussion of the aftermath of this testament.

Zhao, Ziyang. "Report on the Work of the Government." BR, no. 27 (4 July 1983): I–XXIV. At the First Session of the Sixth NPC on 6 June 1983. Part III concerns literature and art policies.

Zheng, Huaizhi . "Guanyu 'Jia' ju yanchu yihou de yixie qingkuang" (Concerning Some Situations After the Performance of *What If I Really Were*?). WHB 2 February 1981: 3.

Zheng, Wen. "Kexue di kandai wenyi de shehui xiaoguo" (Scientifically Consider the Social Effects of Literature and Art). RMRB 23 April 1980 and XHYB(WZB), no. 6 (1980): 184–186.

Zhou, Enlai . "Zai wenyi gongzuo zuotanhui he gushipian chuangzuo huiyi shang de jianghua" (Speech at a Forum of Literary and Art Workers and a Conference on the Creation of Feature Films, 19 June 1961). HQ, no. 3 (1979): 2–16 and ChL, no. 6 (1979): 83–95.

Zhou, Yang . "Xin minge kaituole shige de xin daolu" (New Folk Songs Open a New Road for Poetry). HQ, no. 1 (1958): 33–39. On "Revolutionary Romanticism."

–––––––––. "Sanci weida de sixiang jiefang yundong" (Six Great Movements to Liberate Thinking). RMRB 7 May 1979 and XHYB(WZB), no. 5 (1979): 1–9. Commemoration of the 60th anniversary of the May Fourth Movement.

——————. "Jiwang kailai, fanrong shehui zhuyi xin shiqi de wenyi" (Be Both Successors and Pioneers, Create a Flourishing Literature and Art in the New Period of Socialism). WYB, no. 11–12 (1979): 8–26. Excerpted in BR, no. 50 (14 December 1979): 8–15. Speech of 1 November 1979 at the Fourth Congress of Writers and Artists.

——————. "Zhou Yang on Reality in Literature and Other Questions." ChL, no. 1 (1980): 92–96. October 1979 interview.

——————. "Xuexi Lu Xun, yanzhe Lu Xun de zhandou fangxiang jixu qianjin" (Study Lu Xun, Continue to Go Forward Along Lu Xun's Direction of Struggle). RMRB 27 February 1980 and XHYB(WZB), no. 4 (1980): 174–178. Speech of 8 May 1979 in preparation for Lu Xun Centennial.

——————. "Jiefang sixiang, zhenshidi biaoxian women de shidai" (Emancipate Thinking, Truthfully Reflect Our Age). WYB, no. 4 (1981) and XHWZ, no. 4 (1981): 132–137. Zhou's speech to the Drama Forum of 11 February 1980 was made public in 1981. Partial translation in BR, no. 15 (13 April 1981): 23–25.

——————. "Zhanhao gangshao, danghao yuanding" (Stand Firm at Your Guardposts, Be Good Gardeners). WYB, no. 7 (1980): 2–7. Speech of 5 May 1980 to editorial staff of literary magazines.

——————. "Jianchi Lu Xun de wenhua fangxiang, fayang Lu Xun de zhandou chuantong" (Persist in Lu Xun's Cultural Direction and Develop Lu Xun's Militant Tradition). RMRB 28 September 1981 and ChL, no. 1 (1982): 99–118. Speech at the Lu Xun Centennial.

——————. "Guanyu zhengzhi he wenyi de guanxi" (On the Relationship Between Politics and Literature and Art). RMRB 25 March 1981. Translated in BR, no. 15 (13 April 1981): 23–25.

——————. "Wenxue yao gei renmin yi liliang" (Literature Should Give the People Strength). RMRB 21 April 1981: 2.

——————. "Anzhao renmin de yizhi he yishu de biaojun lai pingjian zuopin" (Appraise Literary Works on the Basis of the People's Desires and Scientific Standards). RMRB 24 June 1981: 5. Zhou's summing up of the lessons of the campaign against Bai Hua.

"Zuojia you quanli tichu shenghuo zhong de wenti" (Writers Have the Right to Raise Questions About Life). WYB, no. 9 (1980).

IV. GENERAL BACKGROUND AND REFERENCE

Abrams, M.H. et al., eds. *The Norton Anthology of English Literature.*
Revised. Vol. 2A. N.Y.: W.W.Norton, 1968.

Aird, John S. "Population Studies and Population Policy in China."
Population and Development Review, vol. 8 (1982): 277–278.
Estimates 23 million extra deaths as a result of the Great Leap
Forward; based on Chinese statistics.

Becker, George J., ed. *Documents of Modern Literary Realism.*
Princeton, NJ: Princeton University Press, 1963.

Bernstein, Thomas P. "Starving to Death in China." *New York
Review of Books* (16 June 1983): 36–38. Partial translation of an
article from *Nongye jingji conkan* (Agricultural Economics
Review), no. 6 (1980): 18–19 which uses "starved to death" (*e-si*)
in describing situation in Anhui during the Great Leap.

Birch, Cyril, ed. *Chinese Communist Literature.* N.Y.: Praeger, 1963.

Bodde, Derk and Clarence Morris. *Law in Imperial China.*
Cambridge, MA: Harvard University Press, 1967.

Bonavia, David. *The Chinese: A Portrait.* London: Allen Lane, 1981.
Chapters 15 and 16 are eyewitness reports on the 1978–79 literary
scene and "democracy wall" movement.

Brown, Edward J. *Russian Literature Since the Revolution.* N.Y.:
MacMillan, 1969.

Butterfield, Fox. *China: Alive in the Bitter Sea.* N.Y.: New York
Times Books, 1982.

Chan, Anita and Jonathan Unger, eds. "The Case of Li I-che[Li
Yizhe]." *Chinese Law and Government*, Vol. X, no. 3 (Fall
1977): entire.

Chang, Parris H. "Chinese Politics: Deng's Turbulent Quest."
Problems of Communism (January–February 1981): 1–21.

Chen, Guangsheng. *Lei Feng: Chairman Mao's Good Fighter.*
Peking: Foreign Languages Press, 1968.

Chiu, Hungdah. "China's New Legal System." *Current History*
(September 1980): 29–32, 44–45.

Coale, Ansley J. "Population Trends, Population Policy, and
Population Studies in China." *Population and Development
Review*, vol. 7 (1981): 89. Estimates 16.5 million extra mortality
during the four years after the Great Leap Forward.

Cohen, Jerome Alan. *The Criminal Process in the People's Republic
of China, 1949–1963.* Cambridge, MA: Harvard University
Press, 1968.

——————. "China's Changing Constitution." CQ, no. 76

(December 1978): 835–837.

"Communique of the Third Plenum." HQ, no. 1 (1979): 14–21 and RMRB 24 December 1978 and *Peking Review*, no. 52 (29 December 1978).

Constitution of the People's Republic of China. Peking: Foreign Languages Press, 1975 and 1978.

Constitution of the People's Republic of China (4 December 1982). Unofficial translation in BR, no. 52 (27 December 1982): 10–29.

Constitution of the Communist Party of China (6 September 1982). Unofficial translation in BR, no. 38 (20 September 1982): 8–21.

Dean, Leonard F. *Shakespeare: Modern Essays in Criticism.* N.Y.: Oxford University Press, 1961.

Dittmer, Lowell. "The 12th Congress of the Communist Party of China." CQ, no. 93 (March 1983): 108–124.

Djlas, Milovan. *The New Class: An Analysis of the Communist System.* N.Y.: Praeger, 1967.

Documents of the First Session of the Fifth National People's Congress of the People's Republic of China. Peking: Foreign Languages Press, 1978. Contains Hua Guofeng's speech mentioned in Chapter One.

Dostoyevsky, Fyodor. *The Idiot.* N.Y.: New American Library, 1969.

Fan, K.H., ed. *The Chinese Cultural Revolution: Selected Documents.* N.Y.: Grove Press, 1968.

Fraser, John. *The Chinese: Portrait of a People.* Toronto: Collins Publishers, 1980. Pages 199–271 are an eyewitness report on the "tiny democracy movement."

Friedman, Edward. "Learning About China after the Revolution . . . for the first time." *Bulletin of Concerned Asian Scholars*, Vol. 13, no. 2 (April–June 1981): 41–48.

Frolic, B. Michael. *Mao's People: Sixteen Portraits of Life in Revolutionary China.* Cambridge, MA: Harvard University Press, 1980.

Frye, Northrop. *Anatomy of Criticism.* Princeton, NJ: Princeton University Press, 1957.

––––––––––. *Romanticism Reconsidered: Selected Papers from the English Institute.* N.Y.: Columbia University Press, 1963.

Garside, Roger. *Coming Alive: China After Mao.* N.Y.: McGraw–Hill, 1981. Chapters 10–17 are eyewitness reports on human rights, literature, and the democracy movement.

Gleckner, Robert F. and Gerald E. Enscoe, eds. *Romanticism: Points of View.* Englewood, NJ: Prentice Hall, second edition, 1970.

Goldman, Merle. *Literary Dissent in Communist China.* Cambridge:

Harvard University Press, 1967.
----------. *Modern Chinese Literature in the May Fourth Era.*
Cambridge: Harvard University Press, 1977.
----------. *China's Intellectuals: Advise and Dissent.*
Cambridge: Harvard University Press, 1981.
Gotz, Michael. *Images of the Worker in Contemporary Chinese Fiction (1949-1964).* Unpublished Ph.D. dissertation, University of California, Berkeley, 1977.
Guillermaz, Jacques. *The Chinese Communist Party in Power, 1949-1976.* Boulder, CO: Westview Press, 1976.
Gunn, Edward M. *Unwelcome Muse: Chinese Literature in Shanghai and Peking, 1937-1945.* N.Y.: Columbia University Press, 1980.
Harvard University Center for International Affairs, ed. *Communist China 1955-1959, Policy Documents with Analysis.* Cambridge: Harvard University Press, 1962.
Hawkes, David. *Ch'u Tz'u: Songs of the South.* Boston: Beacon, 1962.
Hersey, John. "Homecoming." *New Yorker* (10, 17, 24, and 31 May 1982).
Hinton, William. *Shenfan.* N.Y.: Random House, 1983. Complete collaboration of the neo-realist critique of Cultural Revolution rural policies by one who continues to believe in Maoist economics.
Hollowell, John. *Fact and Fiction: the New Journalism and the Nonfiction Novel.* Chapel Hill: University of North Carolina Press, 1977.
Hsia, C.T. *A History of Modern Chinese Fiction.* New Haven, CT: Yale University Press, revised edition, 1971.
----------. *The Classic Chinese Novel.* N.Y.: Columbia University Press, 1968.
----------. "Hsü Chen-ya's *Yü-li hun*: An Essay in Literary History and Criticism." Taibei: Academica Sinica International Sinological Conference reprint (October 1981).
Hsia, T.A. *The Gate of Darkness: Studies in the Leftist Literary Movement in China.* Seattle: University of Washington Press, 1968.
----------. "Twenty Years After the Yenan Forum." CQ, no. 13 (January-March 1963): 226-253.
Huang, Kecheng . "Guanyu dui Mao zhuxi pingjia he dui Mao Zedong Sixiang de taidu wenti" (On the Problems of the Evaluation of Chairman Mao and Our Attitude toward Mao Zedong Thought). JFJB 10 April 1981 and XHWZ, no. 5 (1981): 6-11.

Hugo, Victor. *Quatrevingt-Treize*. Paris: Editions Garnier Freres, 1963.

Important Documents on the Great Proletarian Cultural Revolution in China. Peking: Foreign Languages Press, 1970.

Jenner, W.J.F. "Lu Xun's Last Days and After." CQ, no. 91 (September 1982): 424–445.

Jie, Wen . "Guanyu shehui zhuyi shehui de jieji douzheng he zhuyao maodun" (On Class Struggle in Socialist Society and the Principle Contradiction). HQ, no. 20 (1981) and XHWZ, no. 12 (1981): 25–27.

Keith, Ronald C. "Transcript of Discussions with Wu Daying and Zhang Zhonglin Concerning Legal Change and Civil Rights." CQ, no. 81 (March 1980): 111–121.

––––––––––. "Socialist Legality and Proletarian Democracy in the People's Republic of China." *Canadian Journal of Political Science* (September 1980): 565–582.

Klatt, W. "The Staff of Life: Living Standards in China, 1977–81." CQ, no. 93 (March 1983): 17–50.

Lau, D.C. *The Analects*. Penguin, 1979.

––––––––––. *Mencius*. Penguin, 1970.

Lee, Leo Ou-fan. *The Romantic Generation of Modern Chinese Writers*. Cambridge: Harvard University Press, 1973.

Leng, Shao-chuan. "Criminal Justice in Post-Mao China." CQ, no. 87 (September 1981): 440–469.

Lewis, John Wilson, ed. *Party Leadership and Revolutionary Power in China*. Cambridge, England: Cambridge University Press, 1970.

Li, Victor H. "The Public Security Bureau and Political-Legal Work in Huiyang, 1952–64." In John Wilson Lewis, ed. *The City in Communist China*. Stanford: Stanford University Press, 1971.

Li, Yizhe. "Concerning Socialist Democracy and Legal System." In The 70s, ed. *China: The Revolution is Dead, Long Live the Revolution*. Montreal: Black Rose Books, 1971: 213–241. Written from September 1973 to November 1974.

Lin, Yü-sheng. "The Evolution of the Pre-Confucian Meaning of *Jen* and the Confucian Concept of Moral Autonomy." *Monumenta Serica*, vol. 31 (1974–75): 172–204.

Liu, I-ch'ing . *Shishuo xinyu* (A New Account of Tales of the World). Sibu beiyao. Translated with this title by Richard B. Mather and published by University of Minneapolis Press, 1976.

Liu, James J.Y. *Chinese Theories of Literature*. Chicago: University of Chicago Press, 1975.

Liu, Kwang-ching. "World View and Peasant Rebellion: Reflections on Post–Mao Historiography." *Journal of Asian Studies* (Februrary 1981): 295–326.

Liu, Qing. *Prison Memoirs.* Edited by Stanley Rosen and James Seymour. *Chinese Sociology and Anthropology,* vol.XV, no. 1–2 (Fall–Winter 1982/83): entire.

Lu, Xun . *Lu Xun quanji* . (Complete Works). 16 Vols. Peking: Renmin, 1981.

McDougall, Bonnie S. *The Introduction of Western Literary Theories Into Modern China, 1919–1925.* Tokyo: Centre for East Asian Cultural Studies, 1971.

Mack, Maynard, et al., eds. *The Continental Edition of World Masterpieces.* Vol. 2. N.Y.: Norton, 1966.

Martin, Helmut. *Cult and Canon. The Origin and Development of State Maoism.* Armonk, N.Y.: M.E. Sharpe, 1982.

Marx, Karl and Frederic Engels. *The German Ideology,* Part One. N.Y.: International Publishers, 1970.

Mao, Zedong. *Selected Works of Mao Tse–tung.* Vol. V. Peking: Foreign Languages Press, 1977.

Meisner, Maurice. *Mao's China.* N.Y.: Free Press, 1977.

Milosz, Czeslaw. *The Captive Mind.* N.Y.: Vintage, 1981. 1953 edition.

Moody, Peter R. *Opposition and Dissent in Contemporary China.* Stanford: Hoover Institution Press, 1977.

––––––––––. "Political Liberalization in China: A Struggle Between Two Lines." *Pacific Affairs* (Spring 1984): 26–44.

Panofsky, Erwin. *Meaning in the Visual Arts.* Garden City, NY: Doubleday, 1955.

Peng, Zhen. "Report on the Draft of the Revised Constitution..." BR, no. 50 (13 December 1982): 9–24.

Pickowicz, Paul G. *Marxist Literary Thought in China: The Influence of Ch'ü Ch'iu–pai.* Berkeley: University of California Press, 1981.

Polanyi, Michael. *Personal Knowledge.* Chicago: University of Chicago Press, 1958, 1962.

––––––––––. *Meaning.* Chicago: University of Chicago Press, 1975.

Resolution on Certain Questions in the History of Our Party Since the Founding of the People's Republic of China, BR, no. 27 (6 July 1981).

Schneider, Laurence A. *A Madman of Ch'u.* Berkeley: University of California Press, 1980.

Scholes, Robert and Robert Kellog. *The Nature of Narrative.* N.Y.:

Oxford University Press, 1966.

Schwartz, Benjamin I., ed. *Reflections on the May Fourth Movement: A Symposium.* Cambridge: Harvard University East Asian Research Center, 1972.

Sen, Amartya. "How is India Doing?" *New York Review of Books* (16 December 1982): 41–45. Has statistics on starvation in China during Great Leap and interesting comparason of the handling of famine in democratic India and communist China.

Shakespeare, William. *The Tempest. The Complete Pelican Shakespeare.* Penguin, 1969.

Smith, Hallett, ed. *Twentieth Century Interpretations of "The Tempest."* Englewood Cliffs, NJ: Prentice Hall, 1969.

Silone, Ignazio. *Bread and Wine.* 1955 edition. N.Y.: Signet, 1962.

Spence, Jonathan D. *The Gate of Heavenly Peace: The Chinese and Their Revolution, 1895–1980.* N.Y.: Viking Press, 1981.

Stallknecht, Newton P. and Horst Frenz, eds. *Comparative Literature: Method and Perspective.* Carbondale, IL: Southern Illinois University Press, revised edition, 1971.

Steiner, George. "Marxism and the Literary Critic." In Elizabeth and Tom Burns, eds. *Sociology of Literature and Drama.* Penguin, 1973.

Stevick, Philip, ed. *The Theory of the Novel.* N.Y.: Free Press, 1967.

Swayze, Harold. *Political Control of Literature in the USSR, 1946–1959.* Cambridge: Harvard University Press, 1962.

Terril, Ross, ed. *The China Difference.* N.Y.: Harper Colophon, 1979.

Tong, James, ed. "Underground Journals in China." *Chinese Law and Government,* vol. XIII, no. 3–4 (Fall–Winter 1980–81) and vol. XIV, no. 3 (Fall 1981): entire.

Tu, Wei–ming. "Creative Tension Between *Jen* and *Li.*" *Philosophy East and West* (January–April 1968): 29–39.

Twelfth National Congress of the Communist Party of China (September 1982). Peking: Foreign Languages Press, 1982.

Urban, George. "A Conversation with Leszek Kolakowski: The Devil in History." *Encounter* (January 1981): 9–26.

Waley, Arthur, trans. *The Book of Songs.* N.Y.: Grove Press, 1960.

Watson, Burton, trans. *The Complete Works of Chuang Tzu.* N.Y.: Columbia University Press, 1968.

Wellek, René. *Concepts of Criticism.* New Haven, CT: Yale University Press, 1963.

Womack, Brantly. "Modernization and Democratic Reforms in China." *Journal of Asian Studies* (May 1984): 417–439.

Yao, Mingle. *The Conspiracy and Death of Lin Biao.* N.Y.: Knopf, 1983.

Yu, Loke . "Yu Loke riji zhaichao" (Selections from Yu Loke's Diary). XHYB(WZB), no. 9 (1980): 128–129.

Zhang, Zhixin . "Zhe jiushi yige gongchandangyuan de xuanyan!" (This is a Communist Party Member's Declaration!). GMRB 12 June 1979 and XHYB(WZB), no. 5 (1979): 14–18.

Index

286   Blooming and Contending

168, 171, 172, 173, 174, 175,
178, 181, 202
humanity, 2, 22, 50, 76, 85, 98,
126, 135, 136, 139, 146, 150,
151, 167, 189, 201, 202
Hundred Flowers, 1, 3, 4, 9, 11,
13, 19, 21, 25, 44, 45, 46, 72,
101, 103, 108, 155, 157, 184
hundred schools of thought, 4, 13,
155
idealism, 2, 10, 11, 14, 25, 73, 78,
82, 90, 101, 103, 104, 110, 115,
120, 122, 129, 131, 154, 156,
157, 159, 160, 164, 166, 171,
173, 180, 181, 182, 184, 186,
188, 191, 192, 193, 195, 197,
204, 205
ideology, 2, 5, 7, 8, 12, 13, 19, 21,
22, 24, 25, 27, 40, 42, 49, 52,
57, 60, 62, 64, 82, 85, 87, 91,
92, 93, 94, 109, 116, 120, 121,
122, 124, 126, 149, 154, 155,
160, 164, 169, 173, 181, 190,
199, 206, 207
imagery, 8, 62, 63, 71, 115, 119,
120, 134, 135, 138, 145, 146,
182, 186, 188, 195, 198
imagination, 168, 182
individualism, 1, 8, 11, 17, 23, 25,
52, 57, 96, 161, 173, 183, 184
intellectuals, 1, 2, 3, 4, 14, 15, 16,
22, 24, 27, 53, 57, 58, 73, 82,
83, 84, 85, 96, 100, 101, 127,
130, 141, 142, 144, 147, 150,
153, 154, 155, 157, 159, 171,
179, 180, 181, 185, 189
ironies of history, 100
irony, 14, 23, 42, 67, 68, 72, 73,
77, 80, 85, 86, 87, 91, 92, 93,
94, 95, 98, 99, 100, 101, 102,
108, 111, 115, 120, 121, 122,
129, 130, 131, 132, 139, 147,

157, 158, 168, 170, 173, 187,
199, 205
Jiang Qing, 4, 79, 138
Jiang Zilong, 88, 90, 91, 93
jiefang sixiang, 6 解放思想
Jin Guantao, 186
Jin He, 67, 79
jiushi zhu, 18 救世主
Kong Jiesheng, 66
Kulian, 123
Kuomintang, 52, 71, 76, 110, 130,
140, 142, 143, 187, 199
landlord class, 31, 110
Lao She, 31, 34, 45
Lao Zi, 39, 129
Lee Yee, 108
Lee, Leo Ou-fan, 87, 118, 183
legal system, 25, 26, 54, 56, 57, 58,
121, 122, 127
Lei Feng, 178
Lenin, 5, 7, 8, 13, 17, 26, 32, 57,
65, 102, 121, 122, 123, 124,
154, 160, 161, 168, 170, 174,
178, 180
li, 126 礼
Li Guyi, 41, 42
Li Na, 40
Li Ping, 187, 202, 207
Li sao, 132, 133
Li Shangyin, 183
Li Shoucheng, 14
Li Yizhe, 7
Li Yu, 183
Li Zehou, 185
Li Zhun, 29, 32, 33, 34, 35, 36, 37,
38, 39, 47
Liang Xin, 29, 33, 34, 35
liberalism, 17, 22, 57, 123, 154,
155
Lin Biao, 6, 16, 18, 68, 95, 101,
136, 138
Lin Shu, 183